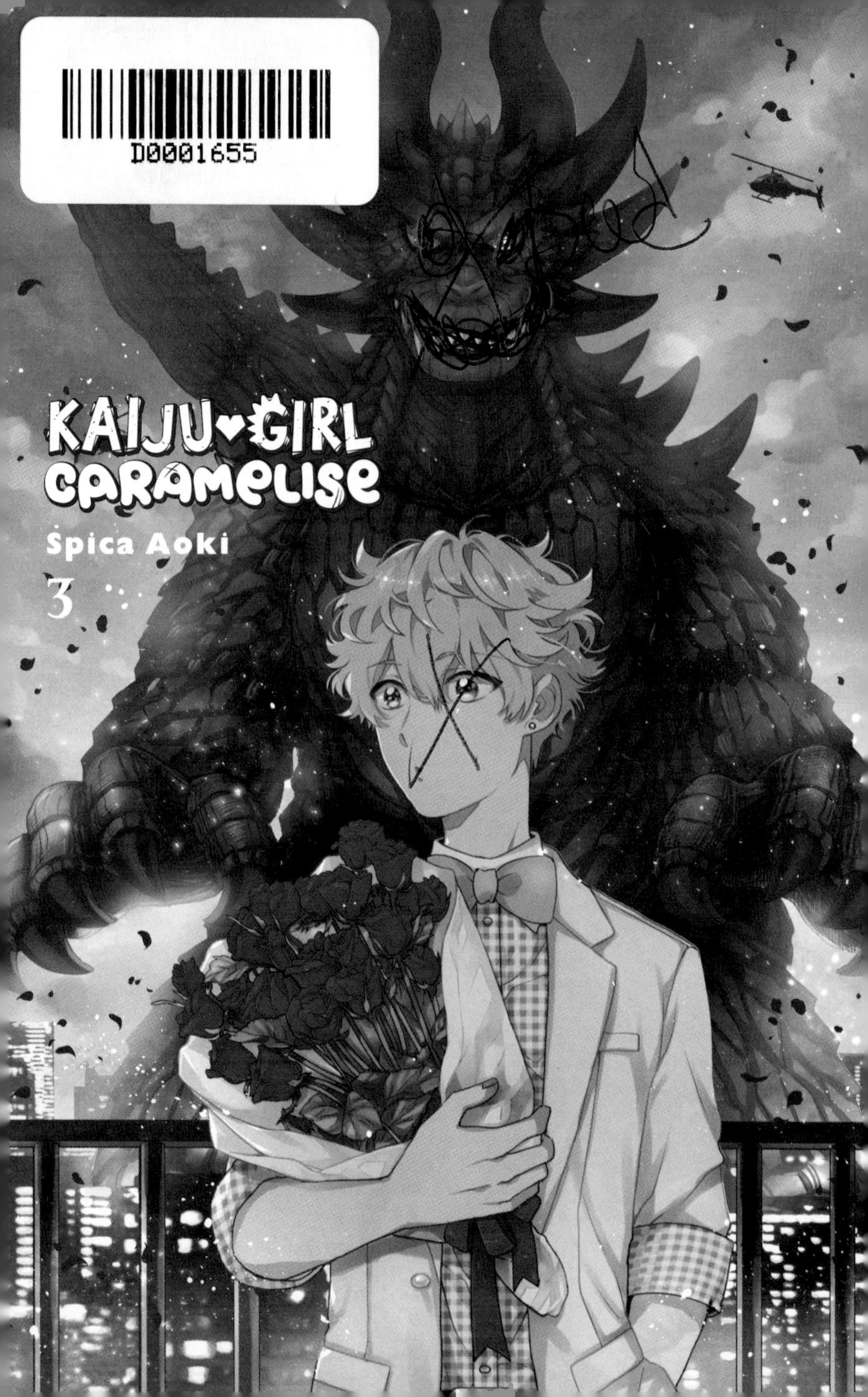
KAIJU♥GIRL
CARAMELISE
Spica Aoki
3

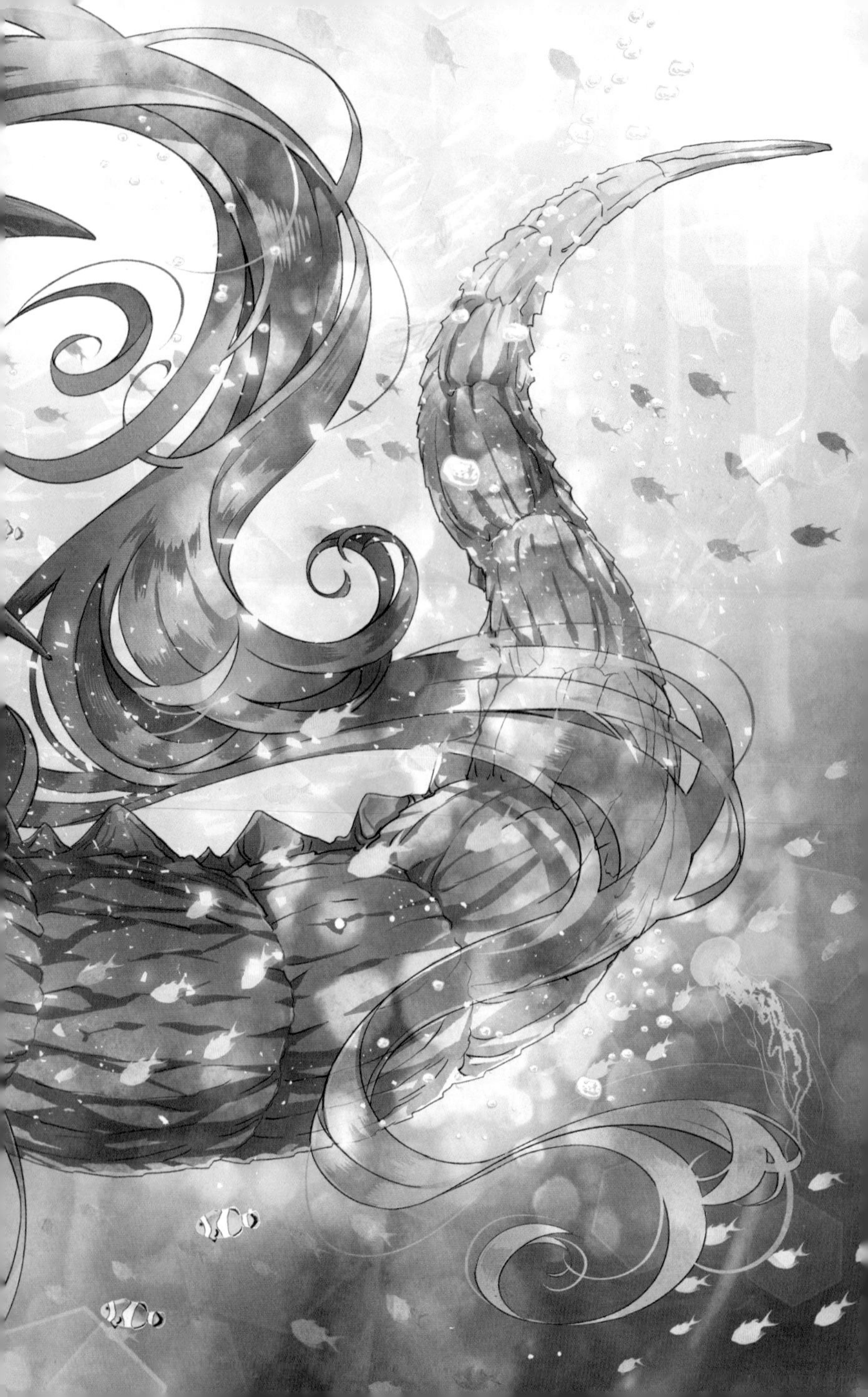

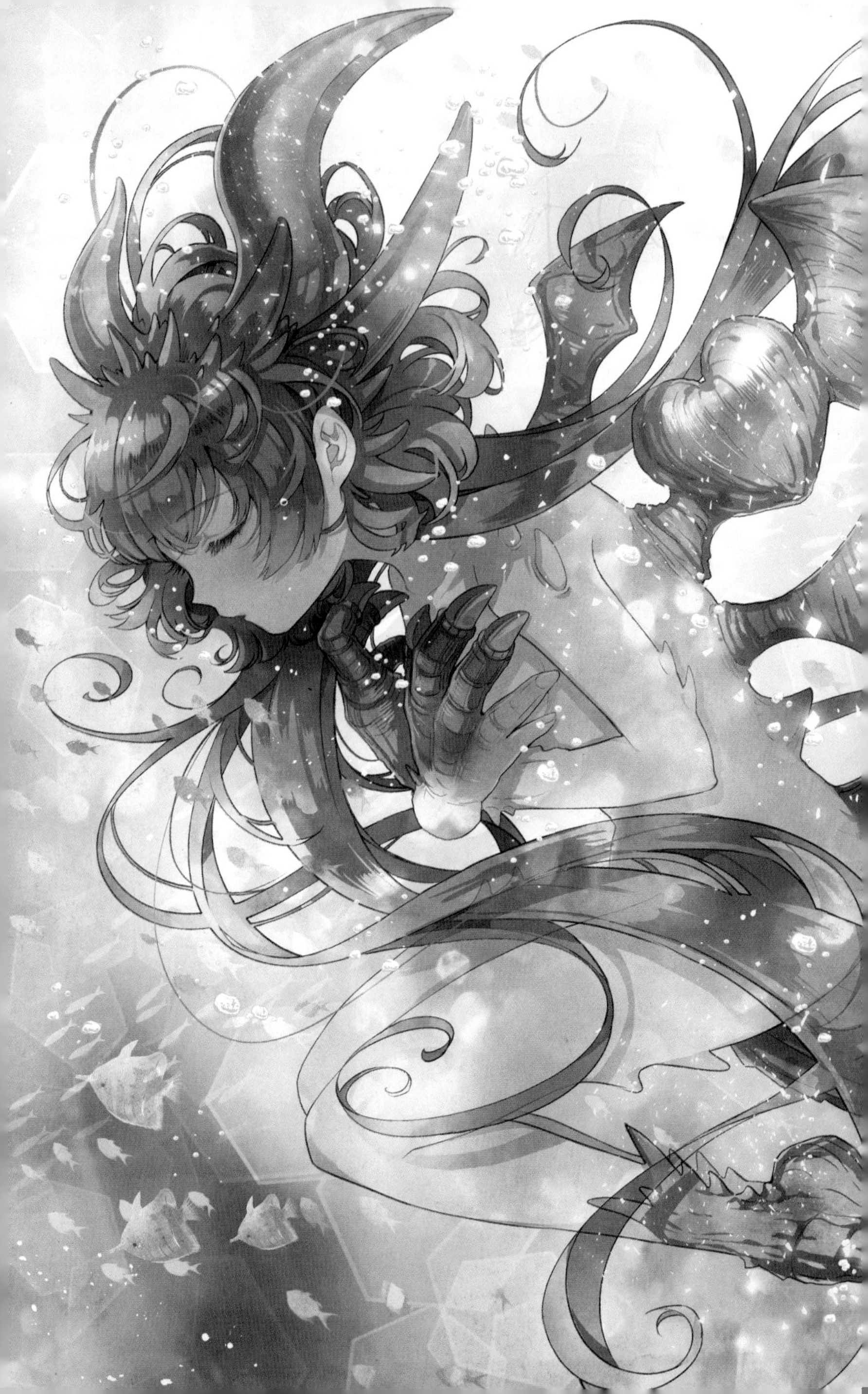

contents

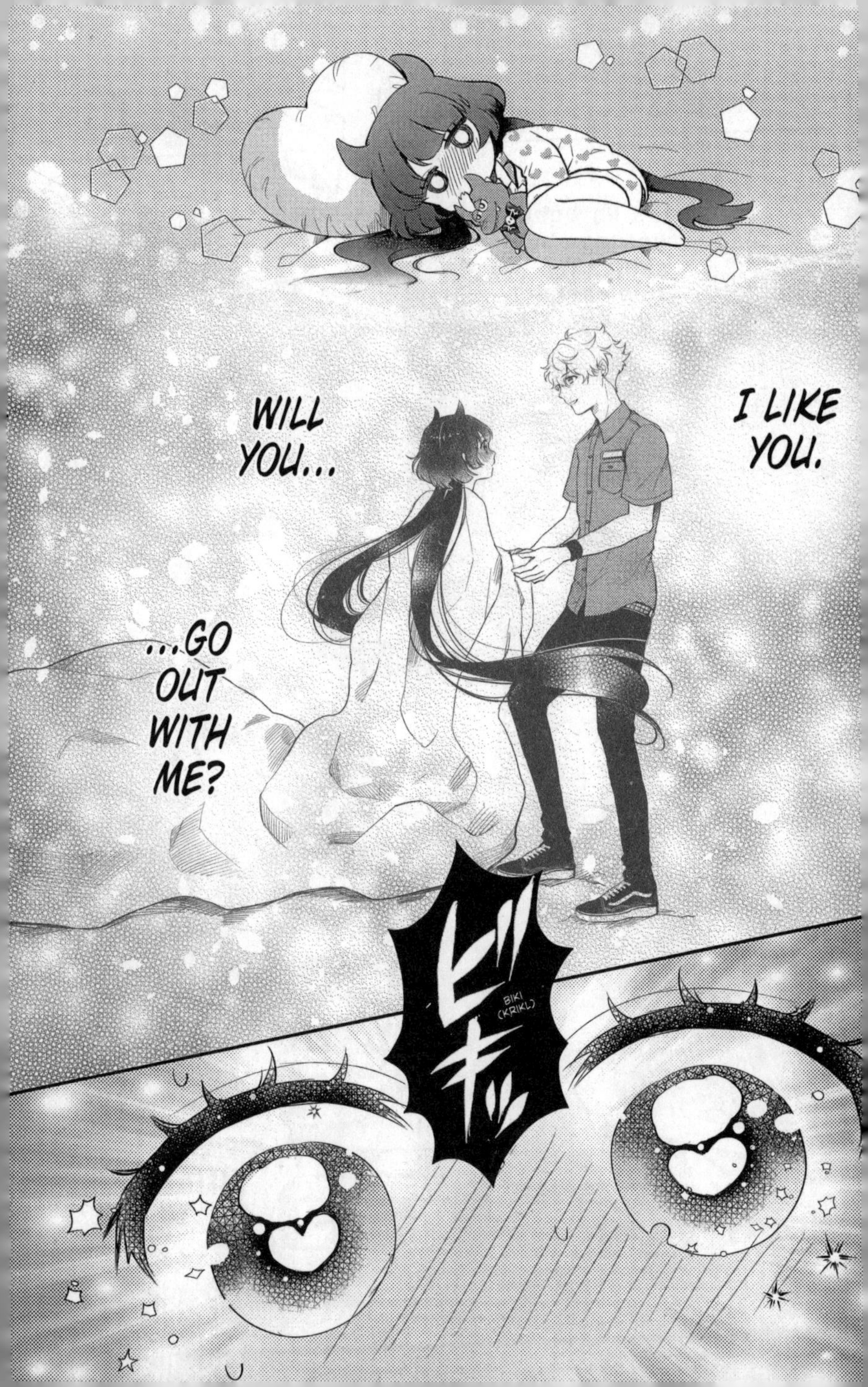
I LIKE YOU.
WILL YOU...
...GO OUT WITH ME?
ビキッ
BIKI (KRIKL)

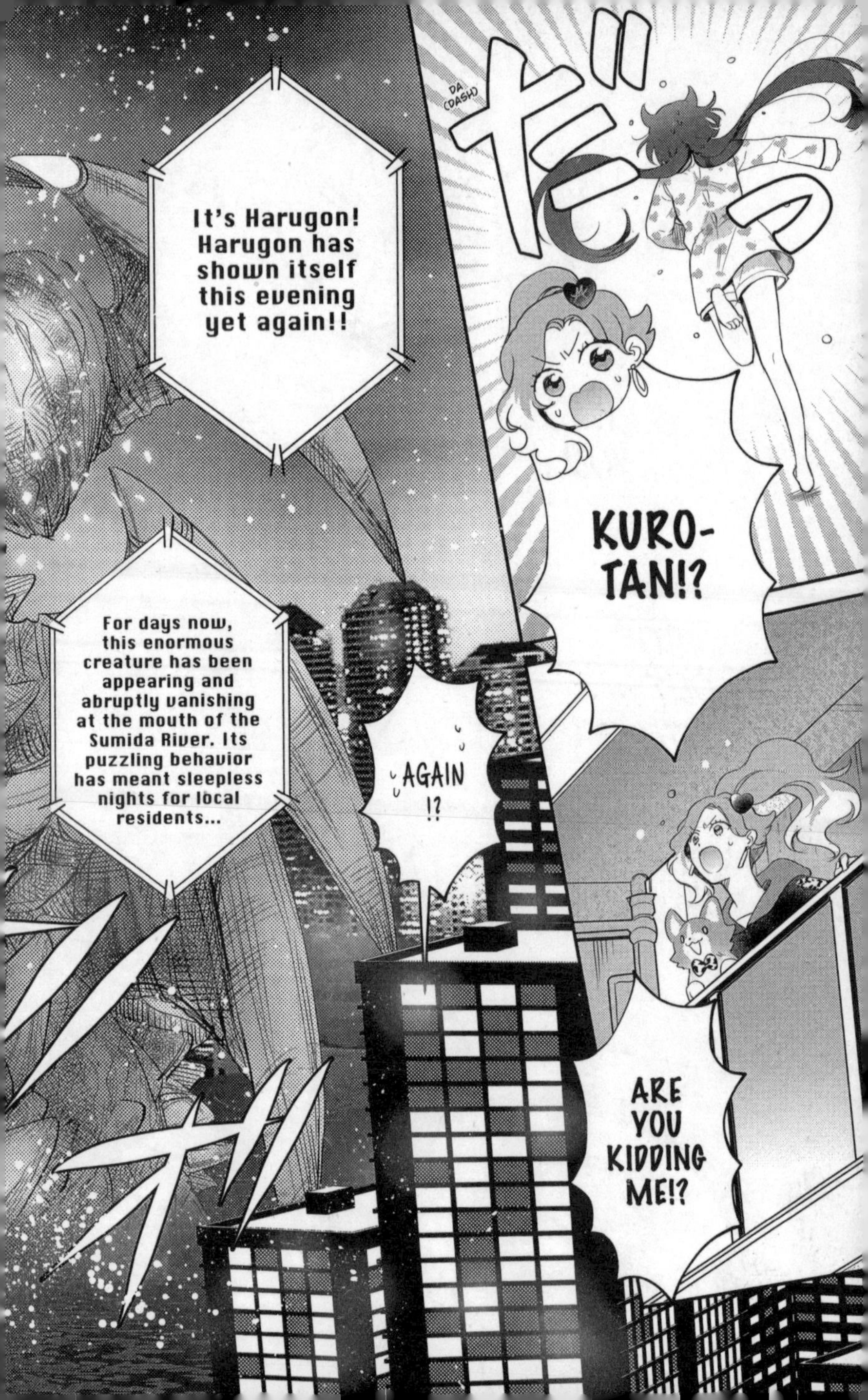
DA (DASH)
KURO-TAN!?
ARE YOU KIDDING ME!?
It's Harugon! Harugon has shown itself this evening yet again!!
For days now, this enormous creature has been appearing and abruptly vanishing at the mouth of the Sumida River. Its puzzling behavior has meant sleepless nights for local residents...
AGAIN !?

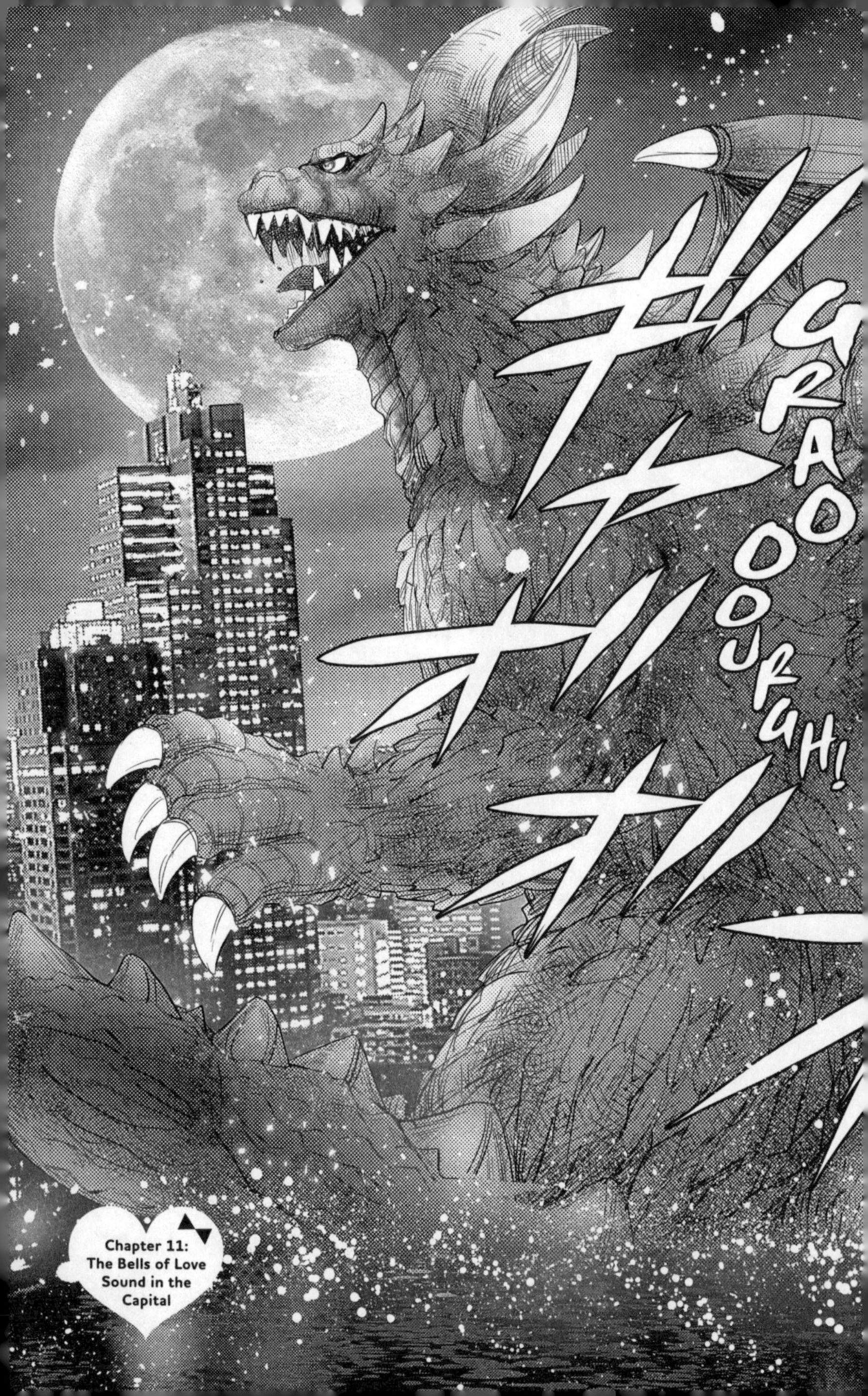
HGURAOOOOURAH!
Chapter 11: The Bells of Love Sound in the Capital

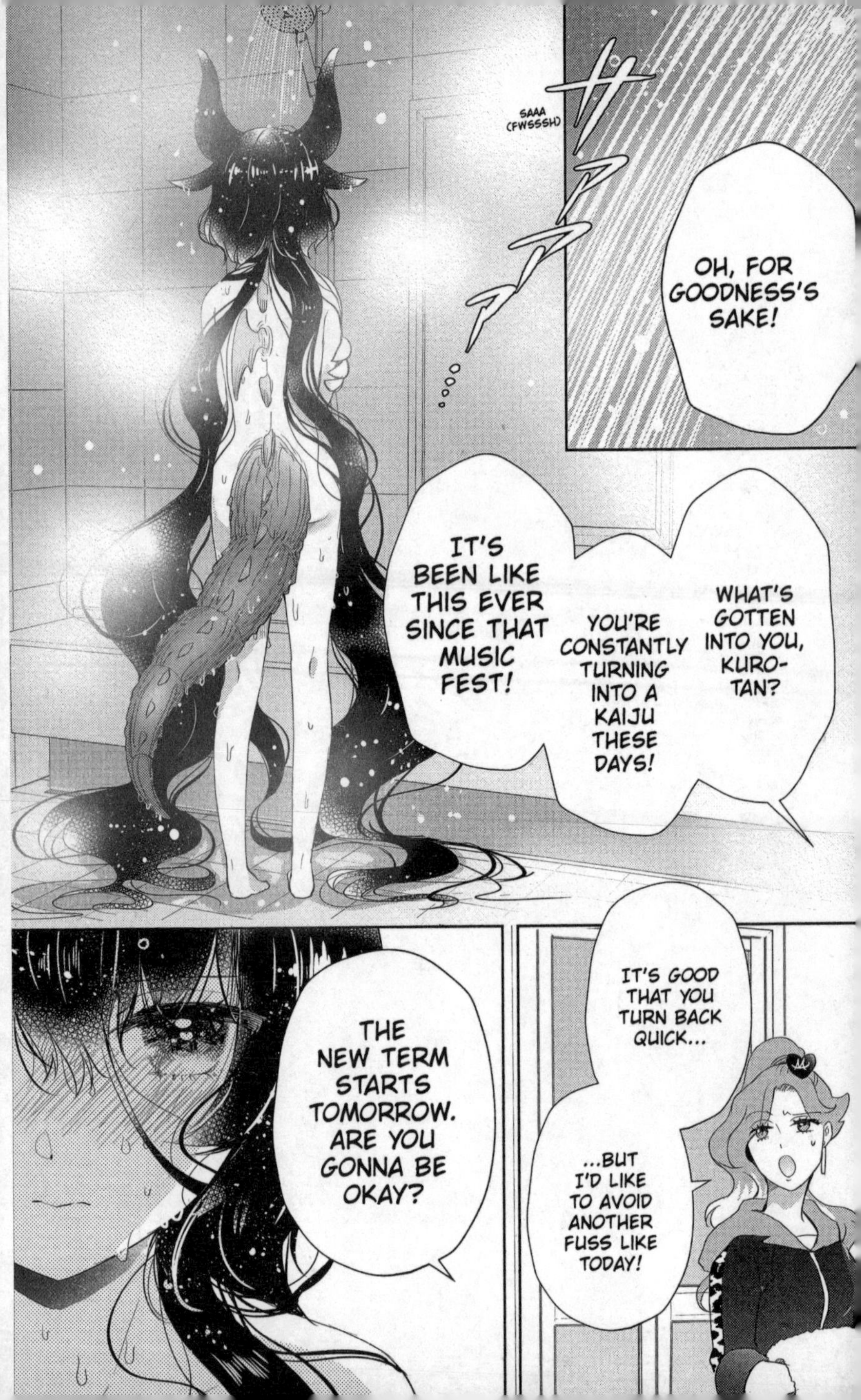
SAAA (FWSSSH)
OH, FOR GOODNESS'S SAKE!
WHAT'S GOTTEN INTO YOU, KURO-TAN?
YOU'RE CONSTANTLY TURNING INTO A KAIJU THESE DAYS!
IT'S BEEN LIKE THIS EVER SINCE THAT MUSIC FEST!
IT'S GOOD THAT YOU TURN BACK QUICK...
...BUT I'D LIKE TO AVOID ANOTHER FUSS LIKE TODAY!
THE NEW TERM STARTS TOMORROW. ARE YOU GONNA BE OKAY?

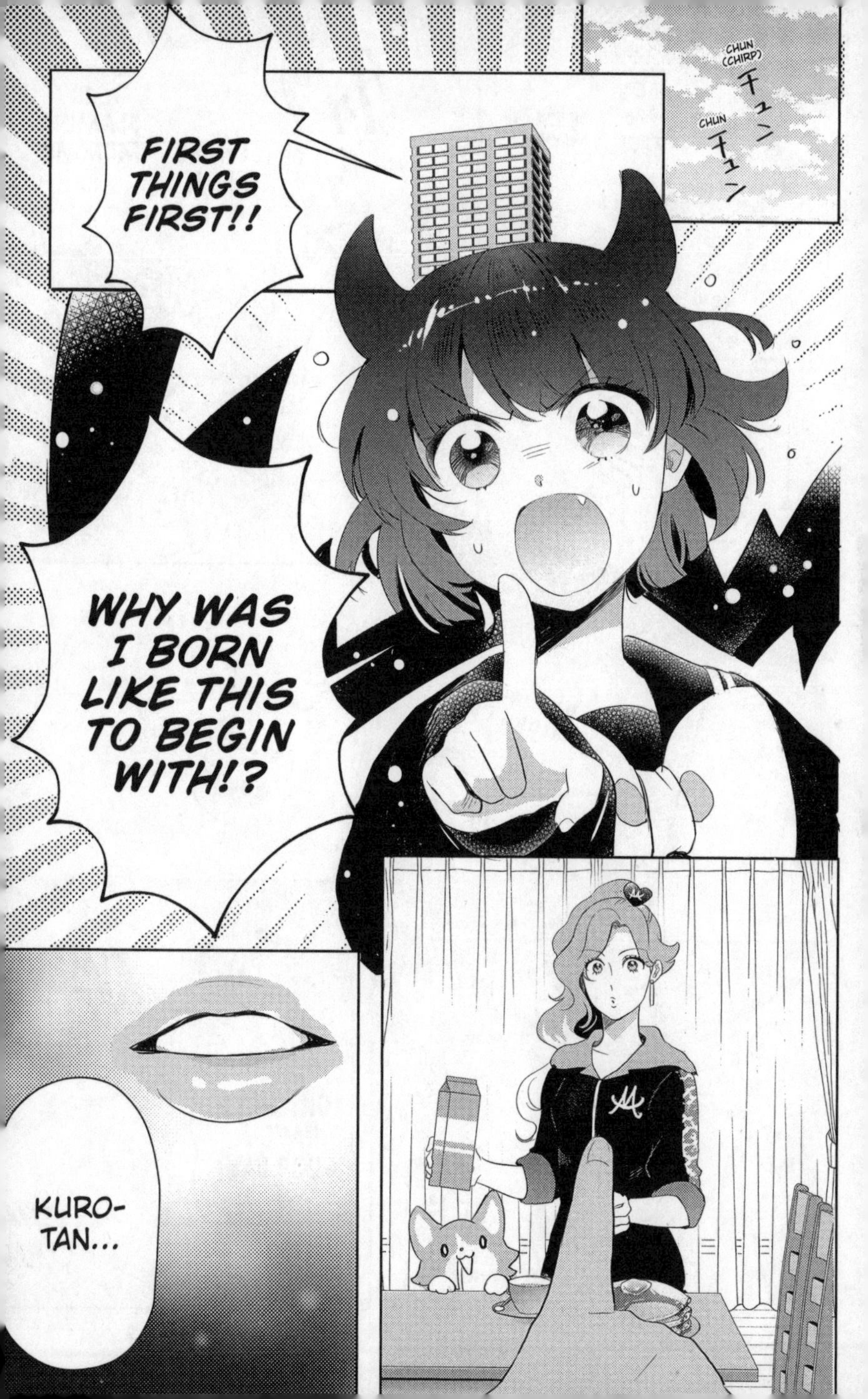
CHUN (CHIRP)
チュン
CHUN
チュン
FIRST THINGS FIRST!!
WHY WAS I BORN LIKE THIS TO BEGIN WITH!?
KURO-TAN...

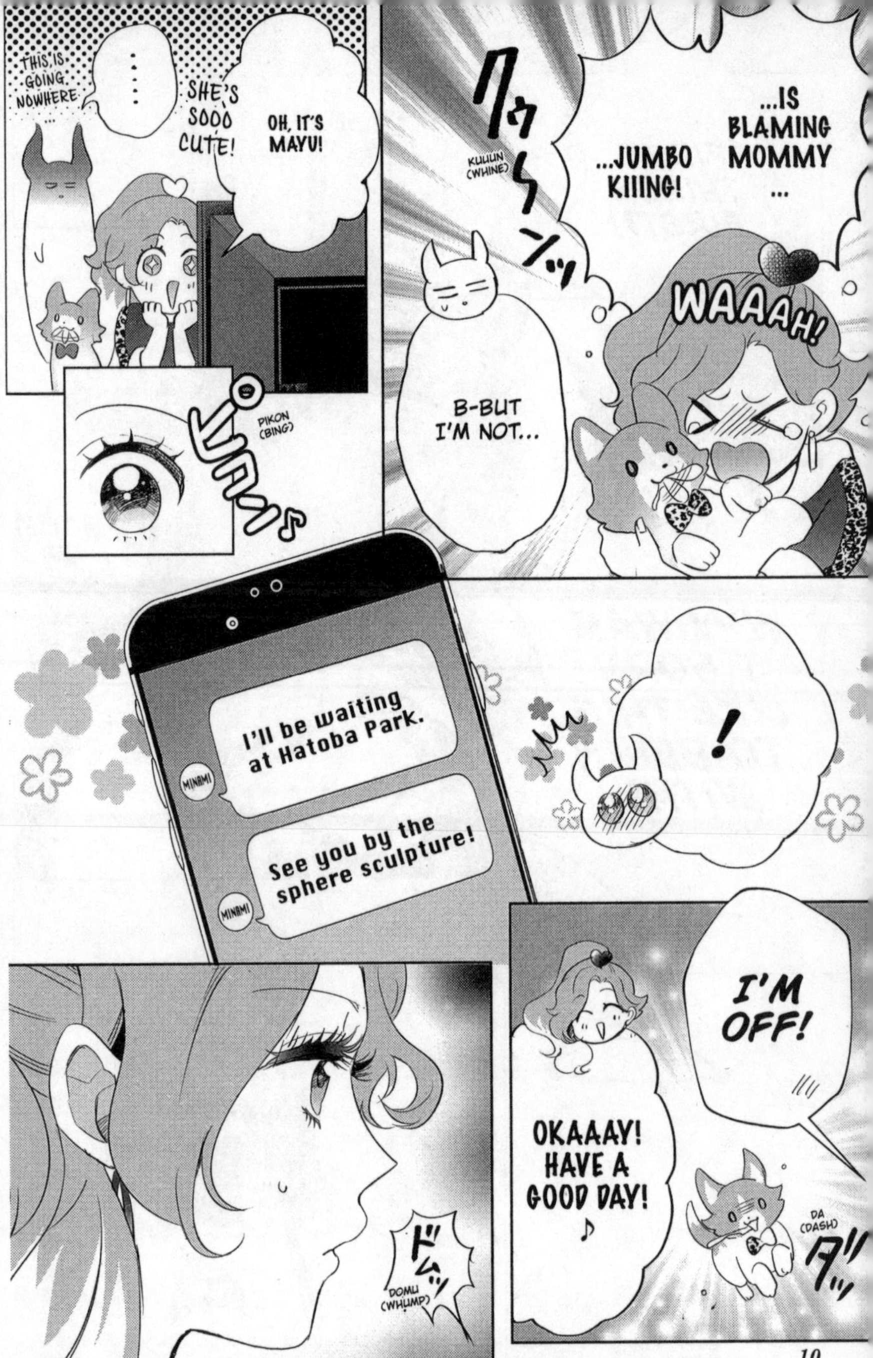

...JUMBO KIIING! ...IS BLAMING MOMMY ...
WAAAH!
KUUUN (WHINE)
B-BUT I'M NOT...
OH, IT'S MAYU!
SHE'S SOOO CUTE!
......
THIS IS GOING NOWHERE ...
PIKON (BING)
!
I'll be waiting at Hatoba Park.
MINAMI
See you by the sphere sculpture!
MINAMI
I'M OFF!
OKAAAY! HAVE A GOOD DAY! ♪
DA (DASH)
DOMU (WHUMP)

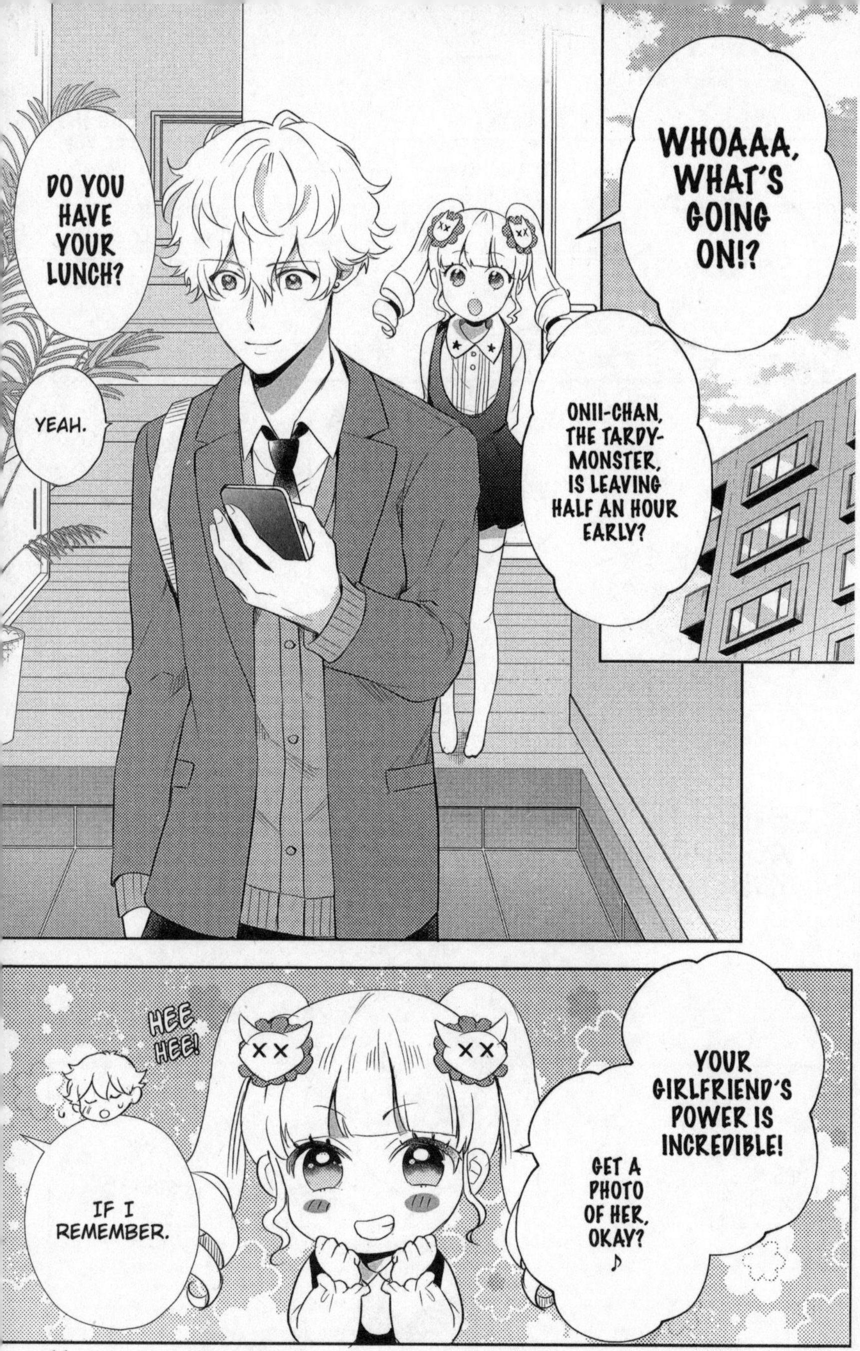
WHOAAA, WHAT'S GOING ON!?
ONII-CHAN, THE TARDY-MONSTER, IS LEAVING HALF AN HOUR EARLY?
DO YOU HAVE YOUR LUNCH?
YEAH.
YOUR GIRLFRIEND'S POWER IS INCREDIBLE!
GET A PHOTO OF HER, OKAY? ♪
HEE HEE!
IF I REMEMBER.

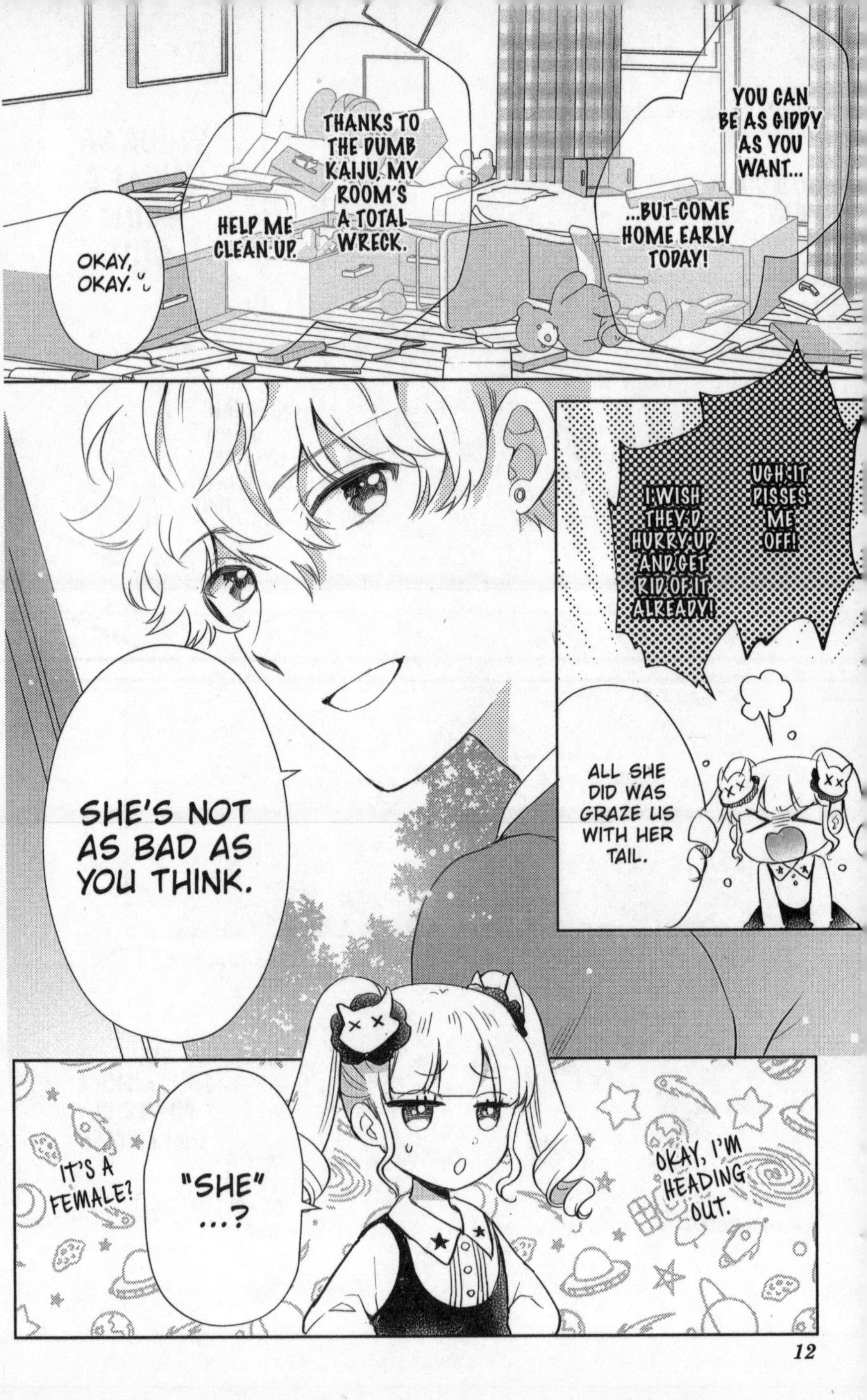

YOU CAN BE AS GIDDY AS YOU WANT...
...BUT COME HOME EARLY TODAY!
THANKS TO THE DUMB KAIJU, MY ROOM'S A TOTAL WRECK.
HELP ME CLEAN UP.
OKAY, OKAY.
UGH, IT PISSES ME OFF!
I WISH THEY'D HURRY UP AND GET RID OF IT ALREADY!
ALL SHE DID WAS GRAZE US WITH HER TAIL.
SHE'S NOT AS BAD AS YOU THINK.
OKAY, I'M HEADING OUT.
"SHE"...?
IT'S A FEMALE?

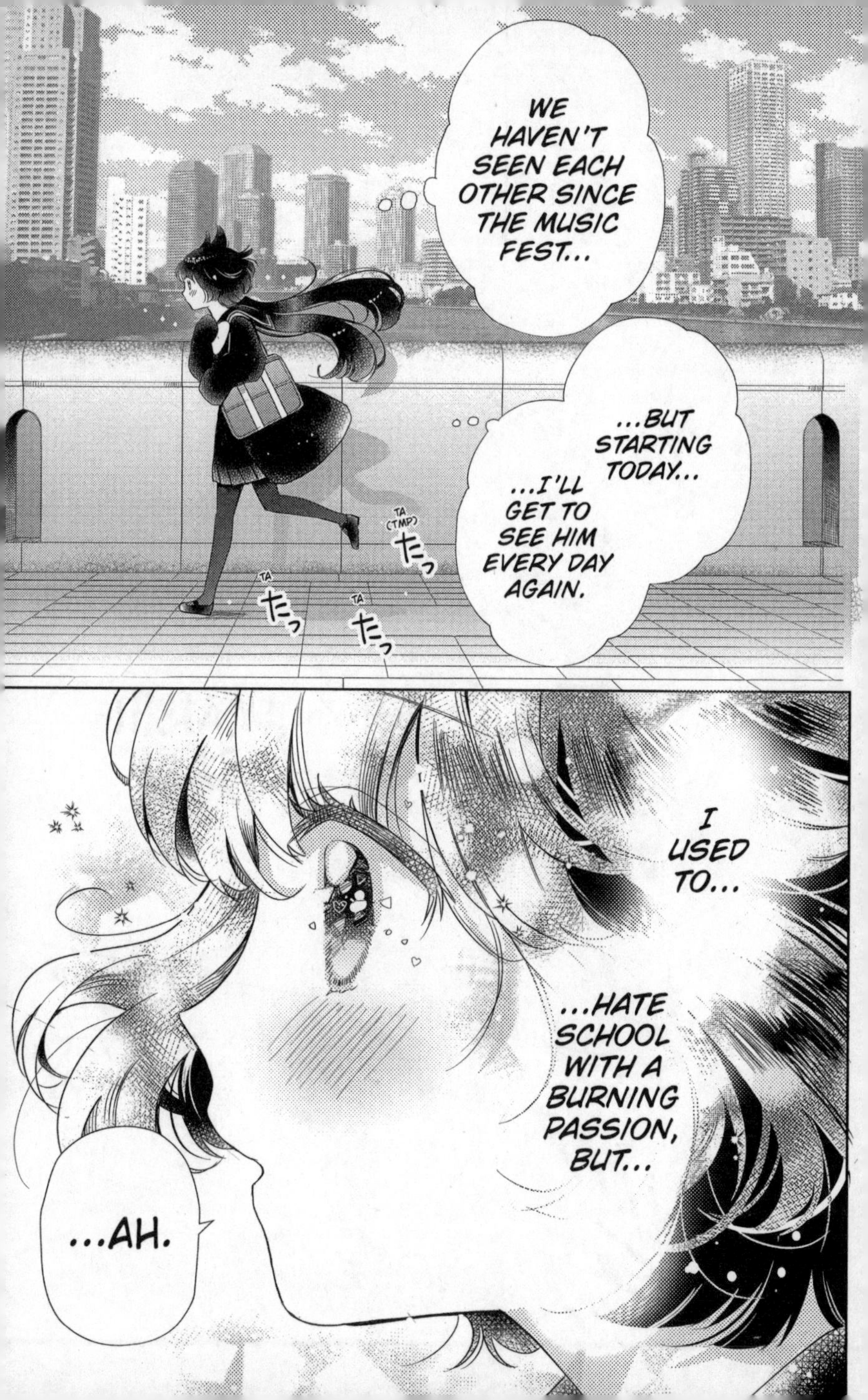
WE HAVEN'T SEEN EACH OTHER SINCE THE MUSIC FEST...
...BUT STARTING TODAY...
...I'LL GET TO SEE HIM EVERY DAY AGAIN.
TA (TMP) たっ
TA たっ
TA たっ
I USED TO...
...HATE SCHOOL WITH A BURNING PASSION, BUT...
...AH.

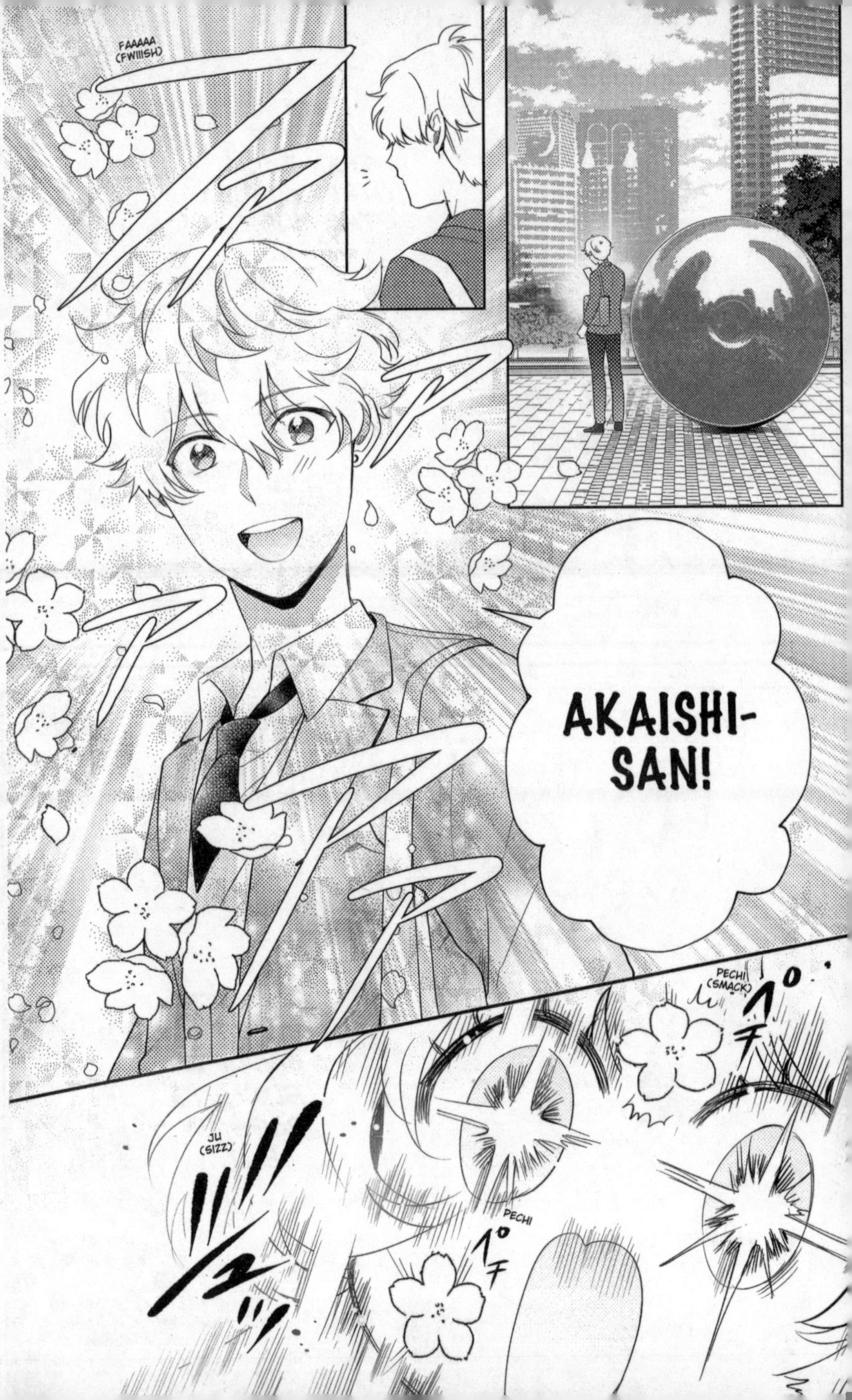
FAAAAA (FWIIISH)
AKAISHI-SAN!
PECHI (SMACK)
JU (SIZZ)
PECHI

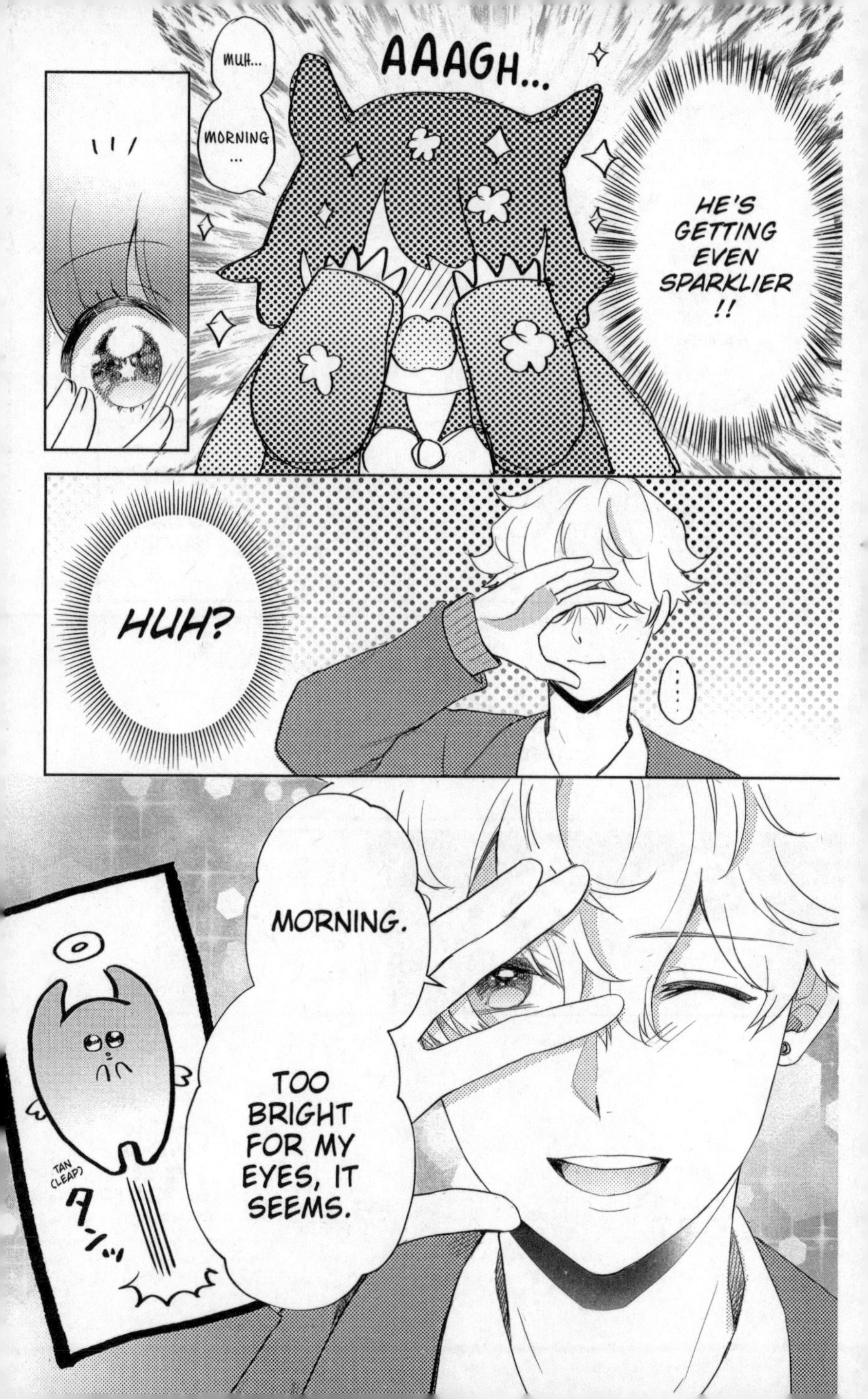
AAAGH...
HE'S GETTING EVEN SPARKLIER!!
MUH... MORNING...
.....
HUH?
MORNING.
TOO BRIGHT FOR MY EYES, IT SEEMS.
TAN (LEAP)

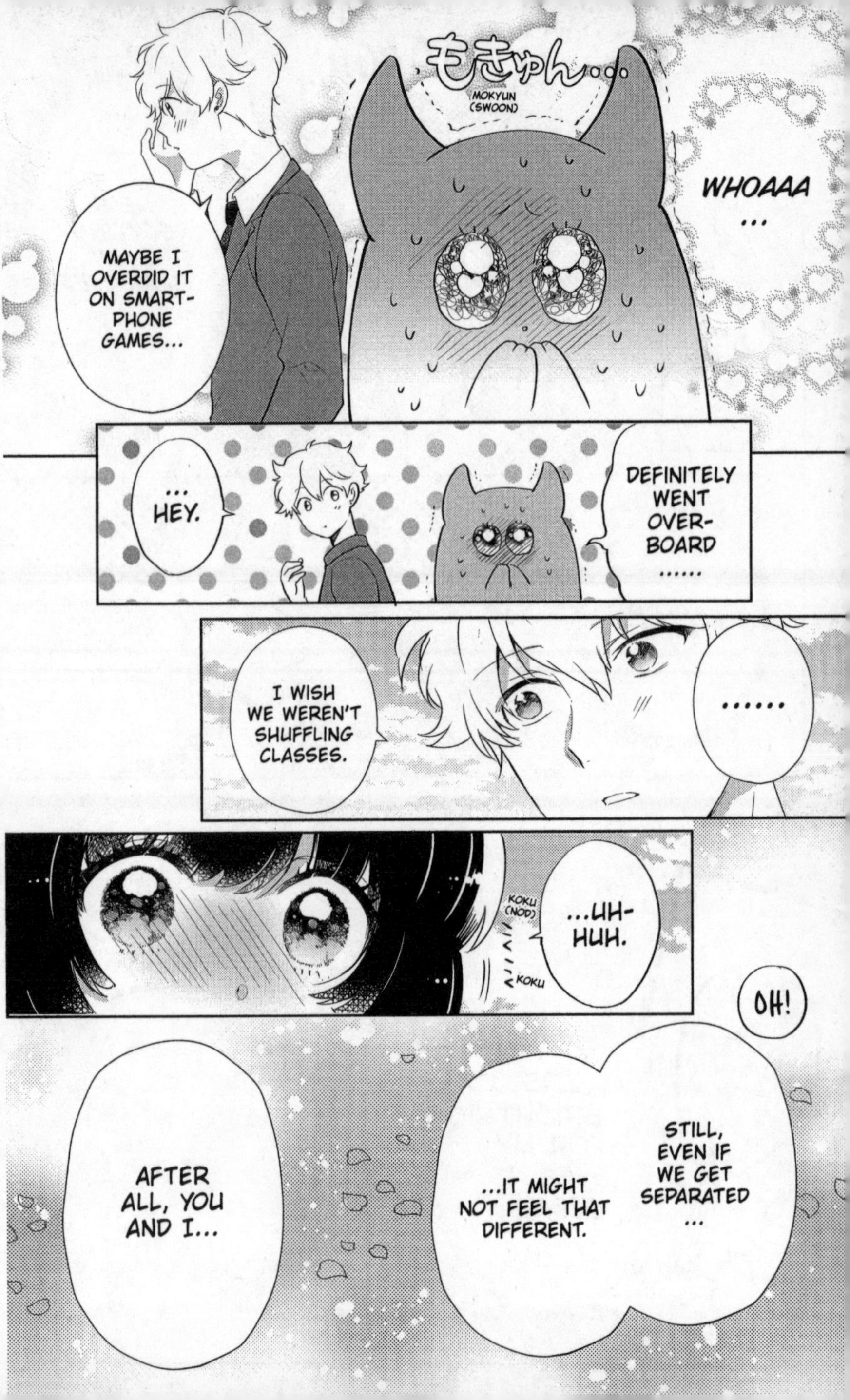
WHOAAA ...
もきゅん…
MOKYUN (SWOON)
MAYBE I OVERDID IT ON SMART-PHONE GAMES...
DEFINITELY WENT OVER-BOARD ......
... HEY.
......
I WISH WE WEREN'T SHUFFLING CLASSES.
...UH-HUH.
KOKU (NOD)
KOKU
OH!
STILL, EVEN IF WE GET SEPARATED ...
...IT MIGHT NOT FEEL THAT DIFFERENT.
AFTER ALL, YOU AND I...

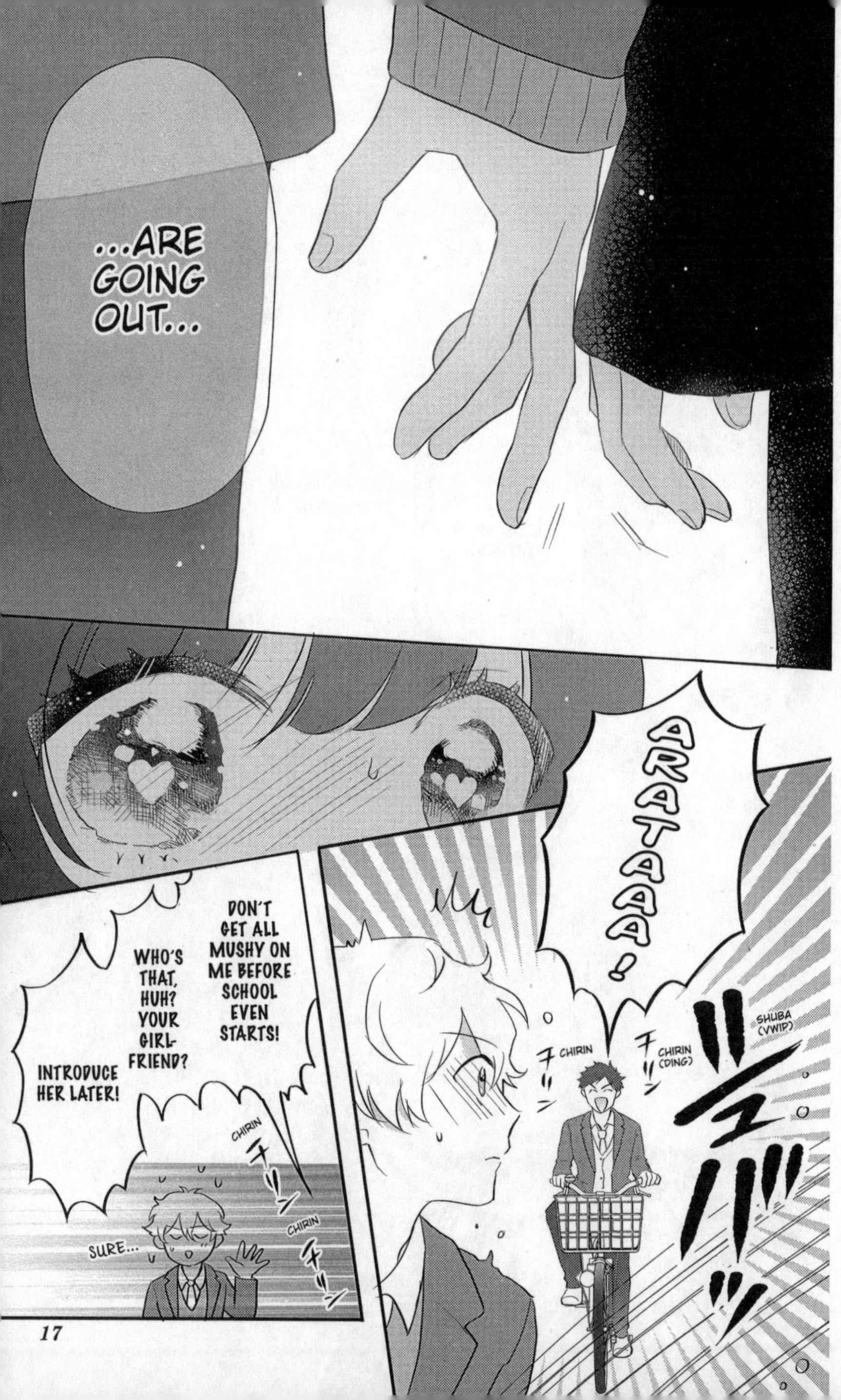
...ARE GOING OUT...
ARATAAAA!
CHIRIN
CHIRIN (DING)
SHUBA (VWIP)
DON'T GET ALL MUSHY ON ME BEFORE SCHOOL EVEN STARTS!
WHO'S THAT, HUH? YOUR GIRL-FRIEND?
INTRODUCE HER LATER!
CHIRIN
CHIRIN
SURE...

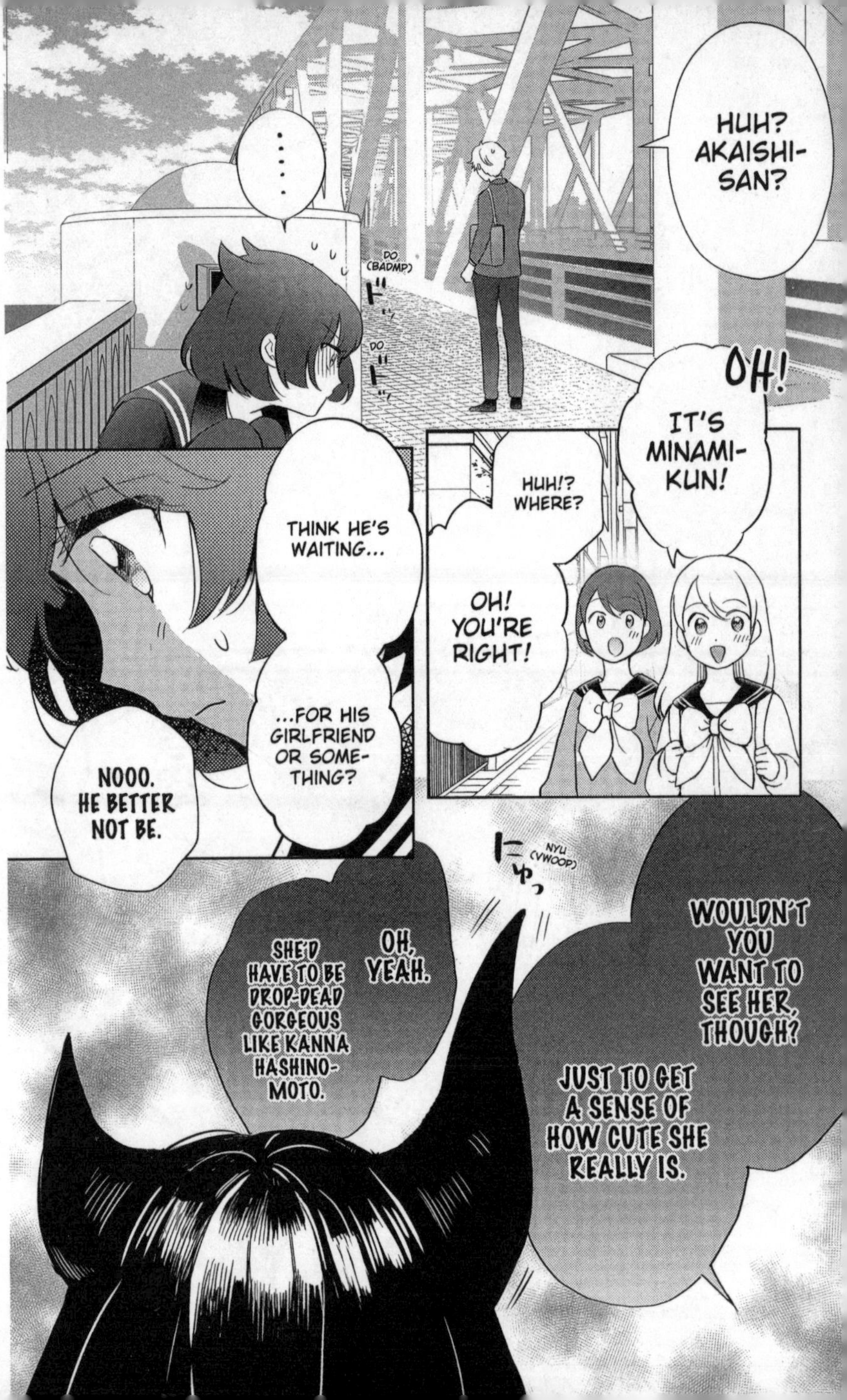
HUH? AKAISHI-SAN?
DO (BADMP)
DO
......
OH!
IT'S MINAMI-KUN!
HUH!? WHERE?
OH! YOU'RE RIGHT!
THINK HE'S WAITING...
...FOR HIS GIRLFRIEND OR SOMETHING?
NOOO. HE BETTER NOT BE.
NYU (VWOOP)
WOULDN'T YOU WANT TO SEE HER, THOUGH?
JUST TO GET A SENSE OF HOW CUTE SHE REALLY IS.
OH, YEAH.
SHE'D HAVE TO BE DROP-DEAD GORGEOUS LIKE KANNA HASHINO-MOTO.

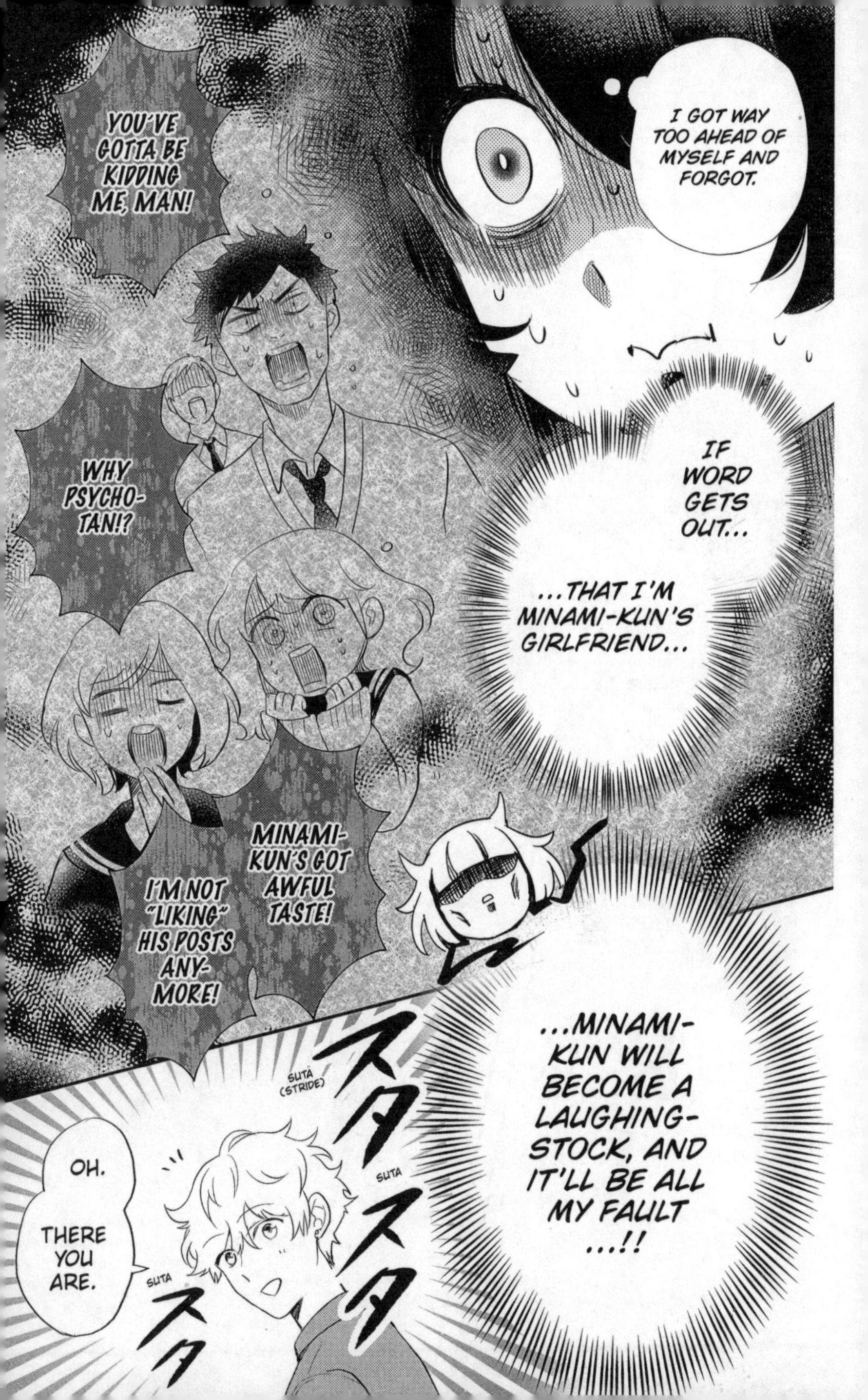
I GOT WAY TOO AHEAD OF MYSELF AND FORGOT.
IF WORD GETS OUT...
...THAT I'M MINAMI-KUN'S GIRLFRIEND...
YOU'VE GOTTA BE KIDDING ME, MAN!
WHY PSYCHO-TAN!?
MINAMI-KUN'S GOT AWFUL TASTE!
I'M NOT "LIKING" HIS POSTS ANYMORE!
...MINAMI-KUN WILL BECOME A LAUGHING-STOCK, AND IT'LL BE ALL MY FAULT ...!!
SUTA (STRIDE)
SUTA
SUTA
OH.
THERE YOU ARE.

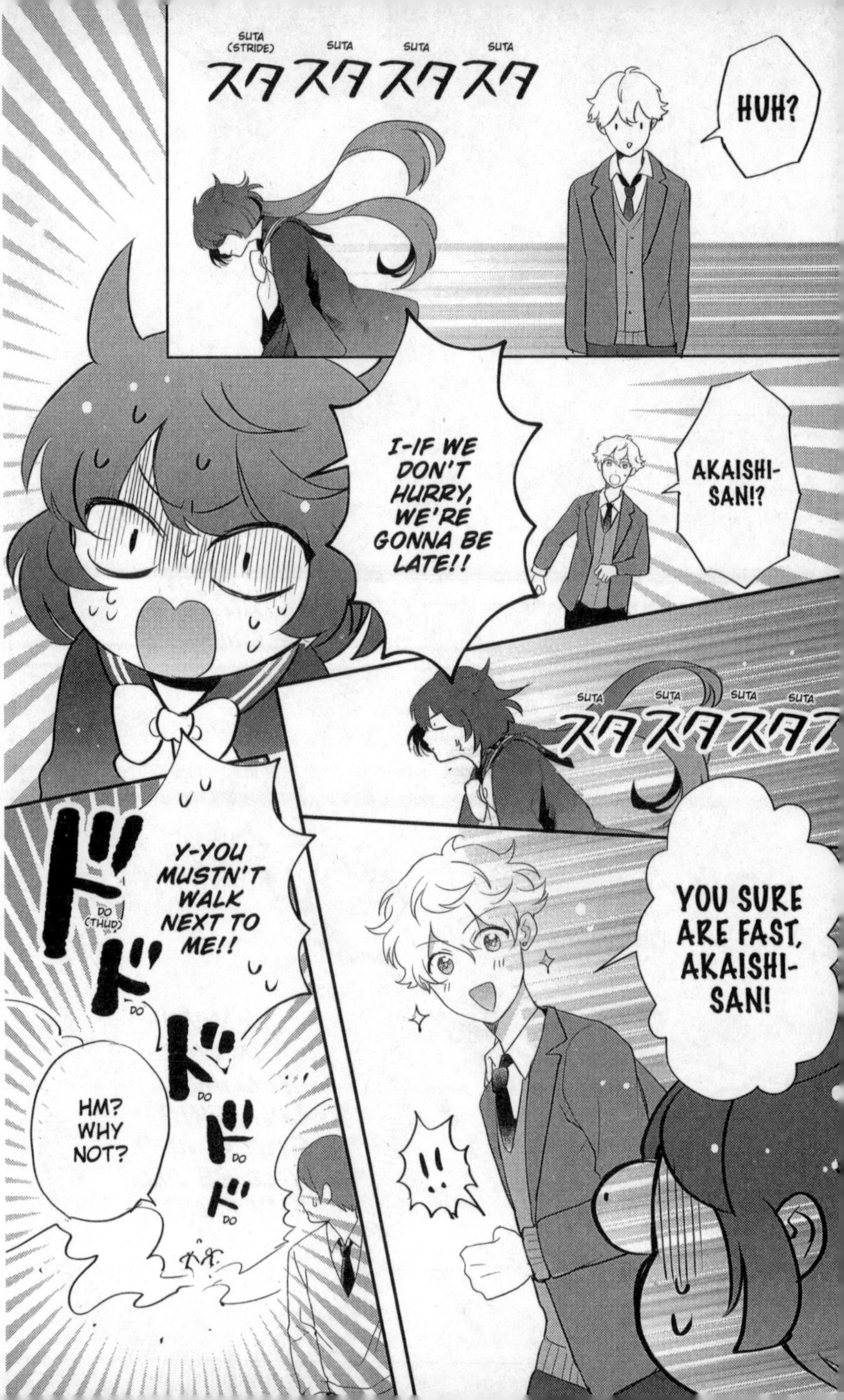
HUH?
SUTA (STRIDE) SUTA SUTA SUTA
スタスタスタスタ
AKAISHI-SAN!?
I-IF WE DON'T HURRY, WE'RE GONNA BE LATE!!
SUTA SUTA SUTA SUTA
スタスタスタス
YOU SURE ARE FAST, AKAISHI-SAN!
!!
Y-YOU MUSTN'T WALK NEXT TO ME!!
ド DO (THUD)
ド DO
ド DO
ド DO
ド DO
HM? WHY NOT?

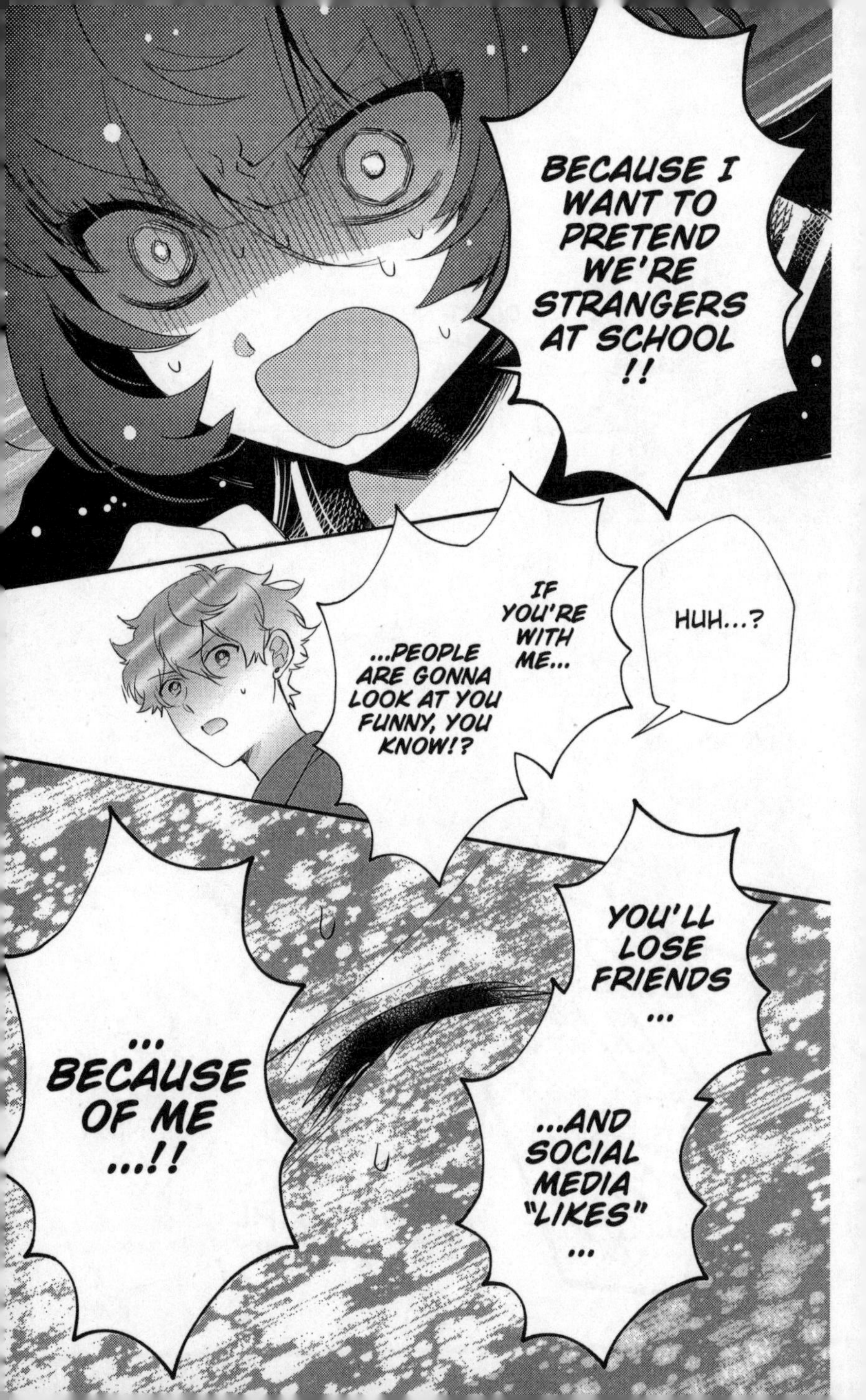
BECAUSE I WANT TO PRETEND WE'RE STRANGERS AT SCHOOL !!
HUH...?
IF YOU'RE WITH ME...
...PEOPLE ARE GONNA LOOK AT YOU FUNNY, YOU KNOW!?
YOU'LL LOSE FRIENDS ...
...AND SOCIAL MEDIA "LIKES" ...
... BECAUSE OF ME ...!!

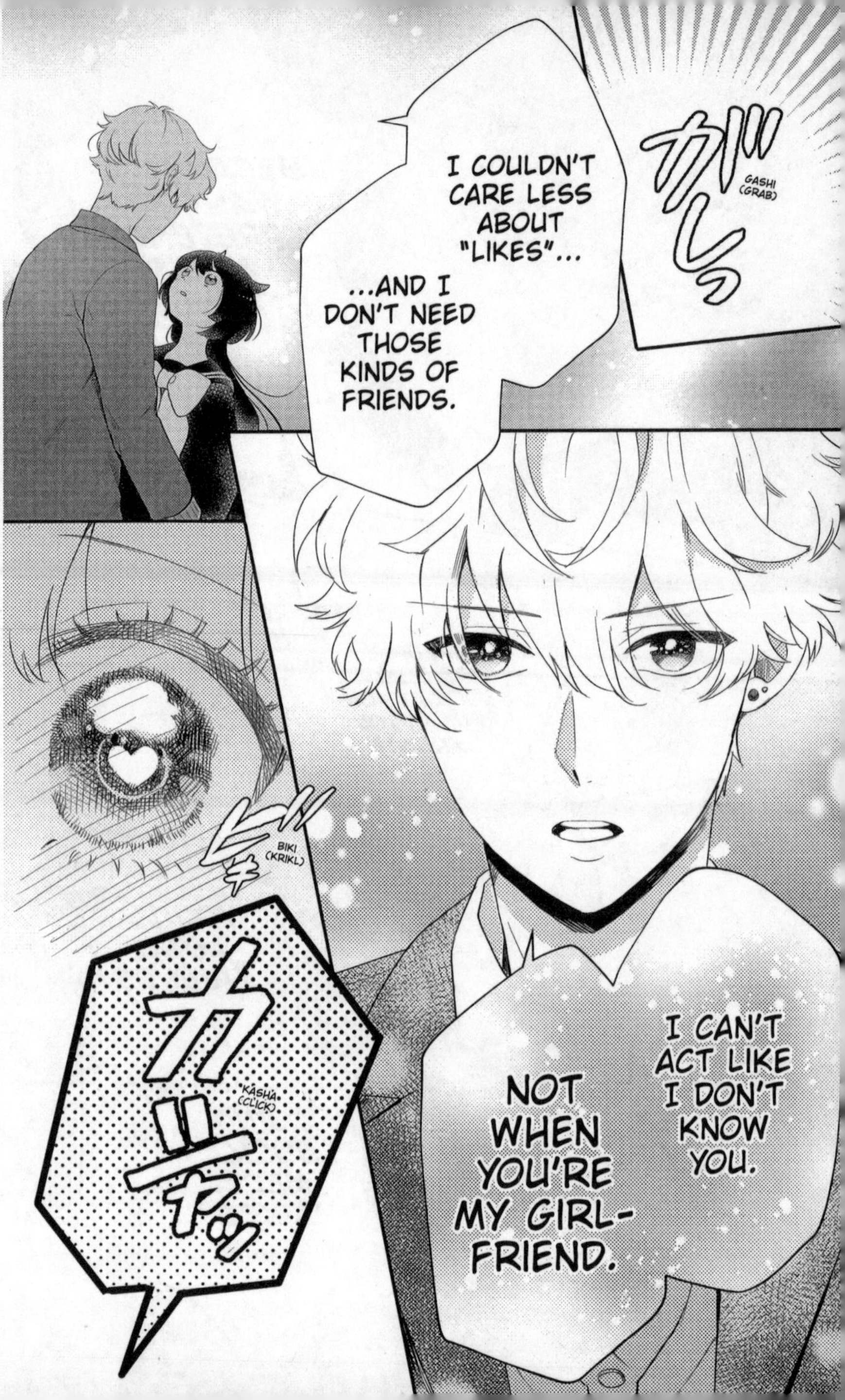
GASHI (GRAB)
I COULDN'T CARE LESS ABOUT "LIKES"...
...AND I DON'T NEED THOSE KINDS OF FRIENDS.
I CAN'T ACT LIKE I DON'T KNOW YOU.
NOT WHEN YOU'RE MY GIRL-FRIEND.
BIKI (KRIKL)
KASHA (CLICK)

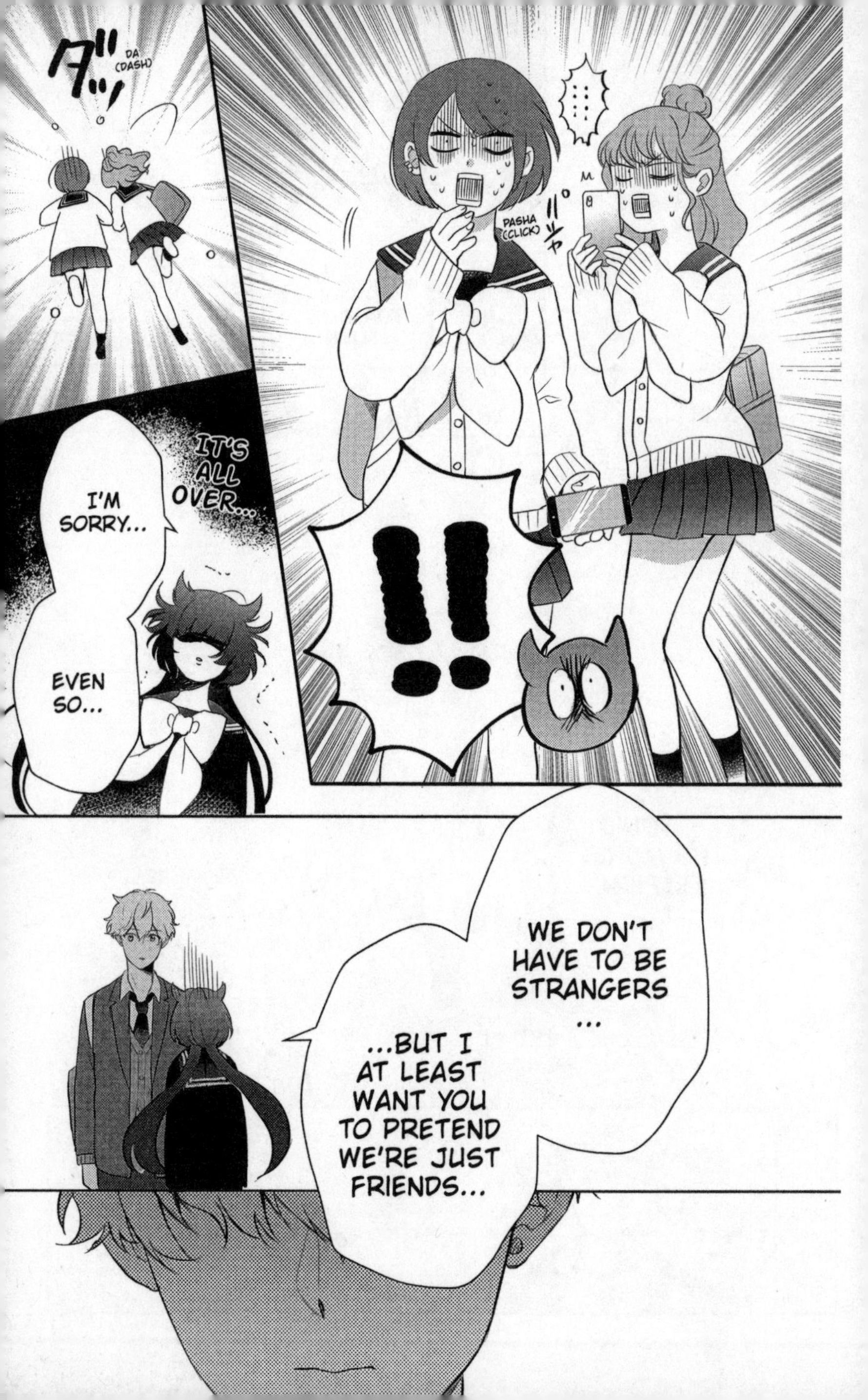
PASHA (CLICK)
!!
DA (DASH)
IT'S ALL OVER...
I'M SORRY...
EVEN SO...
WE DON'T HAVE TO BE STRANGERS...
...BUT I AT LEAST WANT YOU TO PRETEND WE'RE JUST FRIENDS...

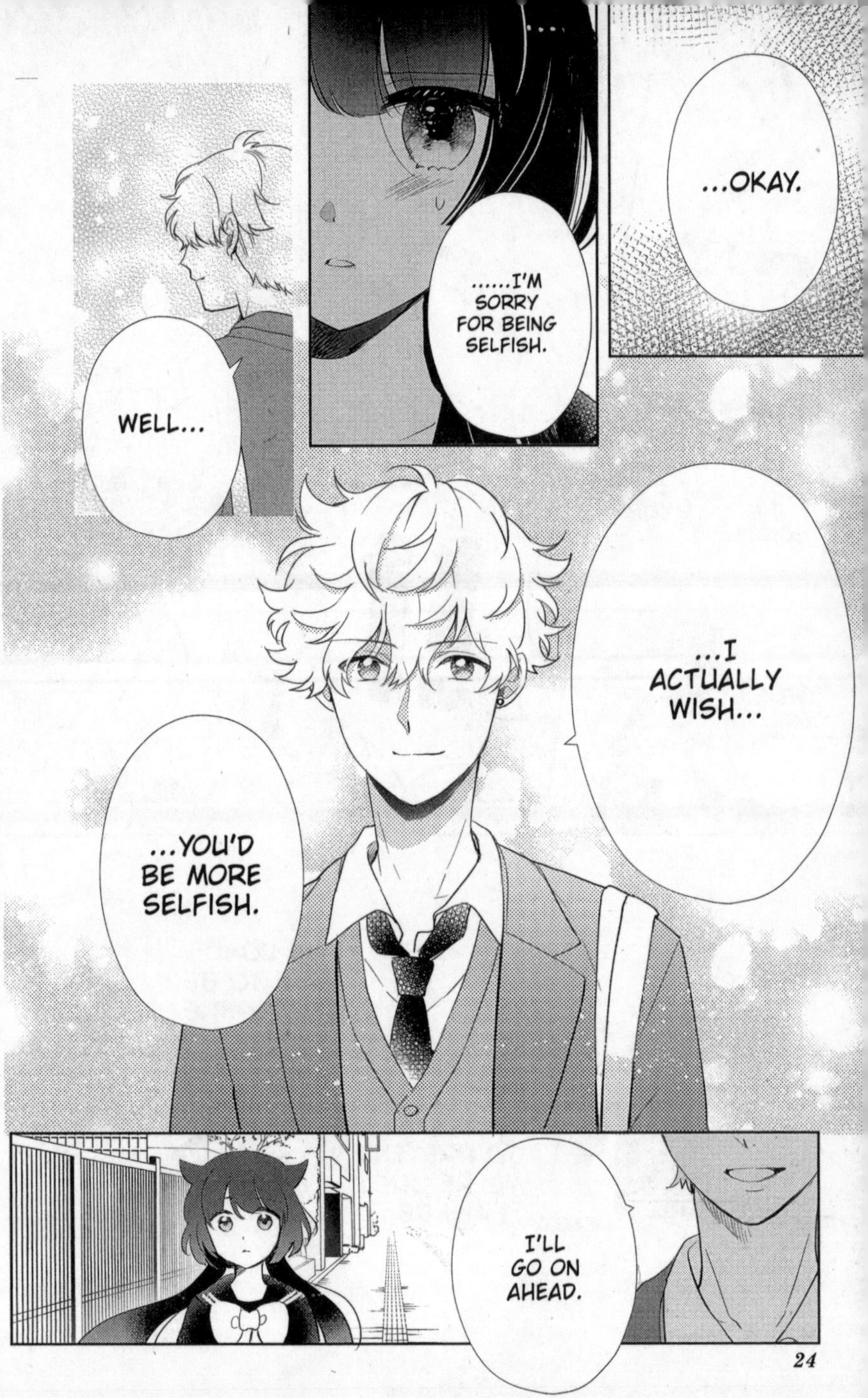
...OKAY.
......I'M SORRY FOR BEING SELFISH.
WELL...
...I ACTUALLY WISH...
...YOU'D BE MORE SELFISH.
I'LL GO ON AHEAD.

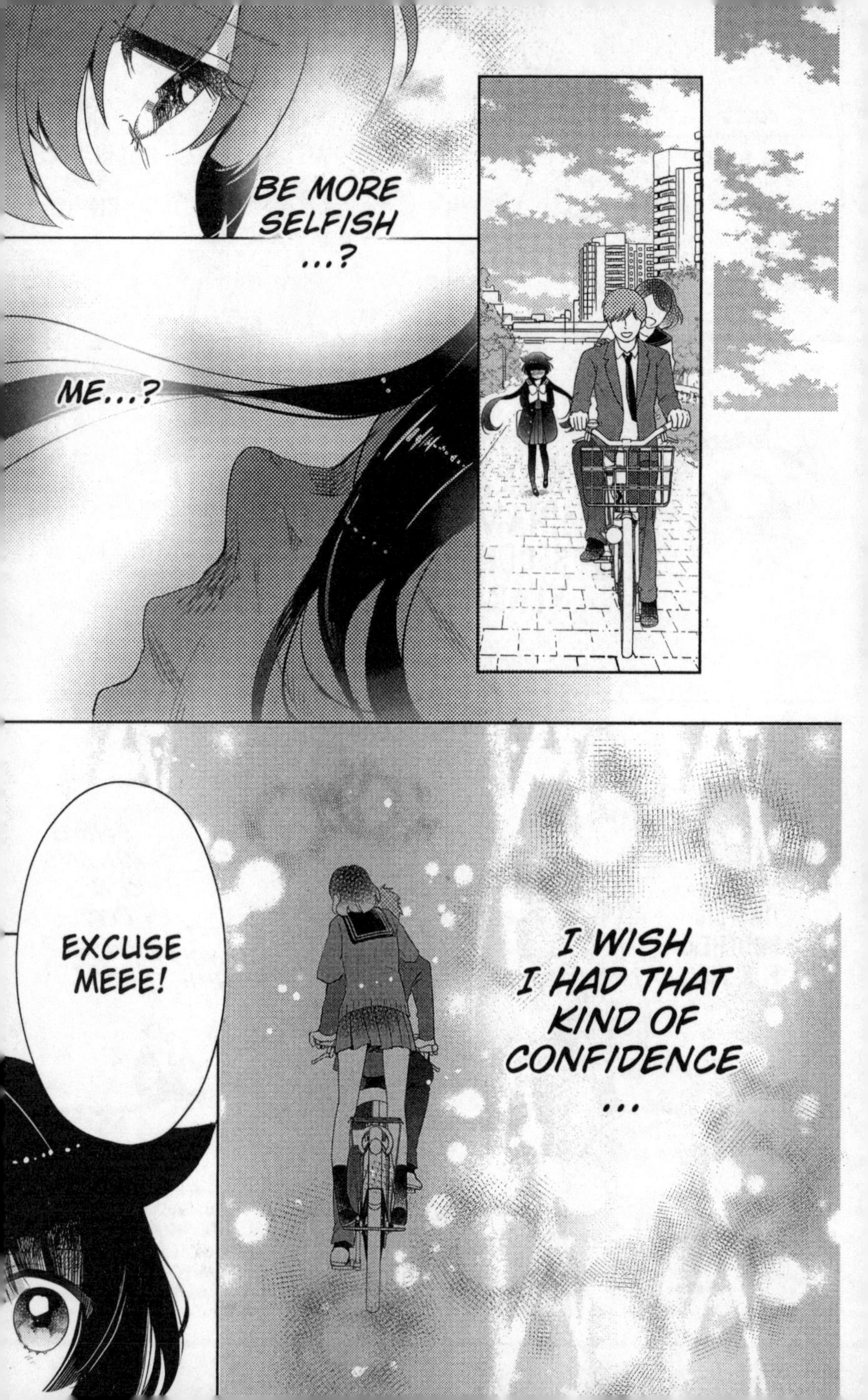
BE MORE SELFISH ...?
ME...?
I WISH I HAD THAT KIND OF CONFIDENCE ...
EXCUSE MEEE!

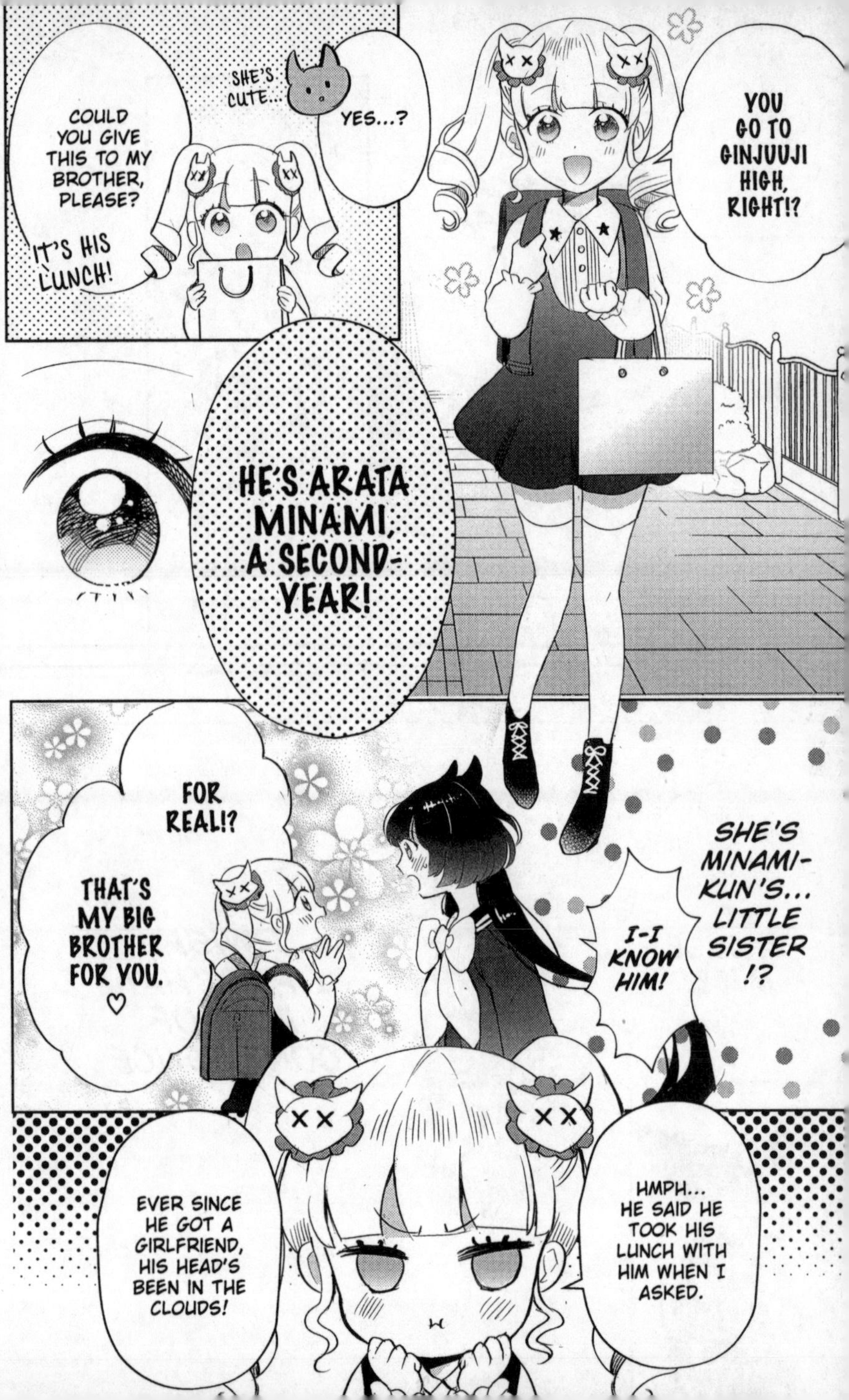
YOU GO TO GINJUUJI HIGH, RIGHT!?
SHE'S CUTE...
YES...?
COULD YOU GIVE THIS TO MY BROTHER, PLEASE?
IT'S HIS LUNCH!
HE'S ARATA MINAMI, A SECOND-YEAR!
SHE'S MINAMI-KUN'S... LITTLE SISTER!?
I-I KNOW HIM!
FOR REAL!?
THAT'S MY BIG BROTHER FOR YOU. ♡
HMPH... HE SAID HE TOOK HIS LUNCH WITH HIM WHEN I ASKED.
EVER SINCE HE GOT A GIRLFRIEND, HIS HEAD'S BEEN IN THE CLOUDS!

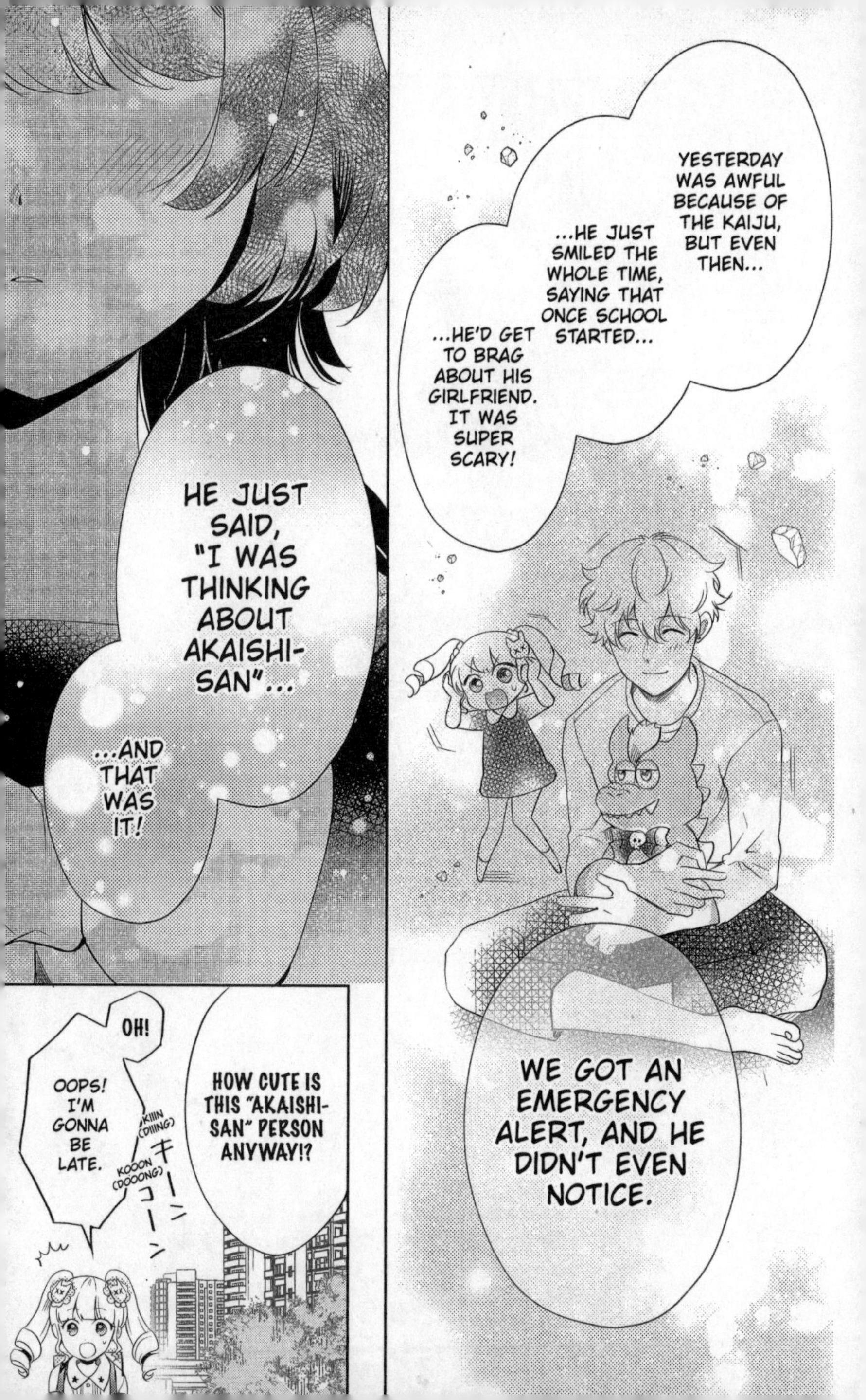
YESTERDAY WAS AWFUL BECAUSE OF THE KAIJU, BUT EVEN THEN...
...HE JUST SMILED THE WHOLE TIME, SAYING THAT ONCE SCHOOL STARTED...
...HE'D GET TO BRAG ABOUT HIS GIRLFRIEND. IT WAS SUPER SCARY!
WE GOT AN EMERGENCY ALERT, AND HE DIDN'T EVEN NOTICE.
HE JUST SAID, "I WAS THINKING ABOUT AKAISHI-SAN"...
...AND THAT WAS IT!
HOW CUTE IS THIS "AKAISHI-SAN" PERSON ANYWAY!?
KIIN (DIIING)
KOOON (DOOONG)
OH!
OOPS! I'M GONNA BE LATE.

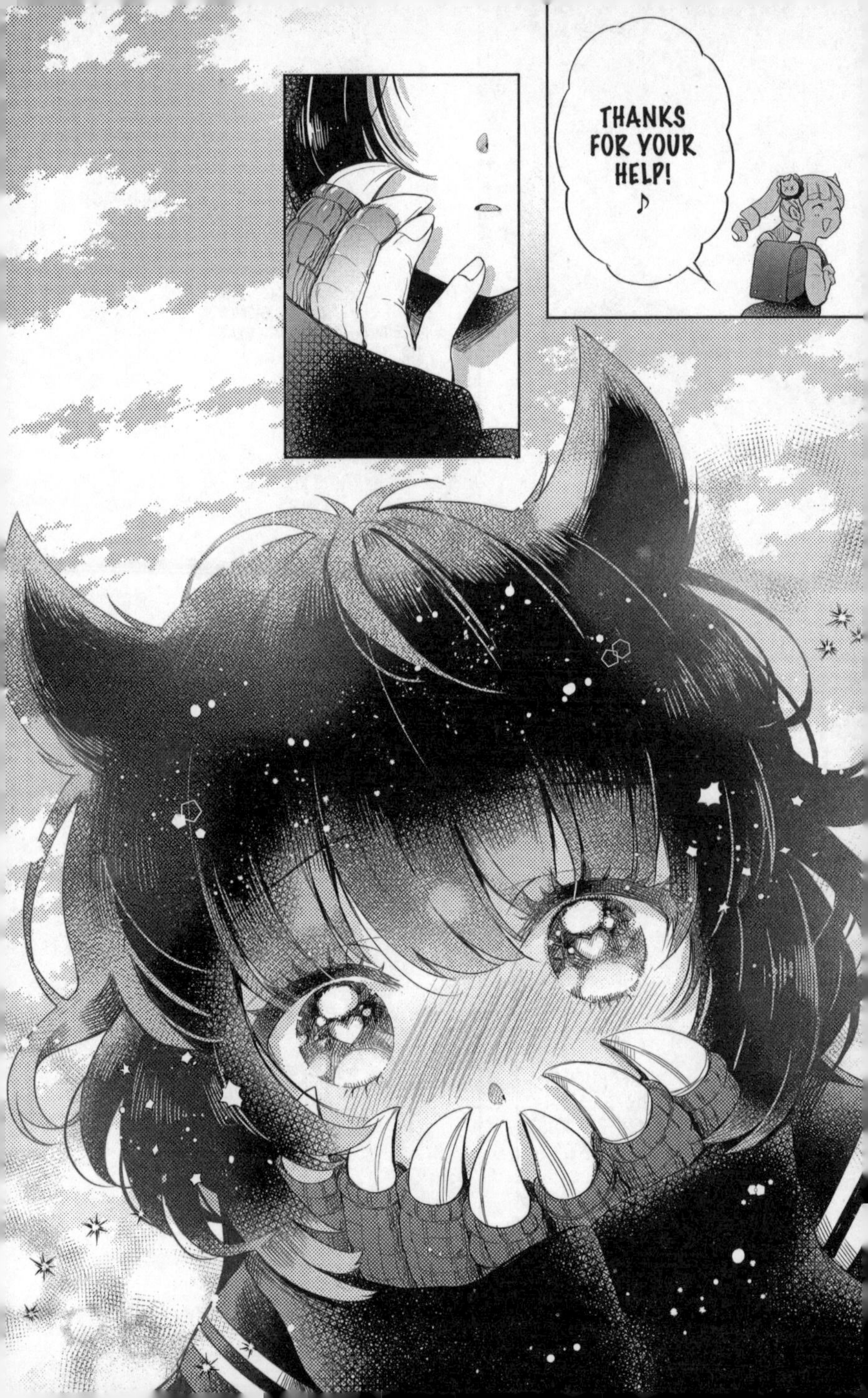
THANKS FOR YOUR HELP! ♪

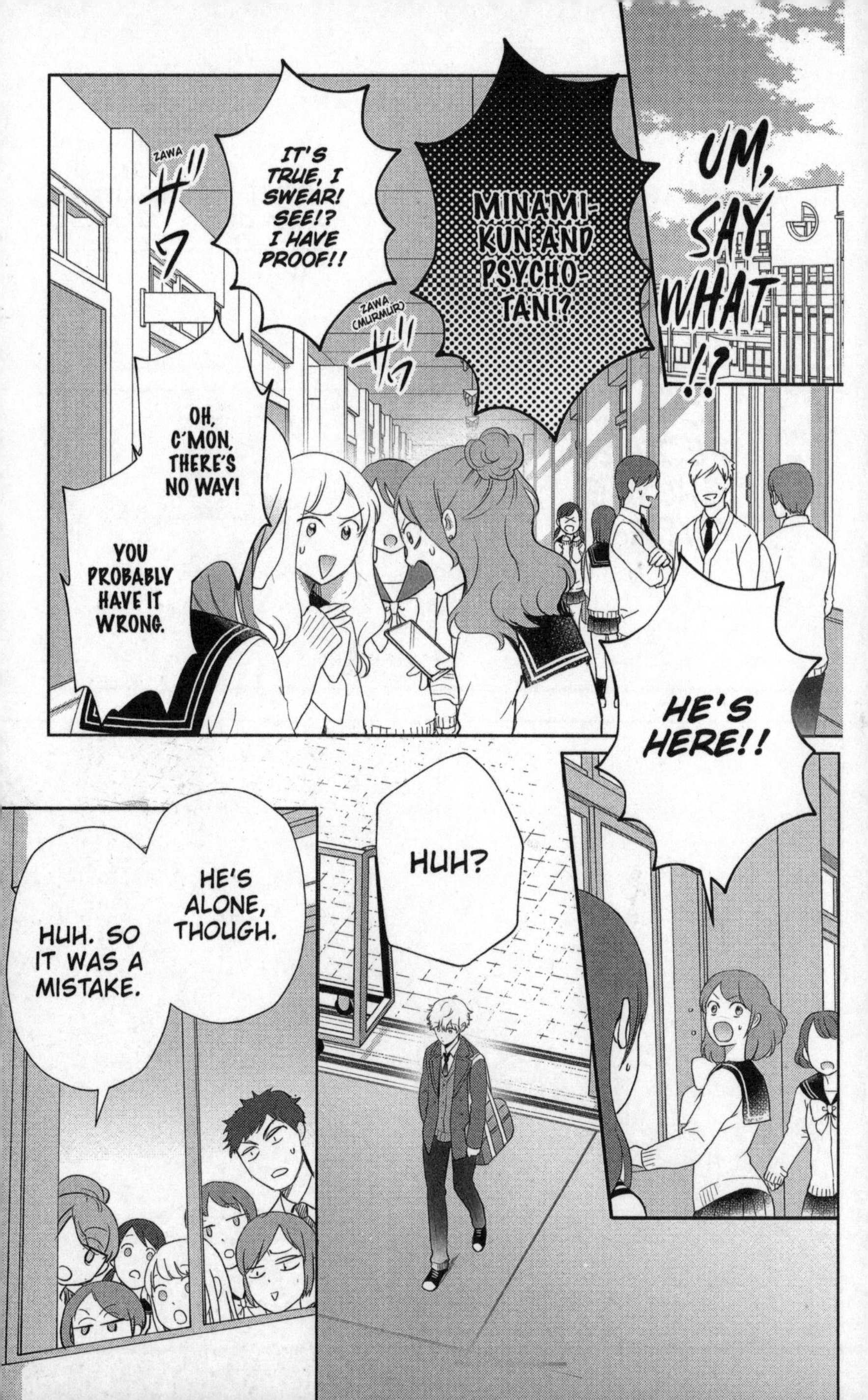
UM, SAY WHAT!?
MINAMI-KUN AND PSYCHO-TAN!?
ZAWA (MURMUR)
IT'S TRUE, I SWEAR! SEE!? I HAVE PROOF!!
ZAWA
OH, C'MON, THERE'S NO WAY!
YOU PROBABLY HAVE IT WRONG.
HE'S HERE!!
HUH?
HE'S ALONE, THOUGH.
HUH. SO IT WAS A MISTAKE.

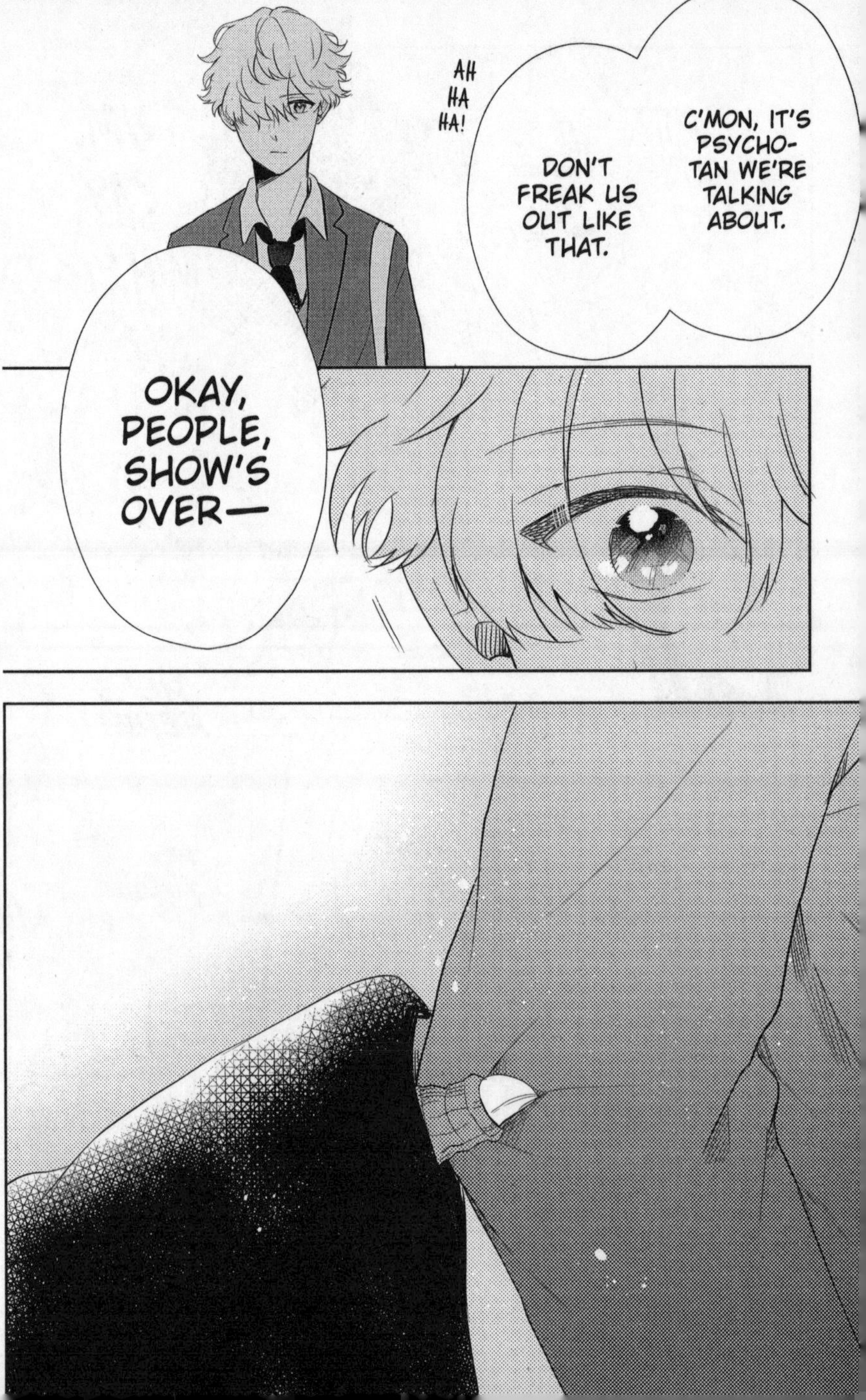
C'MON, IT'S PSYCHO-TAN WE'RE TALKING ABOUT.
DON'T FREAK US OUT LIKE THAT.
AH HA HA!
OKAY, PEOPLE, SHOW'S OVER—

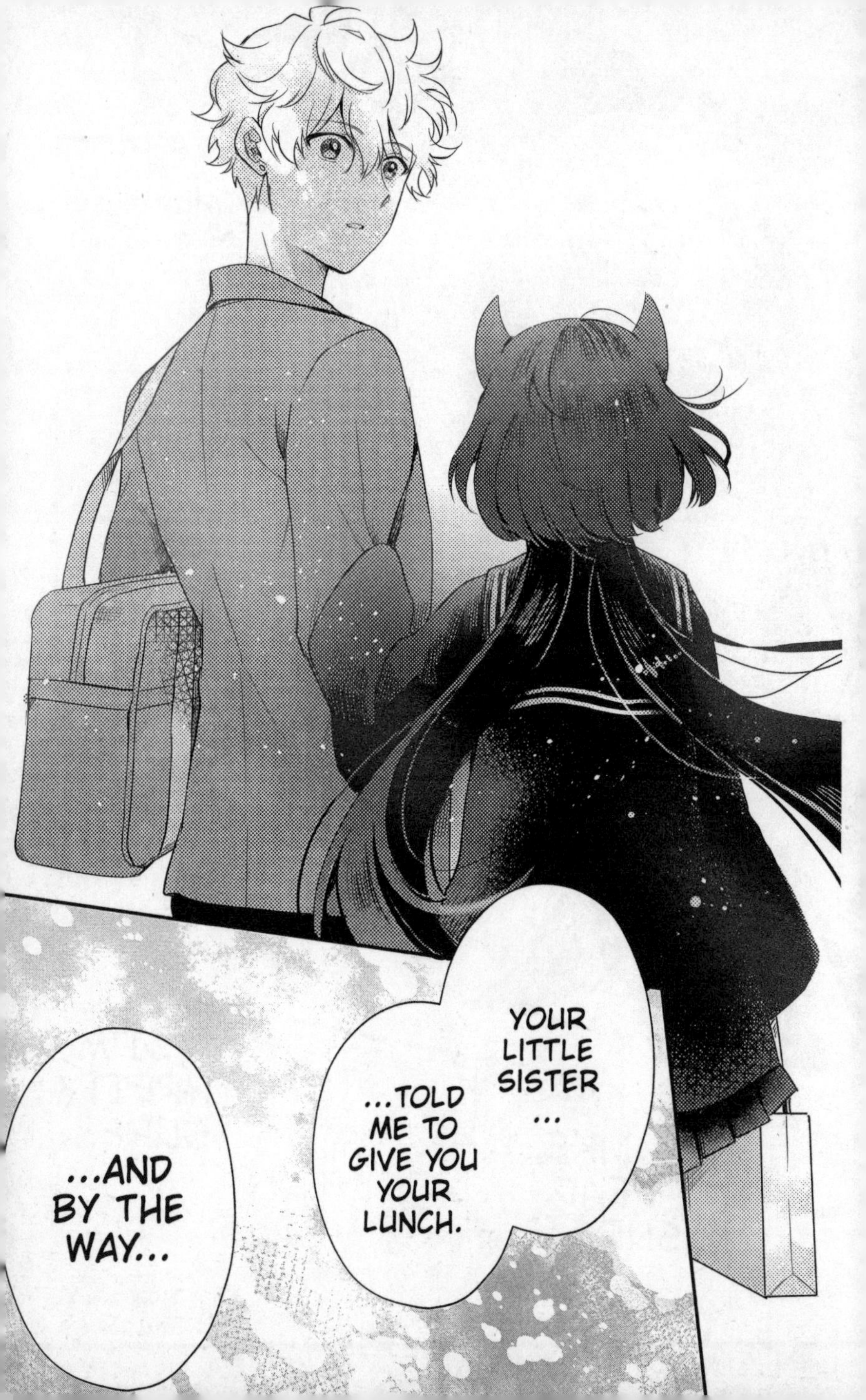
YOUR LITTLE SISTER ...
...TOLD ME TO GIVE YOU YOUR LUNCH.
...AND BY THE WAY...

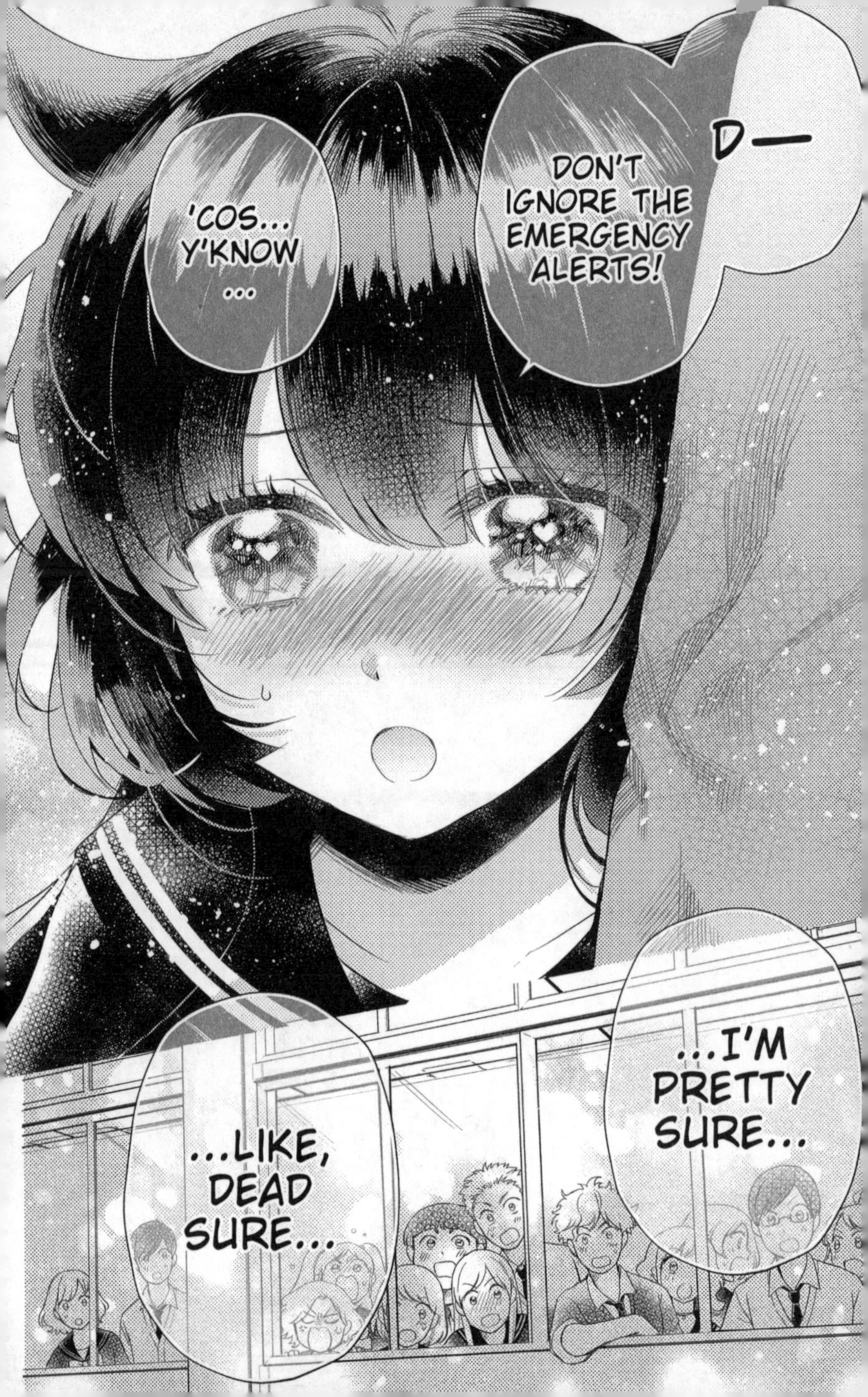
D—
DON'T IGNORE THE EMERGENCY ALERTS!
'COS... Y'KNOW ...
...I'M PRETTY SURE...
...LIKE, DEAD SURE...

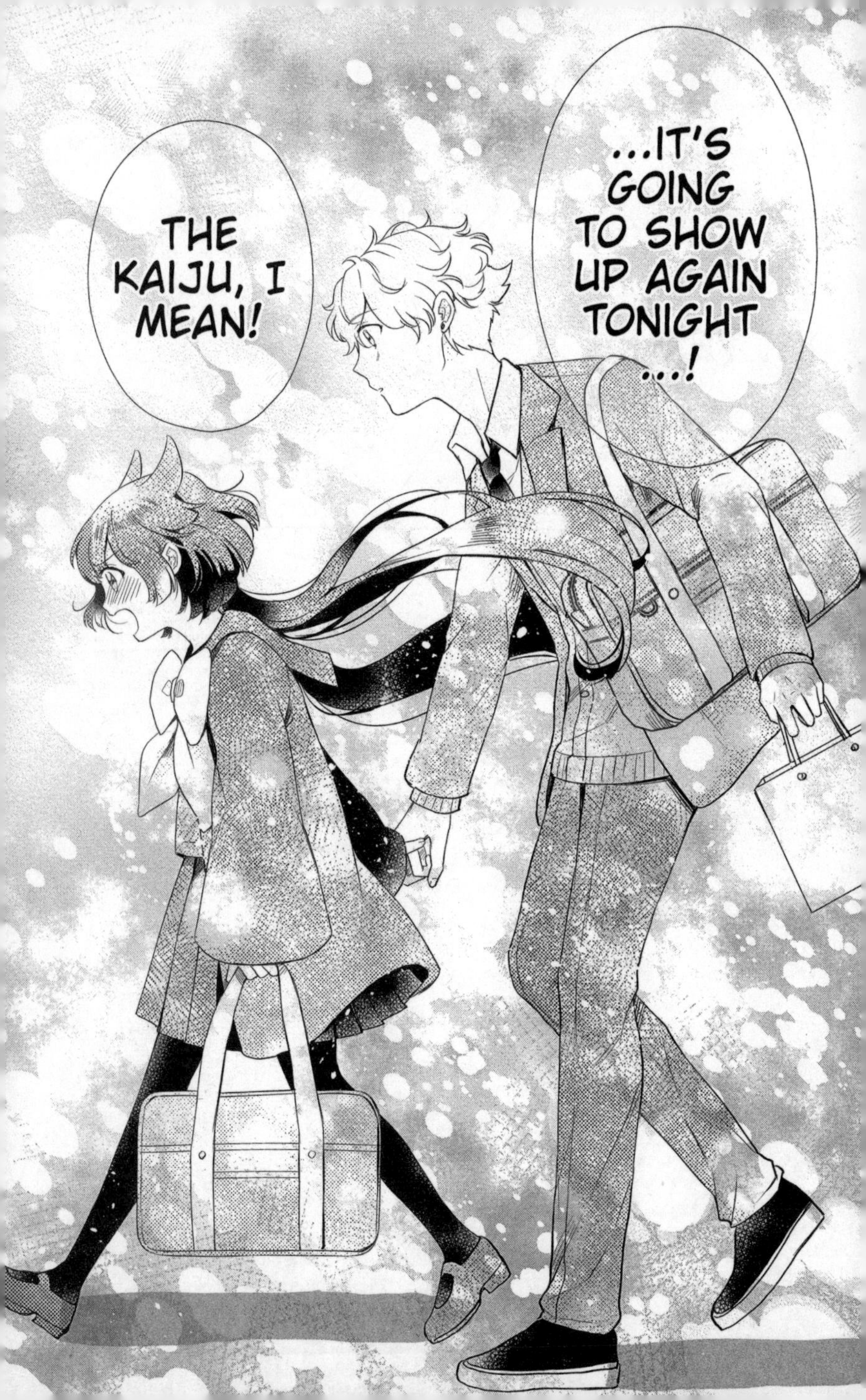
...IT'S GOING TO SHOW UP AGAIN TONIGHT ...!
THE KAIJU, I MEAN!

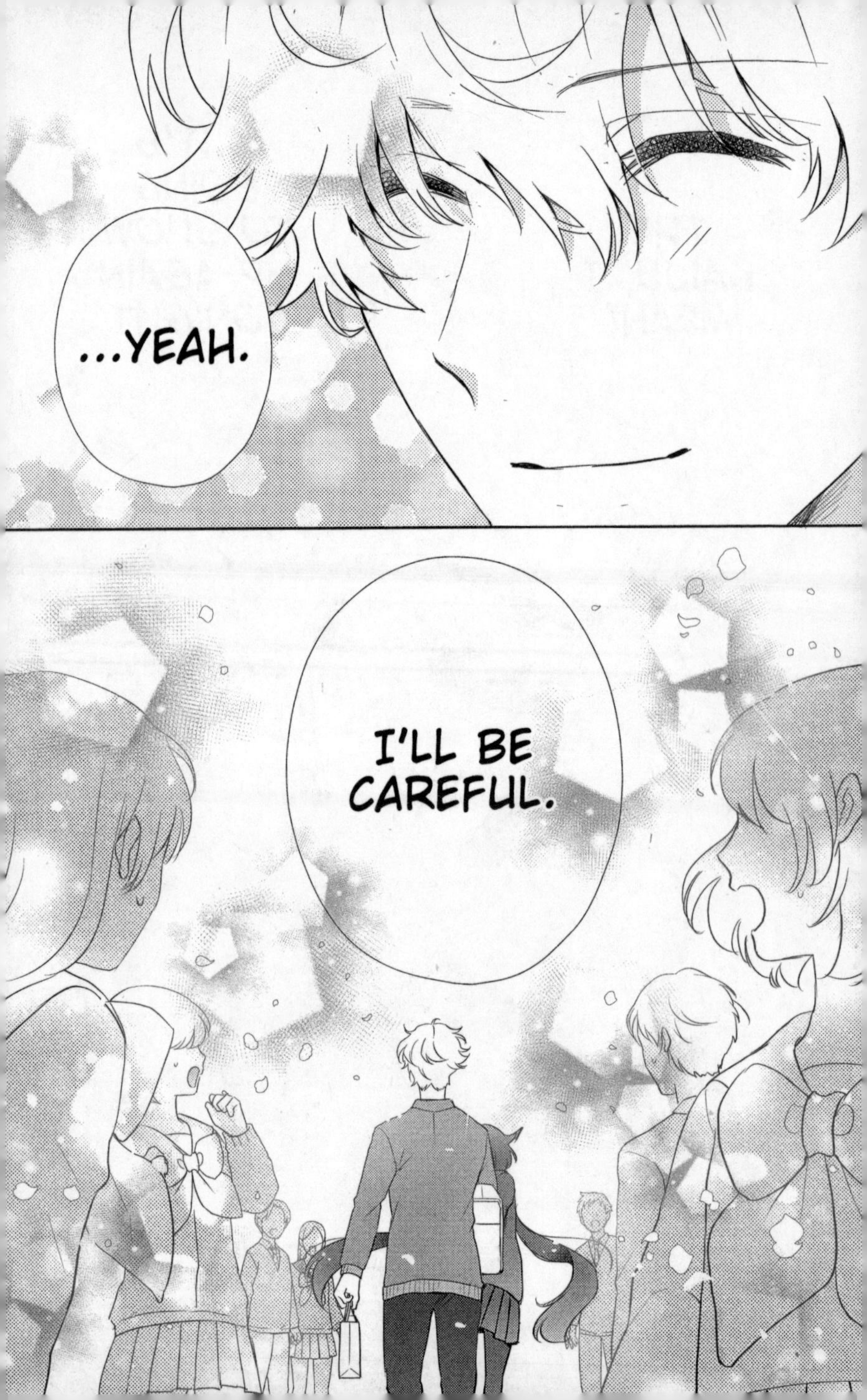
...YEAH.
I'LL BE CAREFUL.

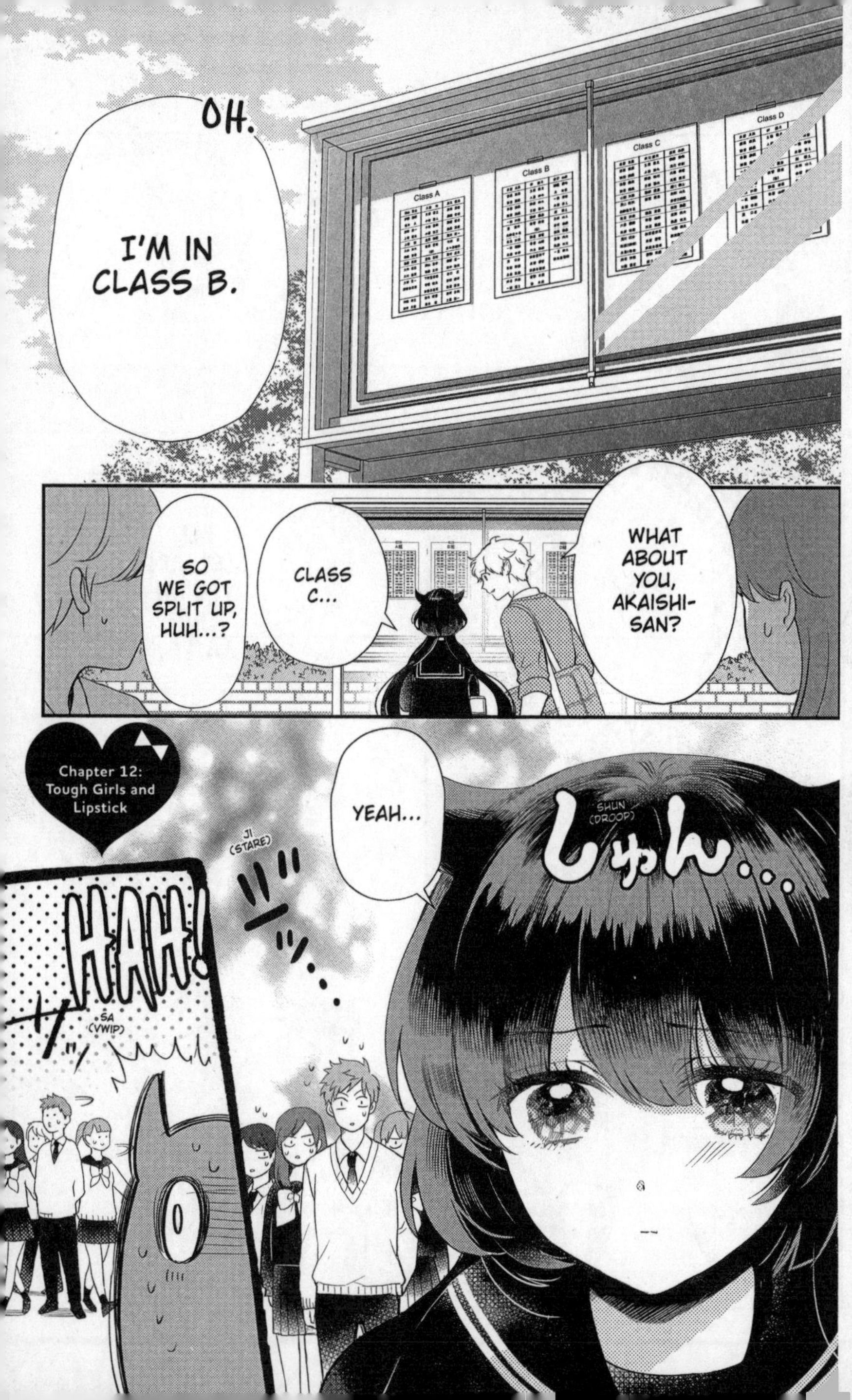
OH.
I'M IN CLASS B.
Class A
Class B
Class C
Class D
WHAT ABOUT YOU, AKAISHI-SAN?
CLASS C...
SO WE GOT SPLIT UP, HUH...?
YEAH...
SHUN (DROOP)
しゅん...
JI (STARE)
Chapter 12: Tough Girls and Lipstick
HAH!
SA (VWIP)

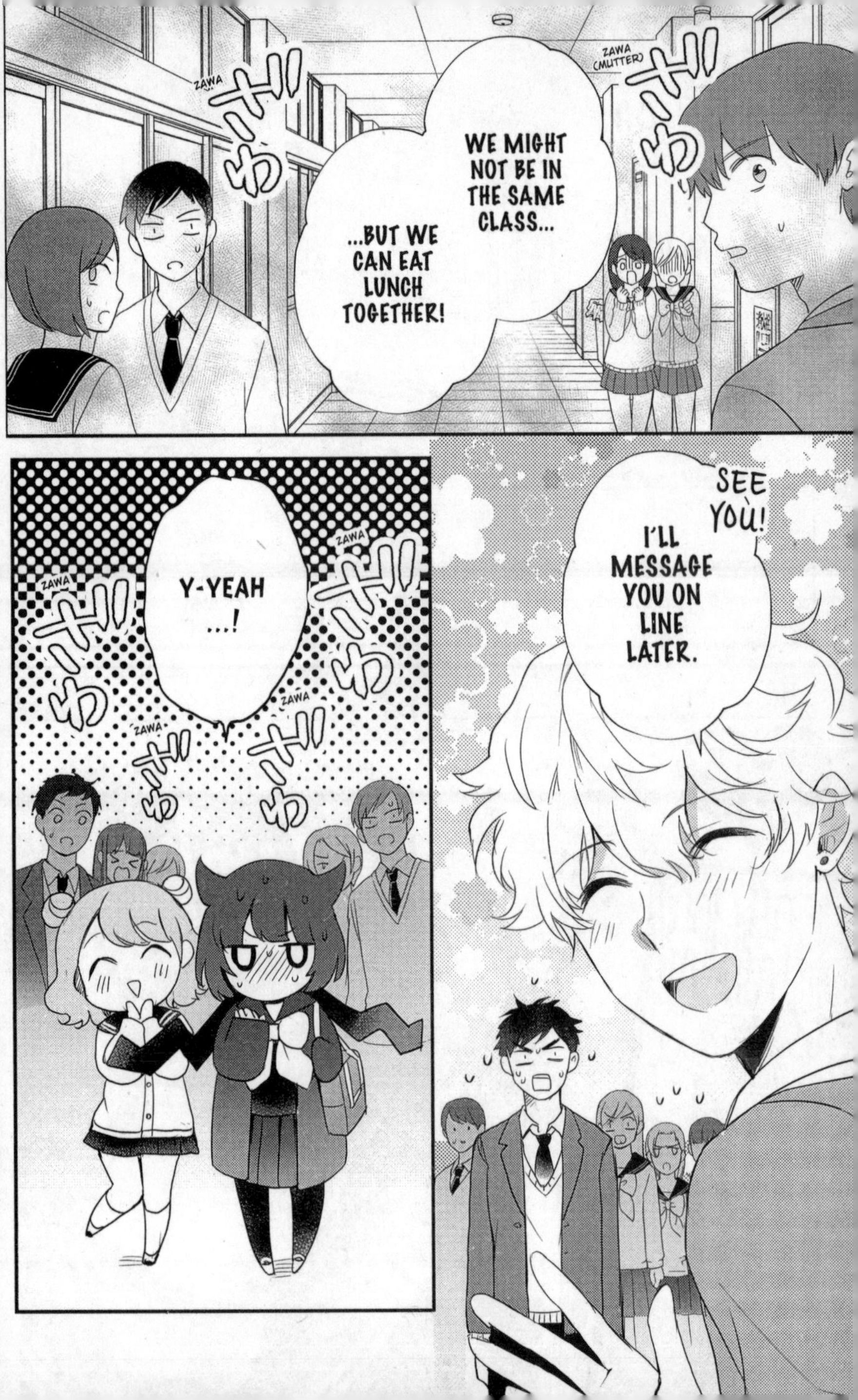
ZAWA (MUTTER)
WE MIGHT NOT BE IN THE SAME CLASS...
...BUT WE CAN EAT LUNCH TOGETHER!
ZAWA
SEE YOU!
I'LL MESSAGE YOU ON LINE LATER.
ZAWA
Y-YEAH ...!
ZAWA
ZAWA
ZAWA

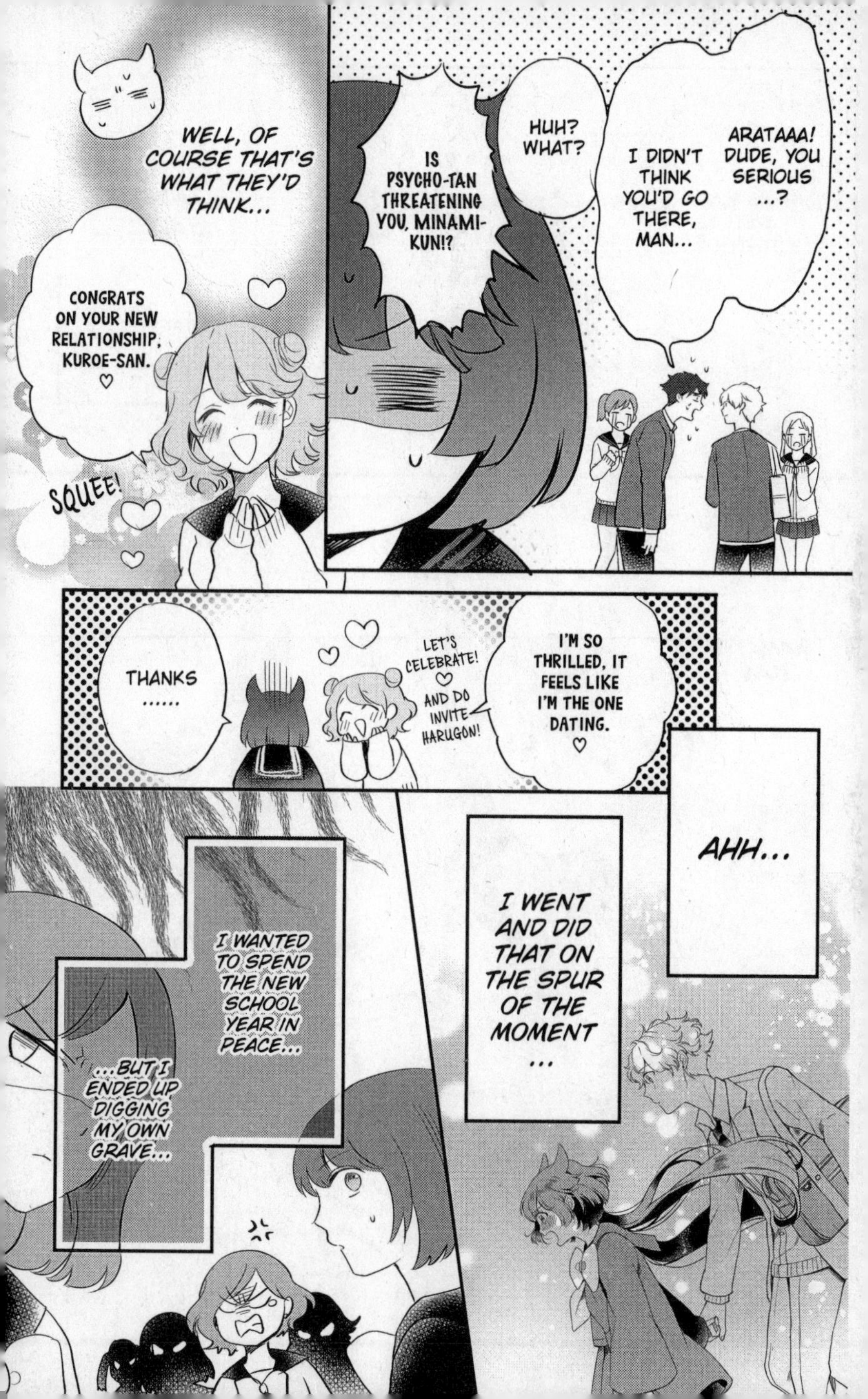
ARATAAA! DUDE, YOU SERIOUS ...?
I DIDN'T THINK YOU'D GO THERE, MAN...
HUH? WHAT?
IS PSYCHO-TAN THREATENING YOU, MINAMI-KUN!?
WELL, OF COURSE THAT'S WHAT THEY'D THINK...
CONGRATS ON YOUR NEW RELATIONSHIP, KUROE-SAN. ♡
SQUEE!
I'M SO THRILLED, IT FEELS LIKE I'M THE ONE DATING. ♡
LET'S CELEBRATE! ♡ AND DO INVITE HARUGON!
THANKS ......
AHH...
I WENT AND DID THAT ON THE SPUR OF THE MOMENT ...
I WANTED TO SPEND THE NEW SCHOOL YEAR IN PEACE...
...BUT I ENDED UP DIGGING MY OWN GRAVE...

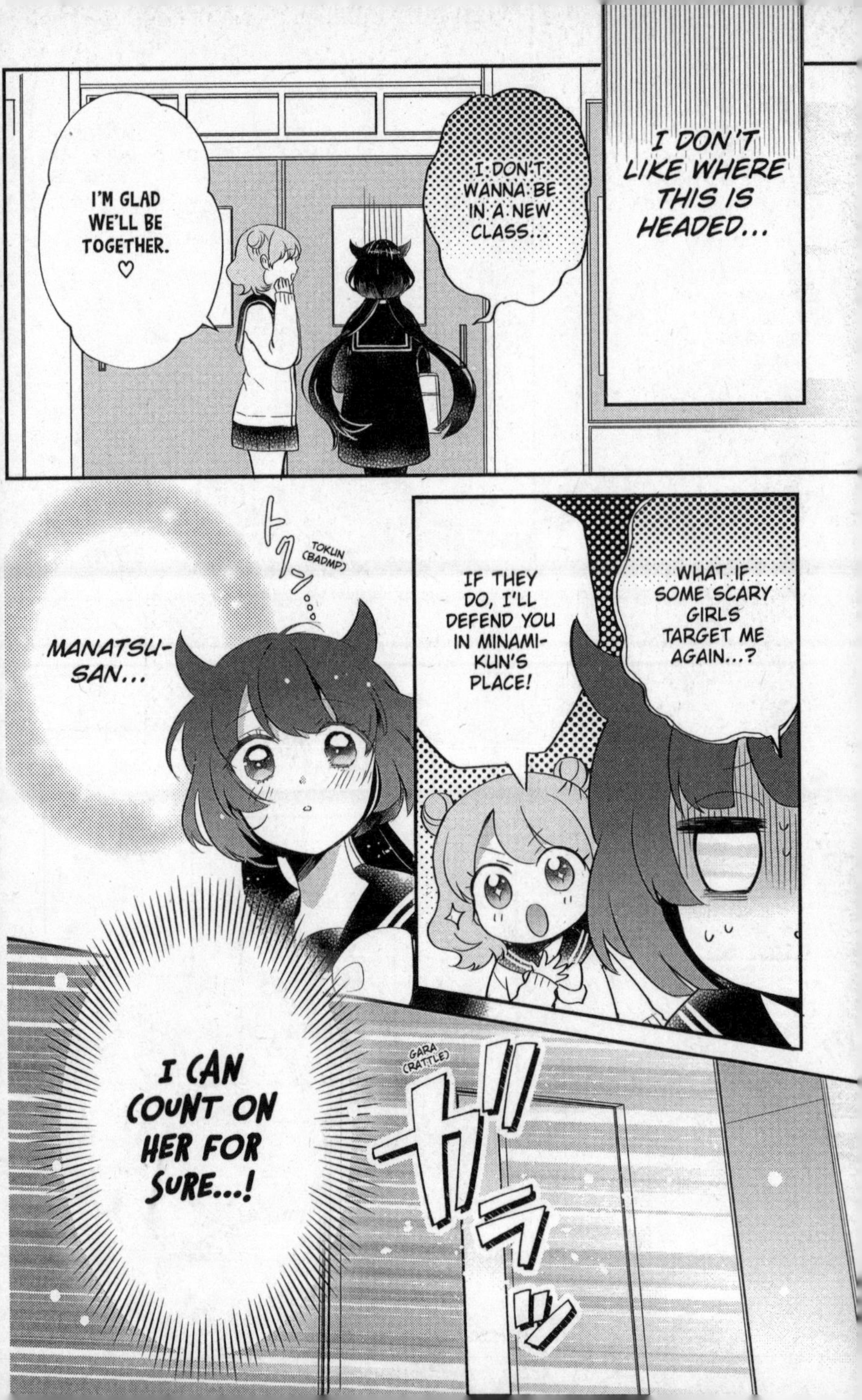
I DON'T LIKE WHERE THIS IS HEADED...
I DON'T WANNA BE IN A NEW CLASS...
I'M GLAD WE'LL BE TOGETHER. ♡
WHAT IF SOME SCARY GIRLS TARGET ME AGAIN...?
IF THEY DO, I'LL DEFEND YOU IN MINAMI-KUN'S PLACE!
トクン
TOKUN (BADMP)
MANATSU-SAN...
I CAN COUNT ON HER FOR SURE...!
ガラッ
GARA (RATTLE)

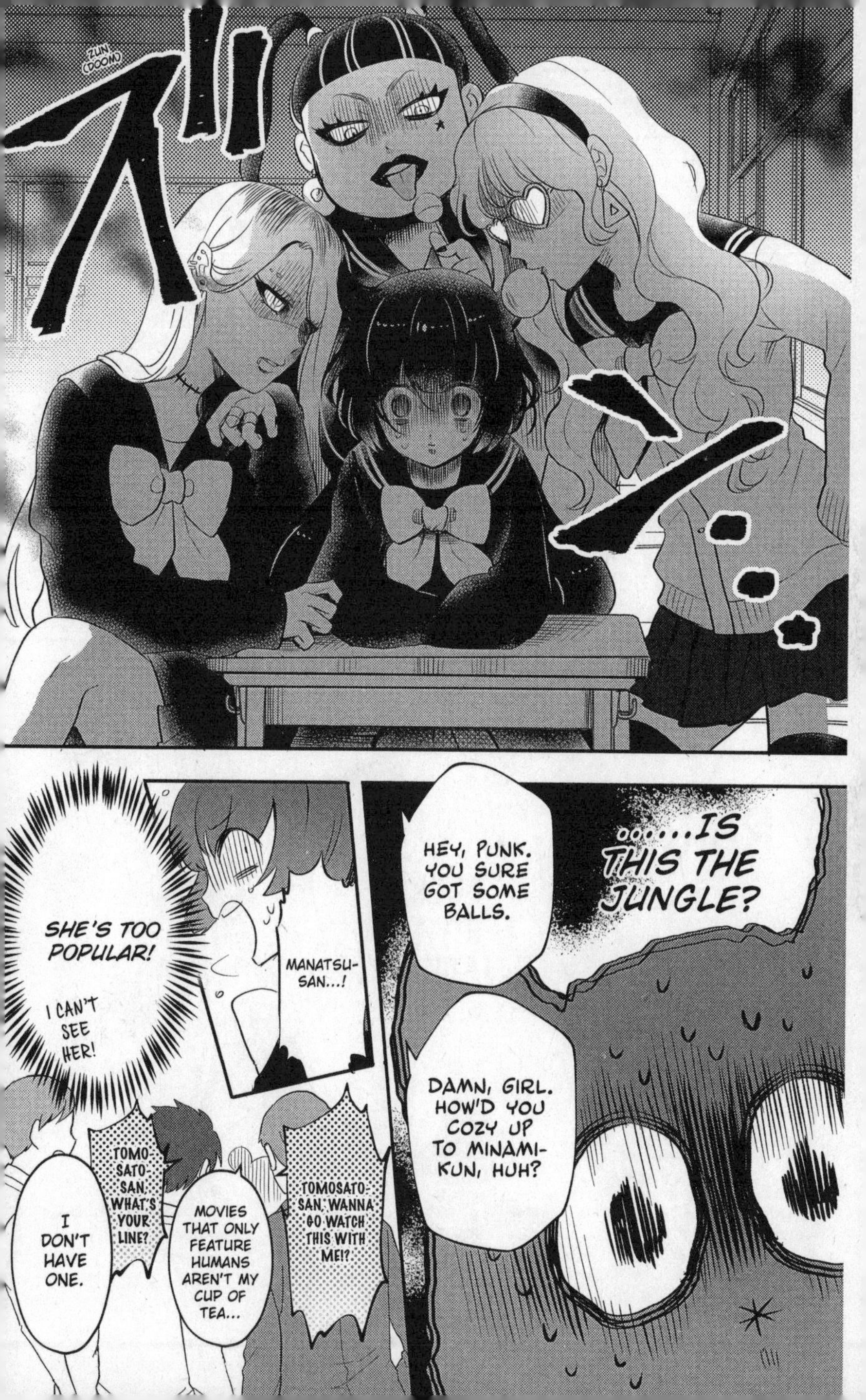
ZUN (DOOM)
......IS THIS THE JUNGLE?
HEY, PUNK. YOU SURE GOT SOME BALLS.
DAMN, GIRL. HOW'D YOU COZY UP TO MINAMI-KUN, HUH?
MANATSU-SAN...!
SHE'S TOO POPULAR!
I CAN'T SEE HER!
TOMOSATO-SAN, WANNA GO WATCH THIS WITH ME!?
MOVIES THAT ONLY FEATURE HUMANS AREN'T MY CUP OF TEA...
TOMO-SATO-SAN, WHAT'S YOUR LINE?
I DON'T HAVE ONE.

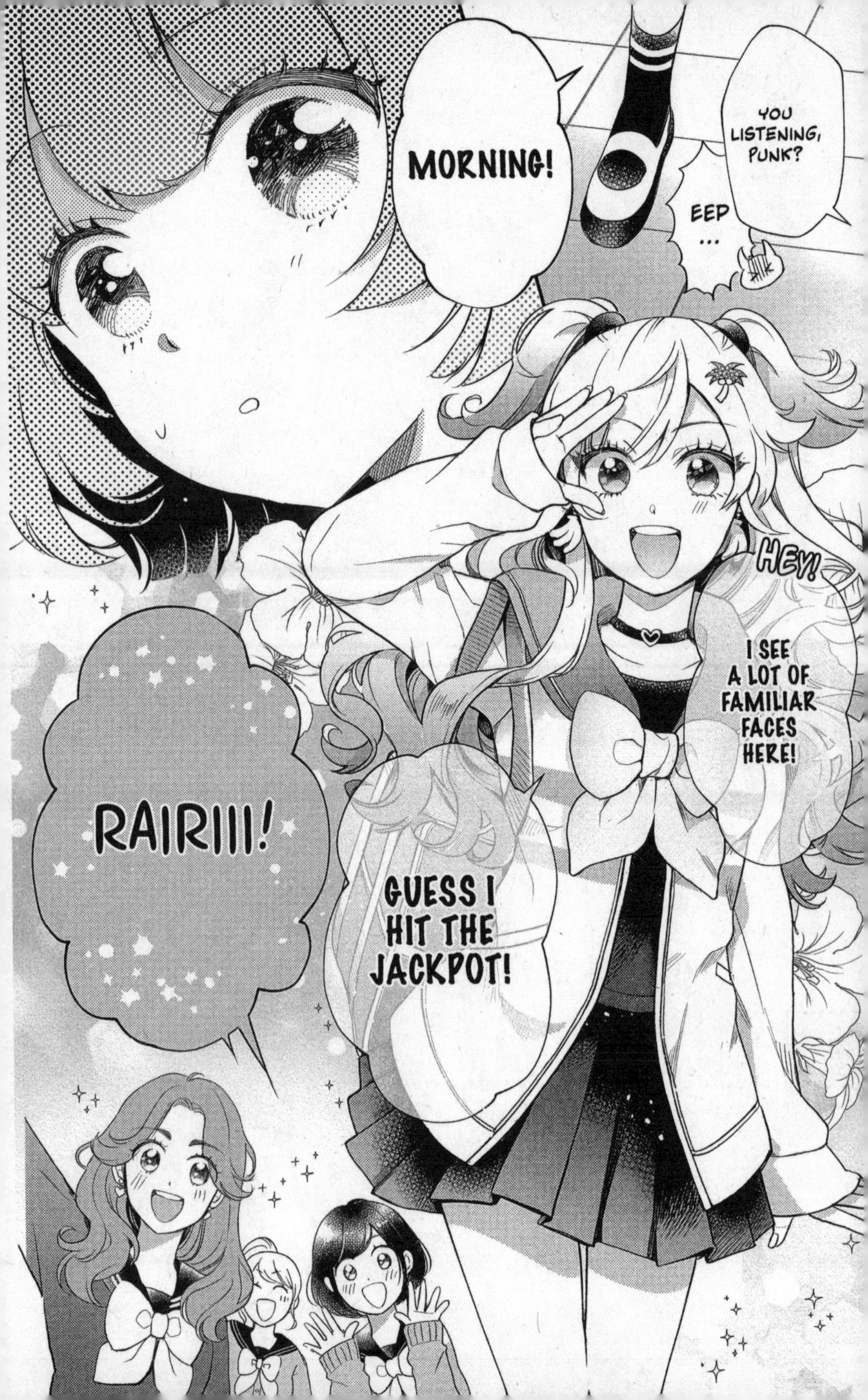
YOU LISTENING, PUNK?
EEP...
MORNING!
HEY!
I SEE A LOT OF FAMILIAR FACES HERE!
GUESS I HIT THE JACKPOT!
RAIRIII!

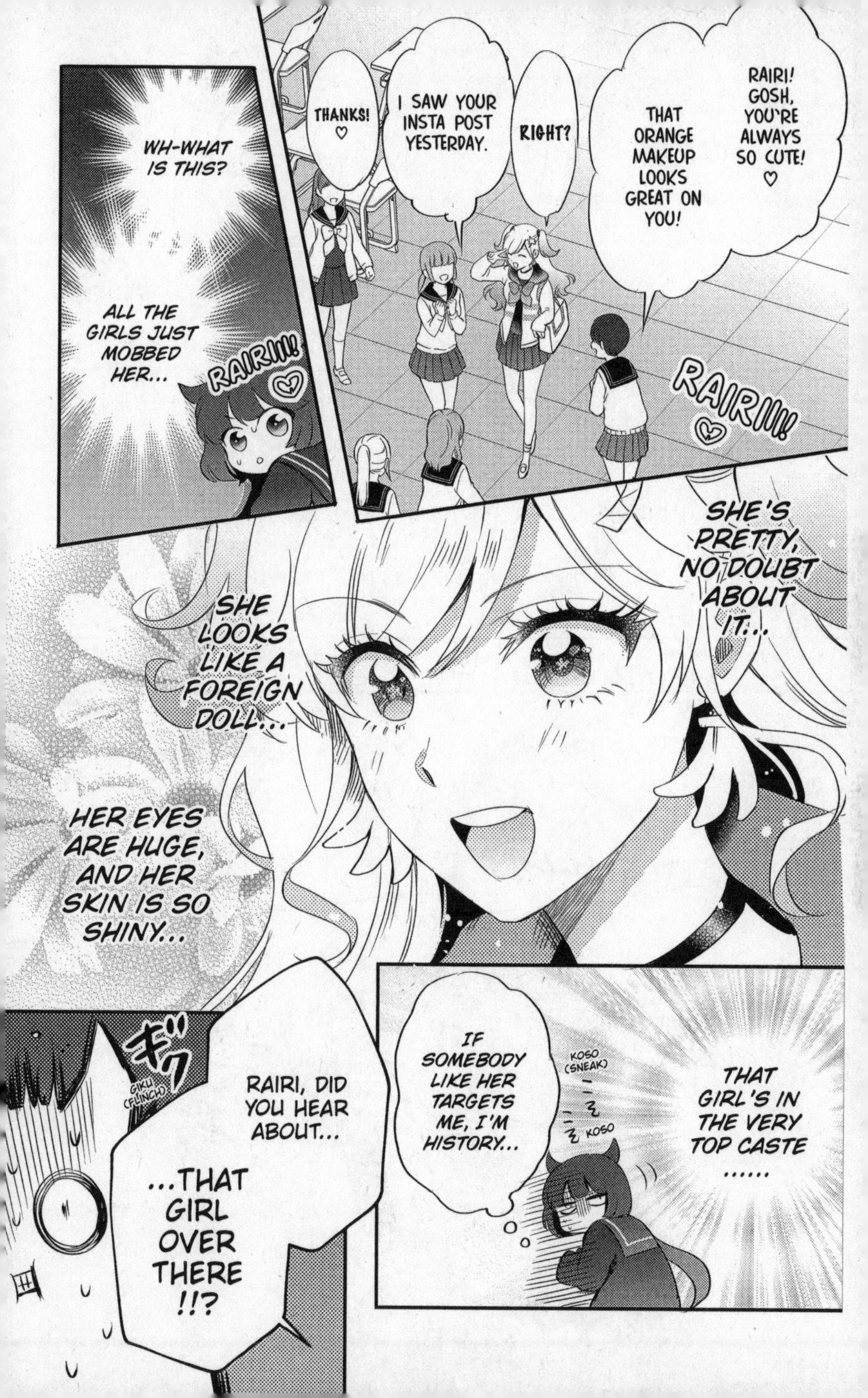
RAIRI! GOSH, YOU'RE ALWAYS SO CUTE! ♡
THAT ORANGE MAKEUP LOOKS GREAT ON YOU!
RIGHT?
I SAW YOUR INSTA POST YESTERDAY.
THANKS! ♡
RAIRI!!! ♡
WH-WHAT IS THIS?
ALL THE GIRLS JUST MOBBED HER...
RAIRI!!! ♡
SHE'S PRETTY, NO DOUBT ABOUT IT...
SHE LOOKS LIKE A FOREIGN DOLL...
HER EYES ARE HUGE, AND HER SKIN IS SO SHINY...
THAT GIRL'S IN THE VERY TOP CASTE ......
KOSO (SNEAK)
KOSO
IF SOMEBODY LIKE HER TARGETS ME, I'M HISTORY...
RAIRI, DID YOU HEAR ABOUT...
...THAT GIRL OVER THERE!!?
ギク
GIKU (FLINCH)

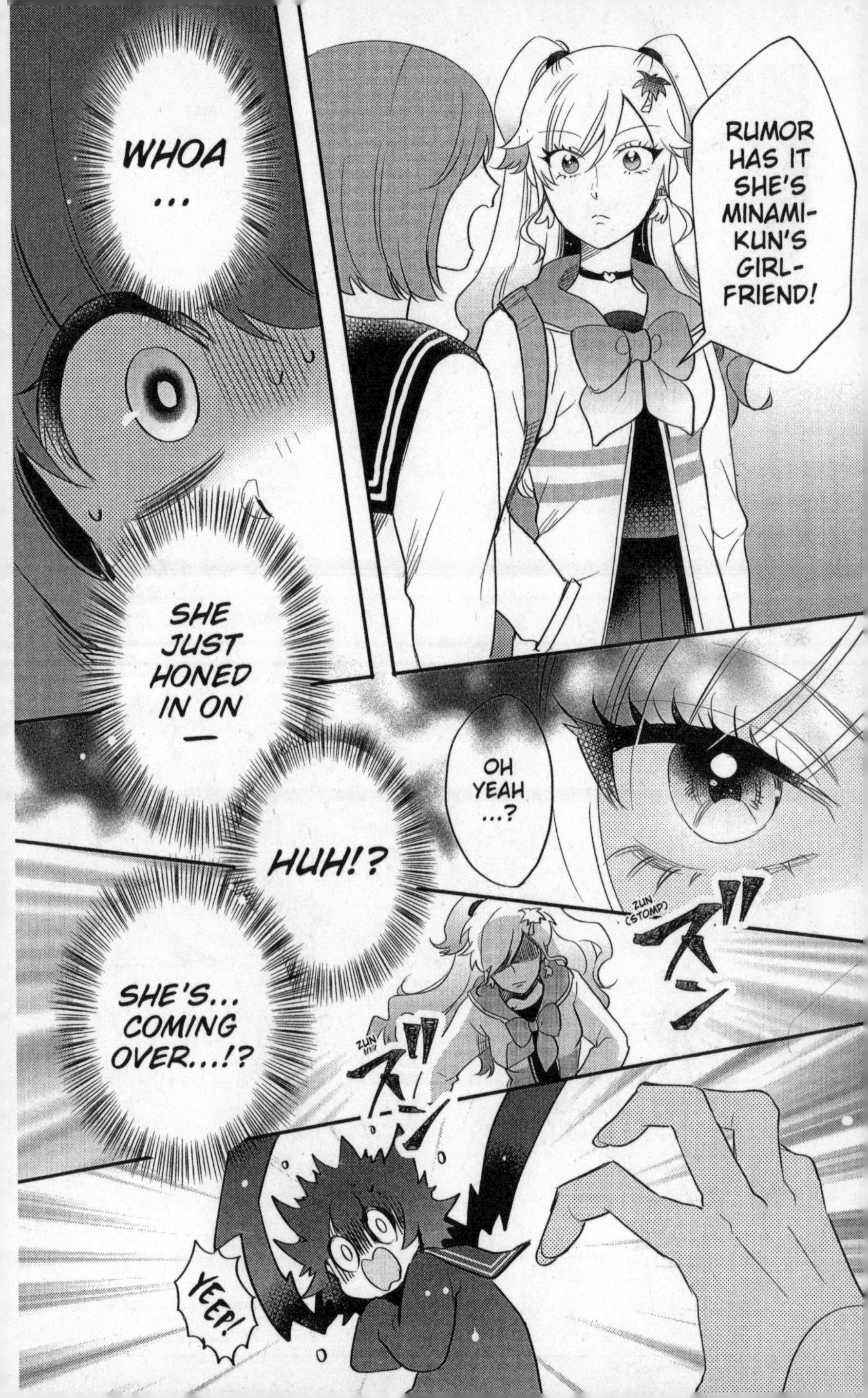
RUMOR HAS IT SHE'S MINAMI-KUN'S GIRL-FRIEND!
WHOA ...
SHE JUST HONED IN ON —
OH YEAH ...?
HUH!?
ZUN (STOMP)
ZUN
SHE'S... COMING OVER...!?
YEEP!

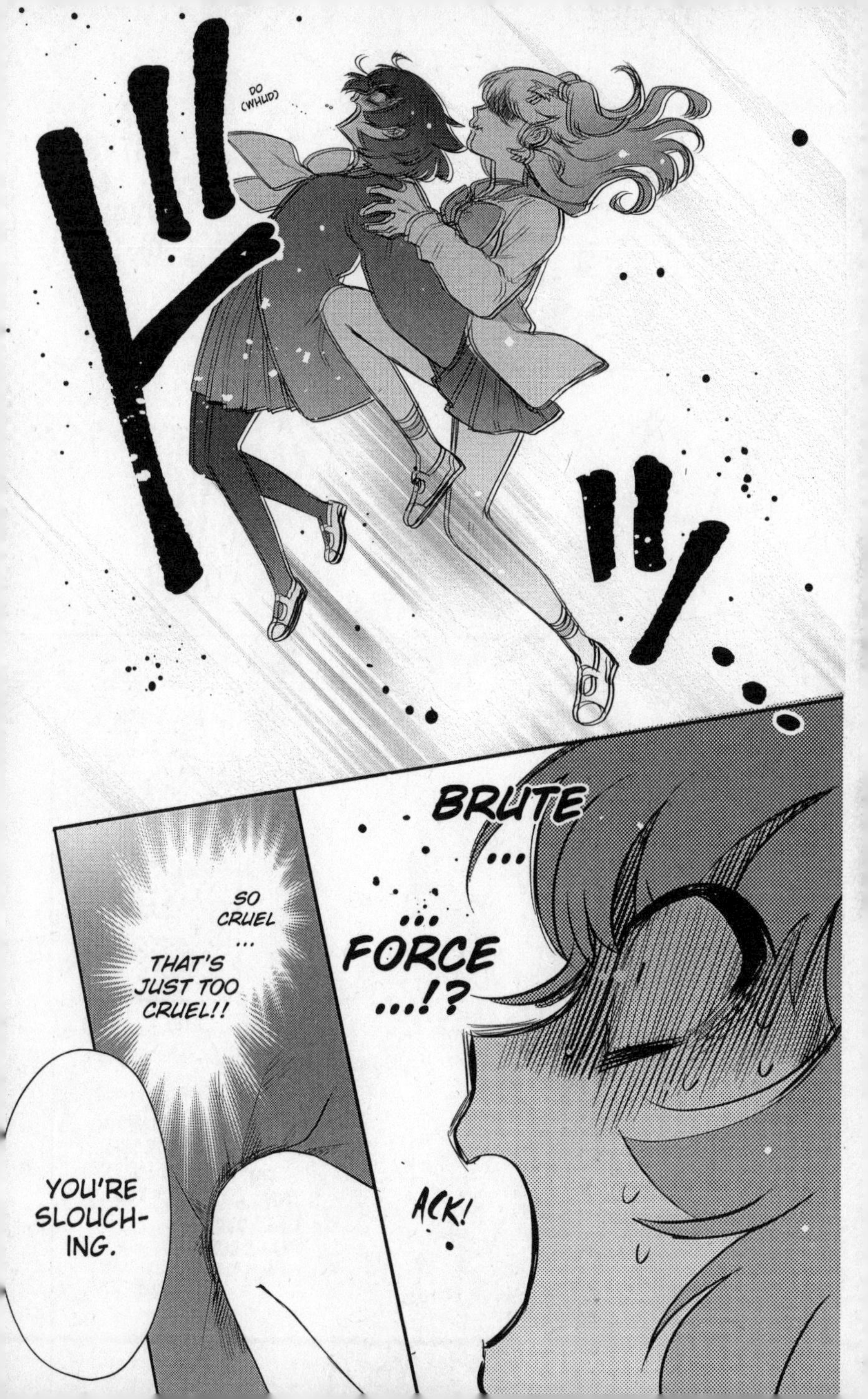
DO (WHUD)
BRUTE ...
... FORCE ...!?
ACK!
SO CRUEL ... THAT'S JUST TOO CRUEL!!
YOU'RE SLOUCH-ING.

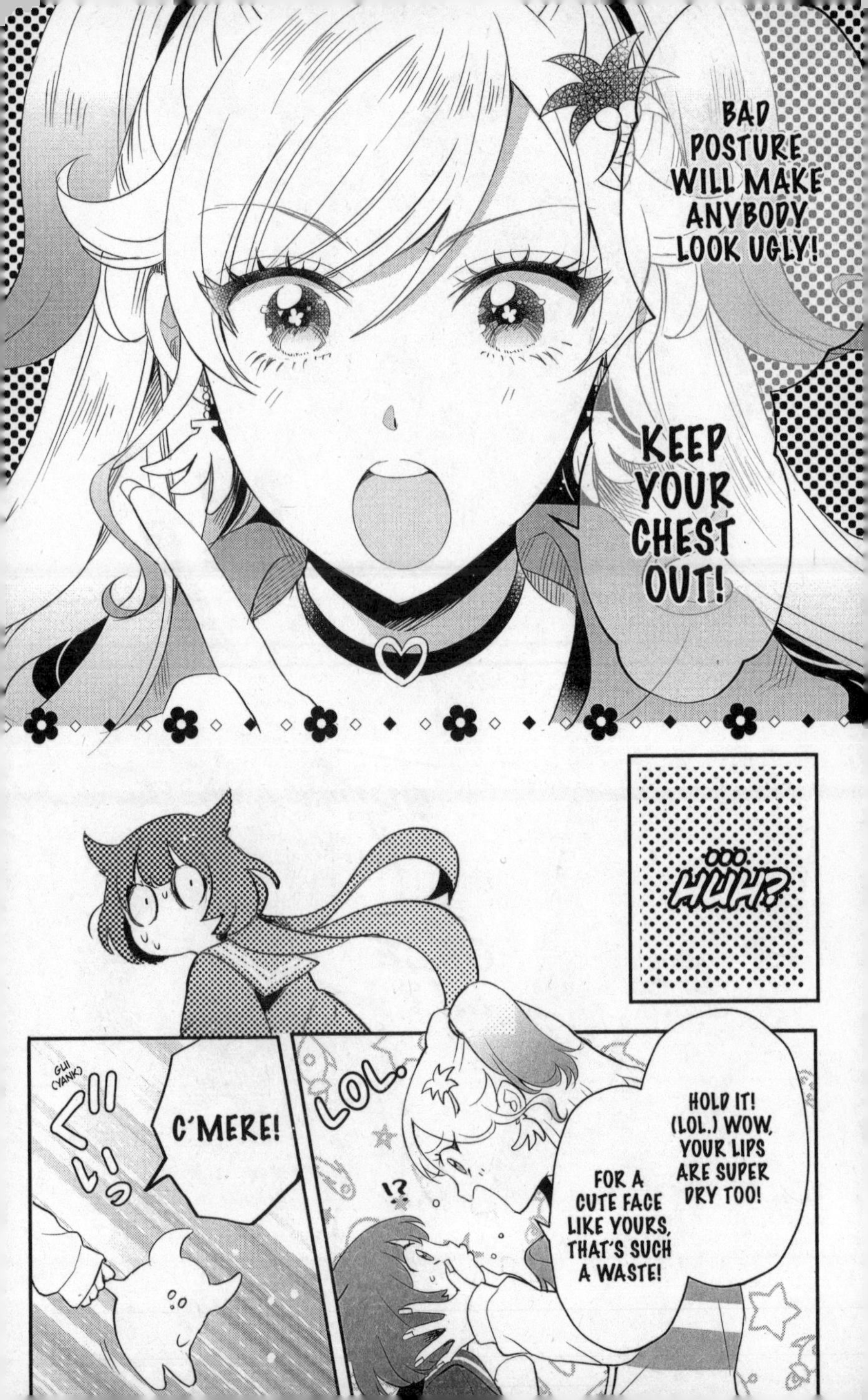
BAD POSTURE WILL MAKE ANYBODY LOOK UGLY!
KEEP YOUR CHEST OUT!
...HUH?
HOLD IT! (LOL.) WOW, YOUR LIPS ARE SUPER DRY TOO!
FOR A CUTE FACE LIKE YOURS, THAT'S SUCH A WASTE!
LOL.
!?
C'MERE!
GUI (YANK)

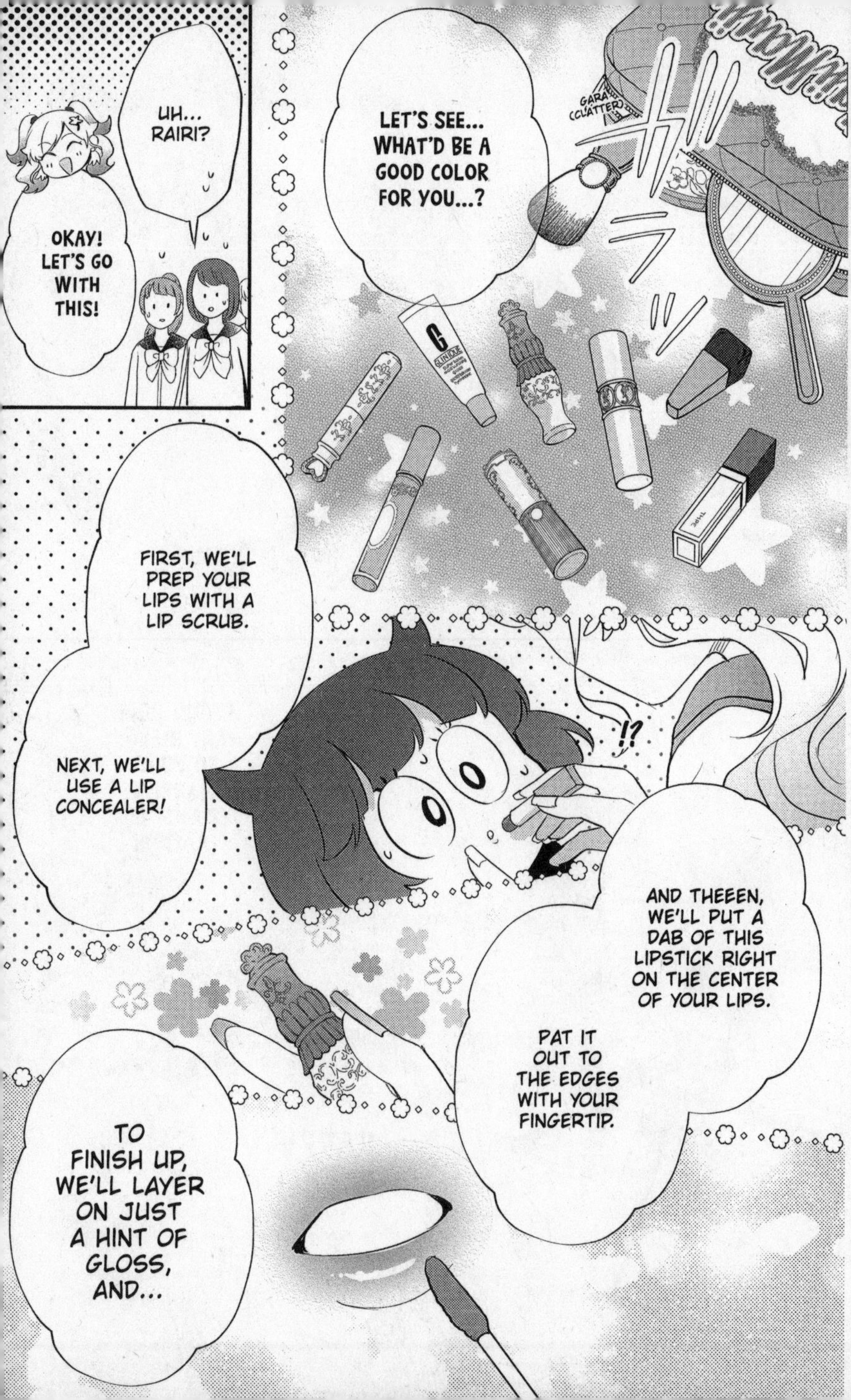
LET'S SEE... WHAT'D BE A GOOD COLOR FOR YOU...?
GARA (CLATTER)
UH... RAIRI?
OKAY! LET'S GO WITH THIS!
FIRST, WE'LL PREP YOUR LIPS WITH A LIP SCRUB.
NEXT, WE'LL USE A LIP CONCEALER!
!?
AND THEEEN, WE'LL PUT A DAB OF THIS LIPSTICK RIGHT ON THE CENTER OF YOUR LIPS.
PAT IT OUT TO THE EDGES WITH YOUR FINGERTIP.
TO FINISH UP, WE'LL LAYER ON JUST A HINT OF GLOSS, AND...

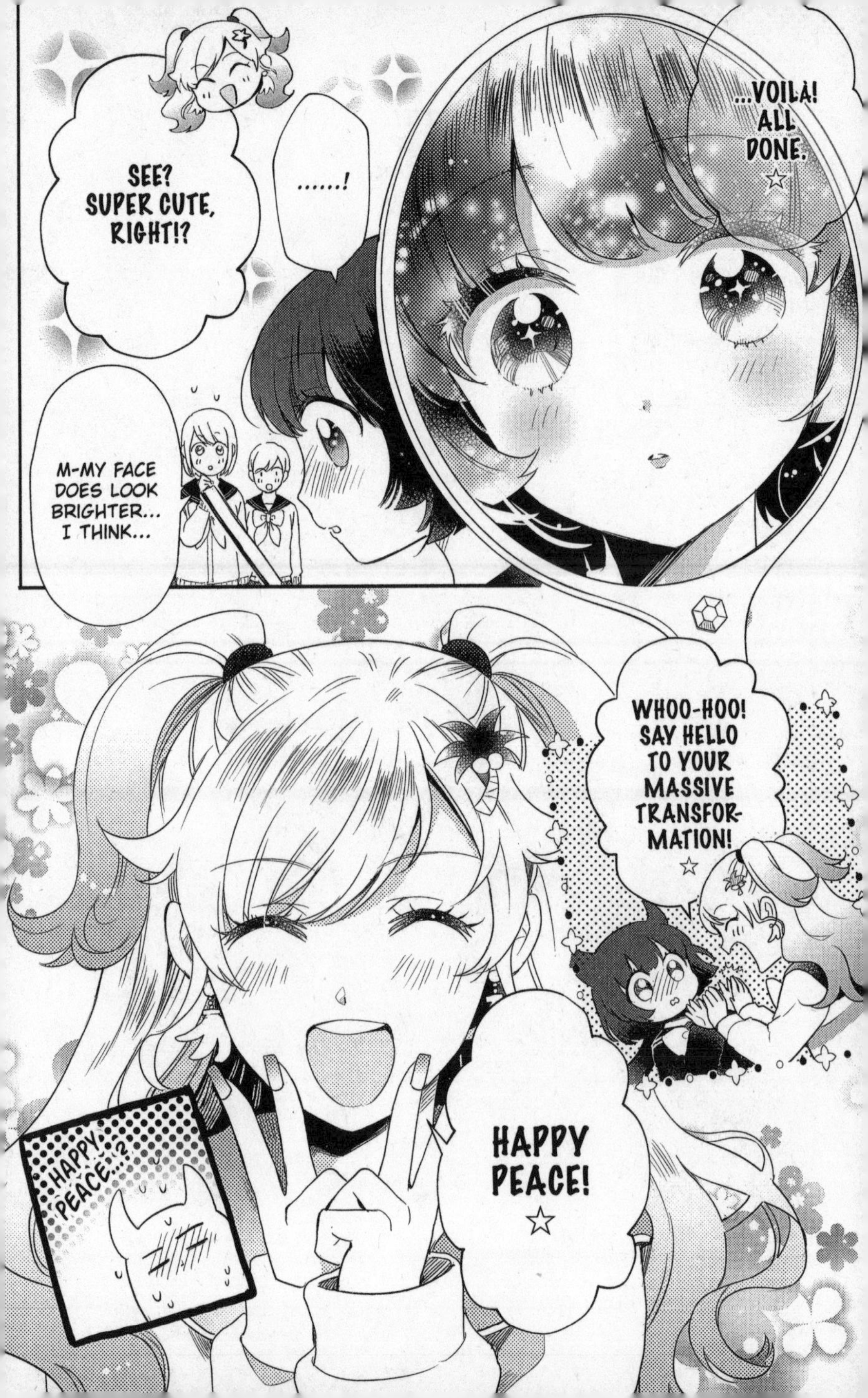
...VOILA! ALL DONE. ☆
......!
SEE? SUPER CUTE, RIGHT!?
M-MY FACE DOES LOOK BRIGHTER... I THINK...
WHOO-HOO! SAY HELLO TO YOUR MASSIVE TRANSFOR-MATION! ☆
HAPPY PEACE! ☆
HAPPY PEACE...?

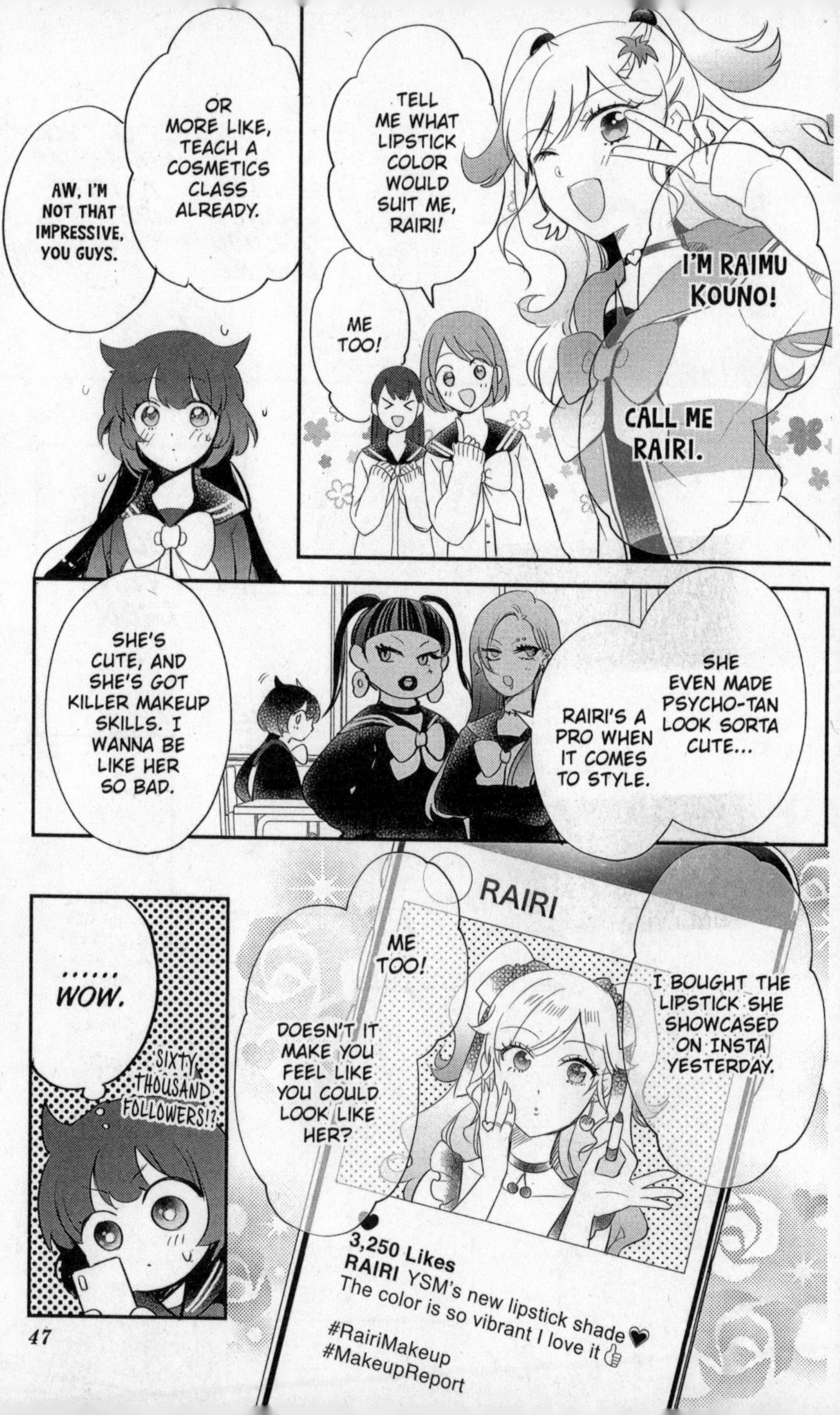
I'M RAIMU KOUNO!
CALL ME RAIRI.
TELL ME WHAT LIPSTICK COLOR WOULD SUIT ME, RAIRI!
ME TOO!
OR MORE LIKE, TEACH A COSMETICS CLASS ALREADY.
AW, I'M NOT THAT IMPRESSIVE, YOU GUYS.
SHE EVEN MADE PSYCHO-TAN LOOK SORTA CUTE...
RAIRI'S A PRO WHEN IT COMES TO STYLE.
SHE'S CUTE, AND SHE'S GOT KILLER MAKEUP SKILLS. I WANNA BE LIKE HER SO BAD.
I BOUGHT THE LIPSTICK SHE SHOWCASED ON INSTA YESTERDAY.
ME TOO!
DOESN'T IT MAKE YOU FEEL LIKE YOU COULD LOOK LIKE HER?
RAIRI
3,250 Likes
RAIRI YSM's new lipstick shade
The color is so vibrant I love it
#RairiMakeup
#MakeupReport
SIXTY THOUSAND FOLLOWERS!?
...... WOW.

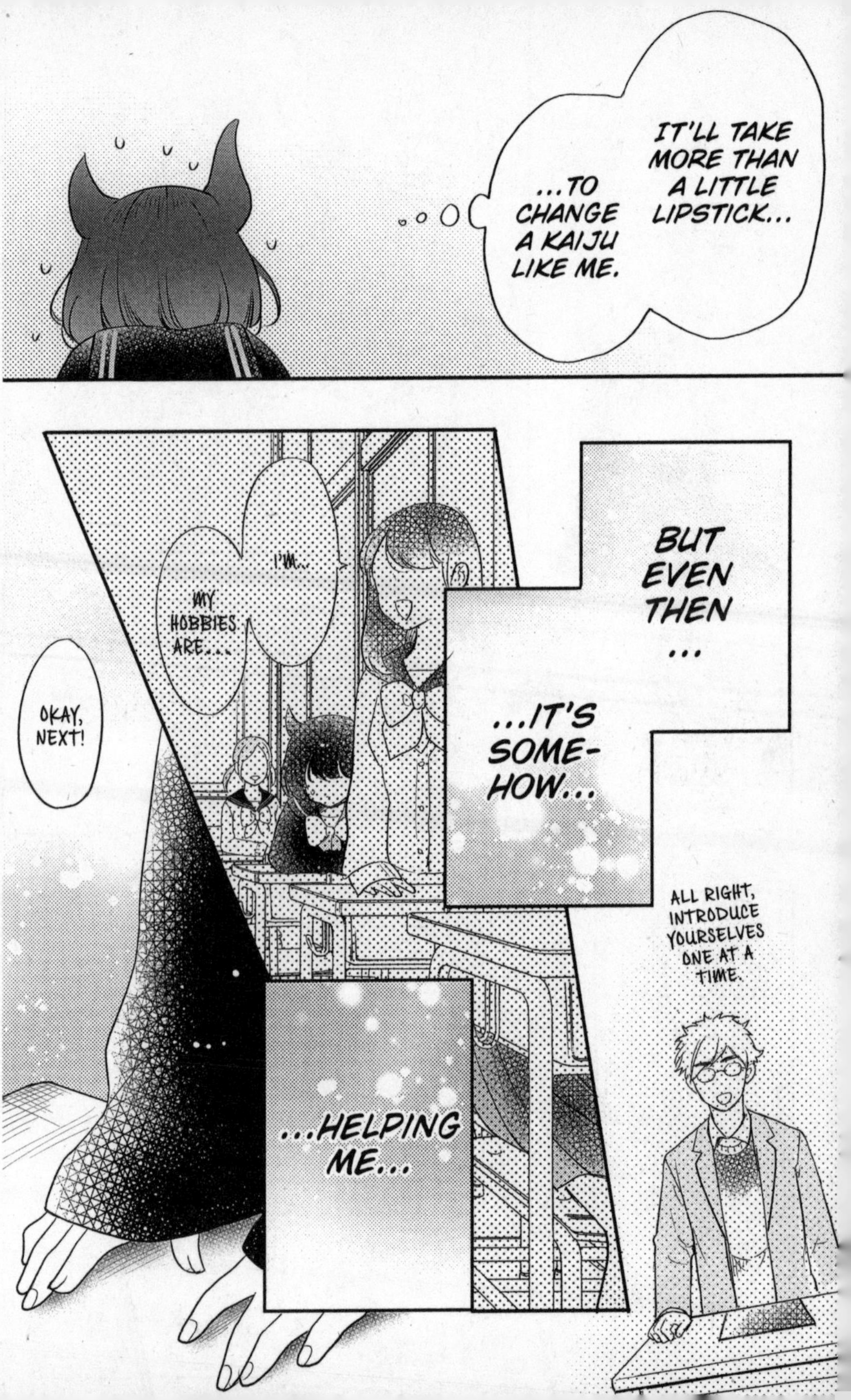
IT'LL TAKE MORE THAN A LITTLE LIPSTICK...
...TO CHANGE A KAIJU LIKE ME.
BUT EVEN THEN...
...IT'S SOME-HOW...
ALL RIGHT, INTRODUCE YOURSELVES ONE AT A TIME.
I'M...
MY HOBBIES ARE...
OKAY, NEXT!
...HELPING ME...

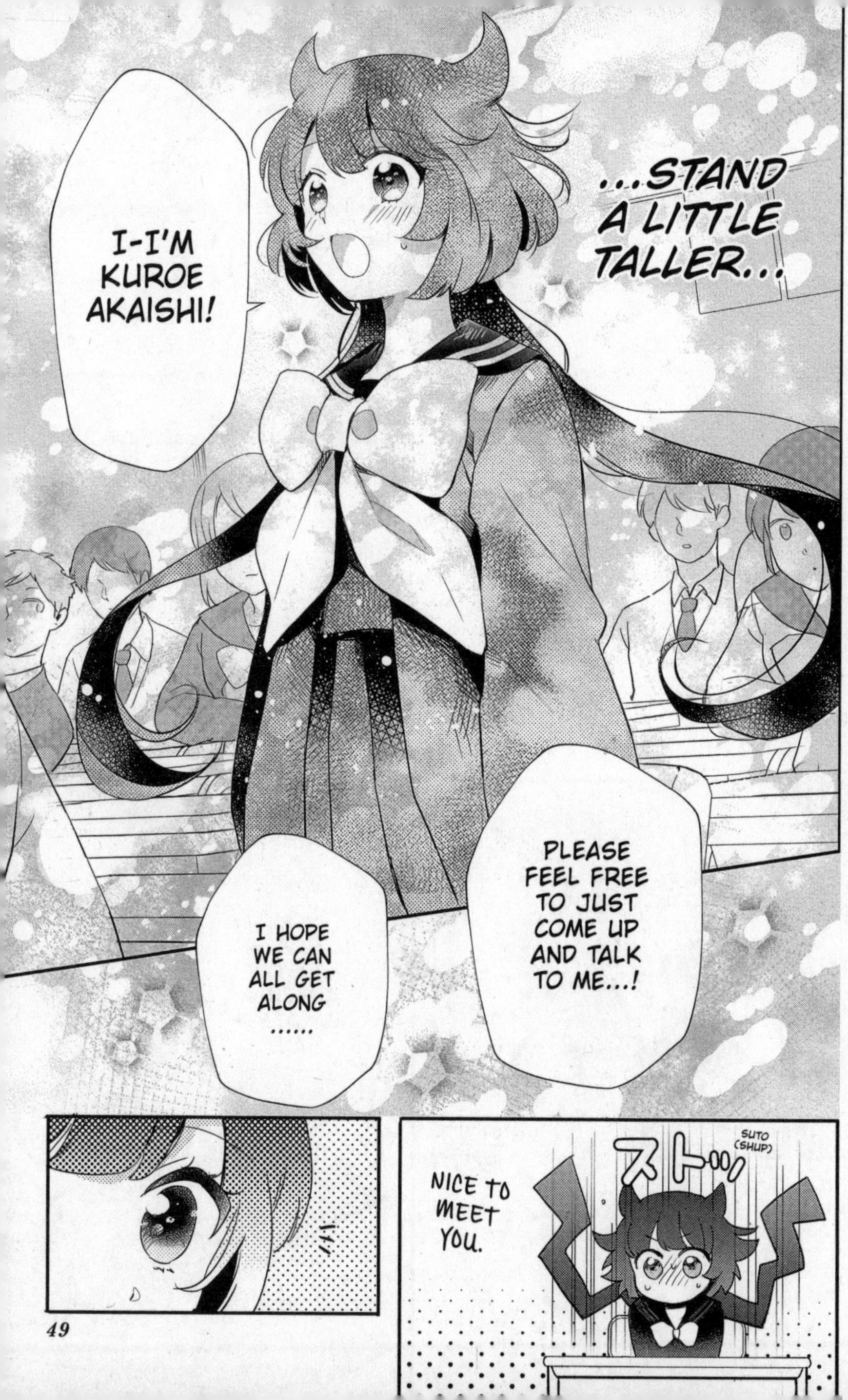
...STAND A LITTLE TALLER...
I-I'M KUROE AKAISHI!
PLEASE FEEL FREE TO JUST COME UP AND TALK TO ME...!
I HOPE WE CAN ALL GET ALONG ......
SUTO (SHUP)
NICE TO MEET YOU.

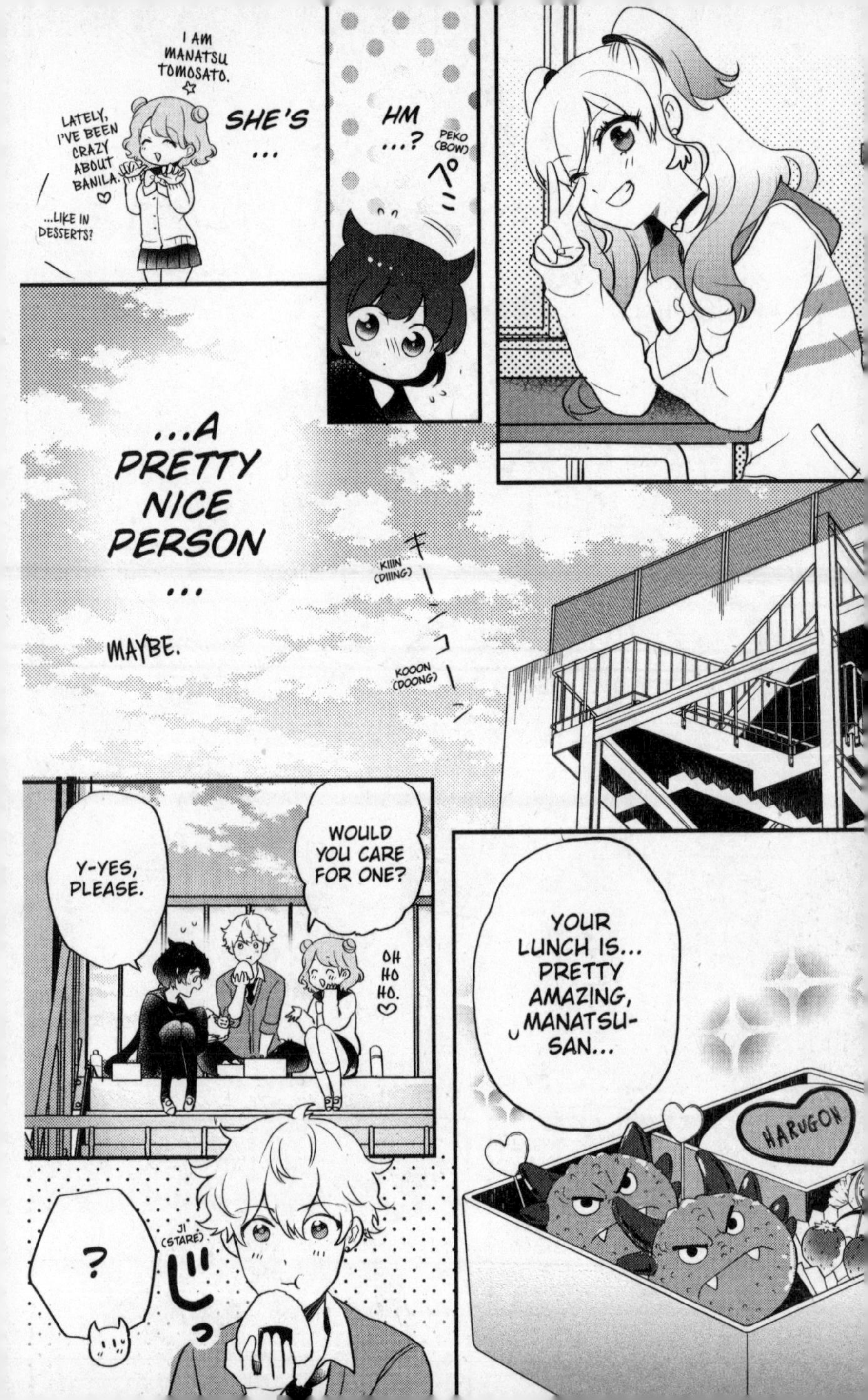
HM ...?
PEKO (BOW)
ぺこ
I AM MANATSU TOMOSATO. ☆
LATELY, I'VE BEEN CRAZY ABOUT BANILA. ♡
...LIKE IN DESSERTS?
SHE'S ...
...A PRETTY NICE PERSON ...
MAYBE.
KIIN (DIIING)
KOOON (DOONG)
キーンコーン
YOUR LUNCH IS... PRETTY AMAZING, MANATSU-SAN...
HARUGON
WOULD YOU CARE FOR ONE?
Y-YES, PLEASE.
OH HO HO. ♡
JI (STARE)
じっ
?

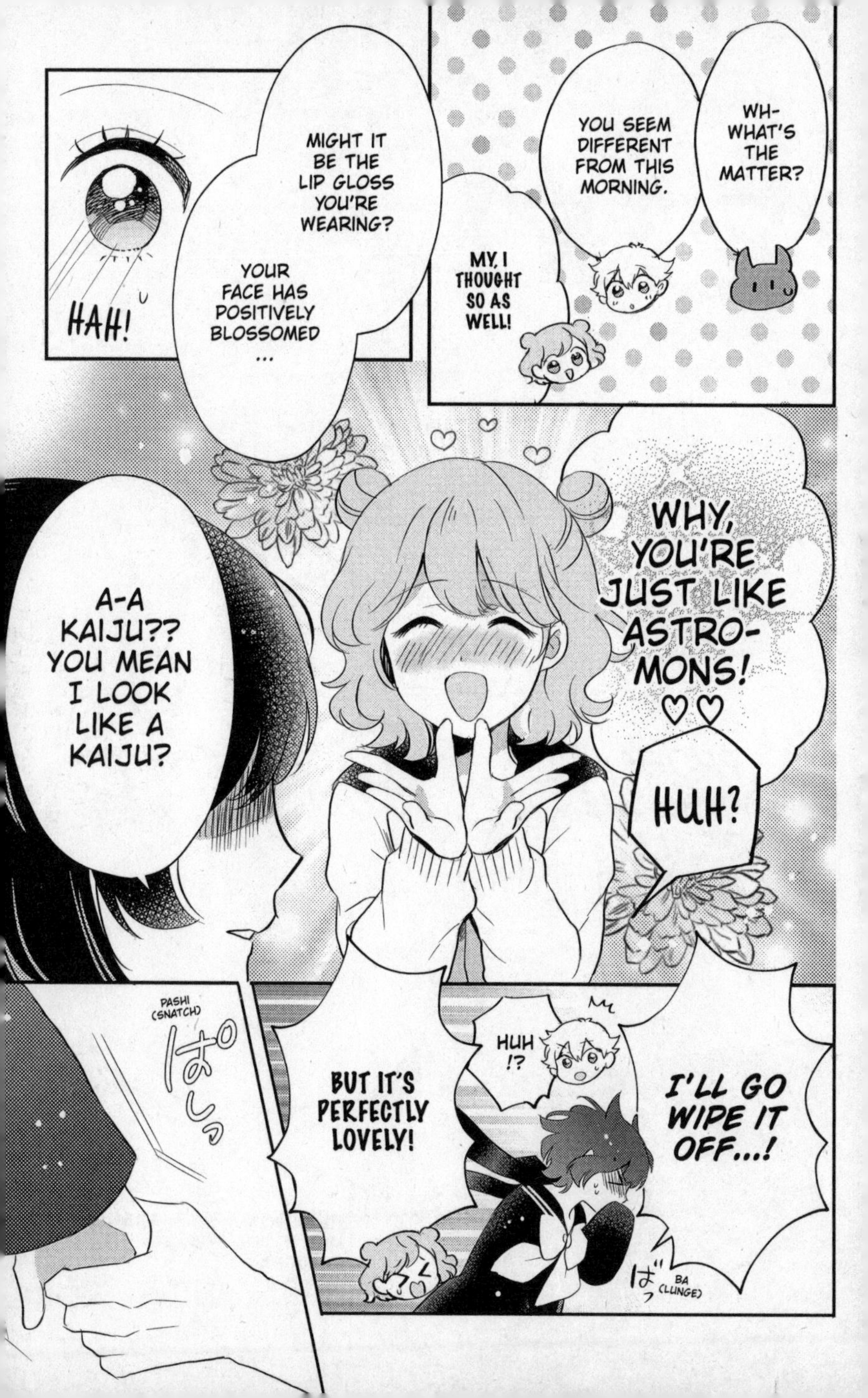
WH-WHAT'S THE MATTER?
YOU SEEM DIFFERENT FROM THIS MORNING.
MY, I THOUGHT SO AS WELL!
MIGHT IT BE THE LIP GLOSS YOU'RE WEARING?
YOUR FACE HAS POSITIVELY BLOSSOMED...
HAH!
WHY, YOU'RE JUST LIKE ASTRO-MONS! ♡♡
HUH?
A-A KAIJU?? YOU MEAN I LOOK LIKE A KAIJU?
I'LL GO WIPE IT OFF...!
HUH!?
BUT IT'S PERFECTLY LOVELY!
ばっ
BA (LUNGE)
ぱしっ
PASHI (SNATCH)

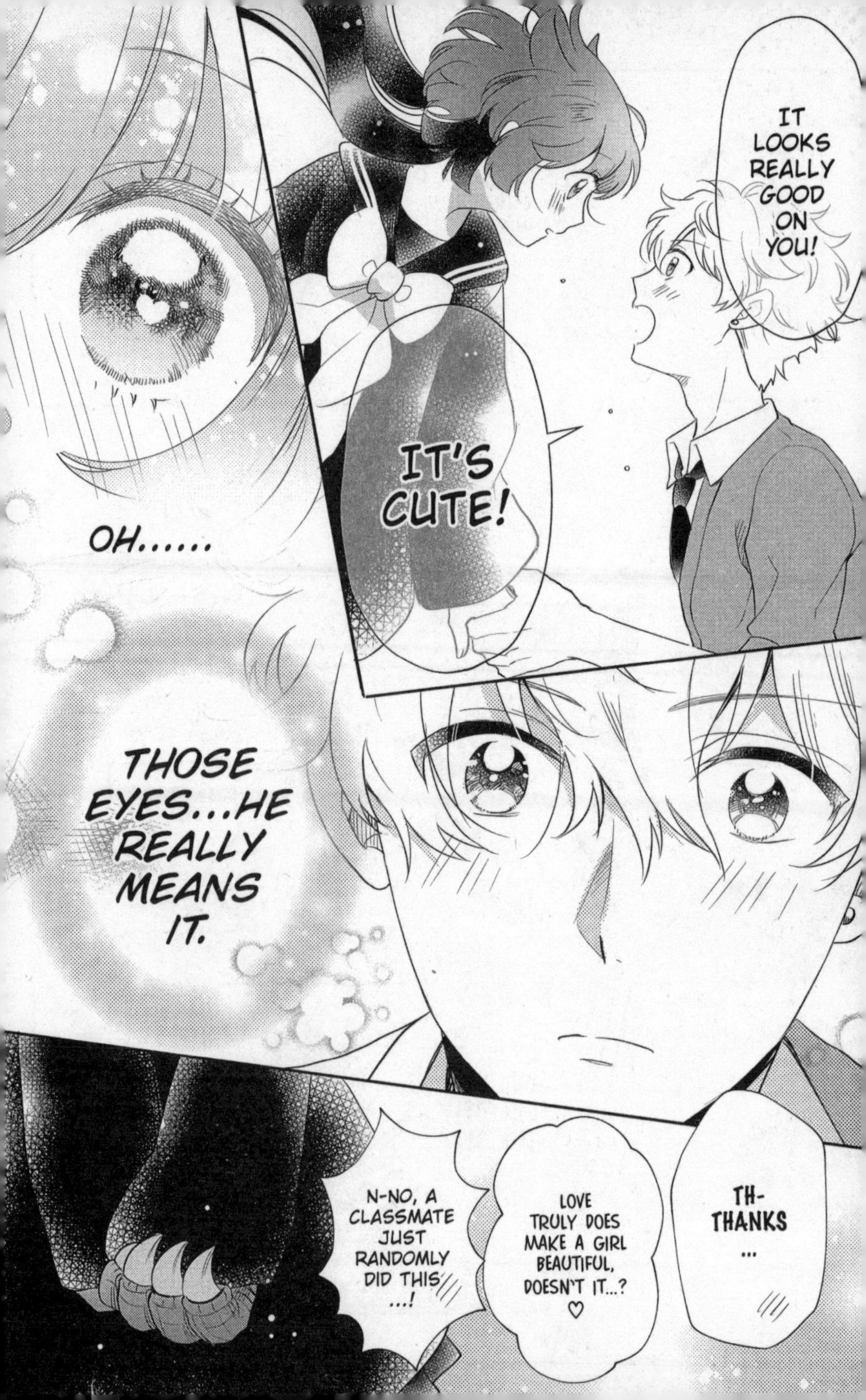
IT LOOKS REALLY GOOD ON YOU!
IT'S CUTE!
OH......
THOSE EYES...HE REALLY MEANS IT.
TH-THANKS...
LOVE TRULY DOES MAKE A GIRL BEAUTIFUL, DOESN'T IT...? ♡
N-NO, A CLASSMATE JUST RANDOMLY DID THIS...!

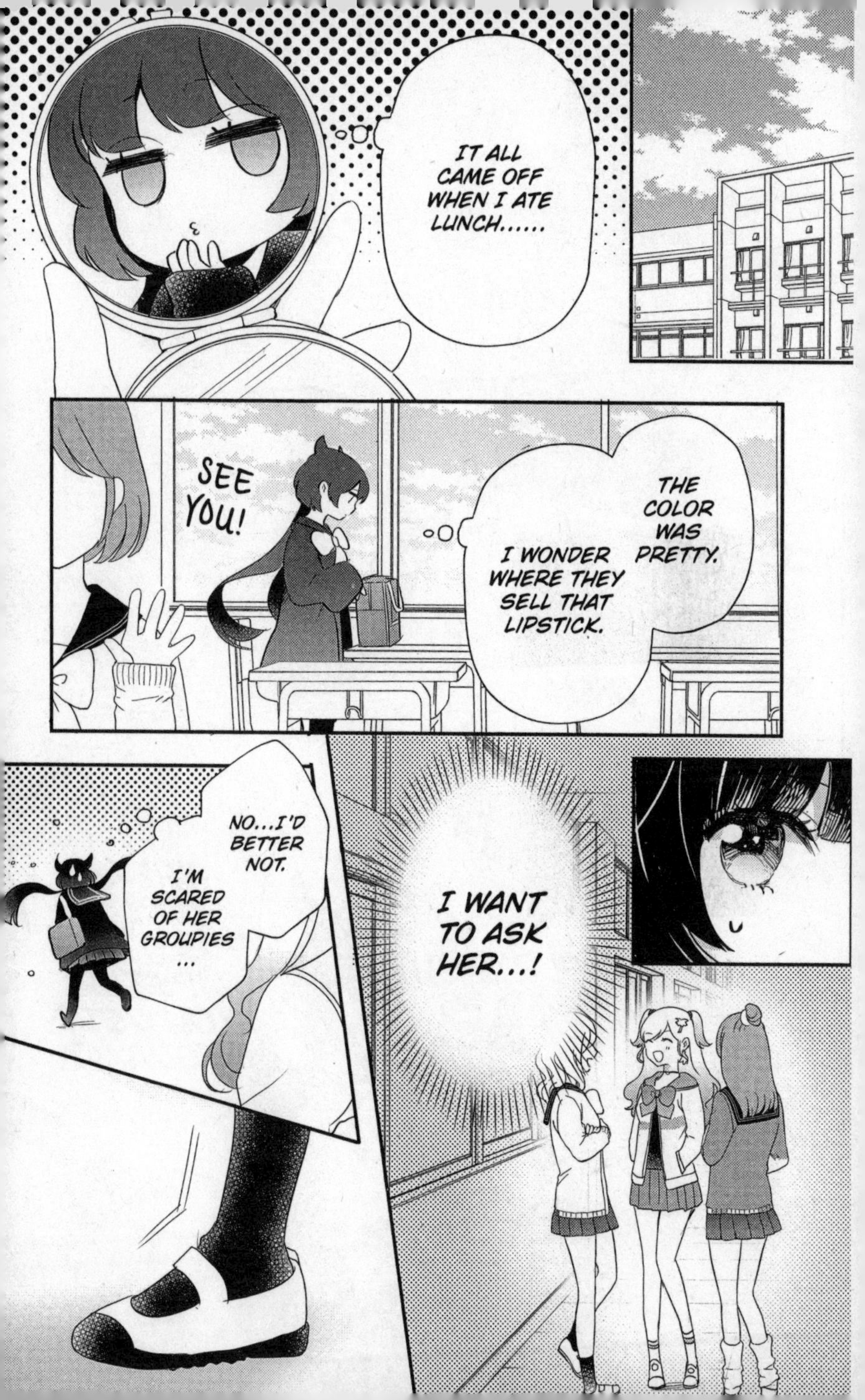
IT ALL CAME OFF WHEN I ATE LUNCH......
THE COLOR WAS PRETTY.
I WONDER WHERE THEY SELL THAT LIPSTICK.
SEE YOU!
I WANT TO ASK HER...!
NO...I'D BETTER NOT.
I'M SCARED OF HER GROUPIES...

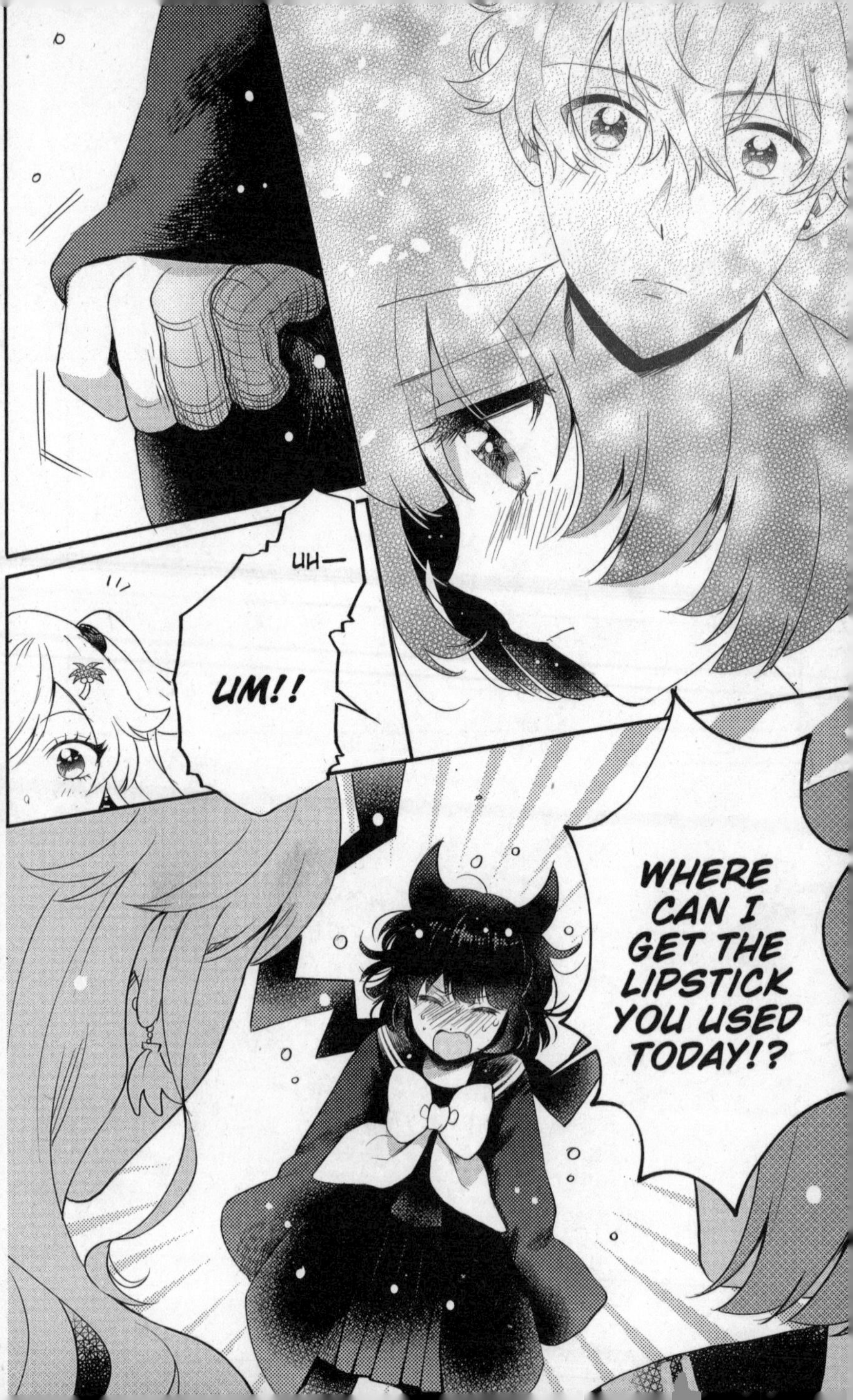
UH—
UM!!
WHERE CAN I GET THE LIPSTICK YOU USED TODAY!?

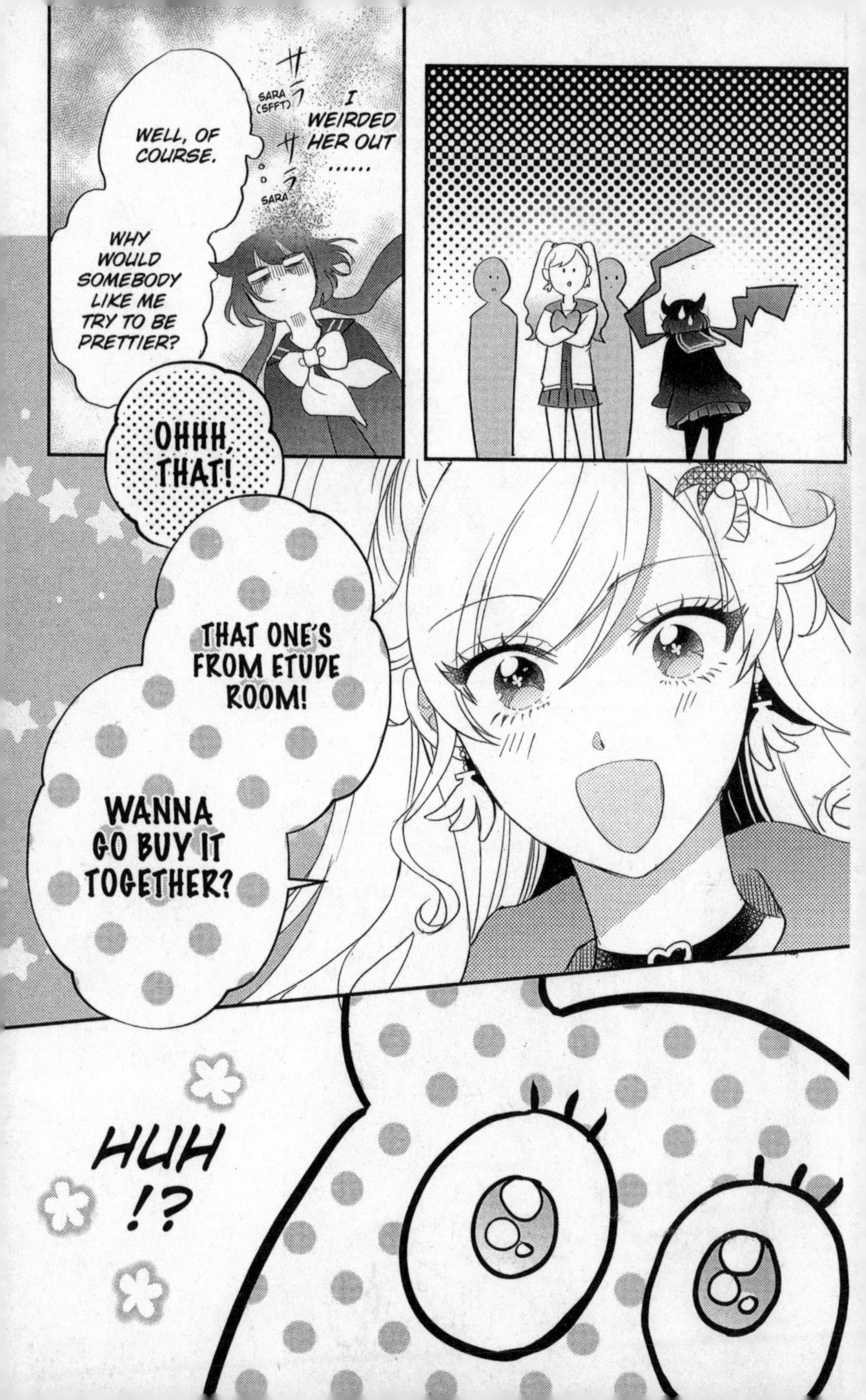

I WEIRDED HER OUT ......
SARA (SFFT)
SARA
WELL, OF COURSE.
WHY WOULD SOMEBODY LIKE ME TRY TO BE PRETTIER?
OHHH, THAT!
THAT ONE'S FROM ETUDE ROOM!
WANNA GO BUY IT TOGETHER?
HUH !?

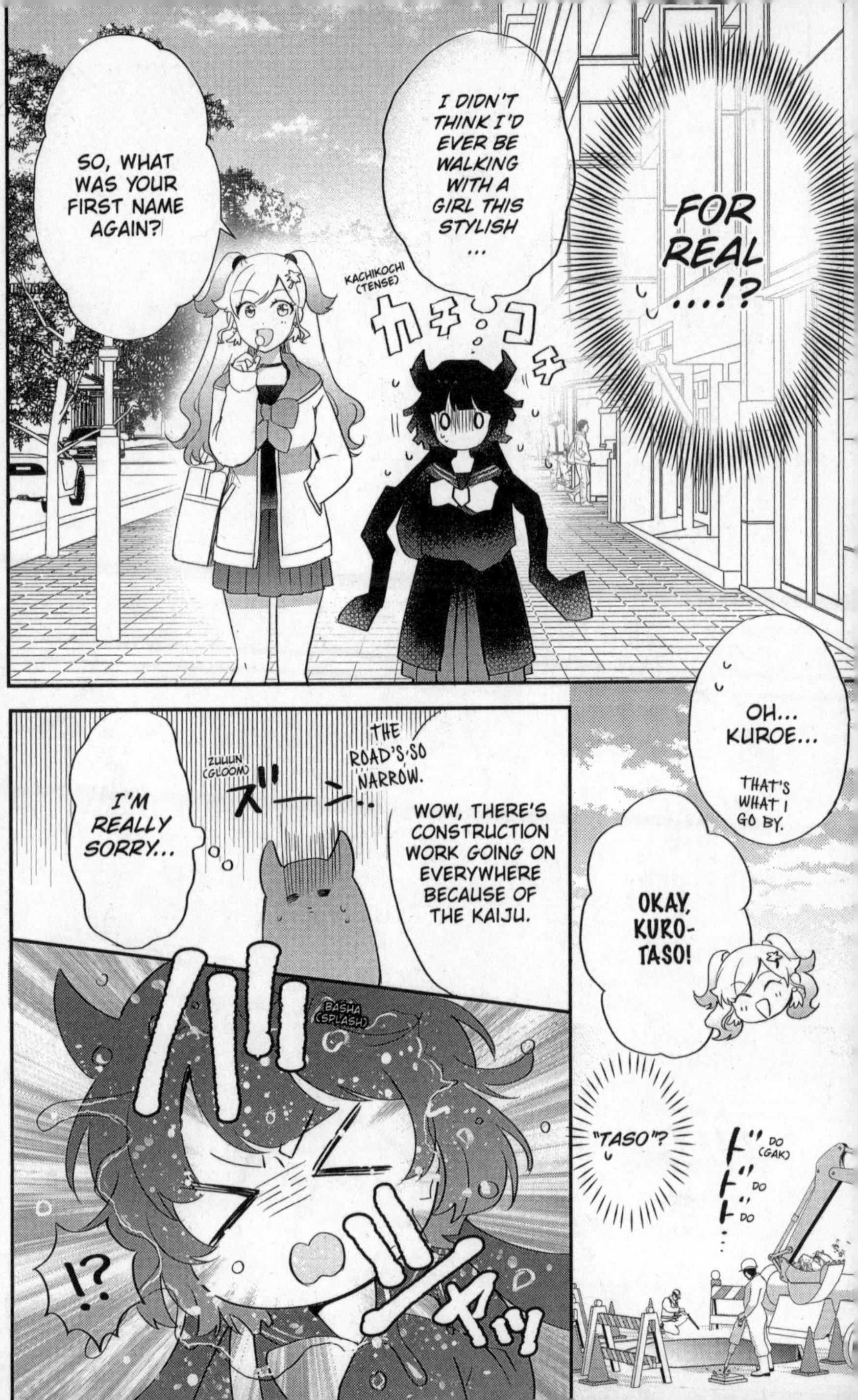
FOR REAL...!?
I DIDN'T THINK I'D EVER BE WALKING WITH A GIRL THIS STYLISH...
KACHIKOCHI (TENSE)
カチコチ
SO, WHAT WAS YOUR FIRST NAME AGAIN?
OH... KUROE...
THAT'S WHAT I GO BY.
OKAY, KURO-TASO!
"TASO"?
DO (GAK)
DO
DO
THE ROAD'S SO NARROW.
WOW, THERE'S CONSTRUCTION WORK GOING ON EVERYWHERE BECAUSE OF THE KAIJU.
ZUUUN (GLOOM)
ズーン
I'M REALLY SORRY...
BASHA (SPLASH)
!?

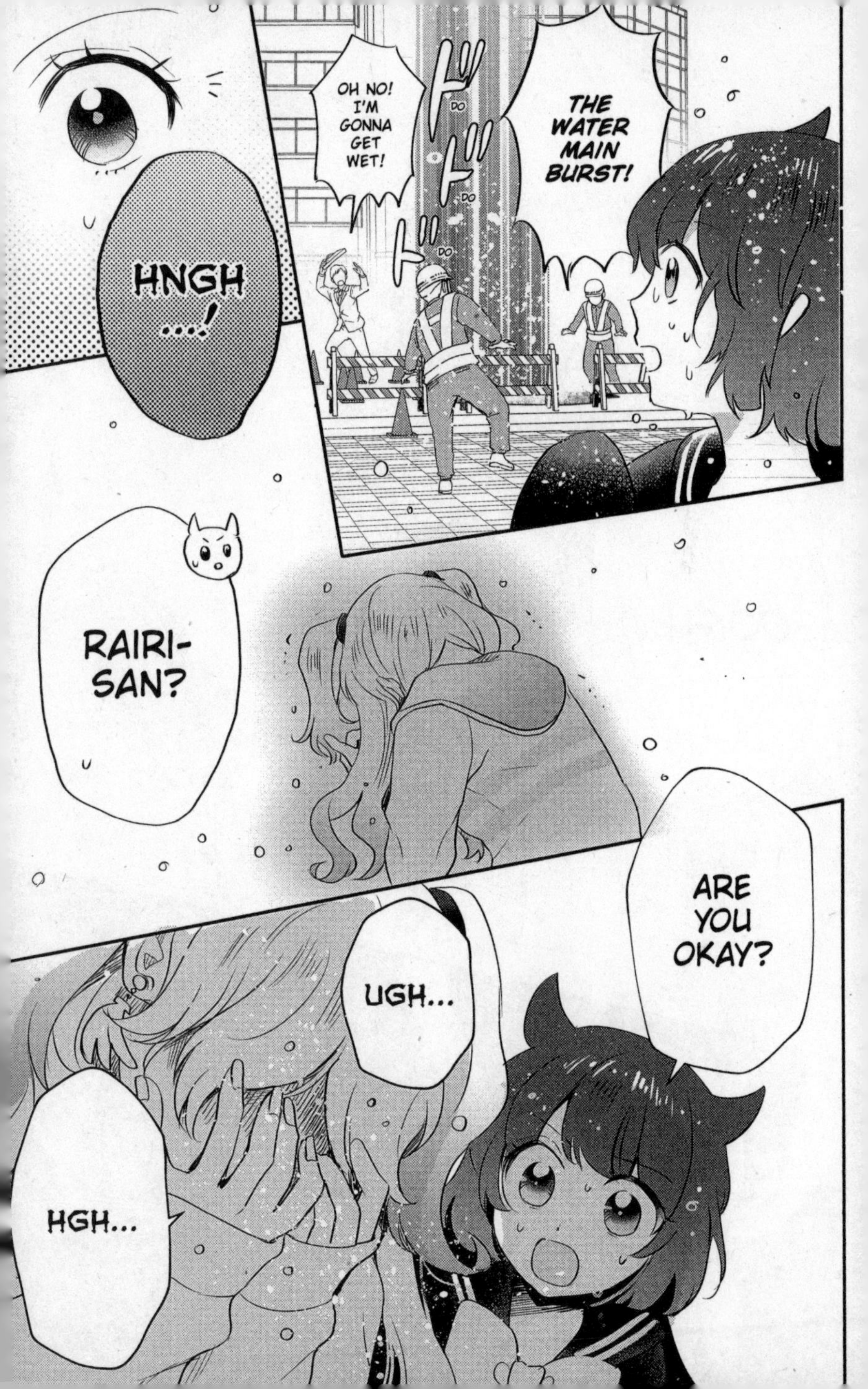
THE WATER MAIN BURST!
OH NO! I'M GONNA GET WET!
DO DO DO
HNGH ...!
RAIRI-SAN?
ARE YOU OKAY?
UGH...
HGH...

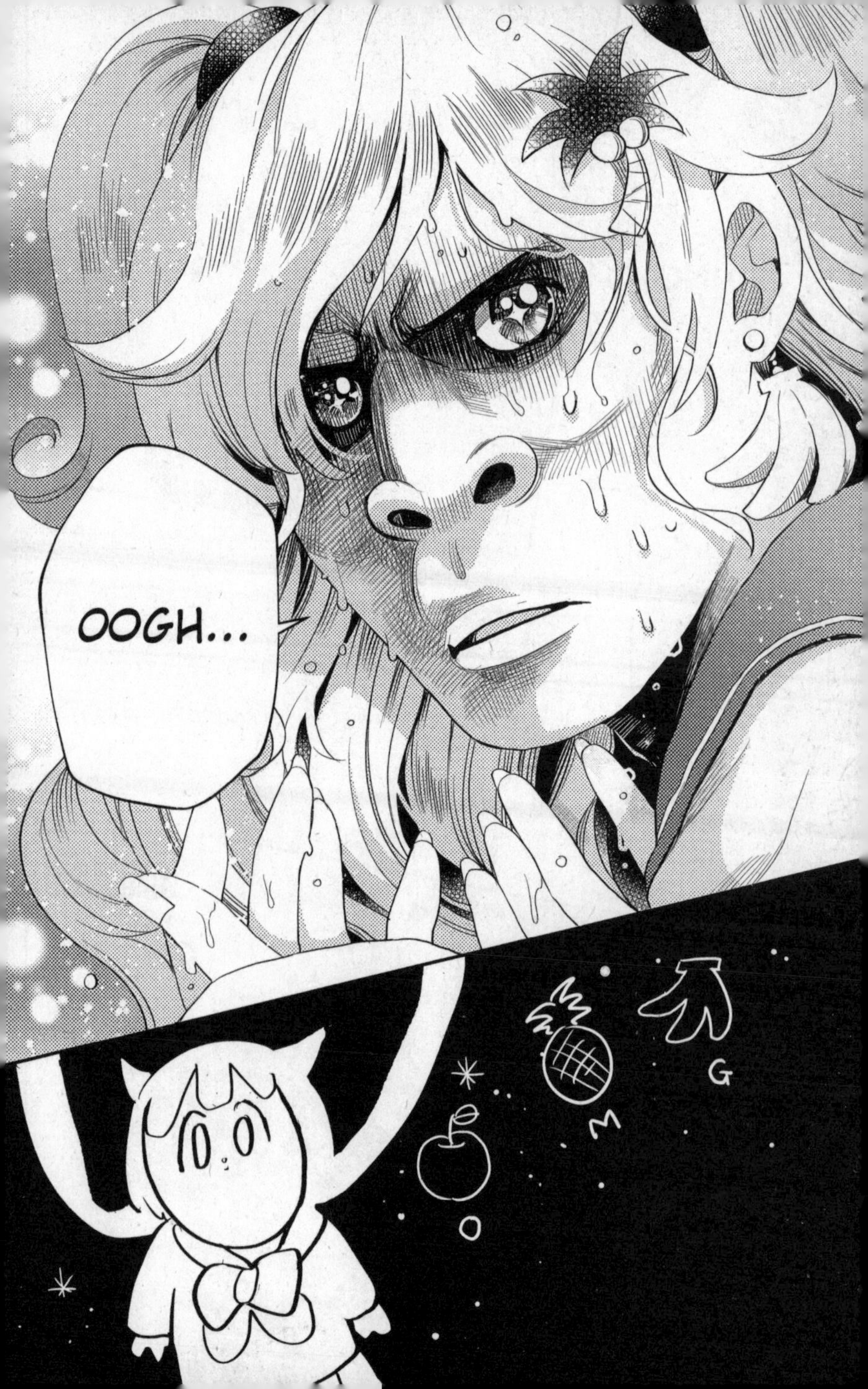
OOGH...
G
M
O

KAIJU♥GIRL
CARAMELISE

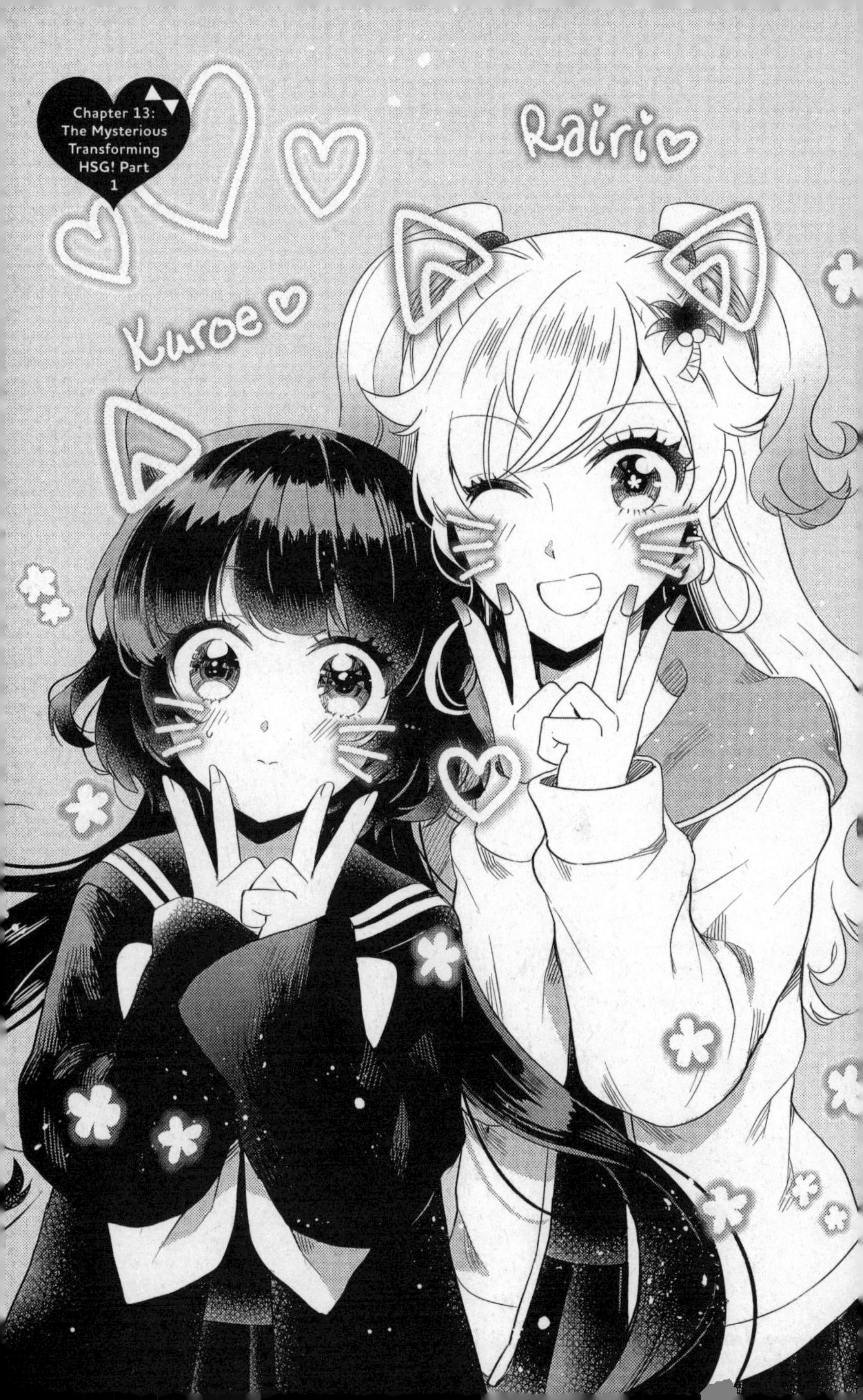
Chapter 13: The Mysterious Transforming HSG! Part 1
Rairi
Kuroe

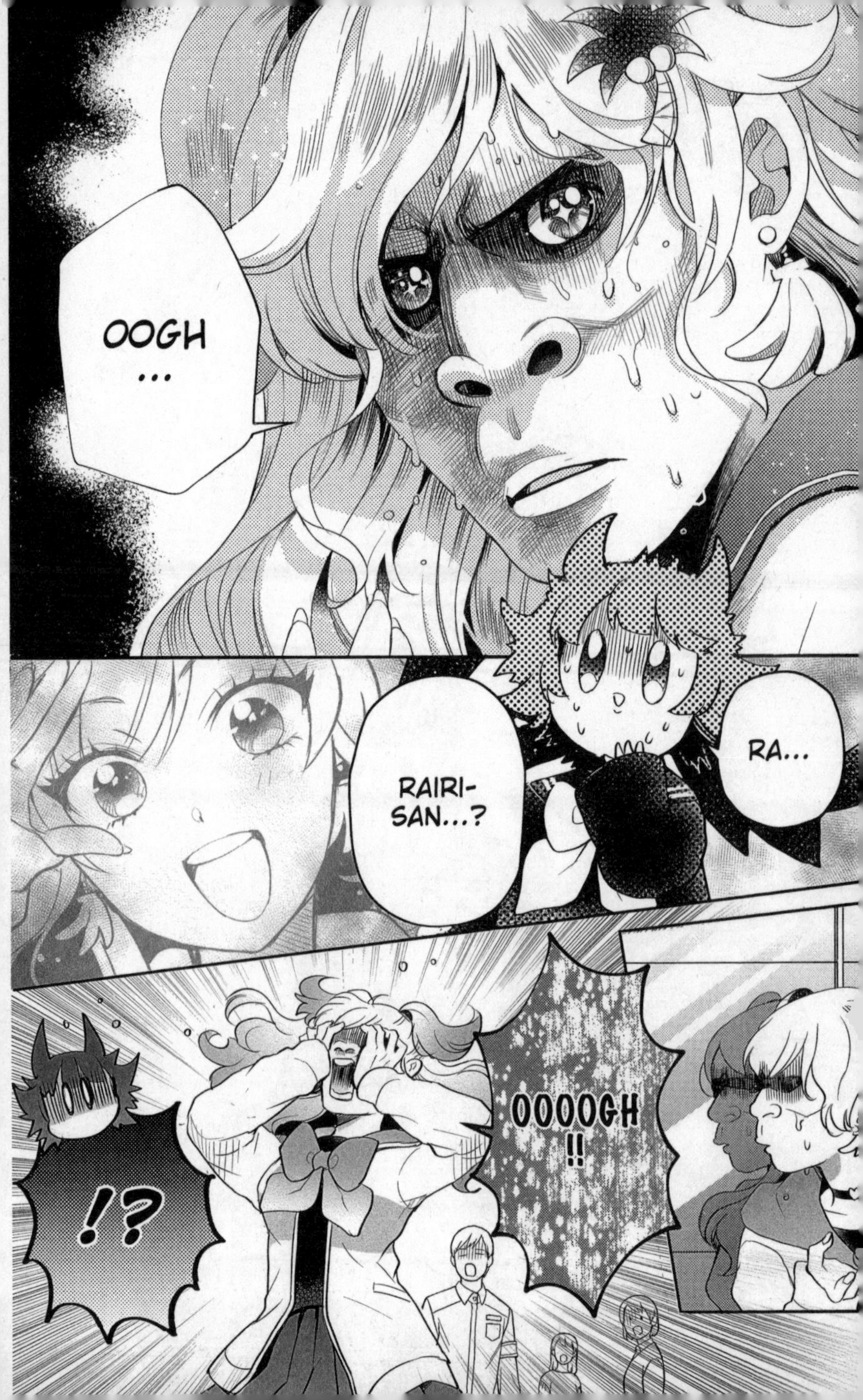
OOGH ...
RA...
RAIRI-SAN...?
OOOOGH !!
!?

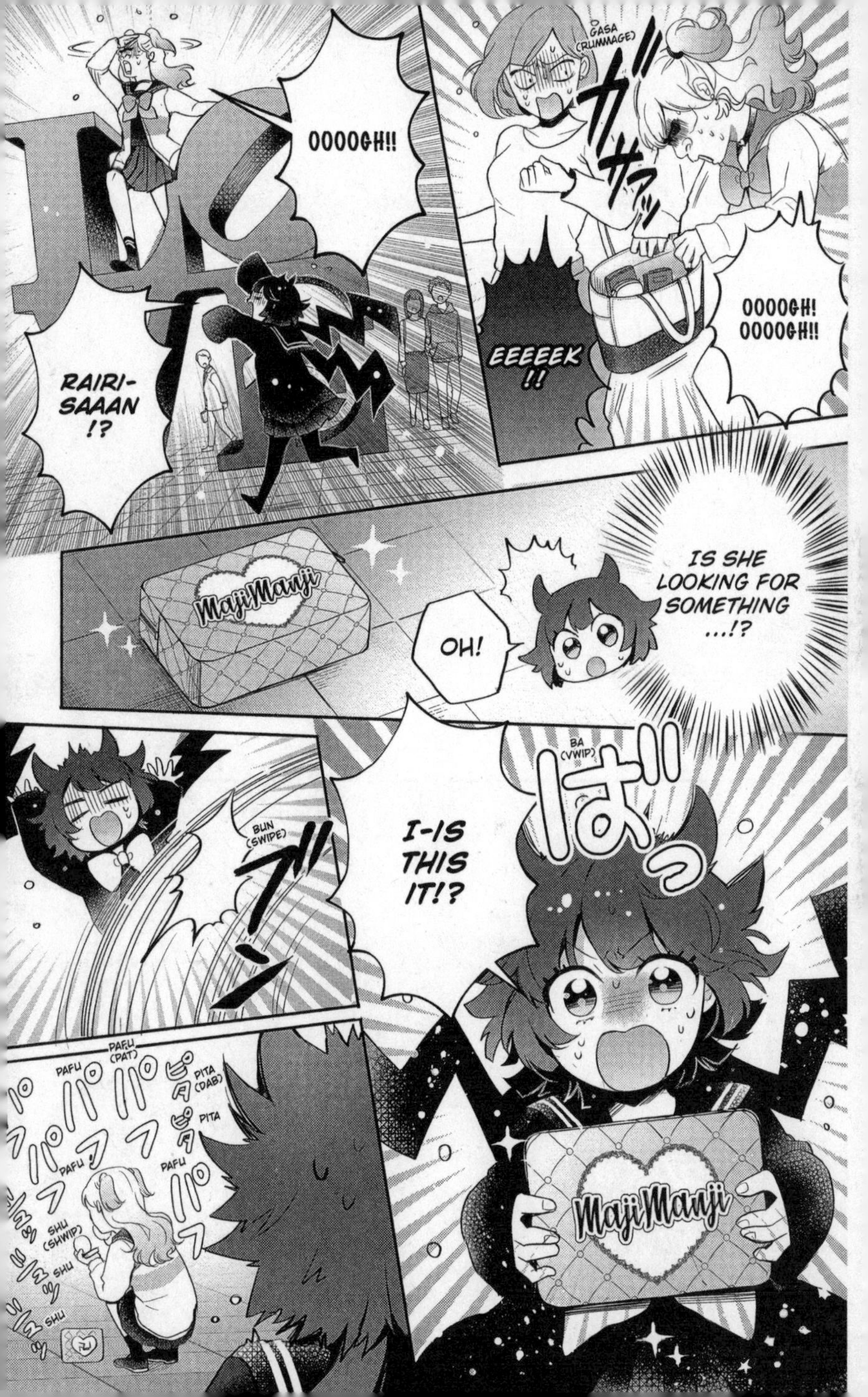
GASA (RUMMAGE)
OOOOGH! OOOOGH!!
EEEEEK!!
OOOOGH!!
RAIRI-SAAAN!?
IS SHE LOOKING FOR SOMETHING...!?
OH!
BA (VWIP)
I-IS THIS IT!?
MajiManji
BUN (SWIPE)
PITA (DAB)
PAFU (PAT)
PAFU
PITA
PAFU
PAFU
SHU (SHWIP)
SHU
SHU

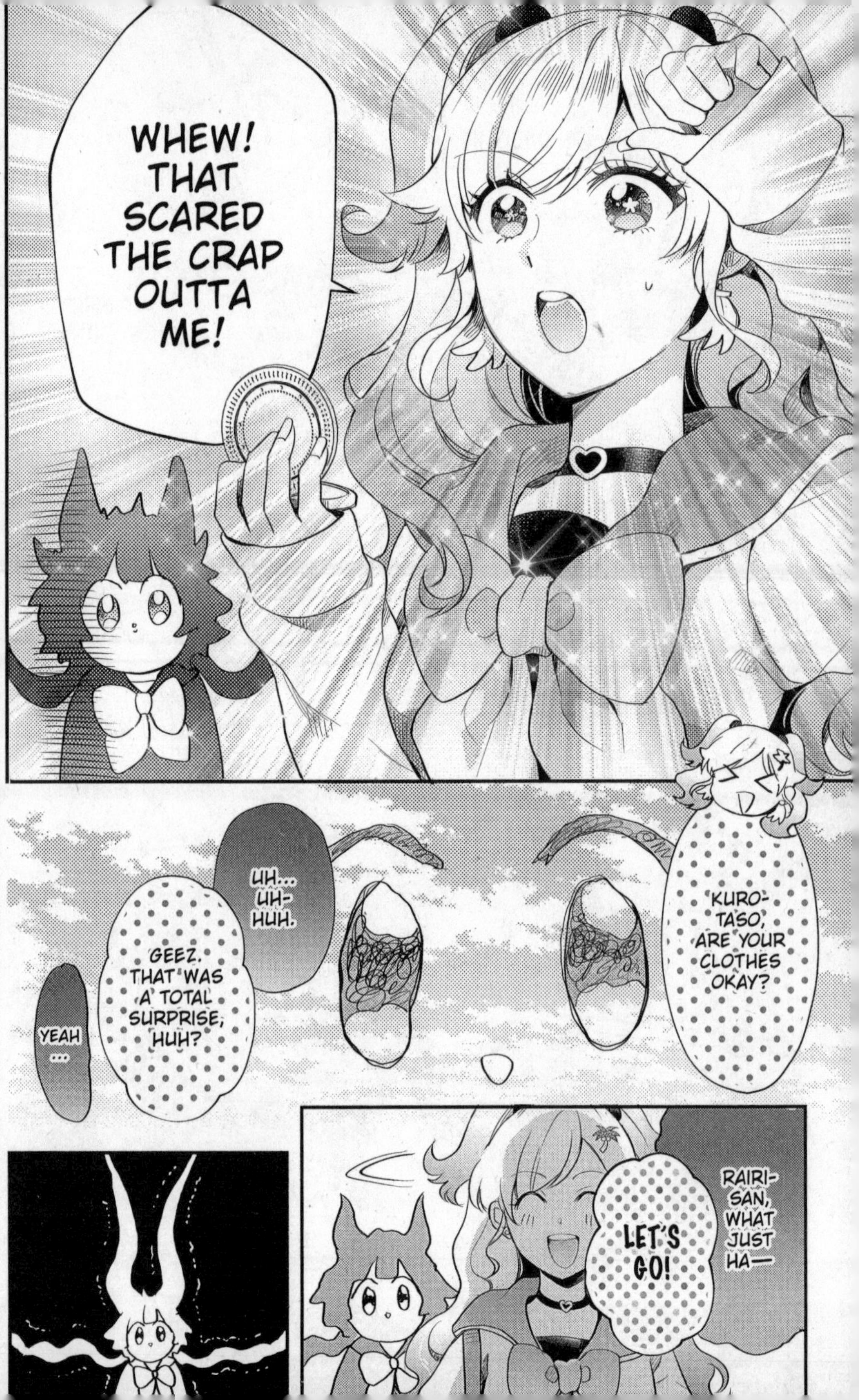
WHEW! THAT SCARED THE CRAP OUTTA ME!
KURO-TASO, ARE YOUR CLOTHES OKAY?
UH... UH-HUH.
GEEZ. THAT WAS A TOTAL SURPRISE, HUH?
YEAH ...
RAIRI-SAN, WHAT JUST HA—
LET'S GO!

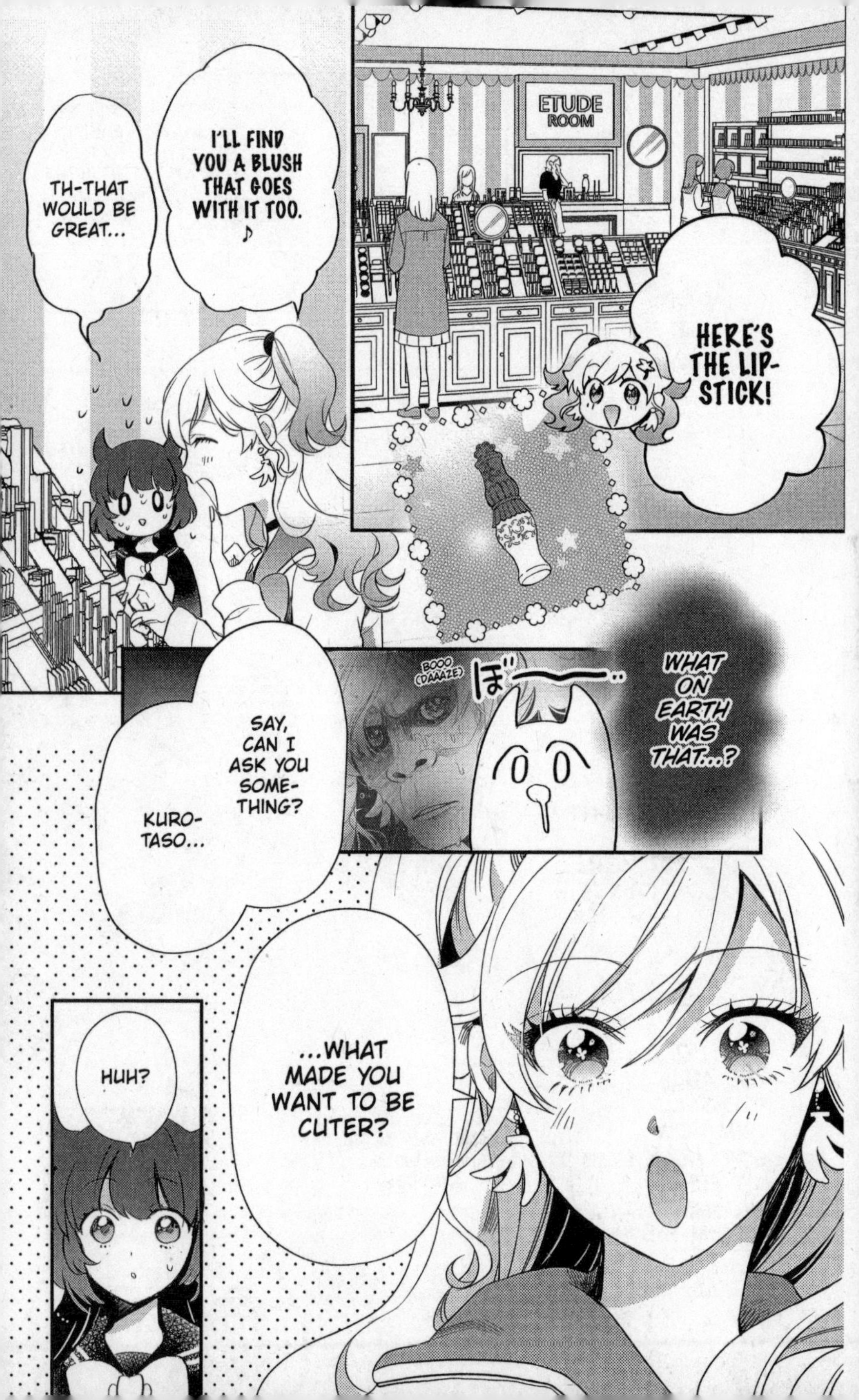
ETUDE ROOM
HERE'S THE LIP-STICK!
I'LL FIND YOU A BLUSH THAT GOES WITH IT TOO. ♪
TH-THAT WOULD BE GREAT...
WHAT ON EARTH WAS THAT...?
ぼーー
BOOO (DAAAZE)
SAY, CAN I ASK YOU SOME-THING?
KURO-TASO...
...WHAT MADE YOU WANT TO BE CUTER?
HUH?

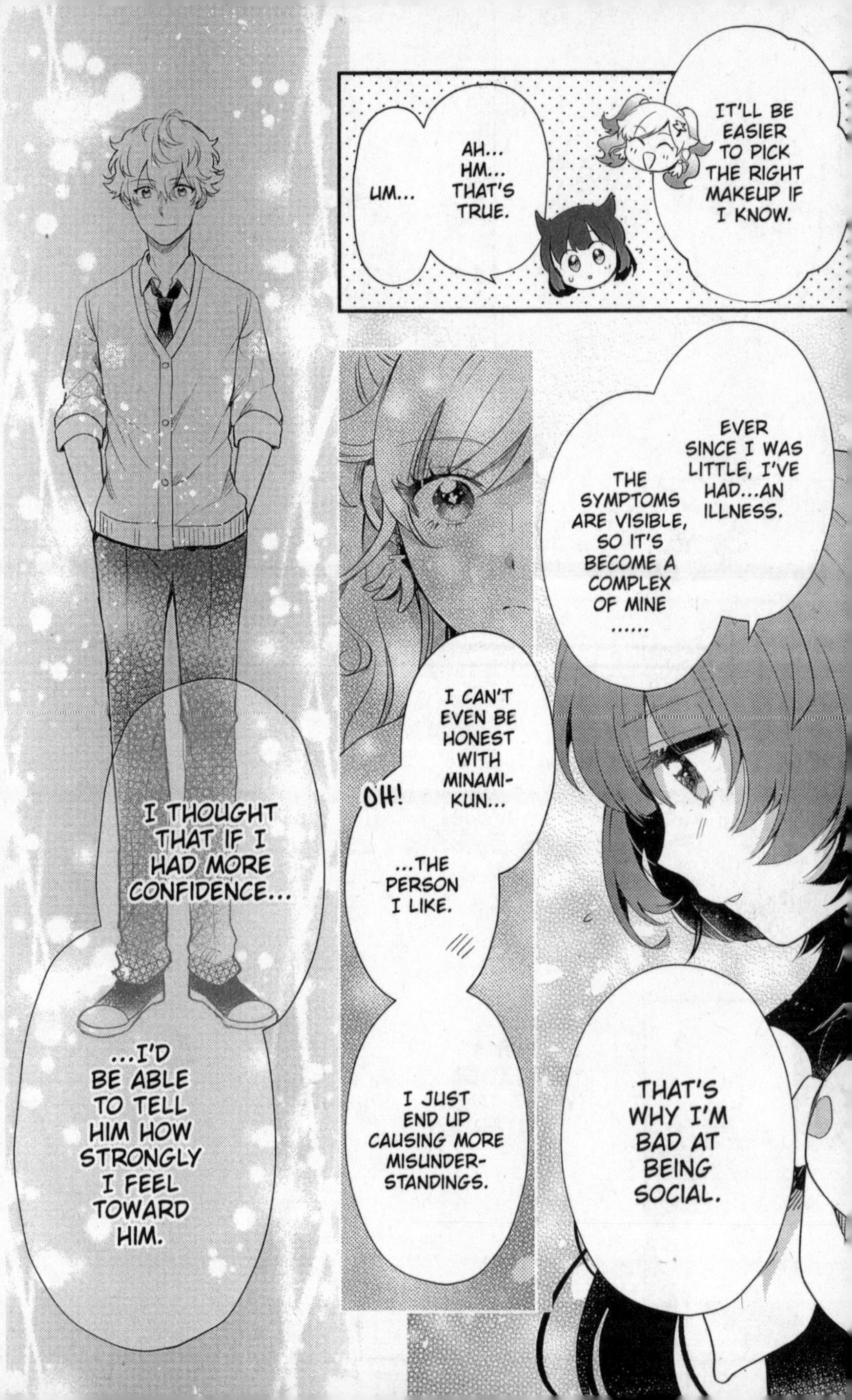
IT'LL BE EASIER TO PICK THE RIGHT MAKEUP IF I KNOW.
AH... HM... THAT'S TRUE.
UM...
EVER SINCE I WAS LITTLE, I'VE HAD...AN ILLNESS.
THE SYMPTOMS ARE VISIBLE, SO IT'S BECOME A COMPLEX OF MINE ......
THAT'S WHY I'M BAD AT BEING SOCIAL.
I CAN'T EVEN BE HONEST WITH MINAMI-KUN...
OH!
...THE PERSON I LIKE.
I JUST END UP CAUSING MORE MISUNDER-STANDINGS.
I THOUGHT THAT IF I HAD MORE CONFIDENCE...
...I'D BE ABLE TO TELL HIM HOW STRONGLY I FEEL TOWARD HIM.

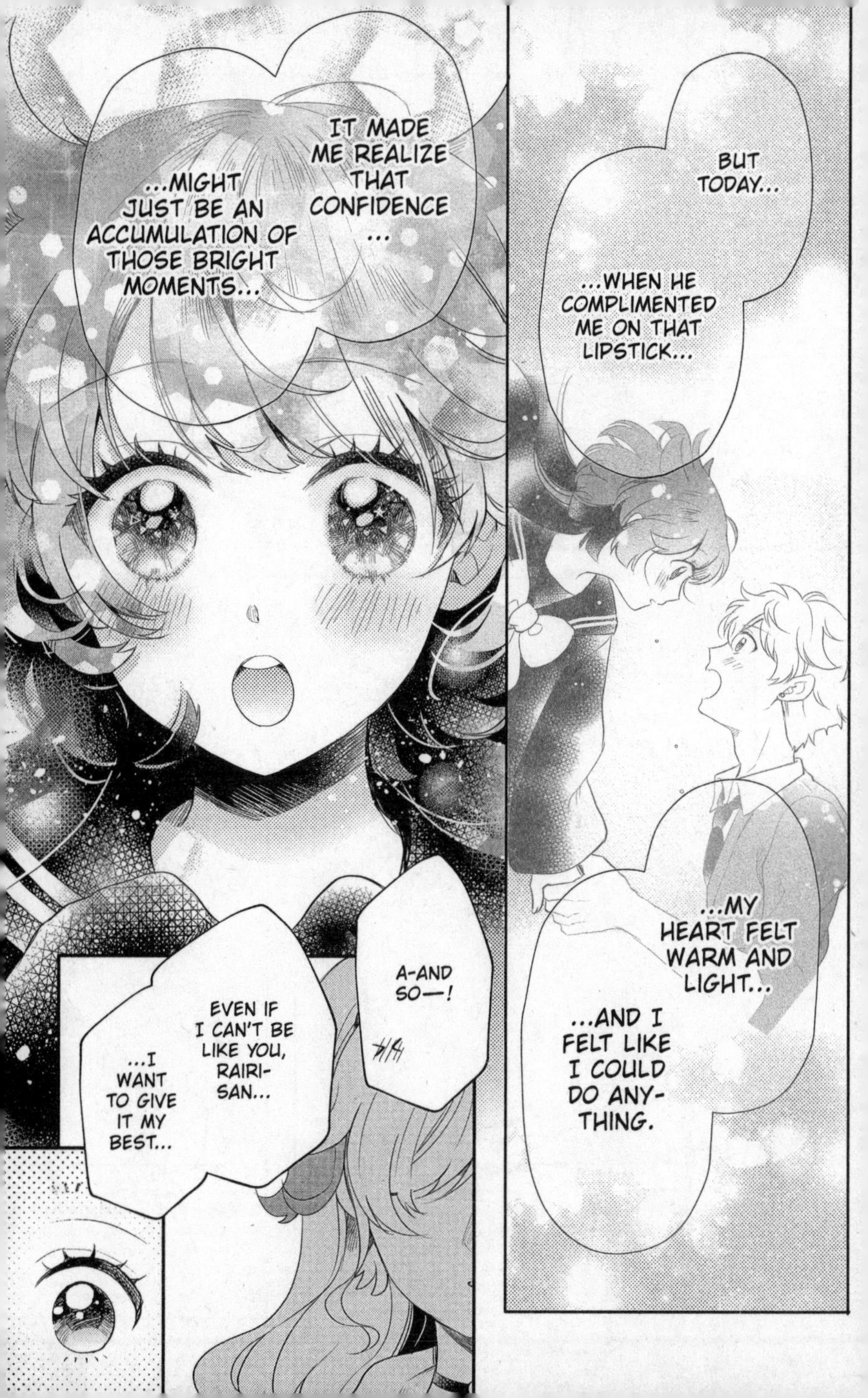
BUT TODAY...
...WHEN HE COMPLIMENTED ME ON THAT LIPSTICK...
...MY HEART FELT WARM AND LIGHT...
...AND I FELT LIKE I COULD DO ANY-THING.
IT MADE ME REALIZE THAT CONFIDENCE ...
...MIGHT JUST BE AN ACCUMULATION OF THOSE BRIGHT MOMENTS...
A-AND SO—!
EVEN IF I CAN'T BE LIKE YOU, RAIRI-SAN...
...I WANT TO GIVE IT MY BEST...

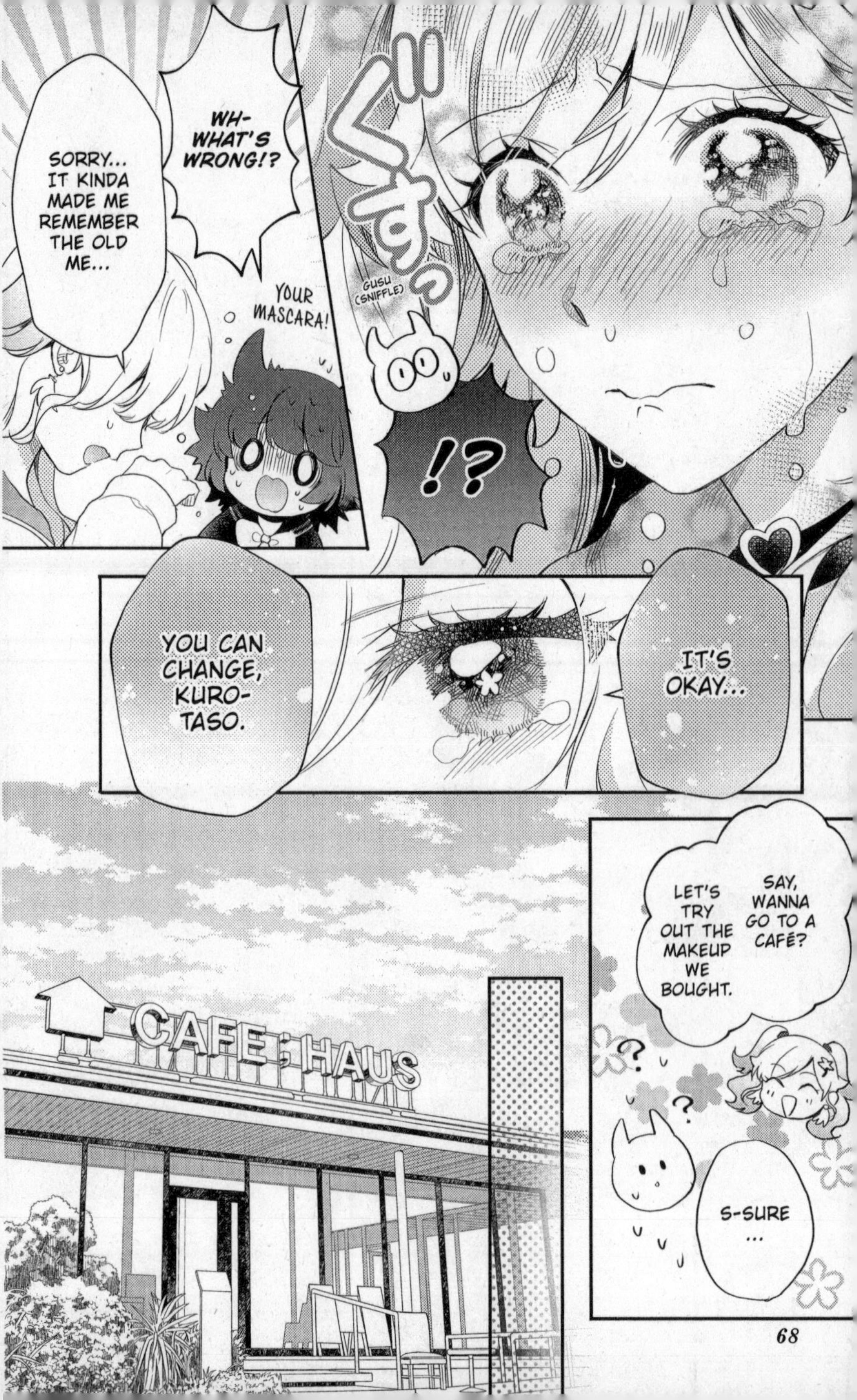
GUSU (SNIFFLE)
!?
YOUR MASCARA!
WH- WHAT'S WRONG!?
SORRY... IT KINDA MADE ME REMEMBER THE OLD ME...
IT'S OKAY...
YOU CAN CHANGE, KURO-TASO.
SAY, WANNA GO TO A CAFÉ?
LET'S TRY OUT THE MAKEUP WE BOUGHT.
S-SURE ...
CAFE HAUS

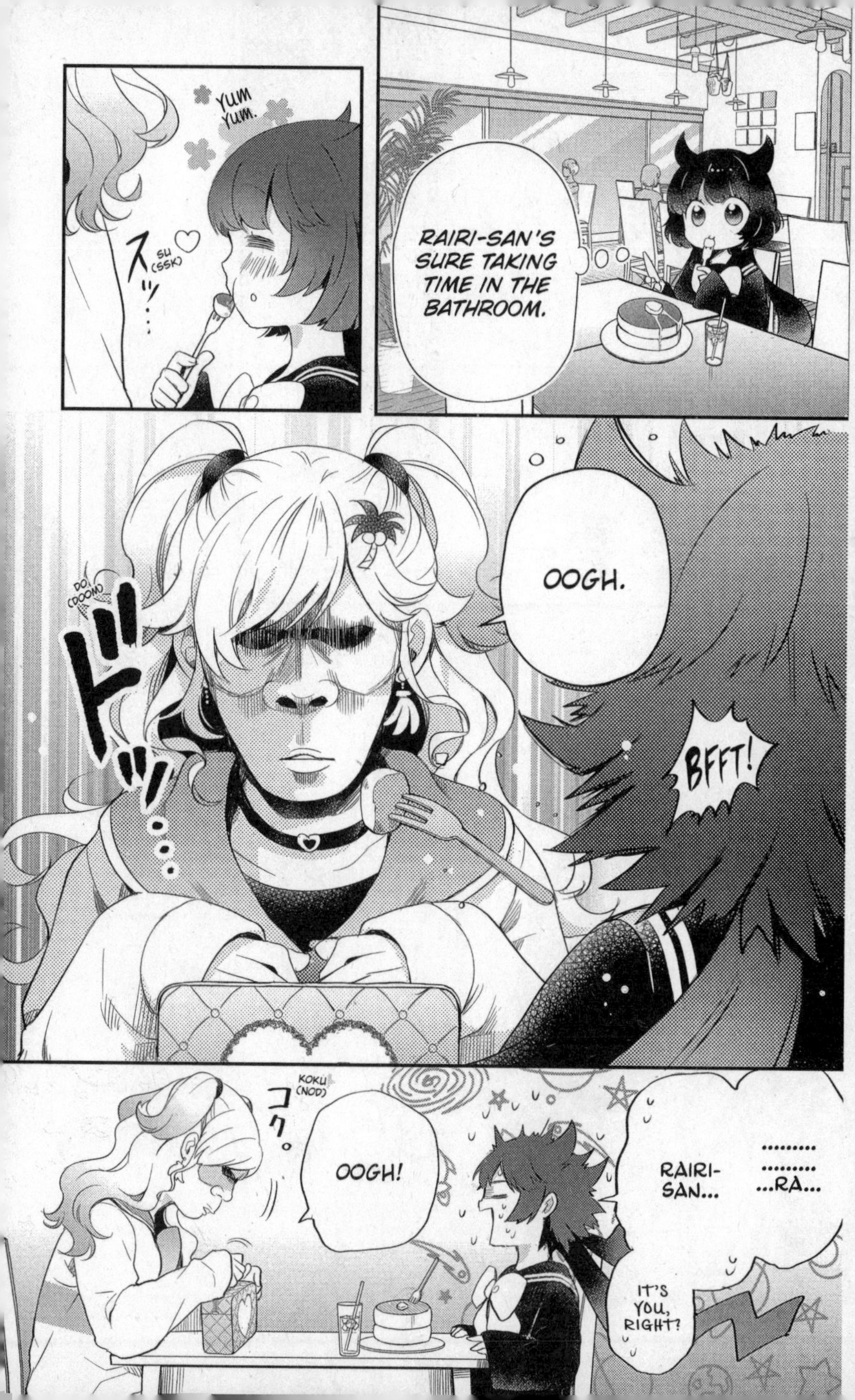
RAIRI-SAN'S SURE TAKING TIME IN THE BATHROOM.
YUM YUM.
SU (SSK)
スッ…
OOGH.
BFFT!
DO (DOOM)
ドッ…
....RA...
RAIRI-SAN...
IT'S YOU, RIGHT?
OOGH!
KOKU (NOD)
コク。

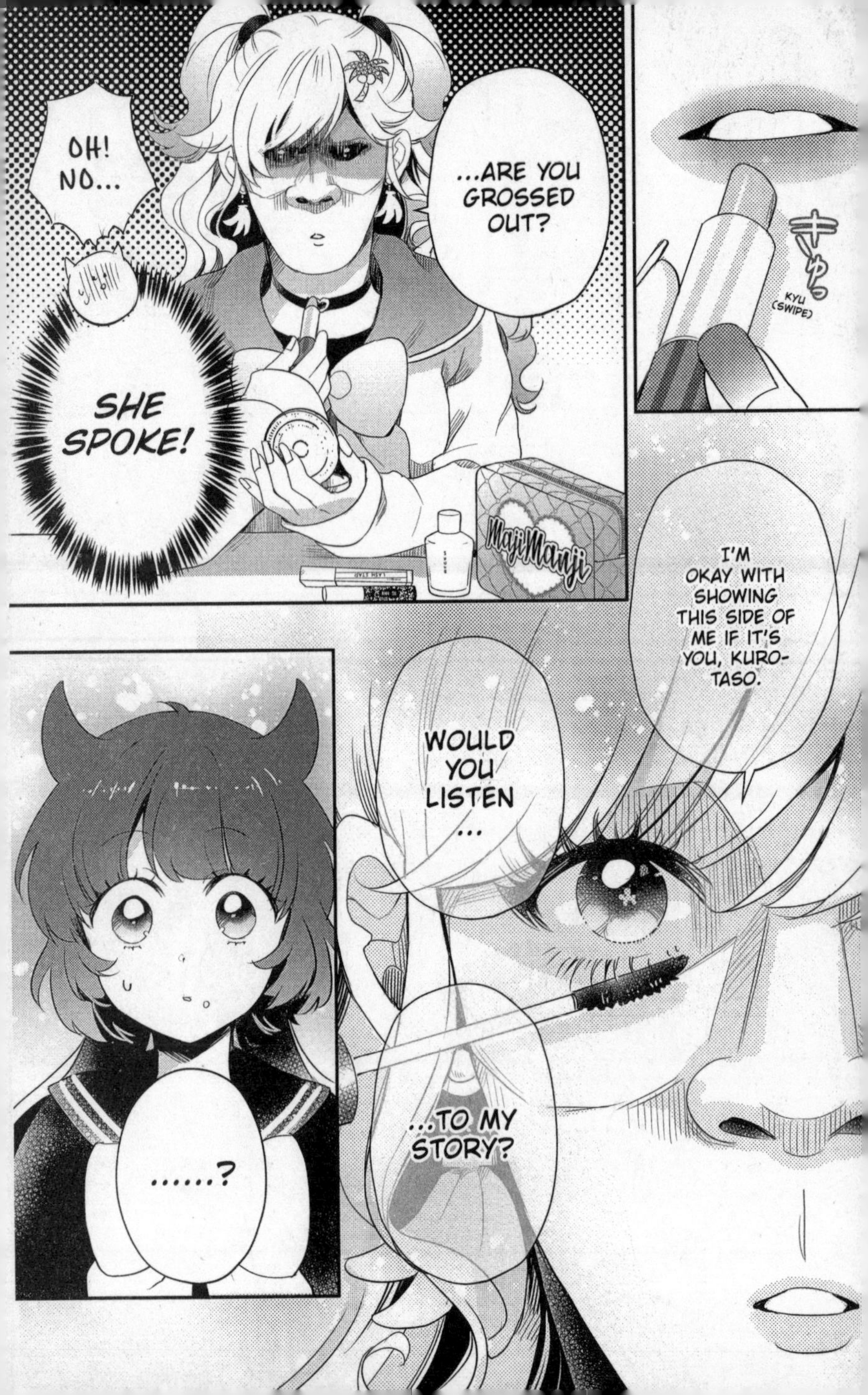
きゅ
KYU (SWIPE)
...ARE YOU GROSSED OUT?
OH! NO...
SHE SPOKE!
I'M OKAY WITH SHOWING THIS SIDE OF ME IF IT'S YOU, KURO-TASO.
WOULD YOU LISTEN...
...TO MY STORY?
......?

Chapter 14: The Mysterious Transforming HSG! Part 2

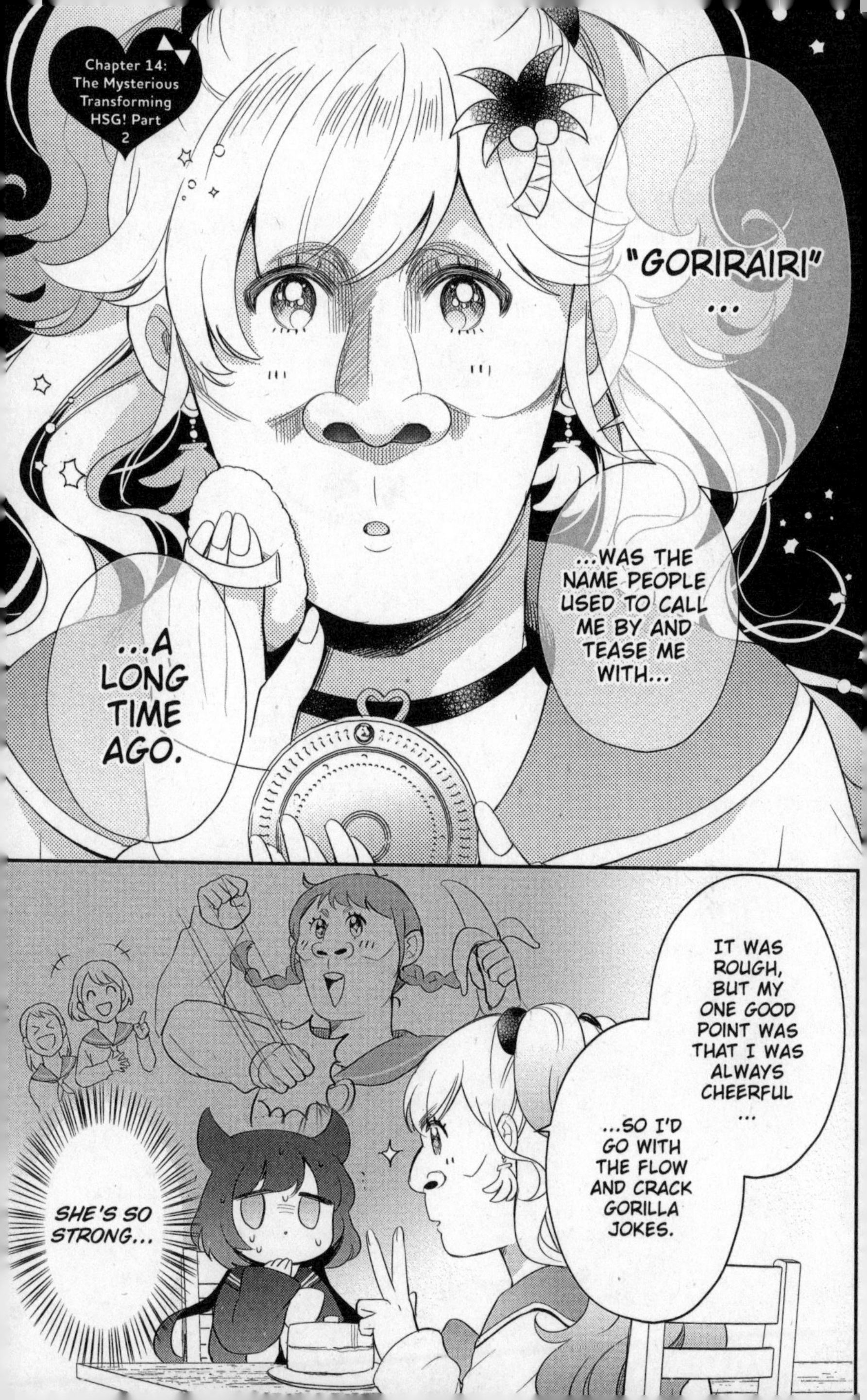
"GORIRAIRI" ...
...WAS THE NAME PEOPLE USED TO CALL ME BY AND TEASE ME WITH...
...A LONG TIME AGO.
IT WAS ROUGH, BUT MY ONE GOOD POINT WAS THAT I WAS ALWAYS CHEERFUL ...
...SO I'D GO WITH THE FLOW AND CRACK GORILLA JOKES.
SHE'S SO STRONG...

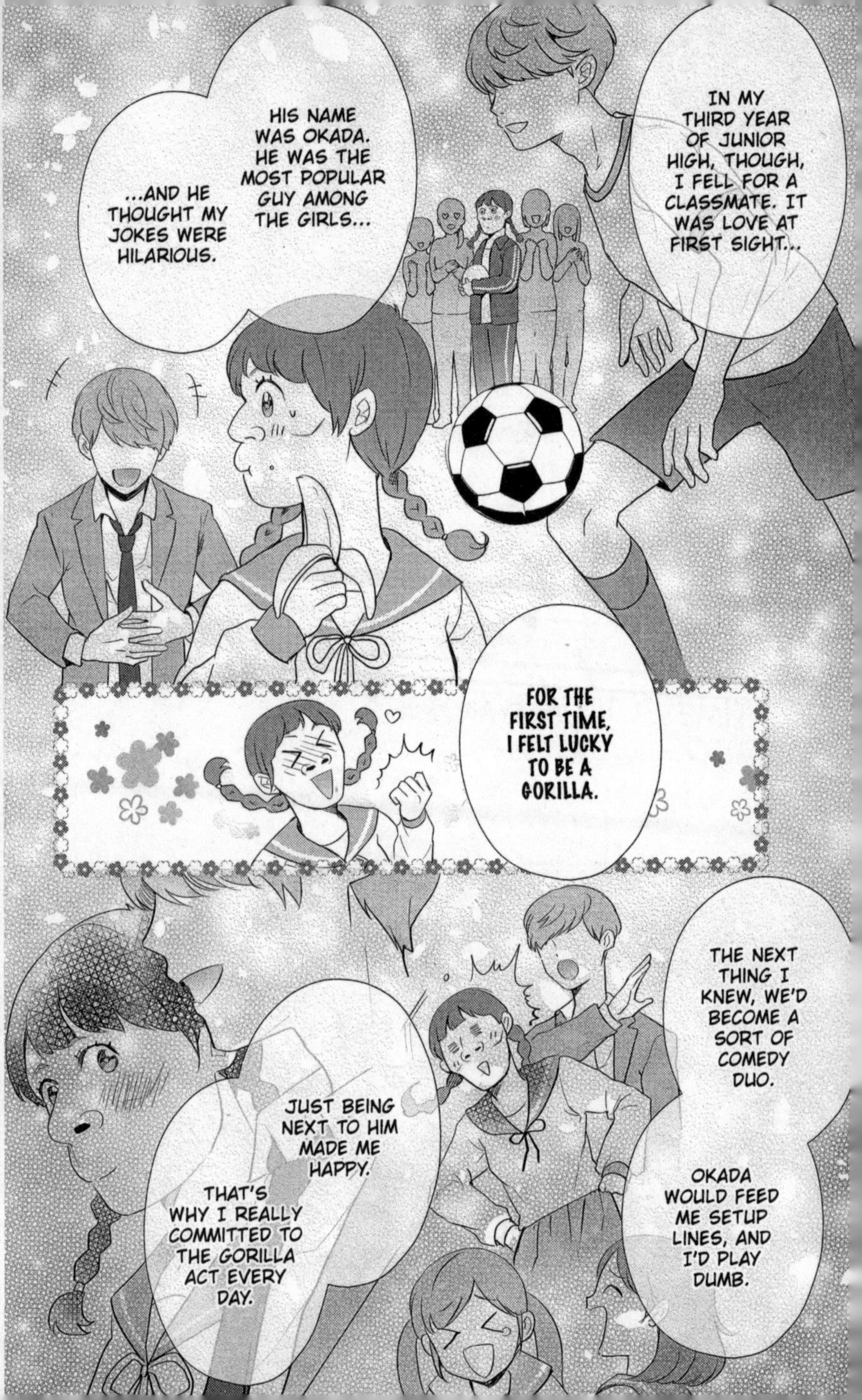
IN MY THIRD YEAR OF JUNIOR HIGH, THOUGH, I FELL FOR A CLASSMATE. IT WAS LOVE AT FIRST SIGHT...
HIS NAME WAS OKADA. HE WAS THE MOST POPULAR GUY AMONG THE GIRLS...
...AND HE THOUGHT MY JOKES WERE HILARIOUS.
FOR THE FIRST TIME, I FELT LUCKY TO BE A GORILLA.
THE NEXT THING I KNEW, WE'D BECOME A SORT OF COMEDY DUO.
OKADA WOULD FEED ME SETUP LINES, AND I'D PLAY DUMB.
JUST BEING NEXT TO HIM MADE ME HAPPY.
THAT'S WHY I REALLY COMMITTED TO THE GORILLA ACT EVERY DAY.

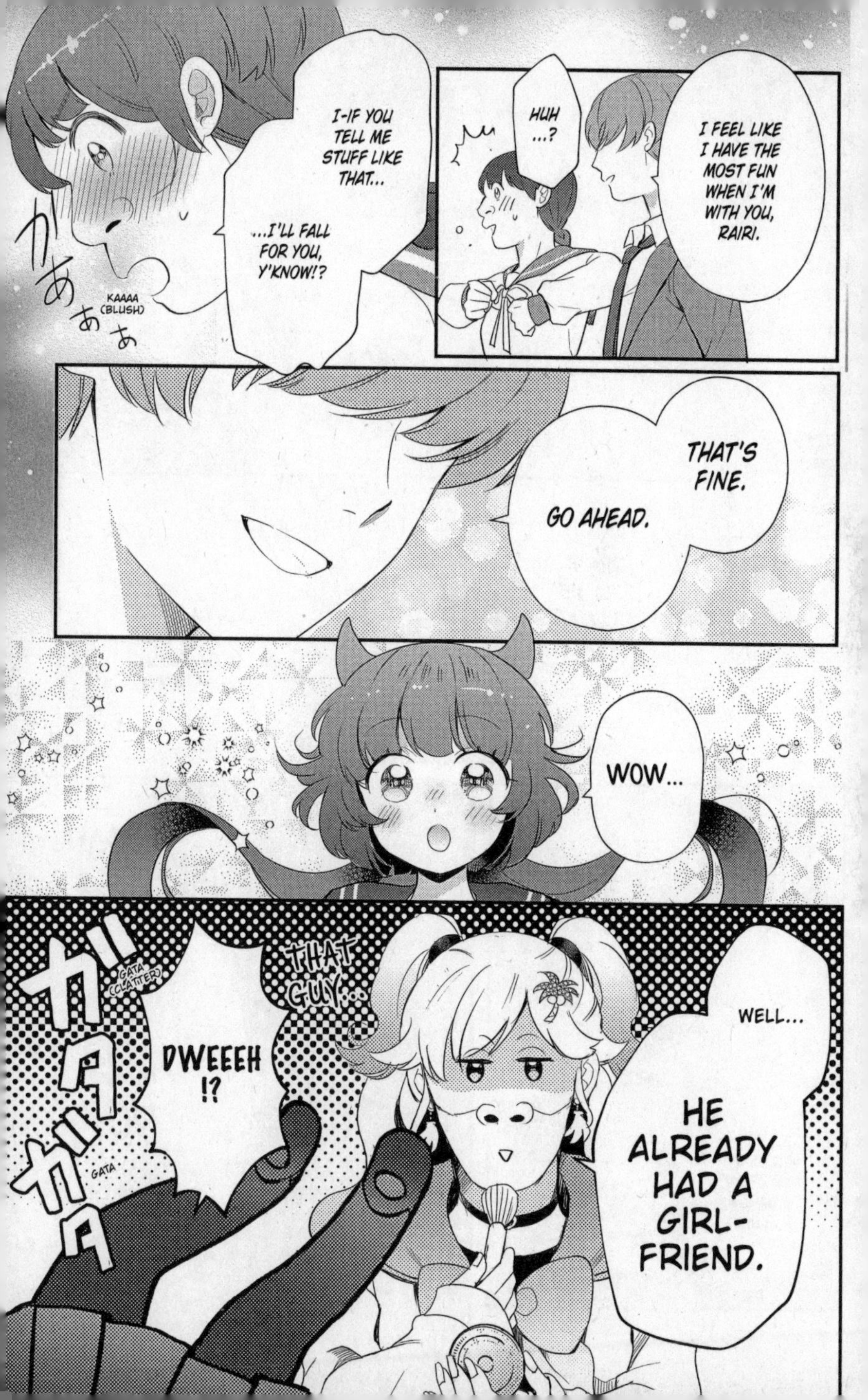
I FEEL LIKE I HAVE THE MOST FUN WHEN I'M WITH YOU, RAIRI.
HUH ...?
I-IF YOU TELL ME STUFF LIKE THAT...
...I'LL FALL FOR YOU, Y'KNOW!?
かあああ
KAAAA (BLUSH)
THAT'S FINE.
GO AHEAD.
WOW...
WELL...
HE ALREADY HAD A GIRL-FRIEND.
THAT GUY...
DWEEEH !?
ガタガタ
GATA (CLATTER)
GATA

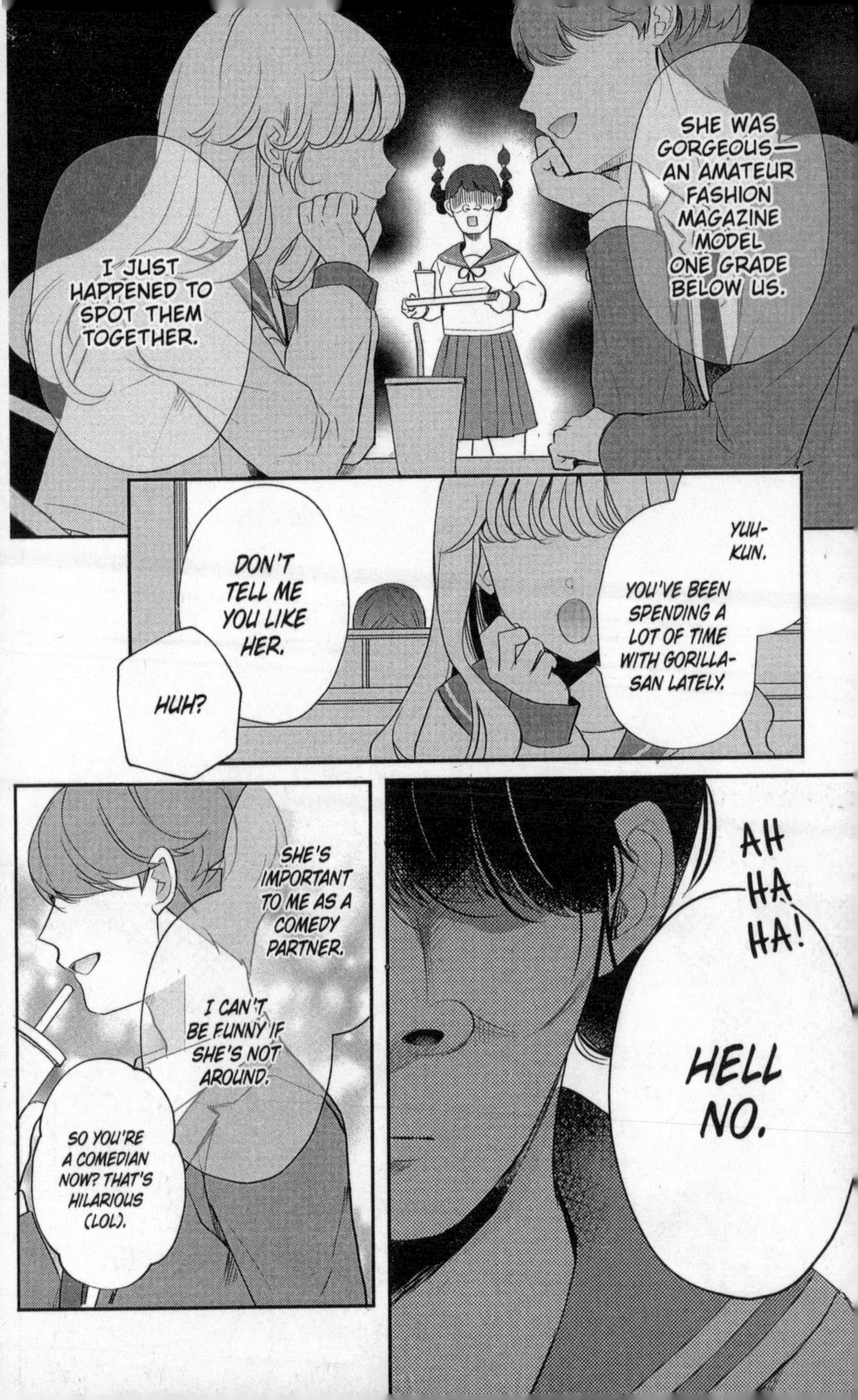
SHE WAS GORGEOUS—AN AMATEUR FASHION MAGAZINE MODEL ONE GRADE BELOW US.
I JUST HAPPENED TO SPOT THEM TOGETHER.
YUU-KUN.
YOU'VE BEEN SPENDING A LOT OF TIME WITH GORILLA-SAN LATELY.
DON'T TELL ME YOU LIKE HER.
HUH?
AH HA HA!
HELL NO.
SHE'S IMPORTANT TO ME AS A COMEDY PARTNER.
I CAN'T BE FUNNY IF SHE'S NOT AROUND.
SO YOU'RE A COMEDIAN NOW? THAT'S HILARIOUS (LOL).

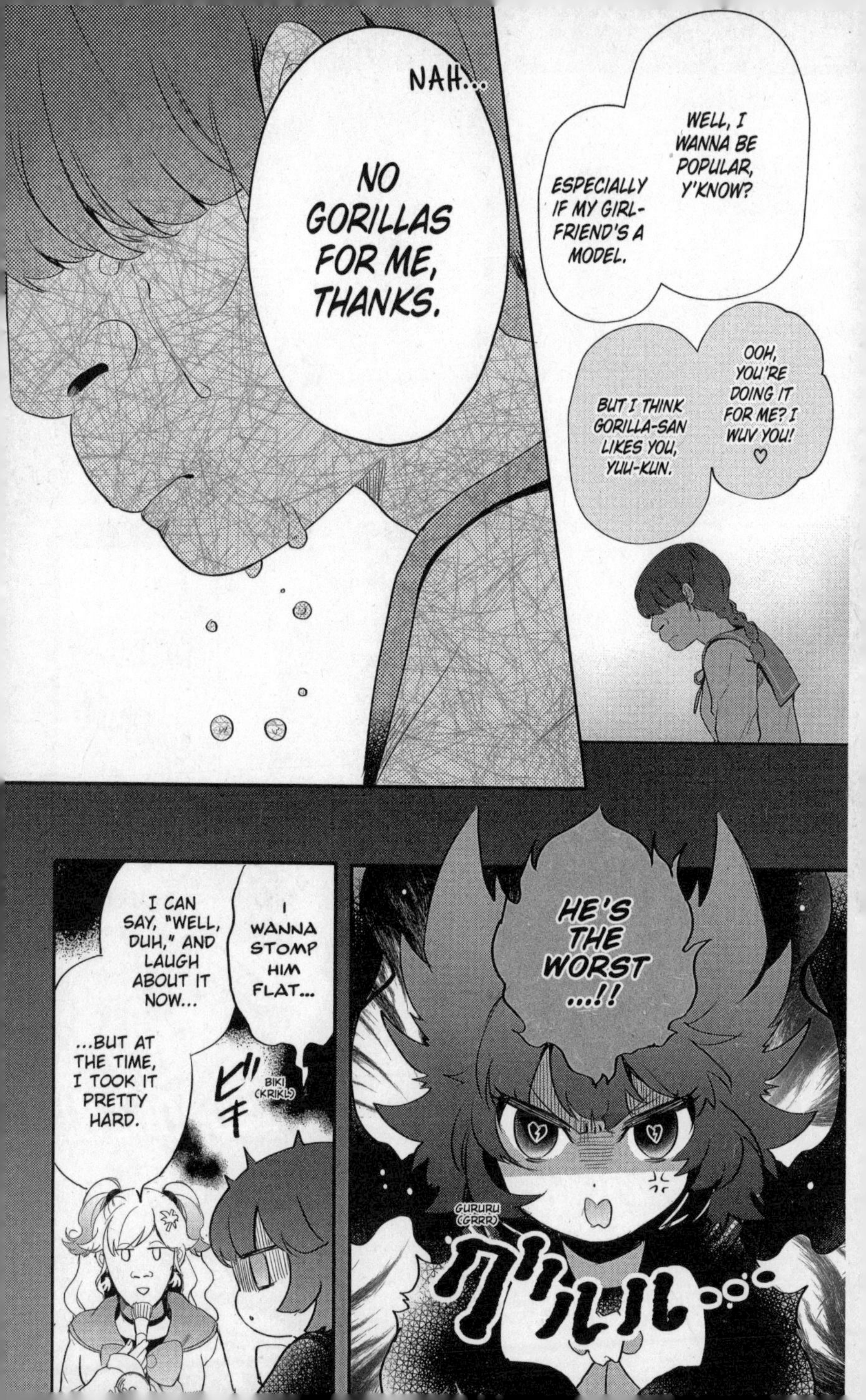
WELL, I WANNA BE POPULAR, Y'KNOW?
ESPECIALLY IF MY GIRL-FRIEND'S A MODEL.
OOH, YOU'RE DOING IT FOR ME? I WUV YOU! ♡
BUT I THINK GORILLA-SAN LIKES YOU, YUU-KUN.
NAH...
NO GORILLAS FOR ME, THANKS.
HE'S THE WORST...!!
GURURU (GRRR)
I WANNA STOMP HIM FLAT...
I CAN SAY, "WELL, DUH," AND LAUGH ABOUT IT NOW...
...BUT AT THE TIME, I TOOK IT PRETTY HARD.
BIKI (KRIKL)

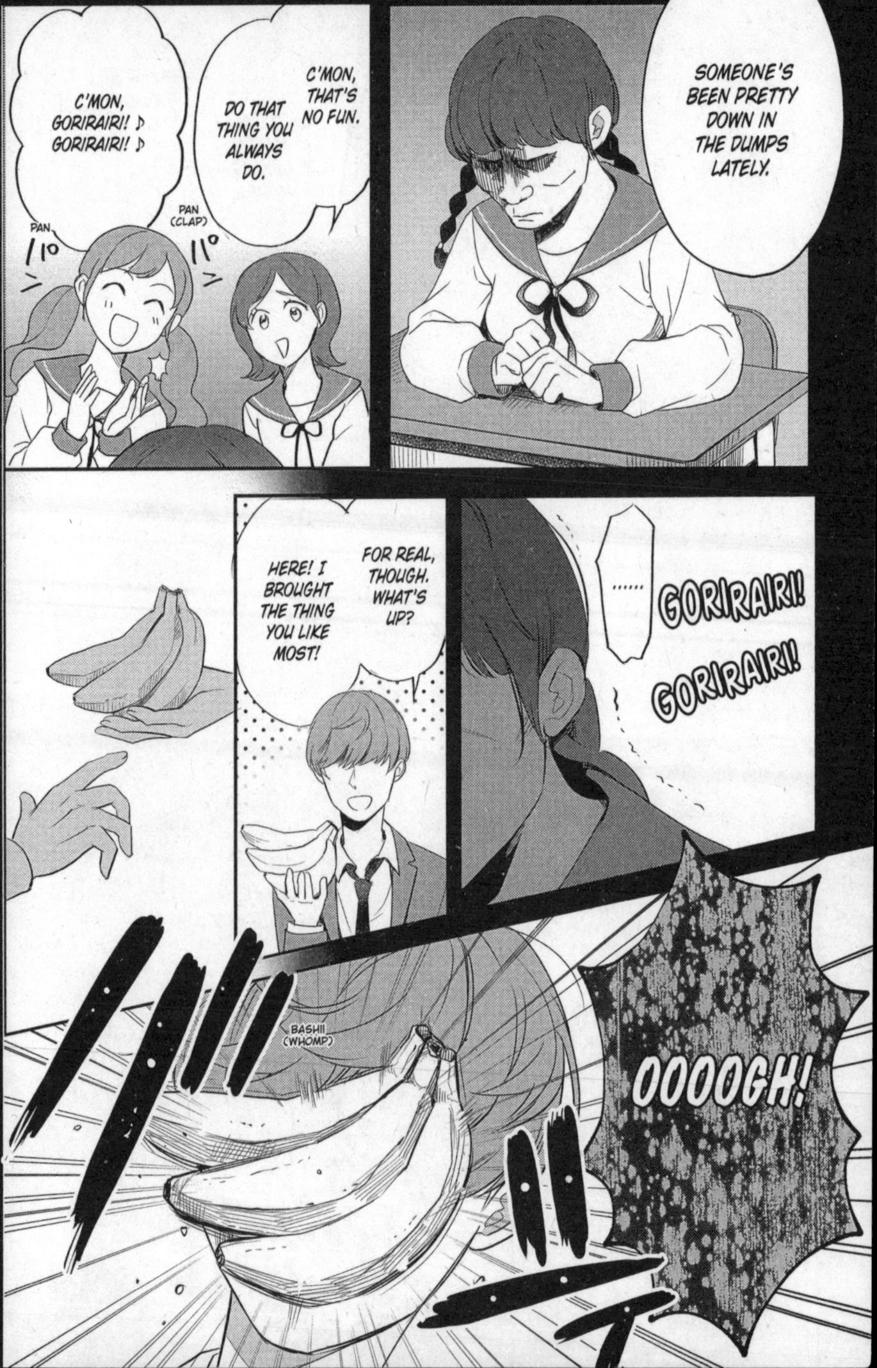
SOMEONE'S BEEN PRETTY DOWN IN THE DUMPS LATELY.
C'MON, THAT'S NO FUN.
DO THAT THING YOU ALWAYS DO.
PAN (CLAP)
C'MON, GORIRAIRI! ♪ GORIRAIRI! ♪
PAN
......
GORIRAIRI!
GORIRAIRI!
FOR REAL, THOUGH. WHAT'S UP?
HERE! I BROUGHT THE THING YOU LIKE MOST!
OOOOGH!
BASHI! (WHOMP)

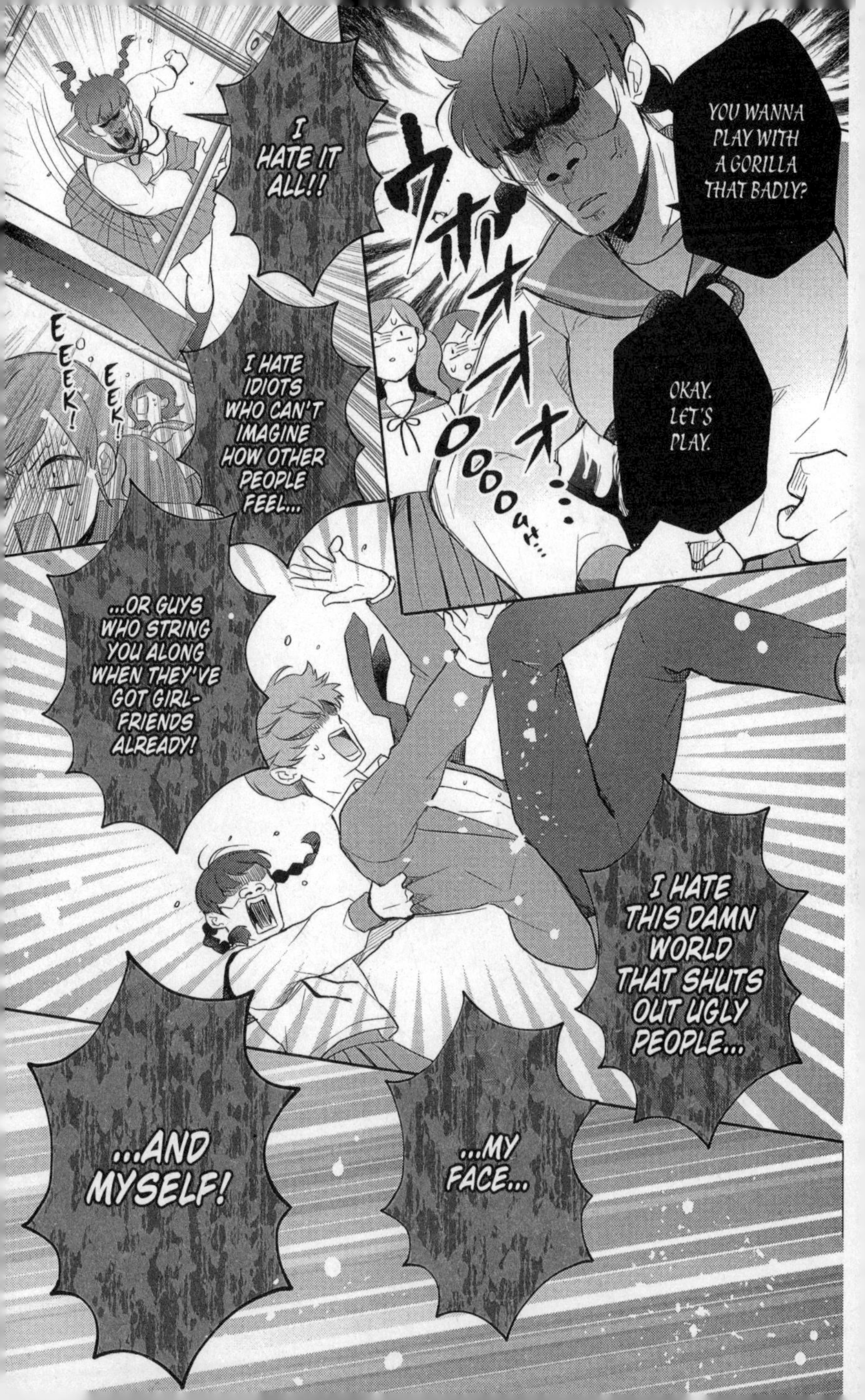
YOU WANNA PLAY WITH A GORILLA THAT BADLY?
OKAY. LET'S PLAY.
ウボオオオ…
OOOOOut...
I HATE IT ALL!!
EEEK!
EEK!
I HATE IDIOTS WHO CAN'T IMAGINE HOW OTHER PEOPLE FEEL...
...OR GUYS WHO STRING YOU ALONG WHEN THEY'VE GOT GIRL-FRIENDS ALREADY!
I HATE THIS DAMN WORLD THAT SHUTS OUT UGLY PEOPLE...
...MY FACE...
...AND MYSELF!

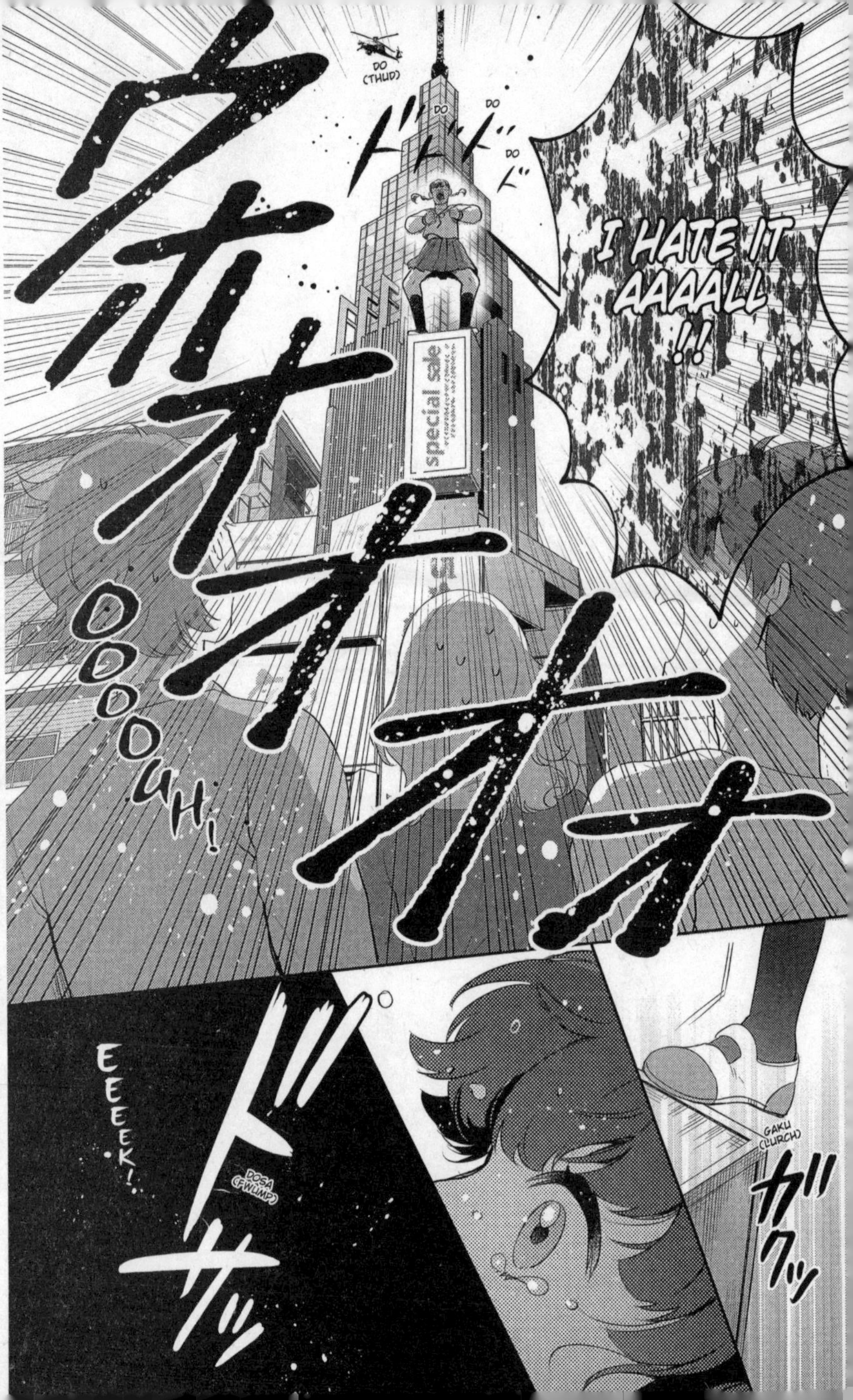
I HATE IT AAAALL!!
DO (THUD)
DO
DO
DO
OOOOUH!
GAKU (LURCH)
DOSA (FWUMP)
EEEEK!

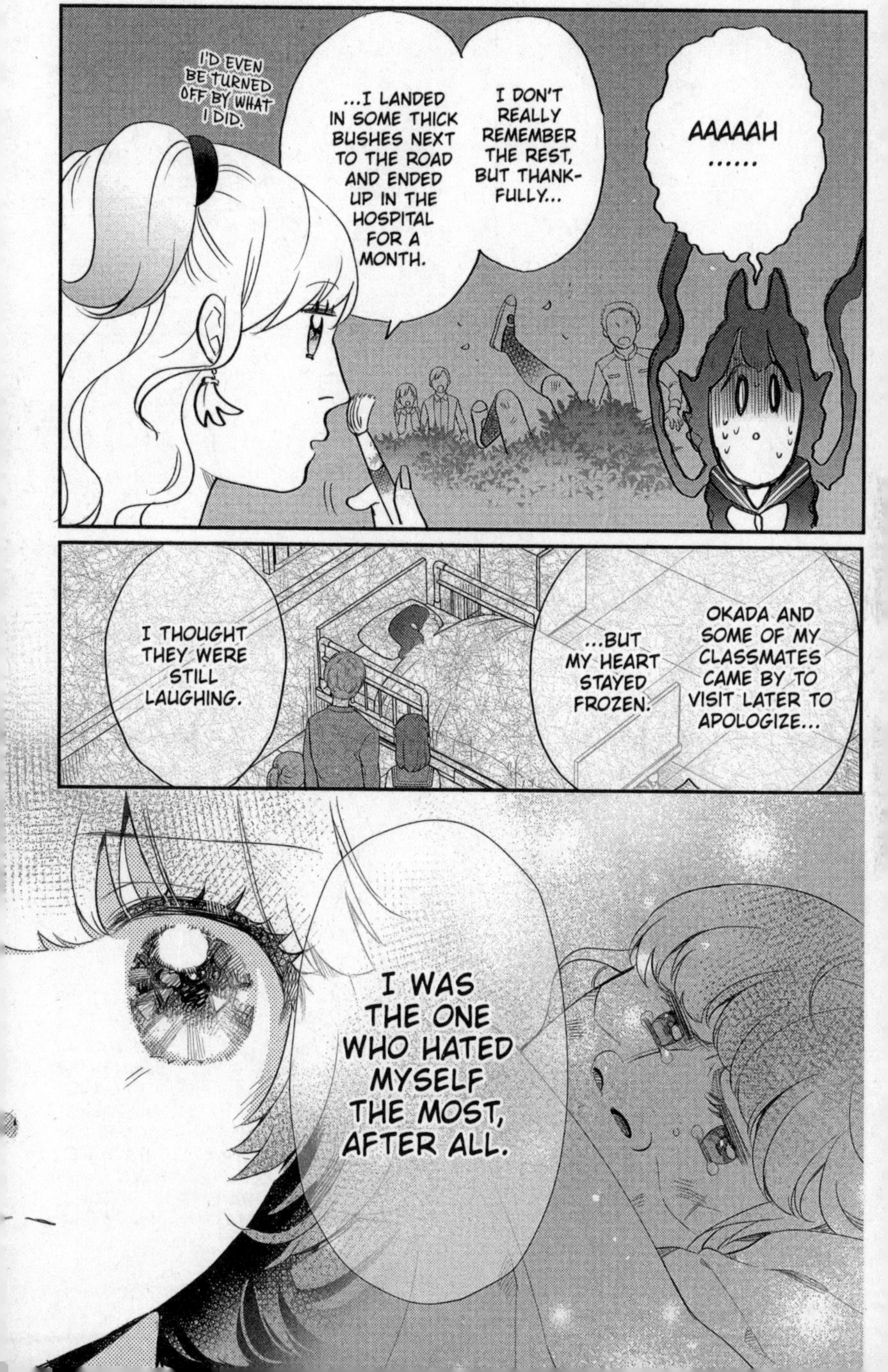
AAAAAH ......
I DON'T REALLY REMEMBER THE REST, BUT THANKFULLY...
...I LANDED IN SOME THICK BUSHES NEXT TO THE ROAD AND ENDED UP IN THE HOSPITAL FOR A MONTH.
I'D EVEN BE TURNED OFF BY WHAT I DID.
OKADA AND SOME OF MY CLASSMATES CAME BY TO VISIT LATER TO APOLOGIZE...
...BUT MY HEART STAYED FROZEN.
I THOUGHT THEY WERE STILL LAUGHING.
I WAS THE ONE WHO HATED MYSELF THE MOST, AFTER ALL.

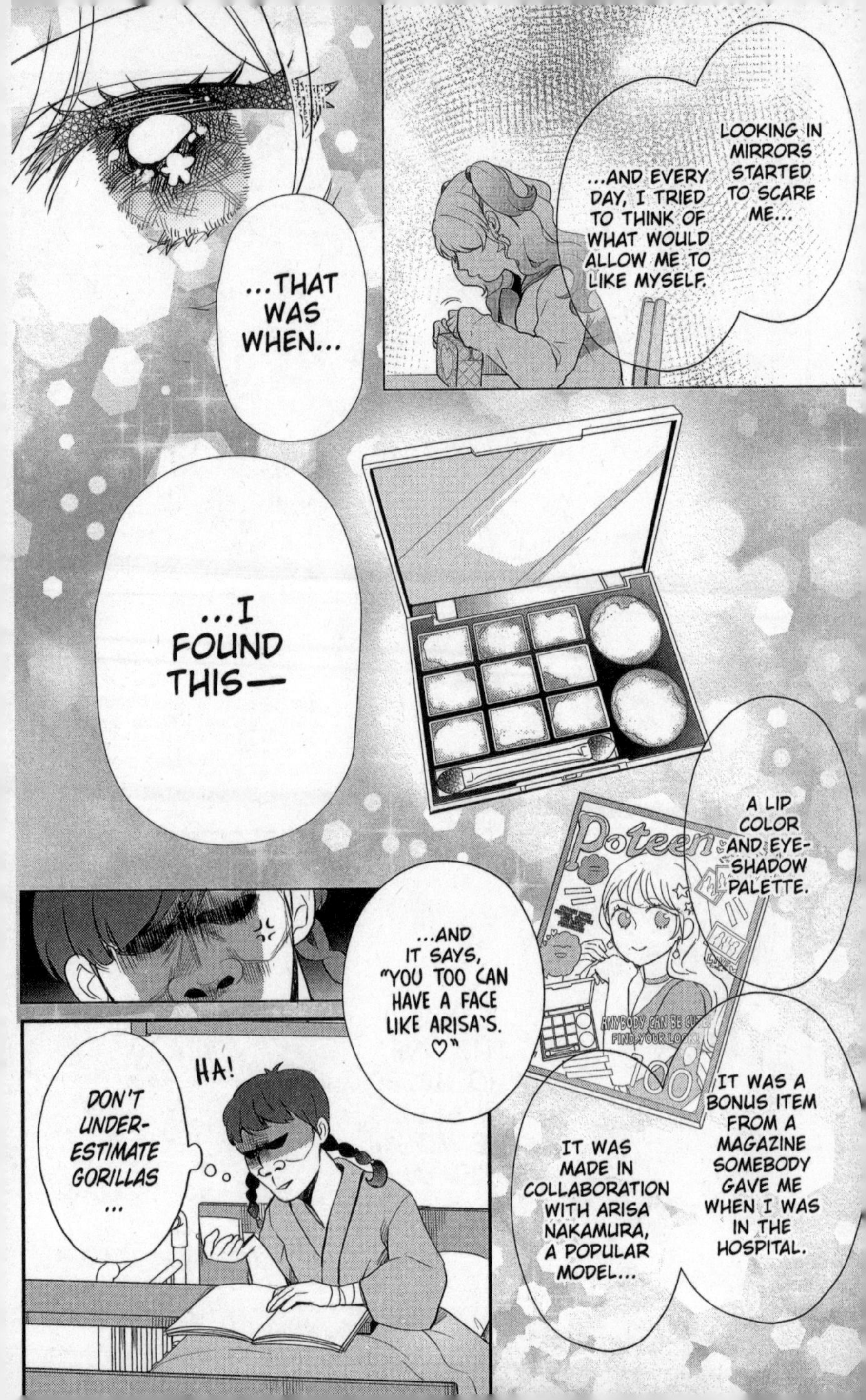
LOOKING IN MIRRORS STARTED TO SCARE ME...
...AND EVERY DAY, I TRIED TO THINK OF WHAT WOULD ALLOW ME TO LIKE MYSELF.
...THAT WAS WHEN...
...I FOUND THIS—
A LIP COLOR AND EYE-SHADOW PALETTE.
IT WAS A BONUS ITEM FROM A MAGAZINE SOMEBODY GAVE ME WHEN I WAS IN THE HOSPITAL.
IT WAS MADE IN COLLABORATION WITH ARISA NAKAMURA, A POPULAR MODEL...
Poteen
ANYBODY CAN BE CUTE!
FIND YOUR LOOK!
100
...AND IT SAYS, "YOU TOO CAN HAVE A FACE LIKE ARISA'S. ♡"
HA!
DON'T UNDER-ESTIMATE GORILLAS...

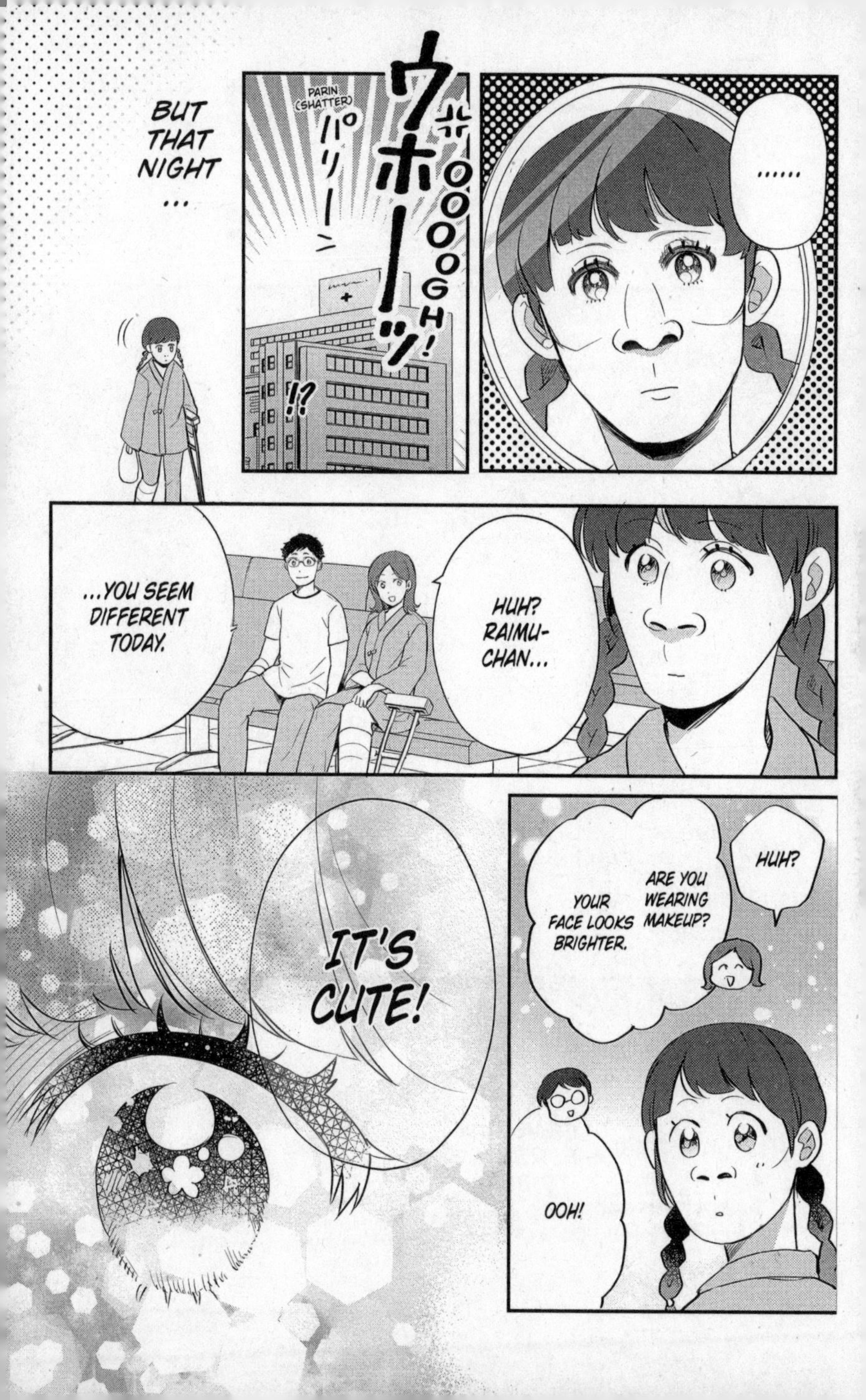
......
PARIN (SHATTER)
パリーン
ウホーーッ
OOOOOGH!
!?
BUT THAT NIGHT ...
HUH? RAIMU-CHAN...
...YOU SEEM DIFFERENT TODAY.
HUH?
ARE YOU WEARING MAKEUP?
YOUR FACE LOOKS BRIGHTER.
OOH!
IT'S CUTE!

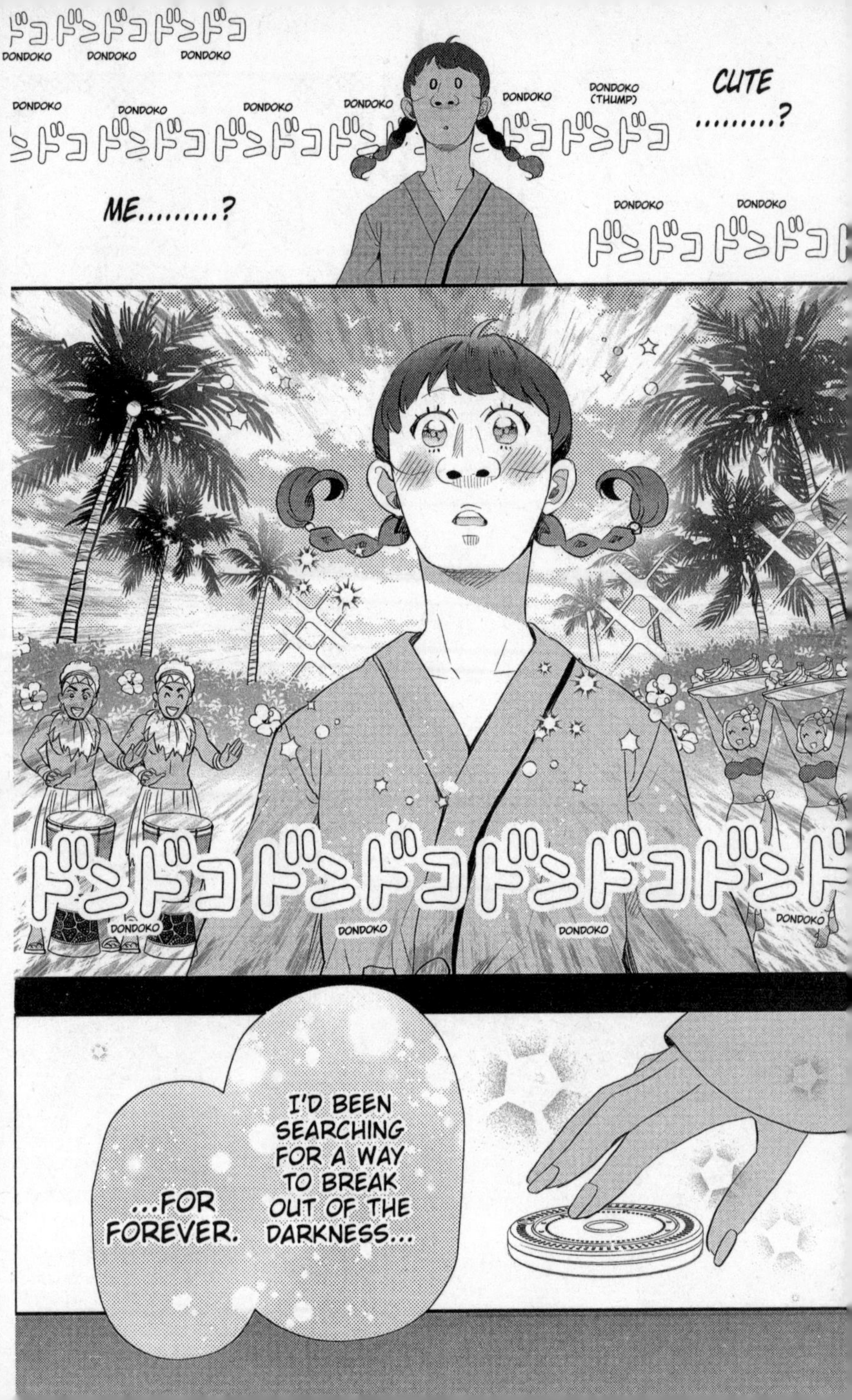
ドコドンドコドンドコ
DONDOKO DONDOKO DONDOKO
DONDOKO (THUMP)
CUTE
.........?
DONDOKO DONDOKO DONDOKO DONDOKO
ドンドコドンドコドンドコドン ドコドンドコ
ME.........?
DONDOKO DONDOKO
ドンドコドンドコ
ドンドコドンドコドンドコドンド
DONDOKO DONDOKO DONDOKO DONDOKO
I'D BEEN SEARCHING FOR A WAY TO BREAK OUT OF THE DARKNESS...
...FOR FOREVER.

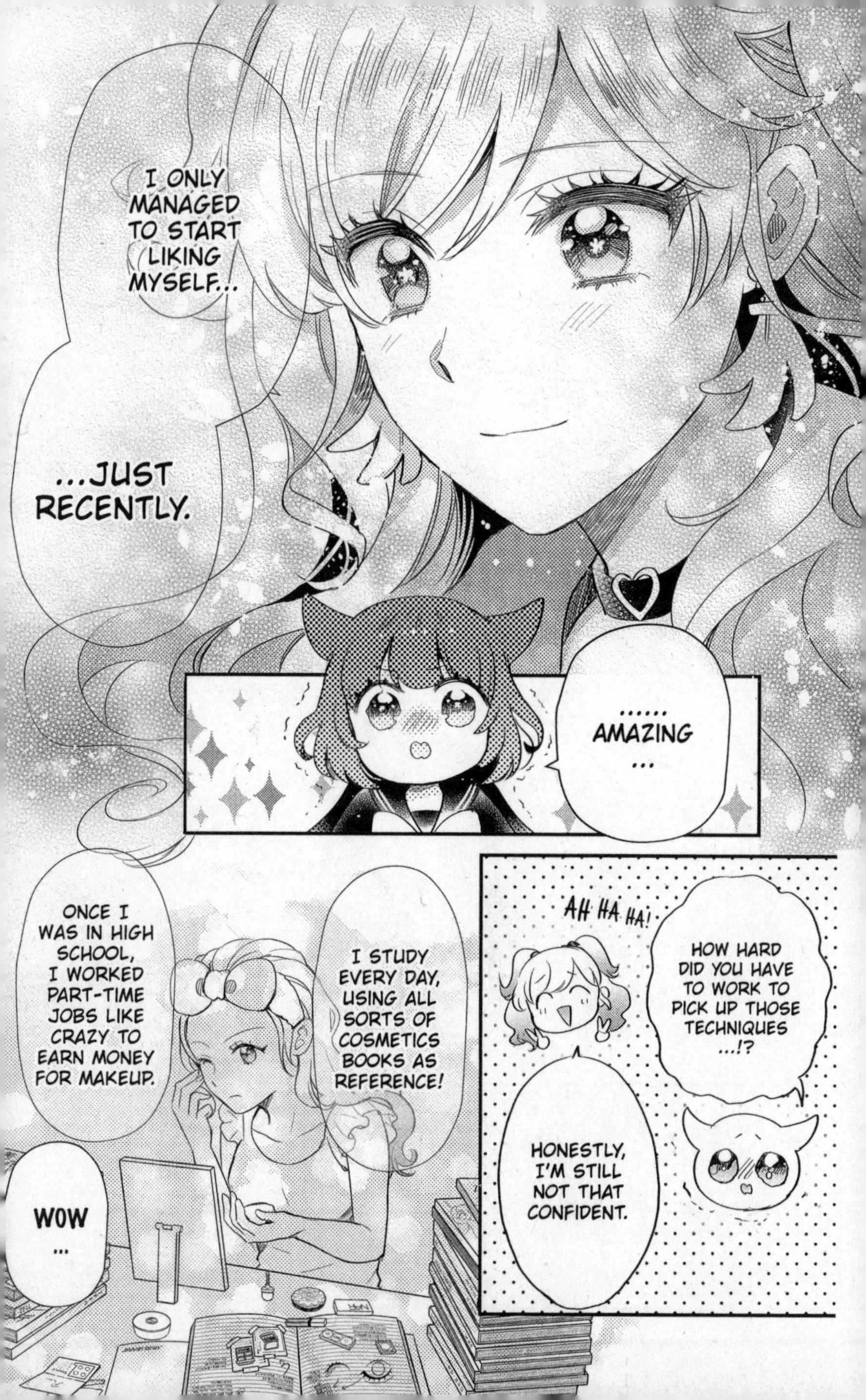
I ONLY MANAGED TO START LIKING MYSELF...
...JUST RECENTLY.
...... AMAZING ...
HOW HARD DID YOU HAVE TO WORK TO PICK UP THOSE TECHNIQUES ...!?
AH HA HA!
HONESTLY, I'M STILL NOT THAT CONFIDENT.
I STUDY EVERY DAY, USING ALL SORTS OF COSMETICS BOOKS AS REFERENCE!
ONCE I WAS IN HIGH SCHOOL, I WORKED PART-TIME JOBS LIKE CRAZY TO EARN MONEY FOR MAKEUP.
WOW ...

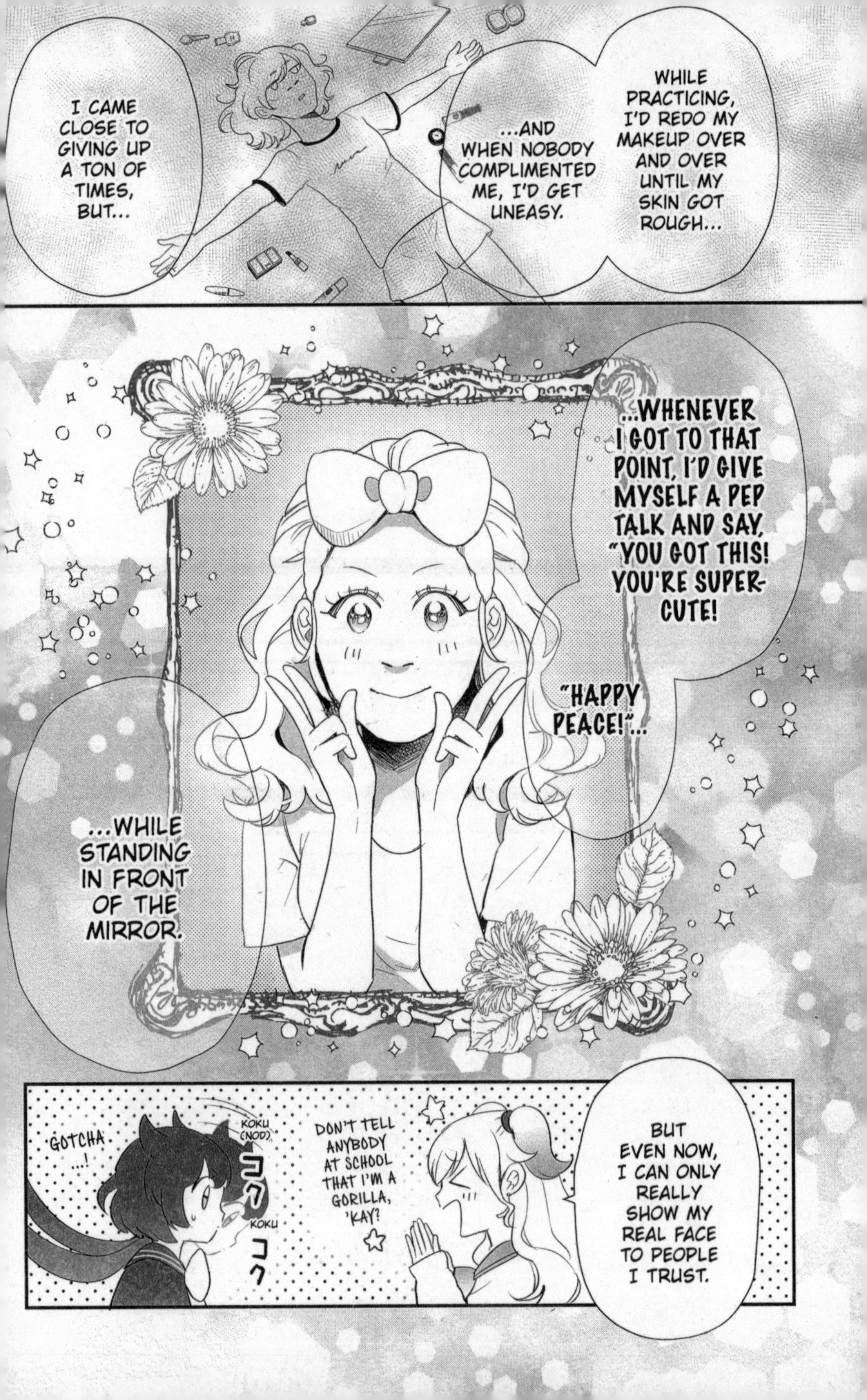
WHILE PRACTICING, I'D REDO MY MAKEUP OVER AND OVER UNTIL MY SKIN GOT ROUGH...
...AND WHEN NOBODY COMPLIMENTED ME, I'D GET UNEASY.
I CAME CLOSE TO GIVING UP A TON OF TIMES, BUT...
...WHENEVER I GOT TO THAT POINT, I'D GIVE MYSELF A PEP TALK AND SAY, "YOU GOT THIS! YOU'RE SUPER-CUTE!
"HAPPY PEACE!"...
...WHILE STANDING IN FRONT OF THE MIRROR.
BUT EVEN NOW, I CAN ONLY REALLY SHOW MY REAL FACE TO PEOPLE I TRUST.
DON'T TELL ANYBODY AT SCHOOL THAT I'M A GORILLA, 'KAY?
KOKU (NOD)
コク
KOKU
コク
GOTCHA ...!

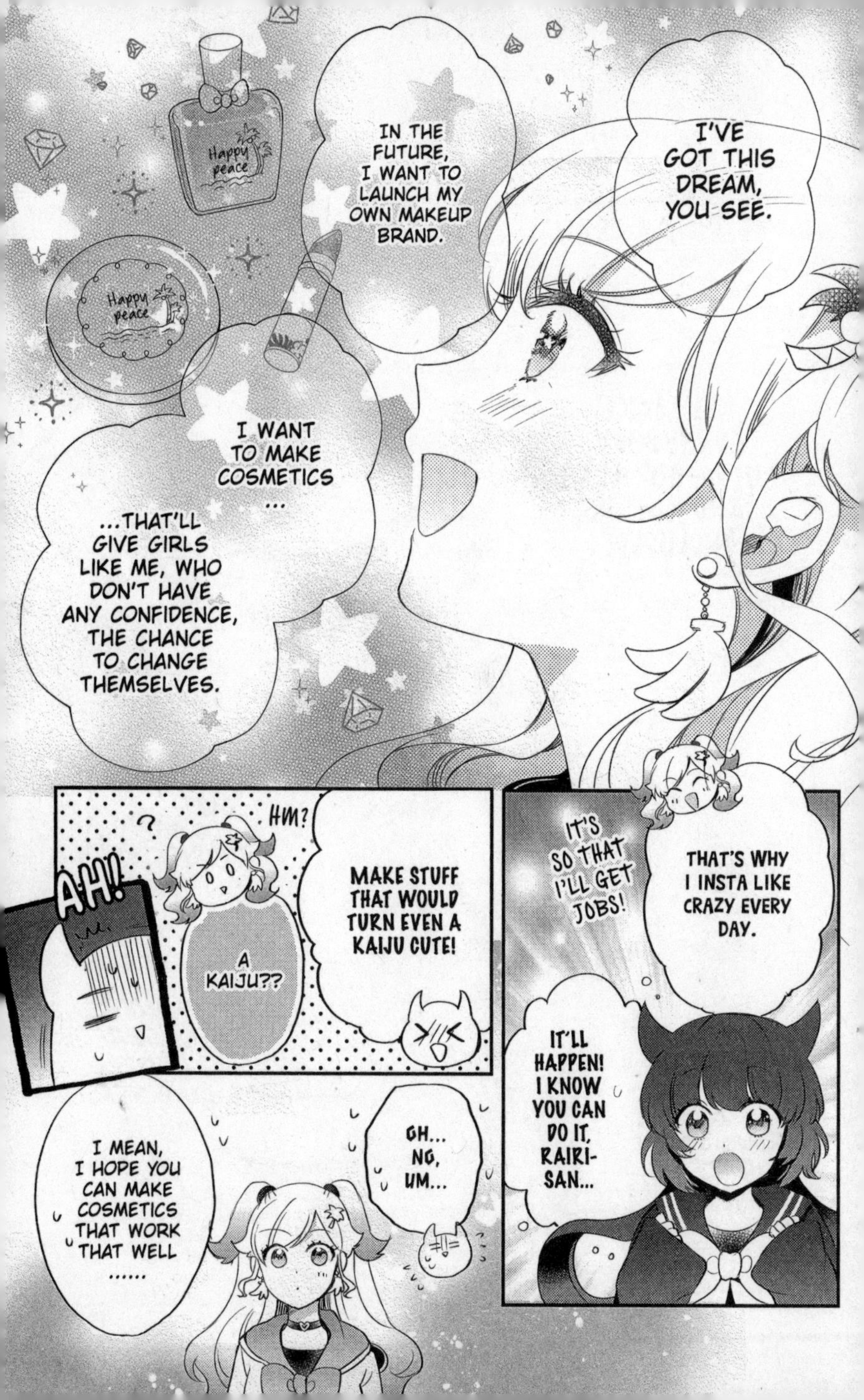
I'VE GOT THIS DREAM, YOU SEE.
IN THE FUTURE, I WANT TO LAUNCH MY OWN MAKEUP BRAND.
Happy peace
Happy peace
I WANT TO MAKE COSMETICS ...
...THAT'LL GIVE GIRLS LIKE ME, WHO DON'T HAVE ANY CONFIDENCE, THE CHANCE TO CHANGE THEMSELVES.
THAT'S WHY I INSTA LIKE CRAZY EVERY DAY.
IT'S SO THAT I'LL GET JOBS!
IT'LL HAPPEN! I KNOW YOU CAN DO IT, RAIRI-SAN...
HM?
MAKE STUFF THAT WOULD TURN EVEN A KAIJU CUTE!
A KAIJU??
AH!
OH... NO, UM...
I MEAN, I HOPE YOU CAN MAKE COSMETICS THAT WORK THAT WELL ......

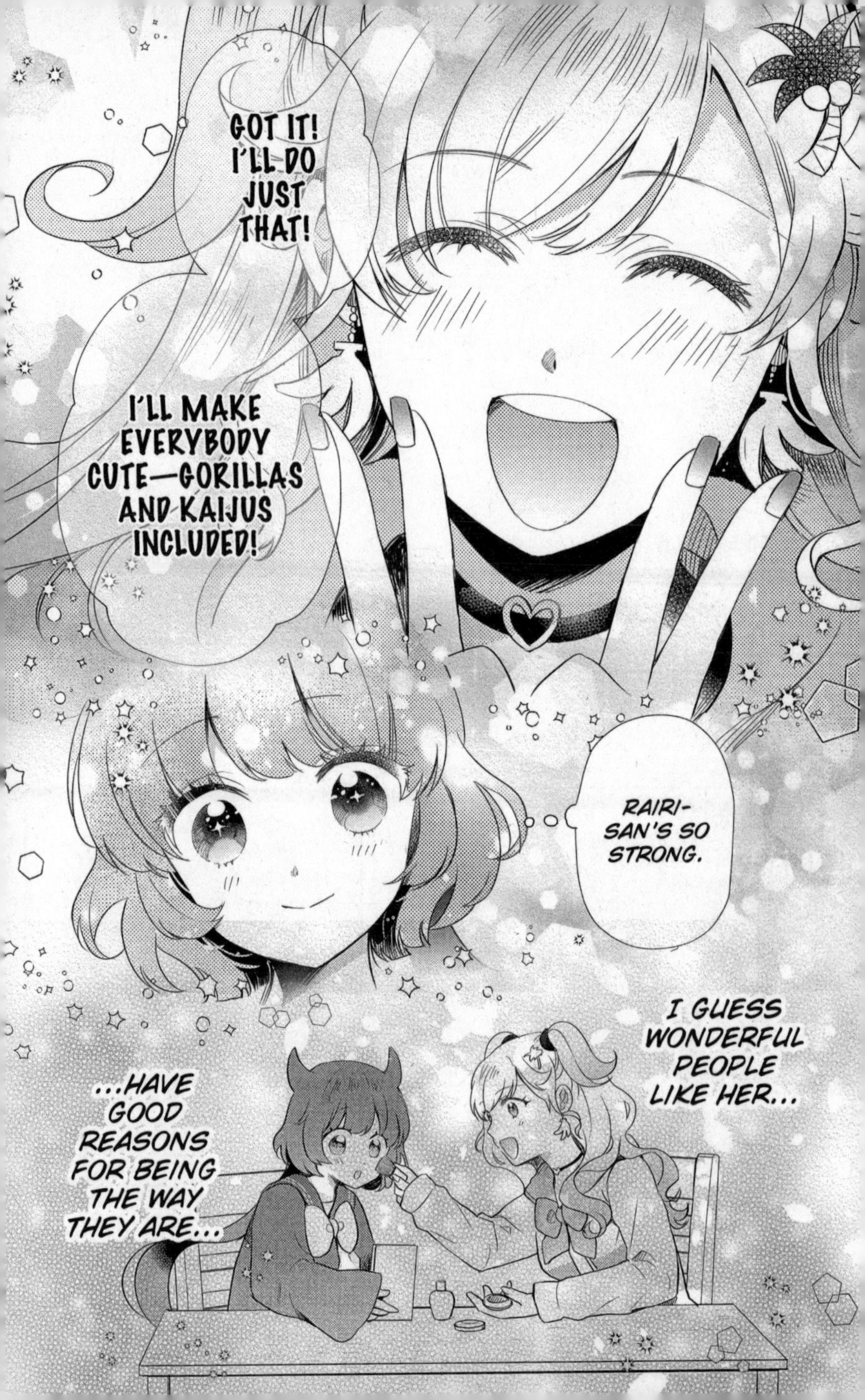
GOT IT! I'LL DO JUST THAT!
I'LL MAKE EVERYBODY CUTE—GORILLAS AND KAIJUS INCLUDED!
RAIRI-SAN'S SO STRONG.
I GUESS WONDERFUL PEOPLE LIKE HER...
...HAVE GOOD REASONS FOR BEING THE WAY THEY ARE...

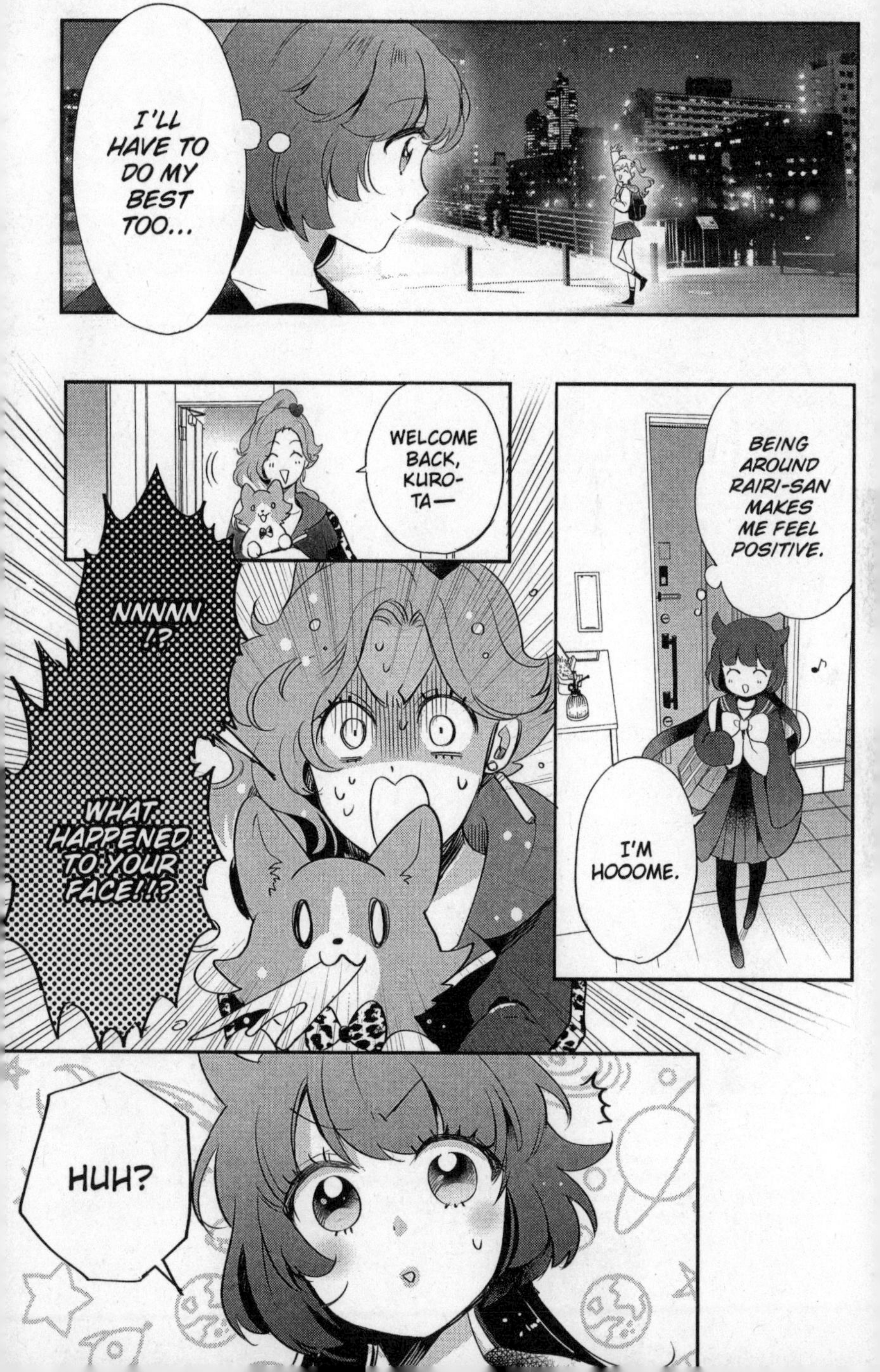
I'LL HAVE TO DO MY BEST TOO...
BEING AROUND RAIRI-SAN MAKES ME FEEL POSITIVE.
I'M HOOOME.
WELCOME BACK, KURO-TA—
NNNNN!?
WHAT HAPPENED TO YOUR FACE!!?
HUH?

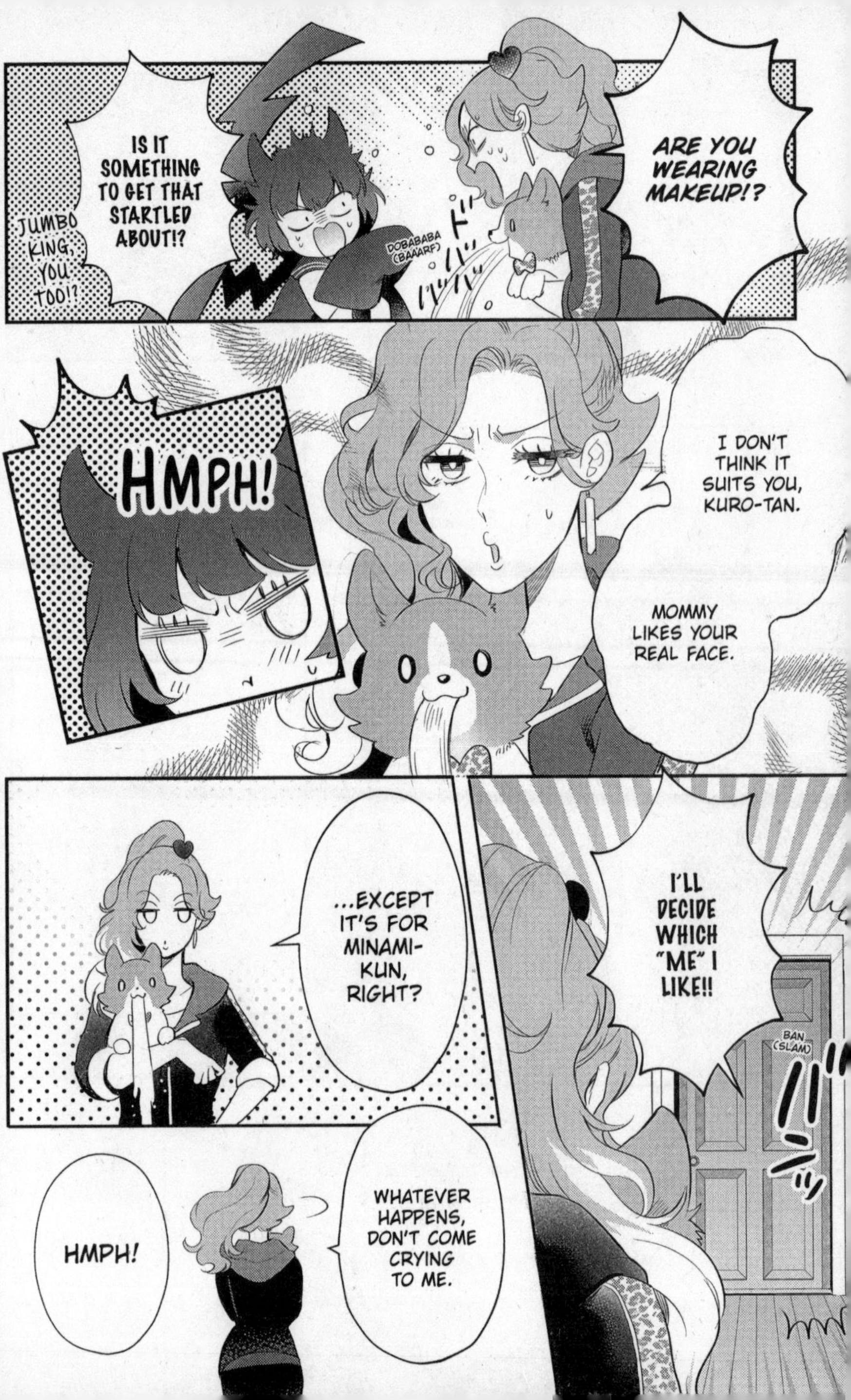
ARE YOU WEARING MAKEUP!?
IS IT SOMETHING TO GET THAT STARTLED ABOUT!?
DOBABABA (BAAARF)
JUMBO KING, YOU TOO!?
I DON'T THINK IT SUITS YOU, KURO-TAN.
MOMMY LIKES YOUR REAL FACE.
HMPH!
I'LL DECIDE WHICH "ME" I LIKE!!
BAN (SLAM)
...EXCEPT IT'S FOR MINAMI-KUN, RIGHT?
WHATEVER HAPPENS, DON'T COME CRYING TO ME.
HMPH!

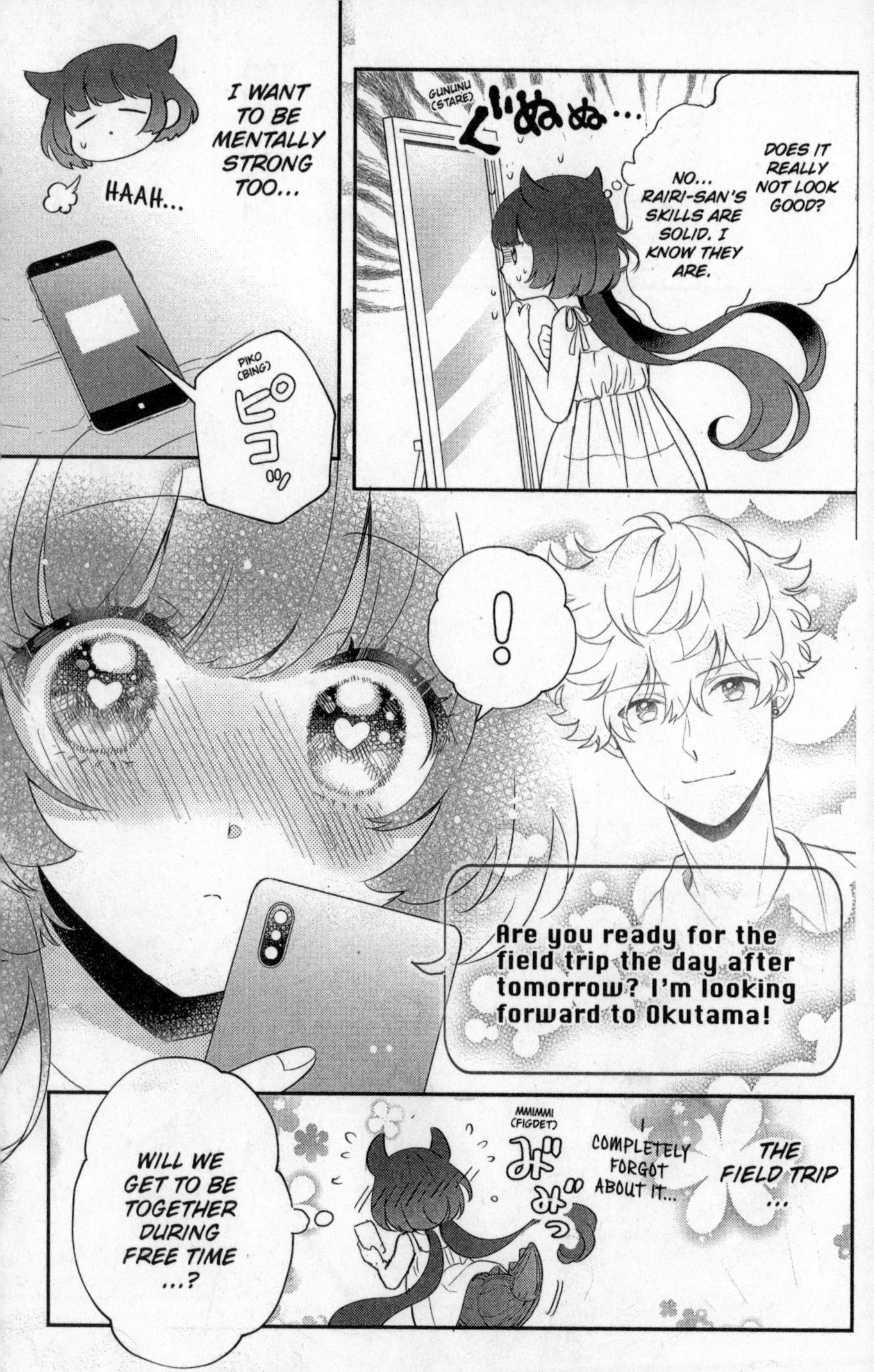
GUNUNU (STARE)
ぐぬぬ…
DOES IT REALLY NOT LOOK GOOD?
NO... RAIRI-SAN'S SKILLS ARE SOLID. I KNOW THEY ARE.
I WANT TO BE MENTALLY STRONG TOO...
HAAH...
PIKO (BING)
ピコッ
!
Are you ready for the field trip the day after tomorrow? I'm looking forward to Okutama!
WILL WE GET TO BE TOGETHER DURING FREE TIME ...?
THE FIELD TRIP ...
I COMPLETELY FORGOT ABOUT IT...
MMIMMI (FIGDET)
みみっ

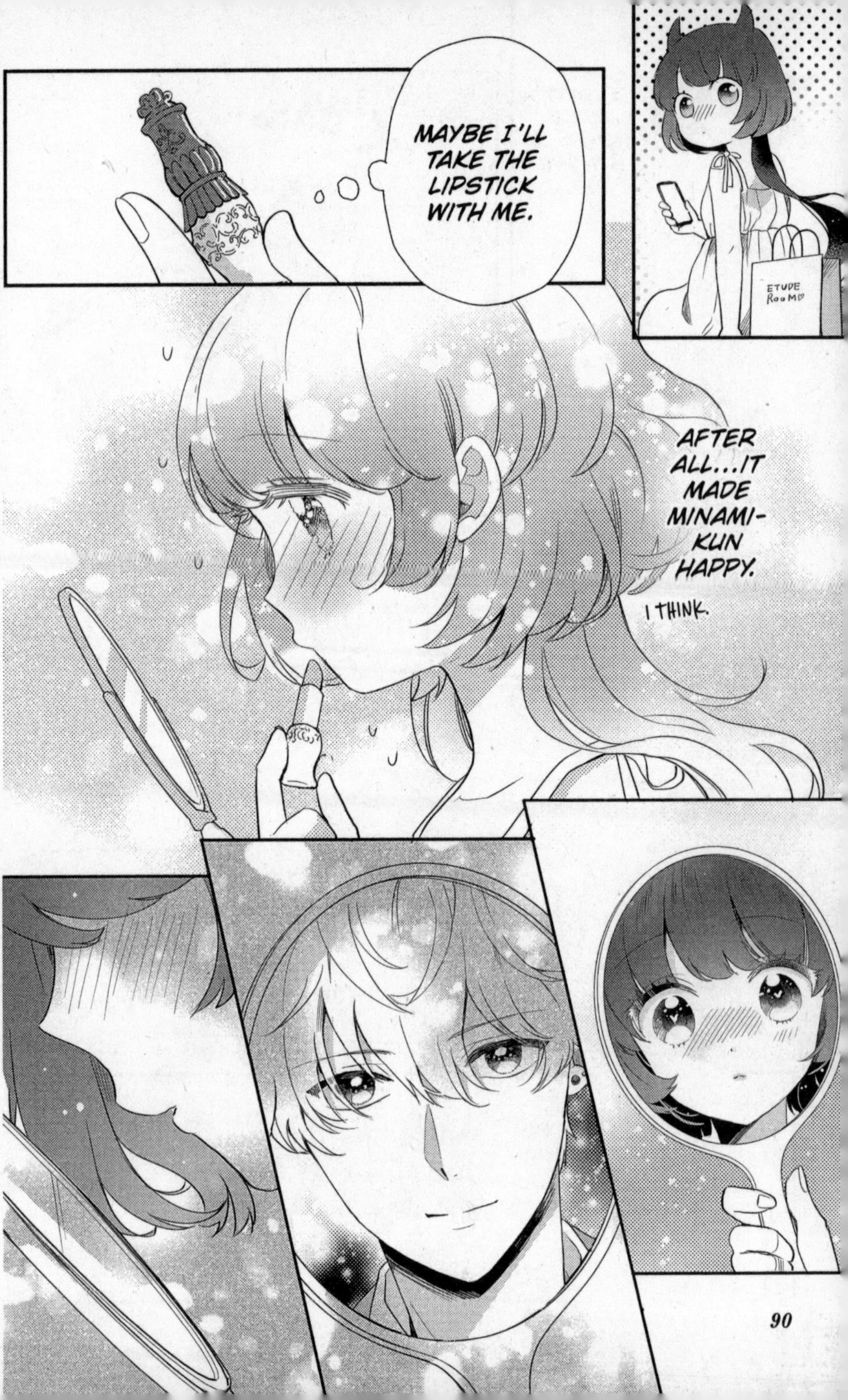

ETUDE RooM
MAYBE I'LL TAKE THE LIPSTICK WITH ME.
AFTER ALL...IT MADE MINAMI-KUN HAPPY.
I THINK.

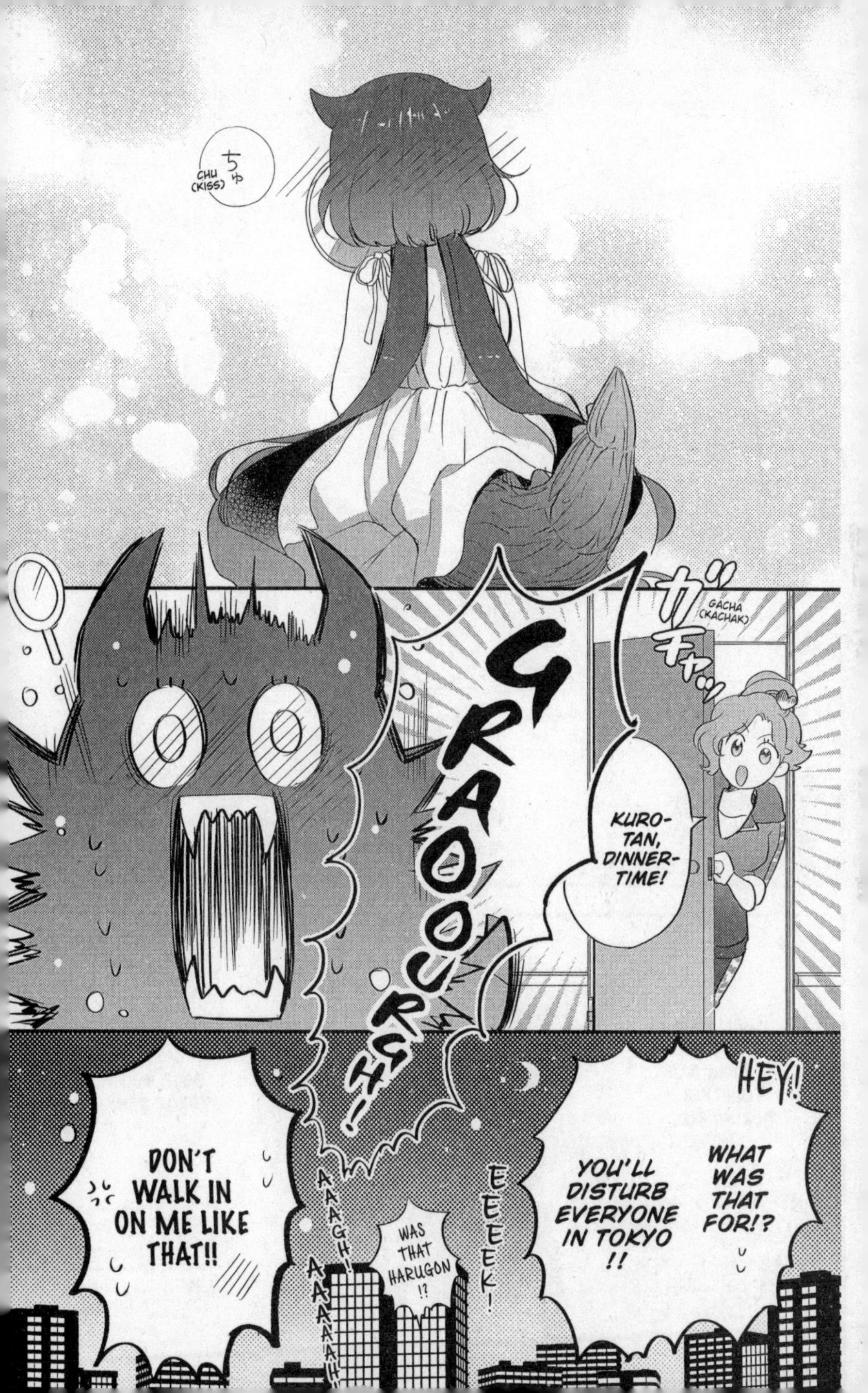
ちゅ
CHU (KISS)
ガチャッ
GACHA (KACHAK)
KURO-TAN, DINNER-TIME!
GRAOOOURSH!
HEY!
WHAT WAS THAT FOR!?
YOU'LL DISTURB EVERYONE IN TOKYO!!
DON'T WALK IN ON ME LIKE THAT!!
EEEEEK!
WAS THAT HARUGON!?
AAAGH!
AAAAAAAH!

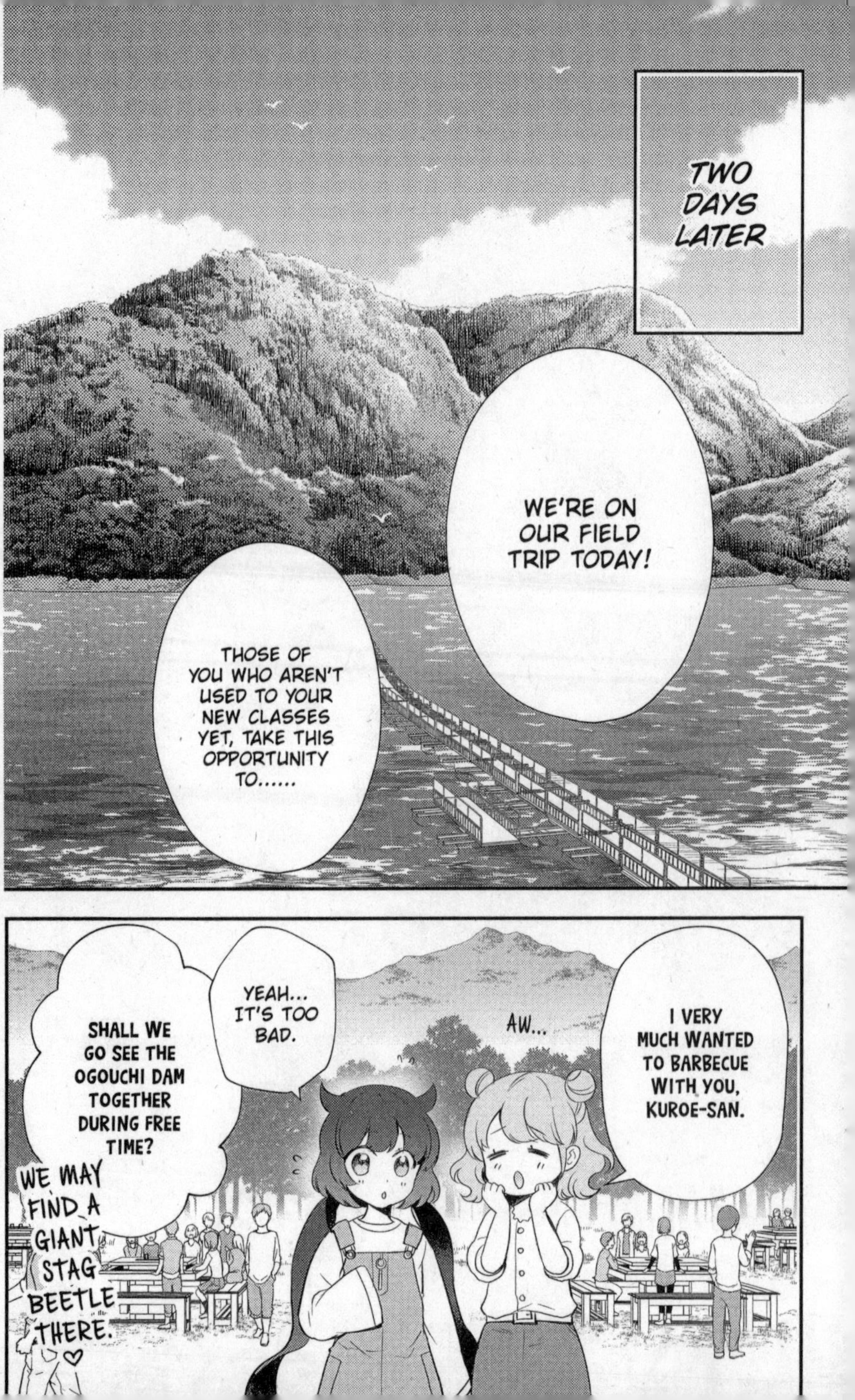
TWO DAYS LATER
WE'RE ON OUR FIELD TRIP TODAY!
THOSE OF YOU WHO AREN'T USED TO YOUR NEW CLASSES YET, TAKE THIS OPPORTUNITY TO......
I VERY MUCH WANTED TO BARBECUE WITH YOU, KUROE-SAN.
AW...
YEAH... IT'S TOO BAD.
SHALL WE GO SEE THE OGOUCHI DAM TOGETHER DURING FREE TIME?
WE MAY FIND A GIANT STAG BEETLE THERE. ♡

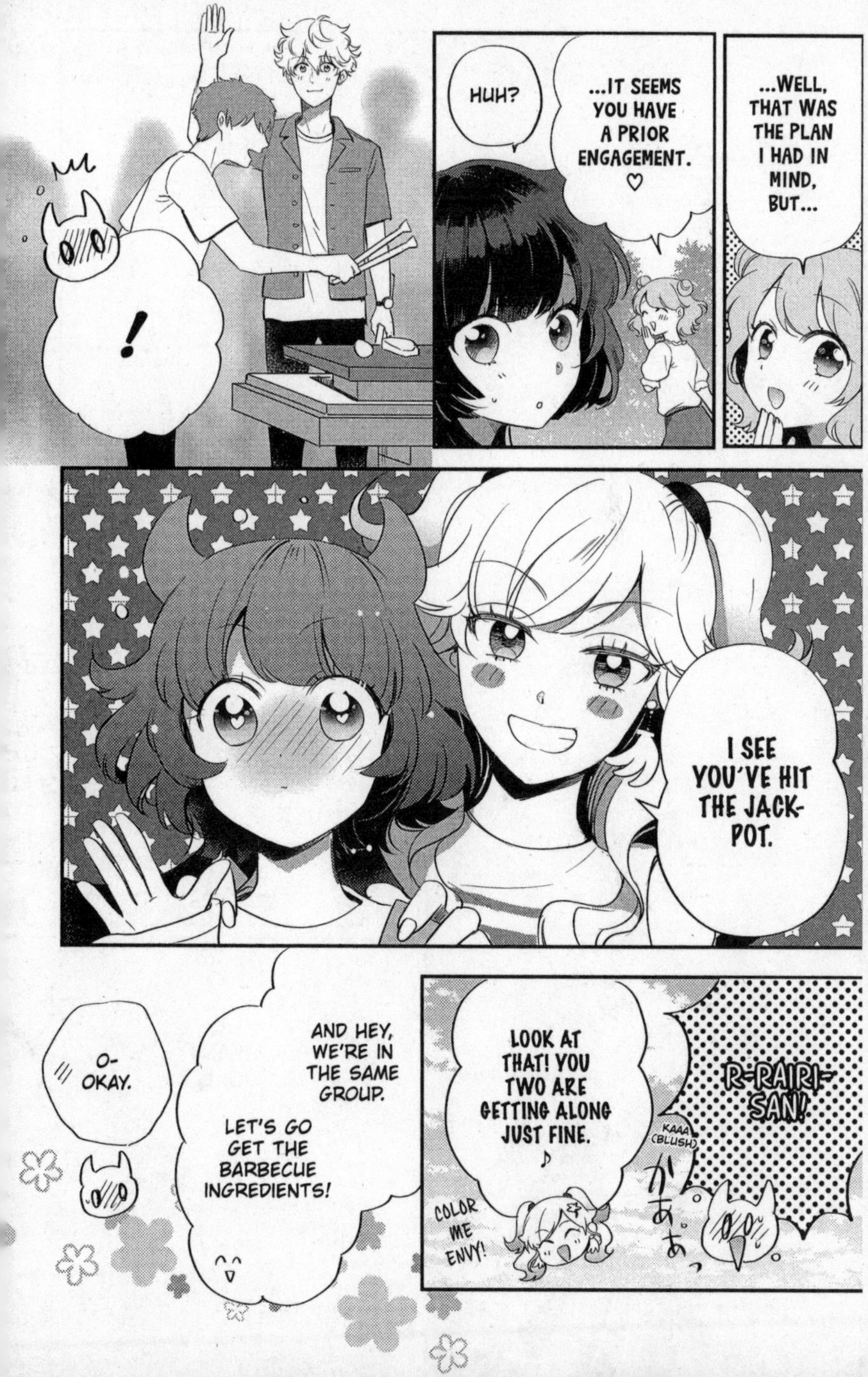
...WELL, THAT WAS THE PLAN I HAD IN MIND, BUT...
...IT SEEMS YOU HAVE A PRIOR ENGAGEMENT. ♡
HUH?
!
I SEE YOU'VE HIT THE JACKPOT.
R-RAIRI-SAN!
LOOK AT THAT! YOU TWO ARE GETTING ALONG JUST FINE. ♪
KAAA (BLUSH)
かあっ
COLOR ME ENVY!
AND HEY, WE'RE IN THE SAME GROUP.
LET'S GO GET THE BARBECUE INGREDIENTS!
O-OKAY.

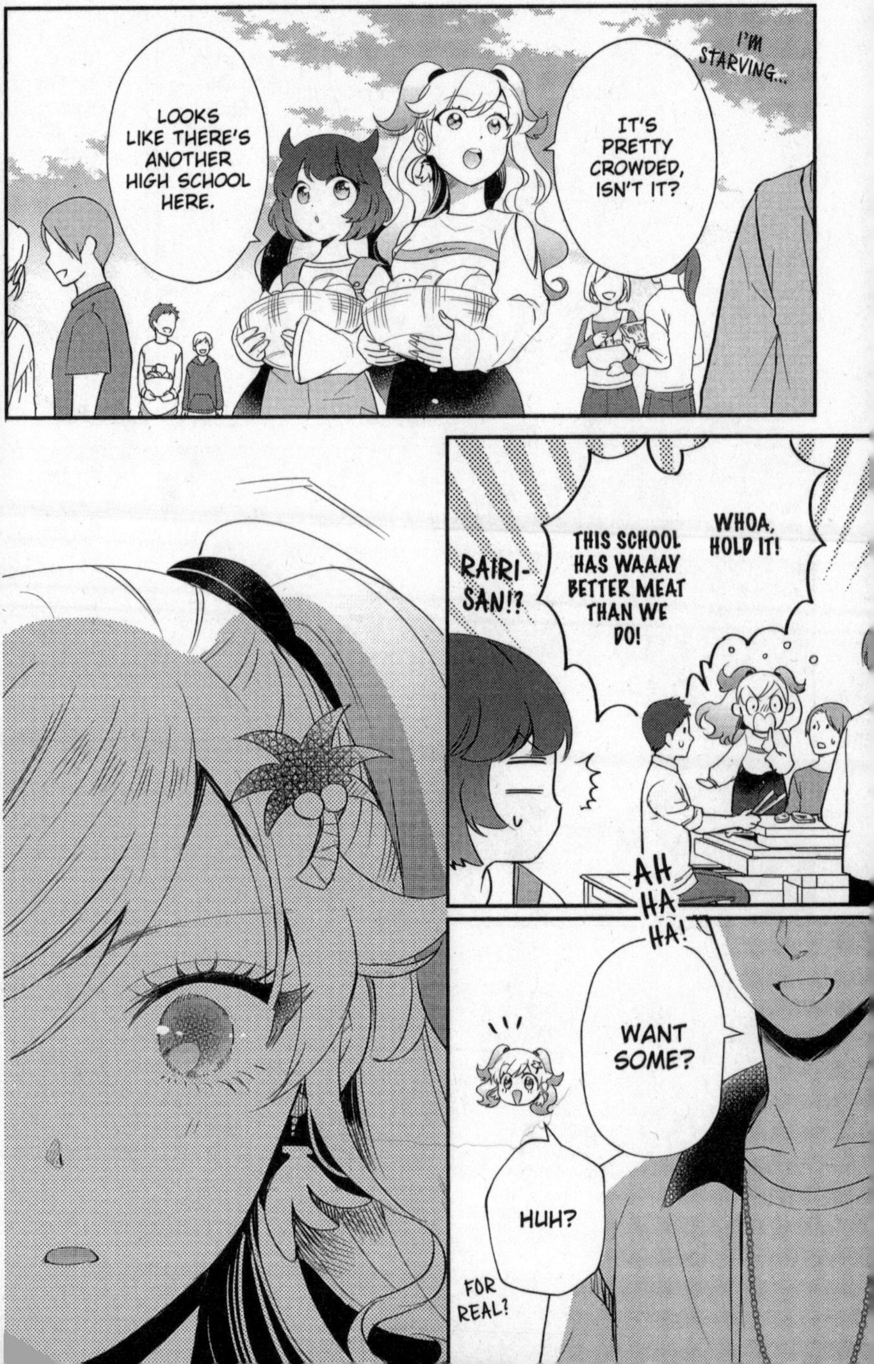
I'M STARVING...
IT'S PRETTY CROWDED, ISN'T IT?
LOOKS LIKE THERE'S ANOTHER HIGH SCHOOL HERE.
WHOA, HOLD IT!
THIS SCHOOL HAS WAAAY BETTER MEAT THAN WE DO!
RAIRI-SAN!?
AH HA HA!
WANT SOME?
HUH?
FOR REAL?

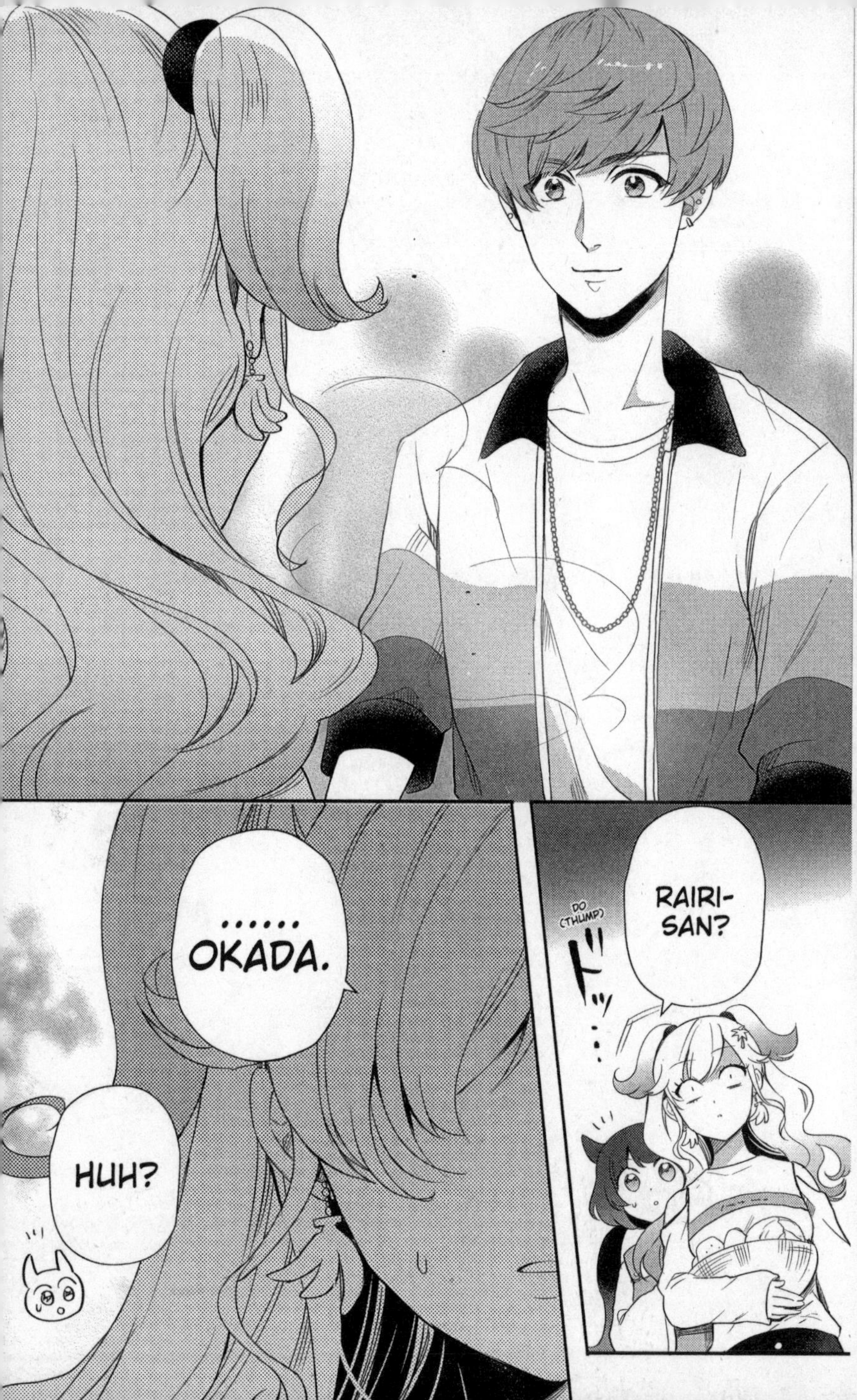
RAIRI-SAN?
DO (THUMP)
......OKADA.
HUH?

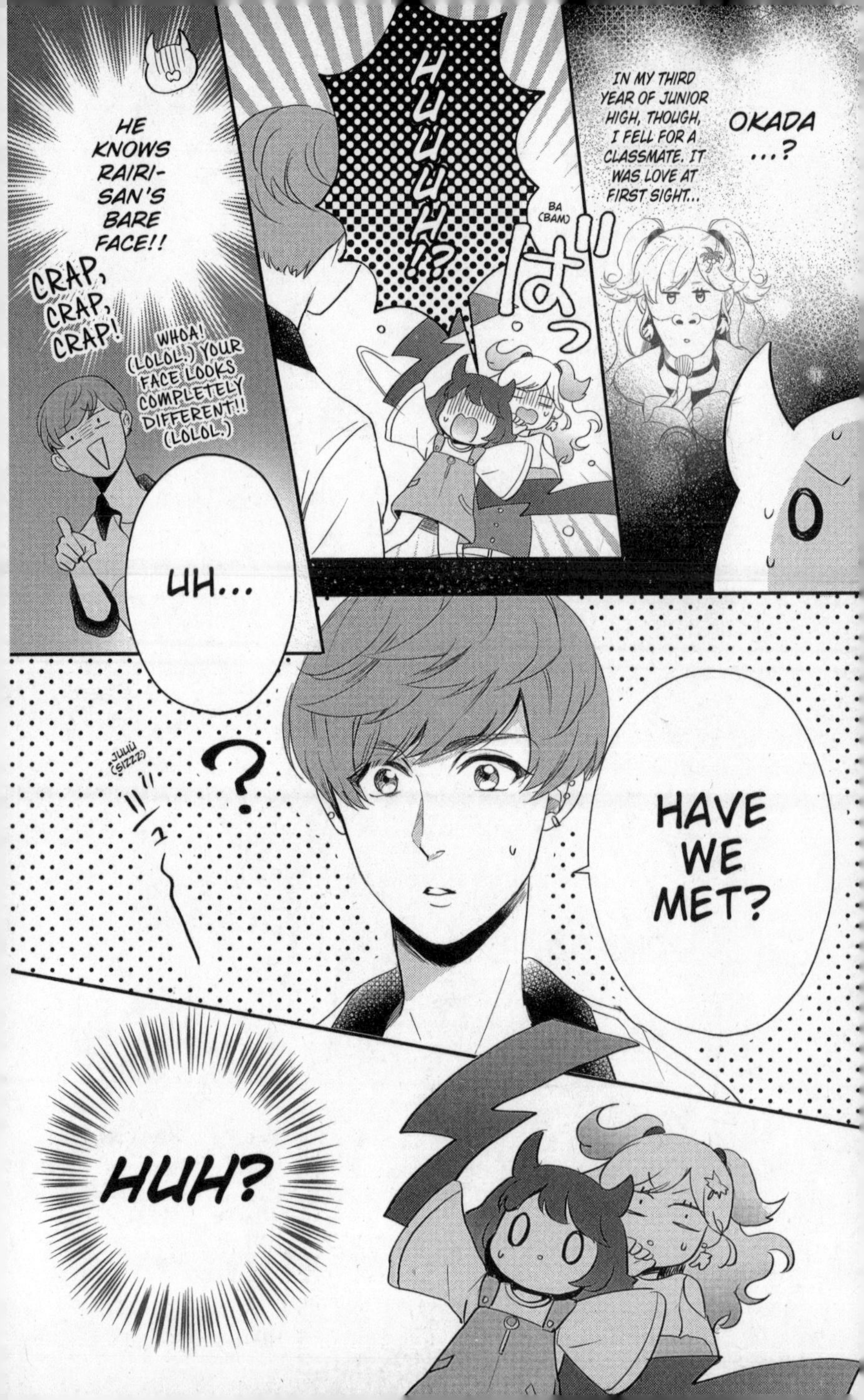
OKADA ...?
IN MY THIRD YEAR OF JUNIOR HIGH, THOUGH, I FELL FOR A CLASSMATE. IT WAS LOVE AT FIRST SIGHT...
HUUUUH!?
ばっ
BA (BAM)
HE KNOWS RAIRI-SAN'S BARE FACE!!
CRAP, CRAP, CRAP!
WHOA! (LOLOL.) YOUR FACE LOOKS COMPLETELY DIFFERENT!! (LOLOL.)
UH...
HAVE WE MET?
?
JUUU (SIZZZ)
HUH?

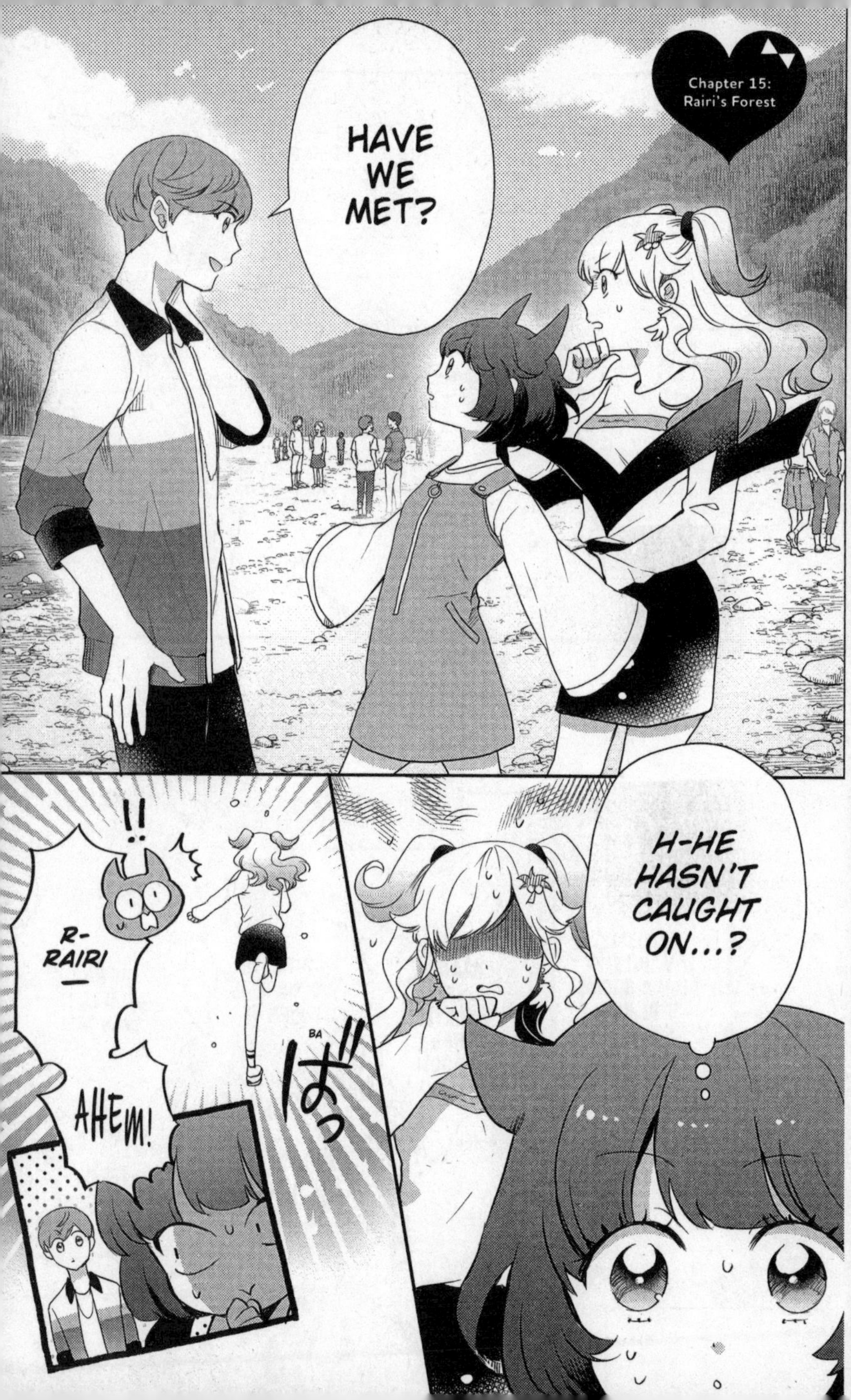
Chapter 15: Rairi's Forest
HAVE WE MET?
H-HE HASN'T CAUGHT ON...?
!!
R-RAIRI —
BA
ばっ
AHEM!

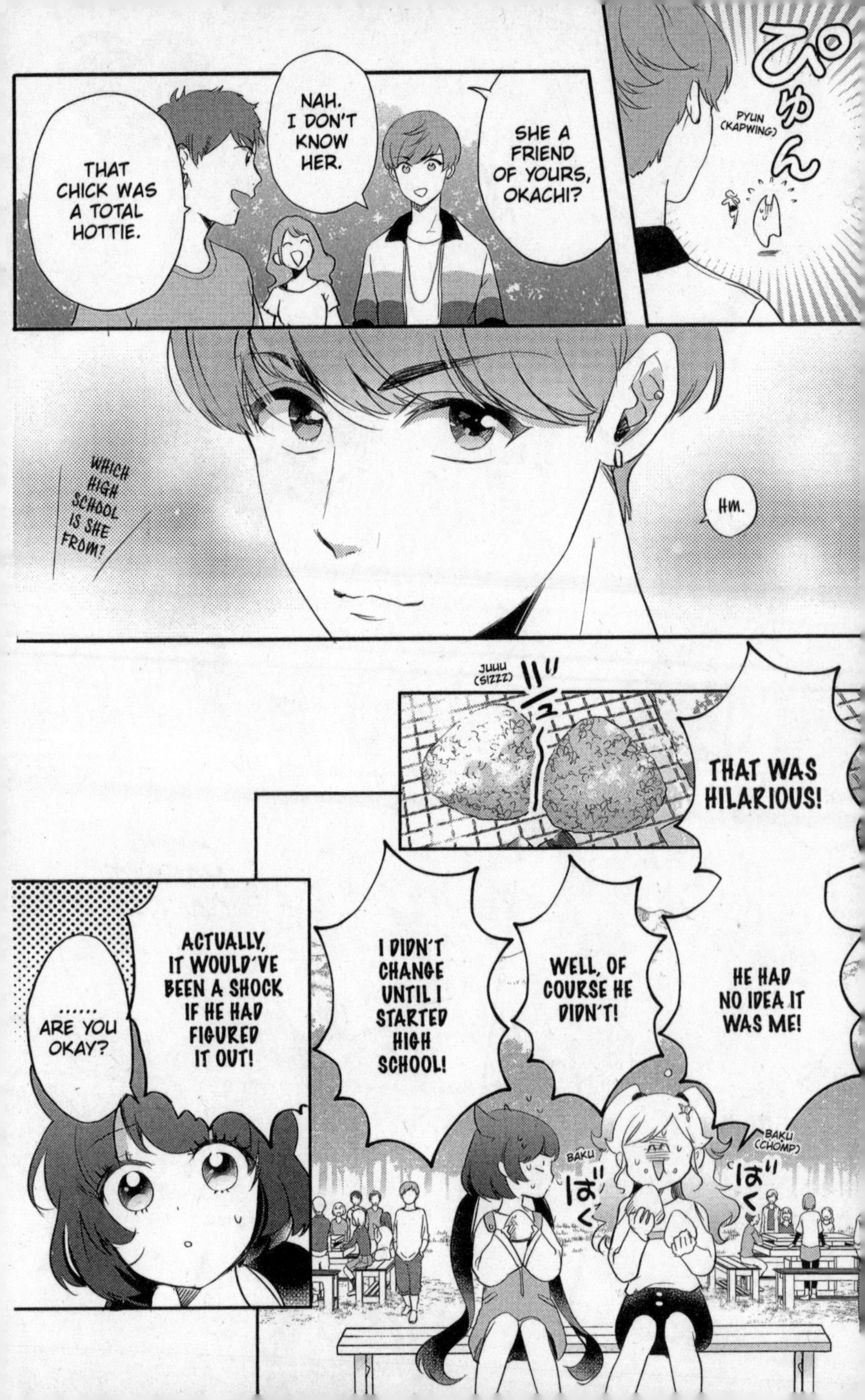
ぴゅん
PYUN (KAPWING)
SHE A FRIEND OF YOURS, OKACHI?
NAH. I DON'T KNOW HER.
THAT CHICK WAS A TOTAL HOTTIE.
Hm.
WHICH HIGH SCHOOL IS SHE FROM?
ジュー
JUUU (SIZZZ)
THAT WAS HILARIOUS!
HE HAD NO IDEA IT WAS ME!
ばく
BAKU (CHOMP)
WELL, OF COURSE HE DIDN'T!
I DIDN'T CHANGE UNTIL I STARTED HIGH SCHOOL!
ばく
BAKU
ACTUALLY, IT WOULD'VE BEEN A SHOCK IF HE HAD FIGURED IT OUT!
...... ARE YOU OKAY?

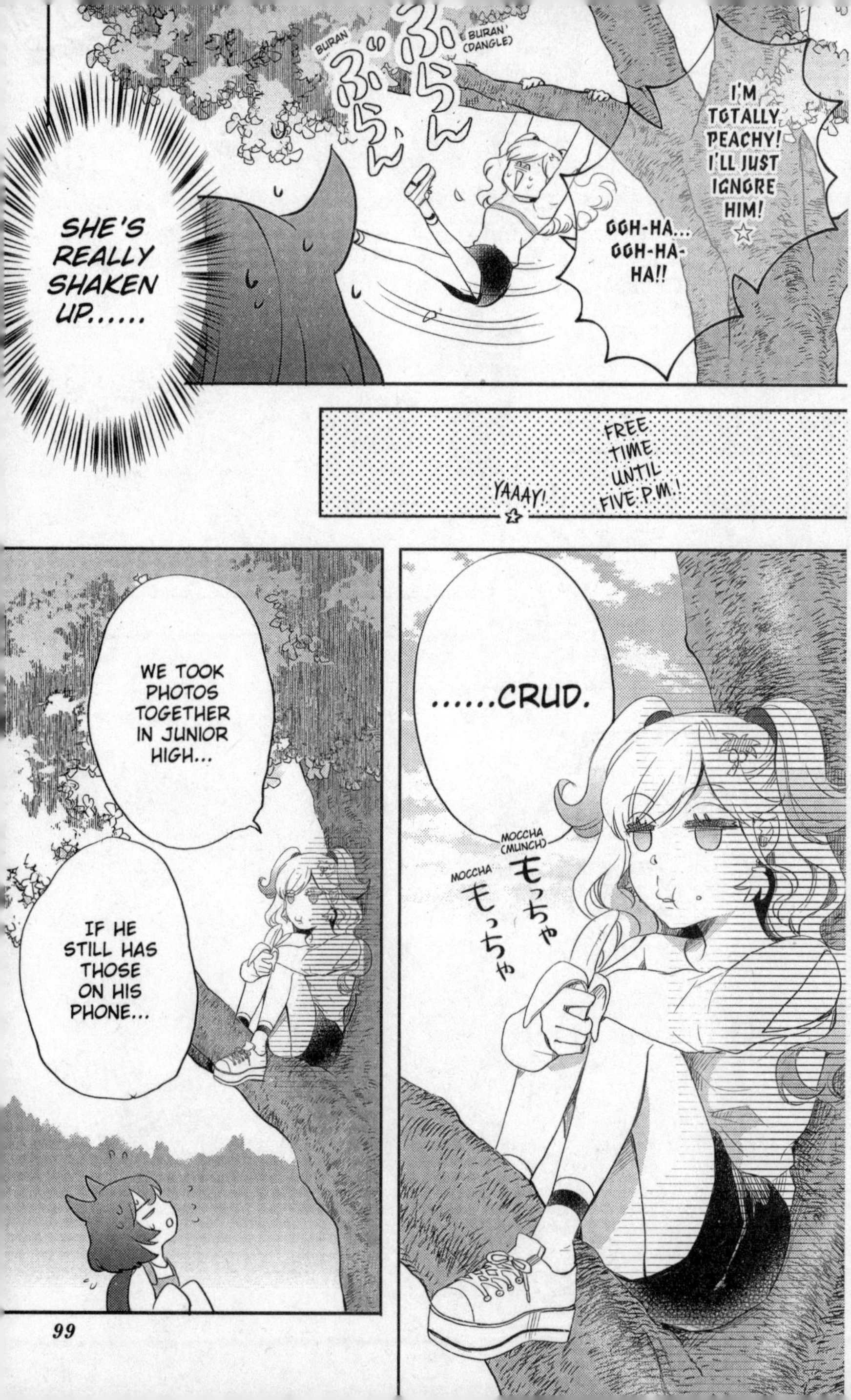
BURAN' (DANGLE)
ぶらん
BURAN
ぶらん
I'M TOTALLY PEACHY! I'LL JUST IGNORE HIM! ☆
OOH-HA... OOH-HA-HA!!
SHE'S REALLY SHAKEN UP......
FREE TIME UNTIL FIVE P.M.!
YAAAY! ☆
......CRUD.
MOCCHA (MUNCH)
もっちゃ
MOCCHA
もっちゃ
WE TOOK PHOTOS TOGETHER IN JUNIOR HIGH...
IF HE STILL HAS THOSE ON HIS PHONE...

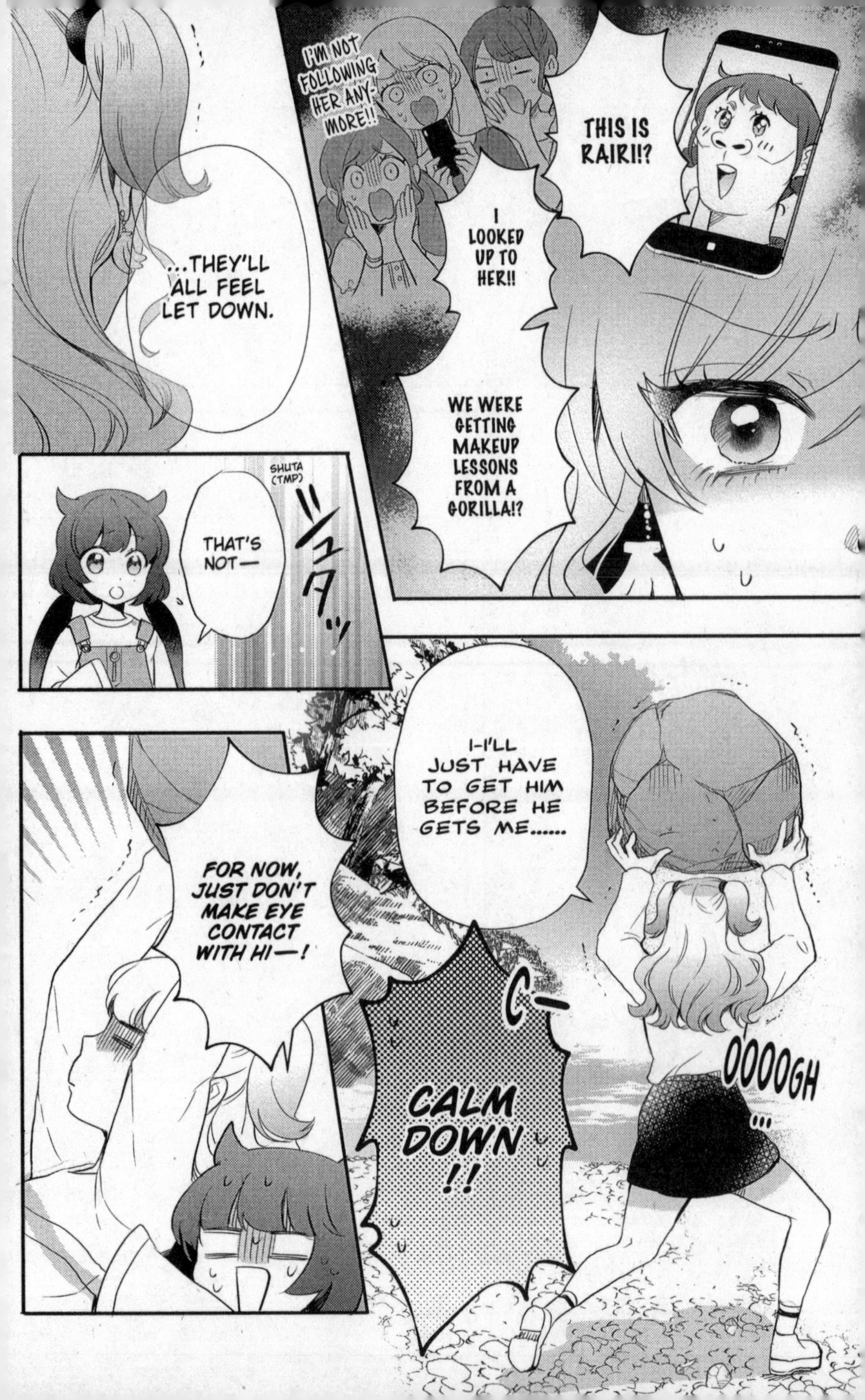
THIS IS RAIR!!?
I'M NOT FOLLOWING HER ANY-MORE!!
I LOOKED UP TO HER!!
WE WERE GETTING MAKEUP LESSONS FROM A GORILLA!?
...THEY'LL ALL FEEL LET DOWN.
SHUTA (TMP)
THAT'S NOT—
I-I'LL JUST HAVE TO GET HIM BEFORE HE GETS ME......
OOOOGH...
C—
CALM DOWN!!
FOR NOW, JUST DON'T MAKE EYE CONTACT WITH HI—!

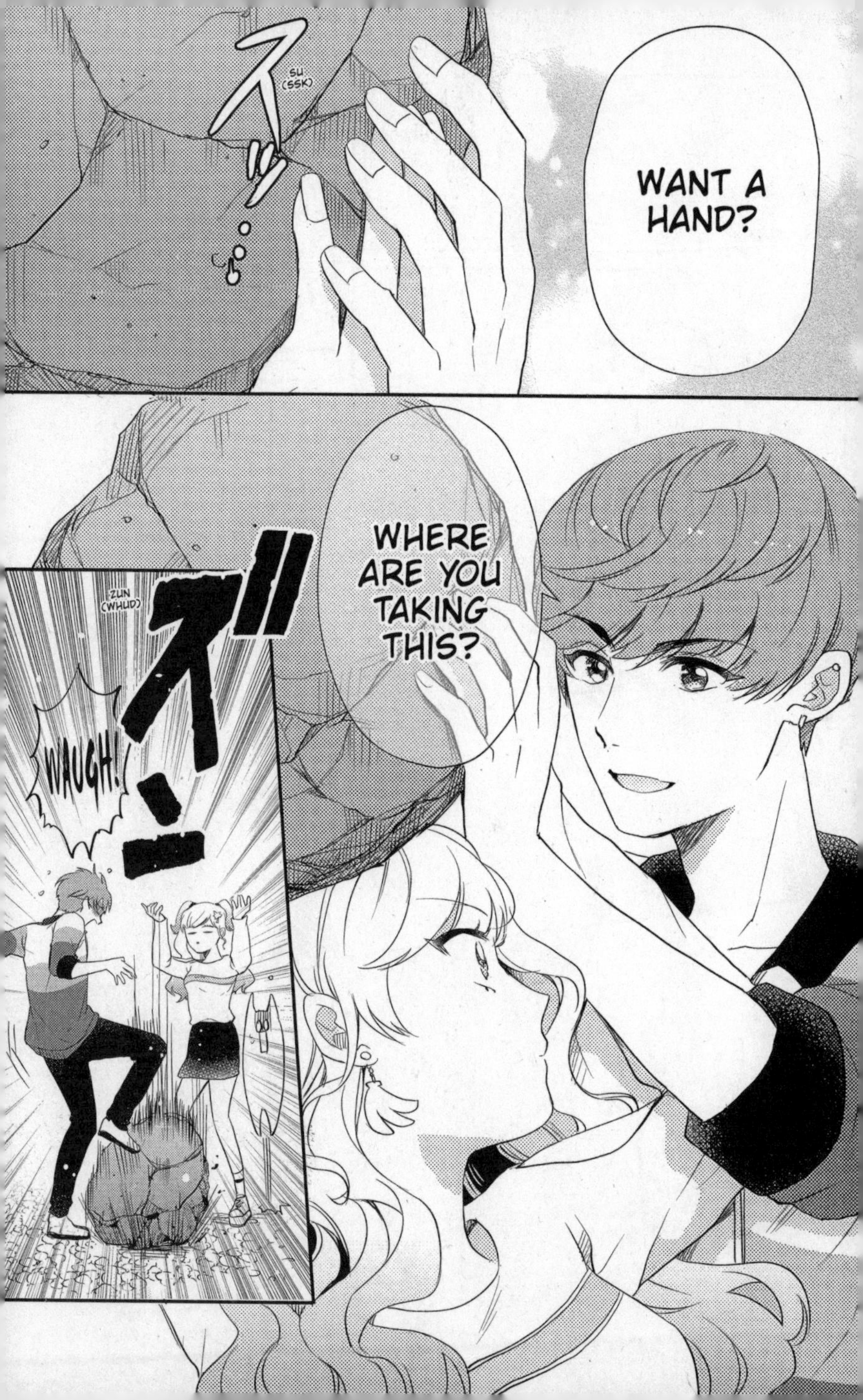
SU (SSK)
WANT A HAND?
WHERE ARE YOU TAKING THIS?
ZUN (WHUD)
WAUGH!

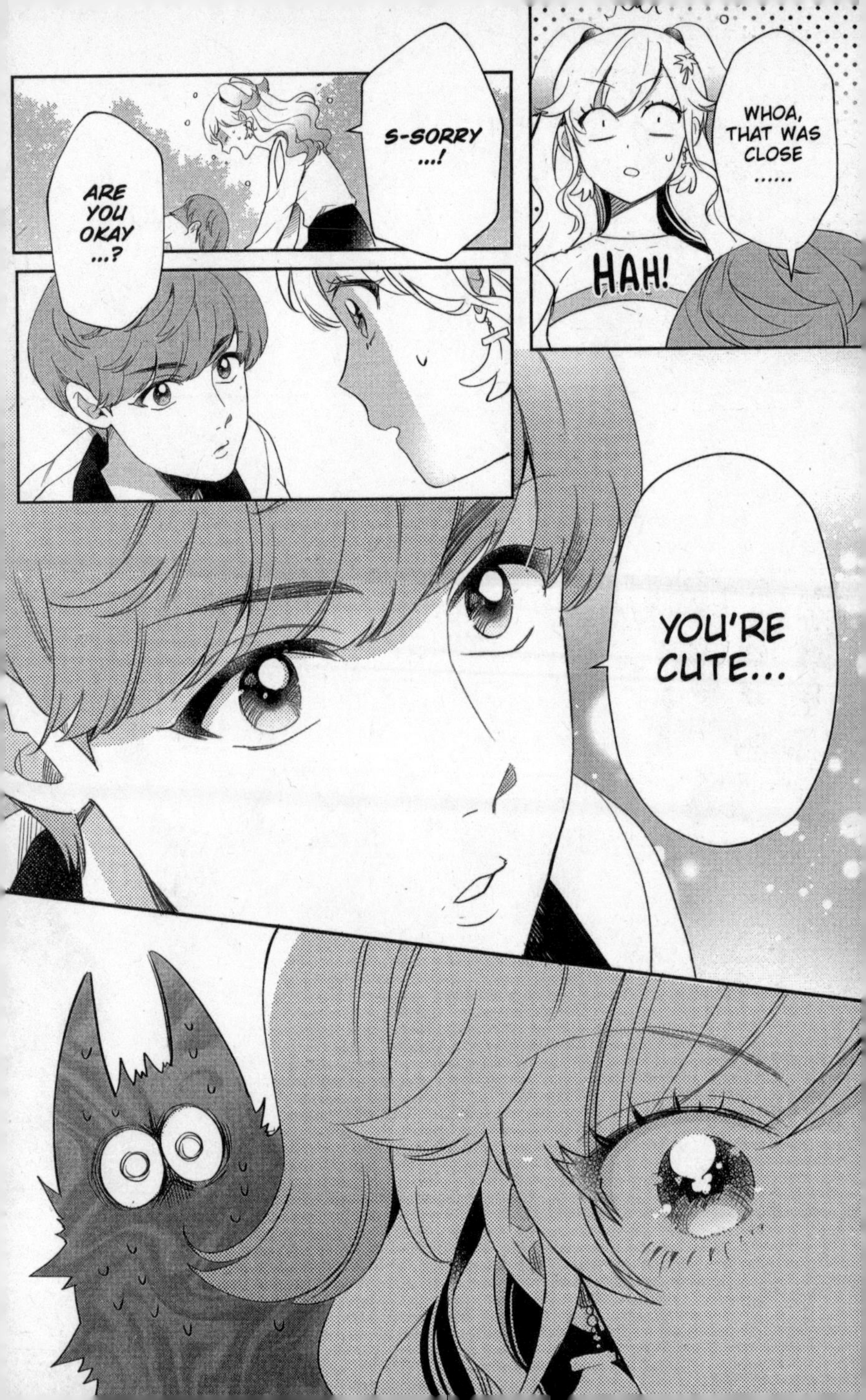
WHOA, THAT WAS CLOSE ......
HAH!
S-SORRY ...!
ARE YOU OKAY ...?
YOU'RE CUTE...

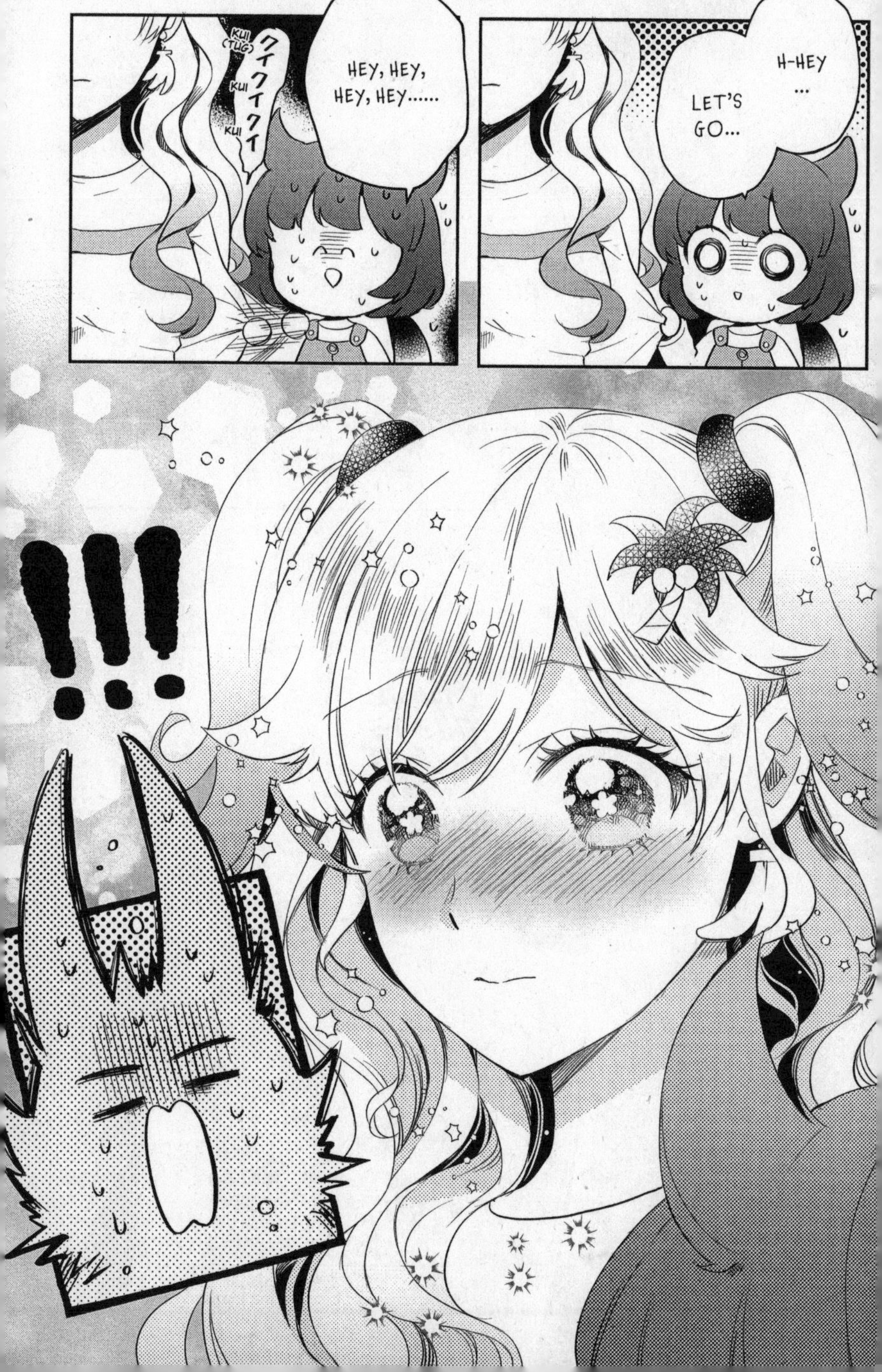
H-HEY ... LET'S GO...
HEY, HEY, HEY, HEY......
クイクイクイ
KUI (TUG) KUI KUI
!!!

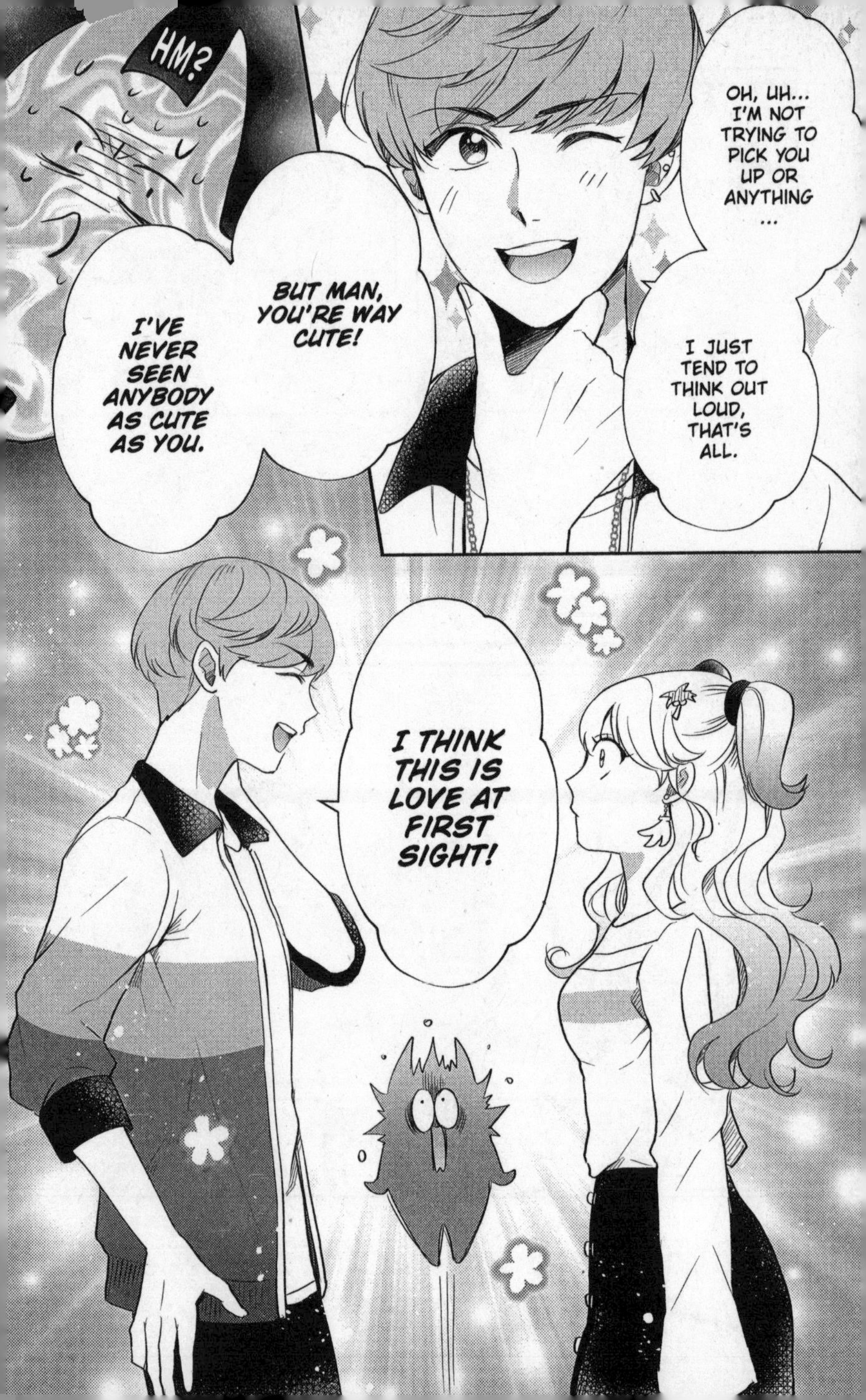

OH, UH... I'M NOT TRYING TO PICK YOU UP OR ANYTHING...
I JUST TEND TO THINK OUT LOUD, THAT'S ALL.
BUT MAN, YOU'RE WAY CUTE!
I'VE NEVER SEEN ANYBODY AS CUTE AS YOU.
HM?
I THINK THIS IS LOVE AT FIRST SIGHT!

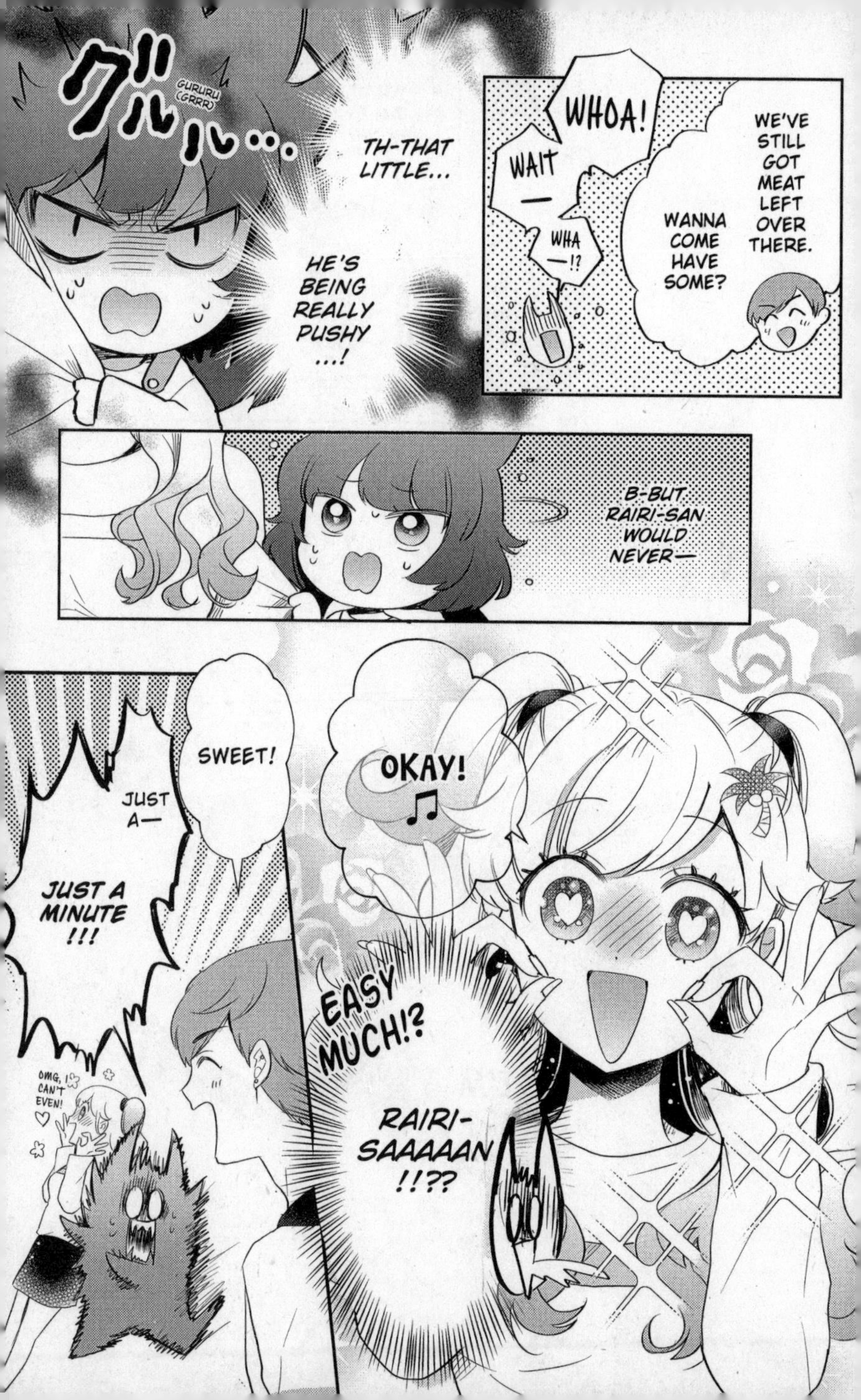
WE'VE STILL GOT MEAT LEFT OVER THERE.
WANNA COME HAVE SOME?
WHOA!
WAIT—
WHA—!?
TH-THAT LITTLE...
グルル…
GURURU (GRRR)
HE'S BEING REALLY PUSHY...!
B-BUT RAIRI-SAN WOULD NEVER—
OKAY! ♫
EASY MUCH!?
RAIRI-SAAAAAN!!??
SWEET!
JUST A—
JUST A MINUTE!!!
OMG, I CAN'T EVEN! ♡

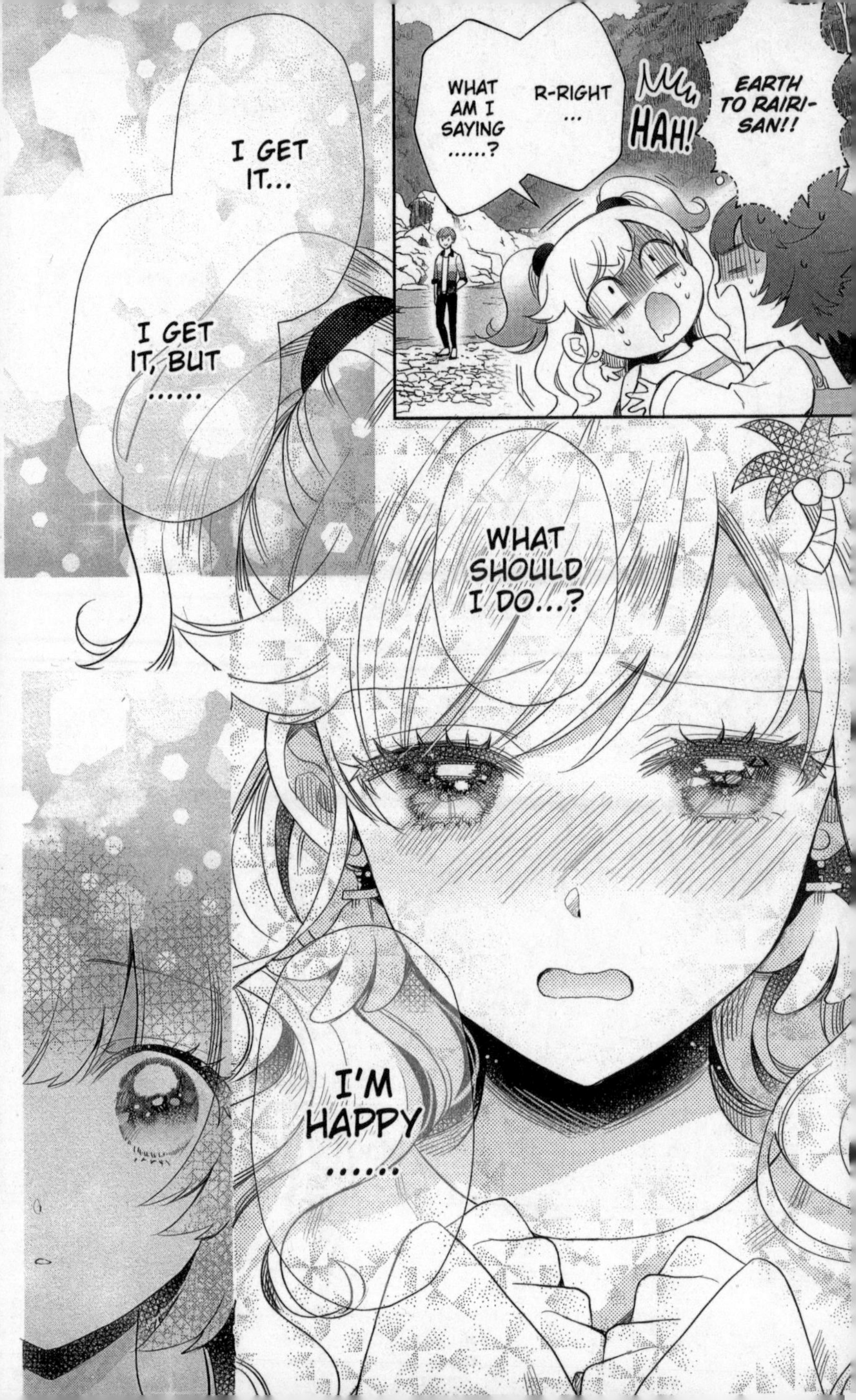
EARTH TO RAIRI-SAN!!
HAH!
R-RIGHT...
WHAT AM I SAYING......?
I GET IT...
I GET IT, BUT......
WHAT SHOULD I DO...?
I'M HAPPY......

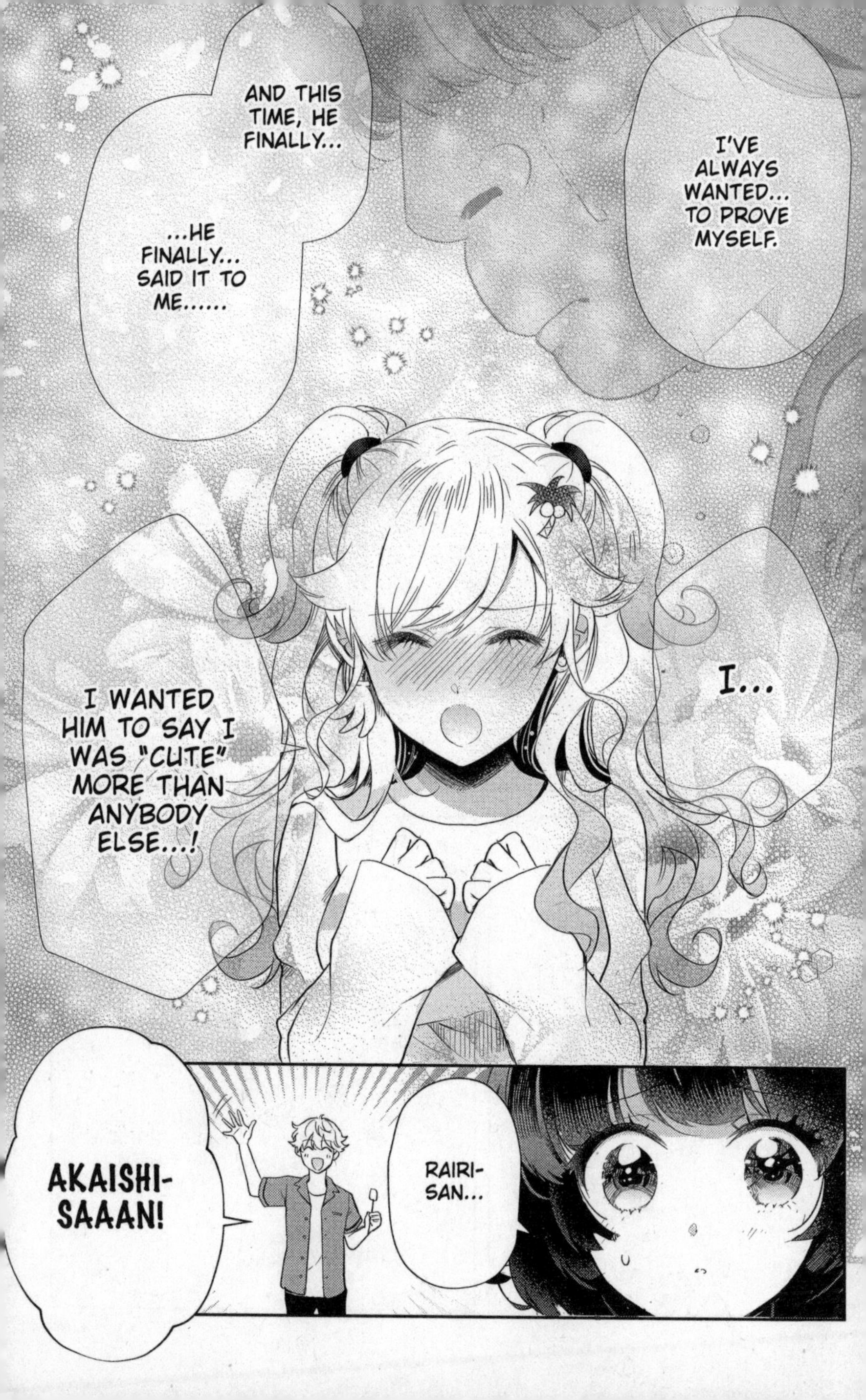
I'VE ALWAYS WANTED... TO PROVE MYSELF.
AND THIS TIME, HE FINALLY...
...HE FINALLY... SAID IT TO ME......
I...
I WANTED HIM TO SAY I WAS "CUTE" MORE THAN ANYBODY ELSE...!
RAIRI-SAN...
AKAISHI-SAAAN!

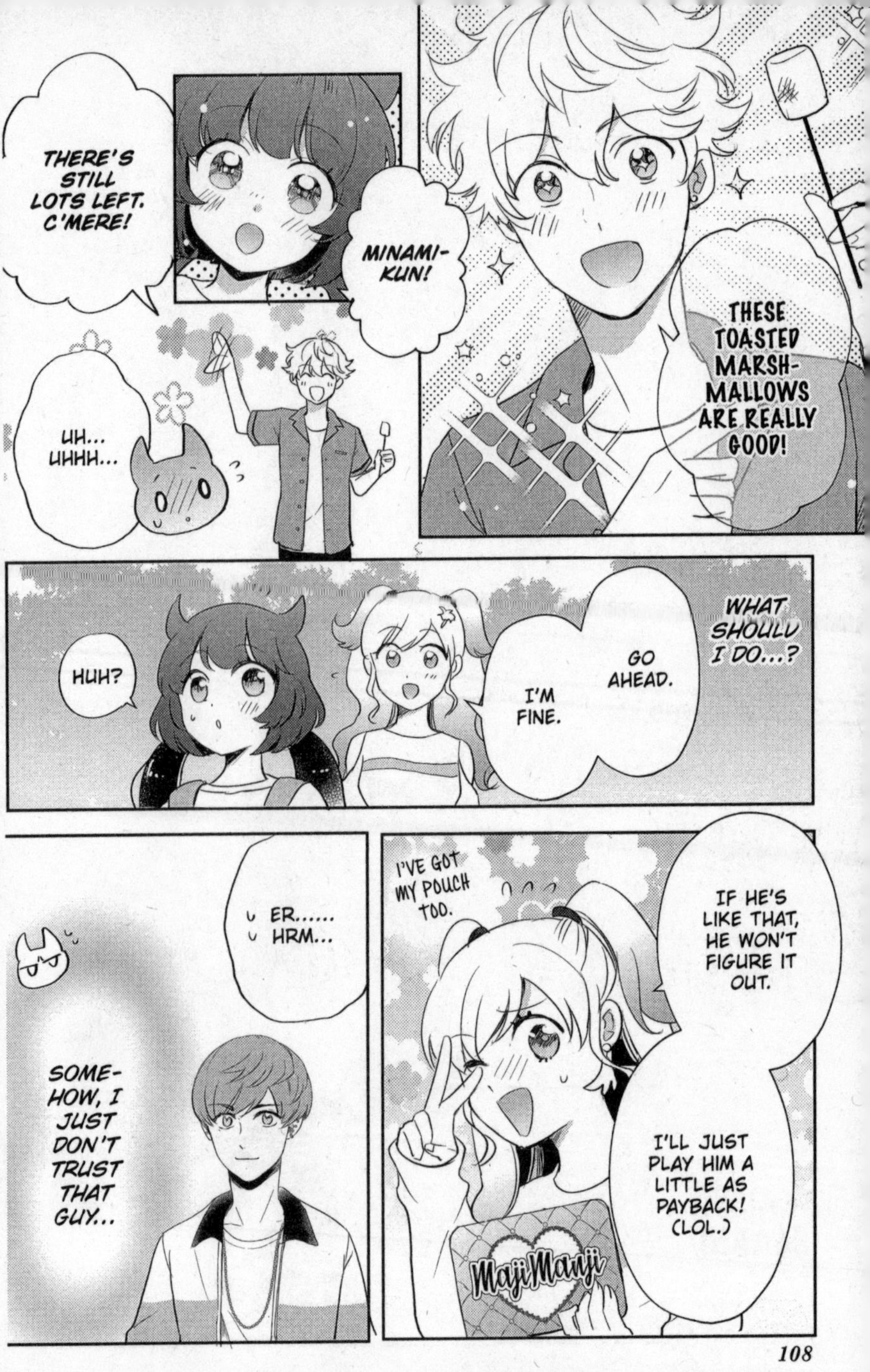
THESE TOASTED MARSH-MALLOWS ARE REALLY GOOD!
MINAMI-KUN!
THERE'S STILL LOTS LEFT. C'MERE!
UH... UHHH...
WHAT SHOULD I DO...?
GO AHEAD. I'M FINE.
HUH?
IF HE'S LIKE THAT, HE WON'T FIGURE IT OUT.
I'VE GOT MY POUCH TOO.
I'LL JUST PLAY HIM A LITTLE AS PAYBACK! (LOL.)
MajiManji
ER...... HRM...
SOME-HOW, I JUST DON'T TRUST THAT GUY...

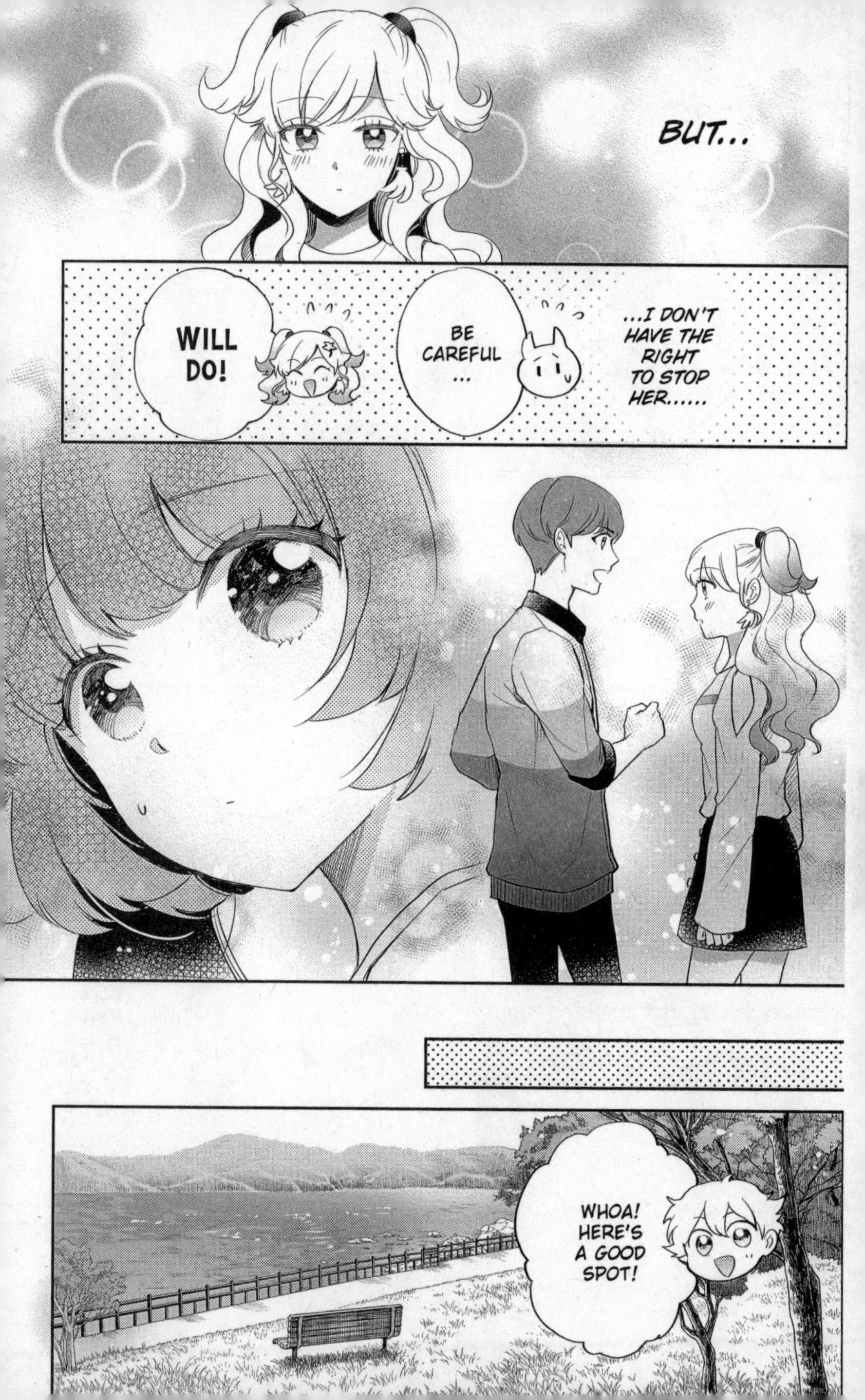
BUT...
...I DON'T HAVE THE RIGHT TO STOP HER......
BE CAREFUL ...
WILL DO!
WHOA! HERE'S A GOOD SPOT!

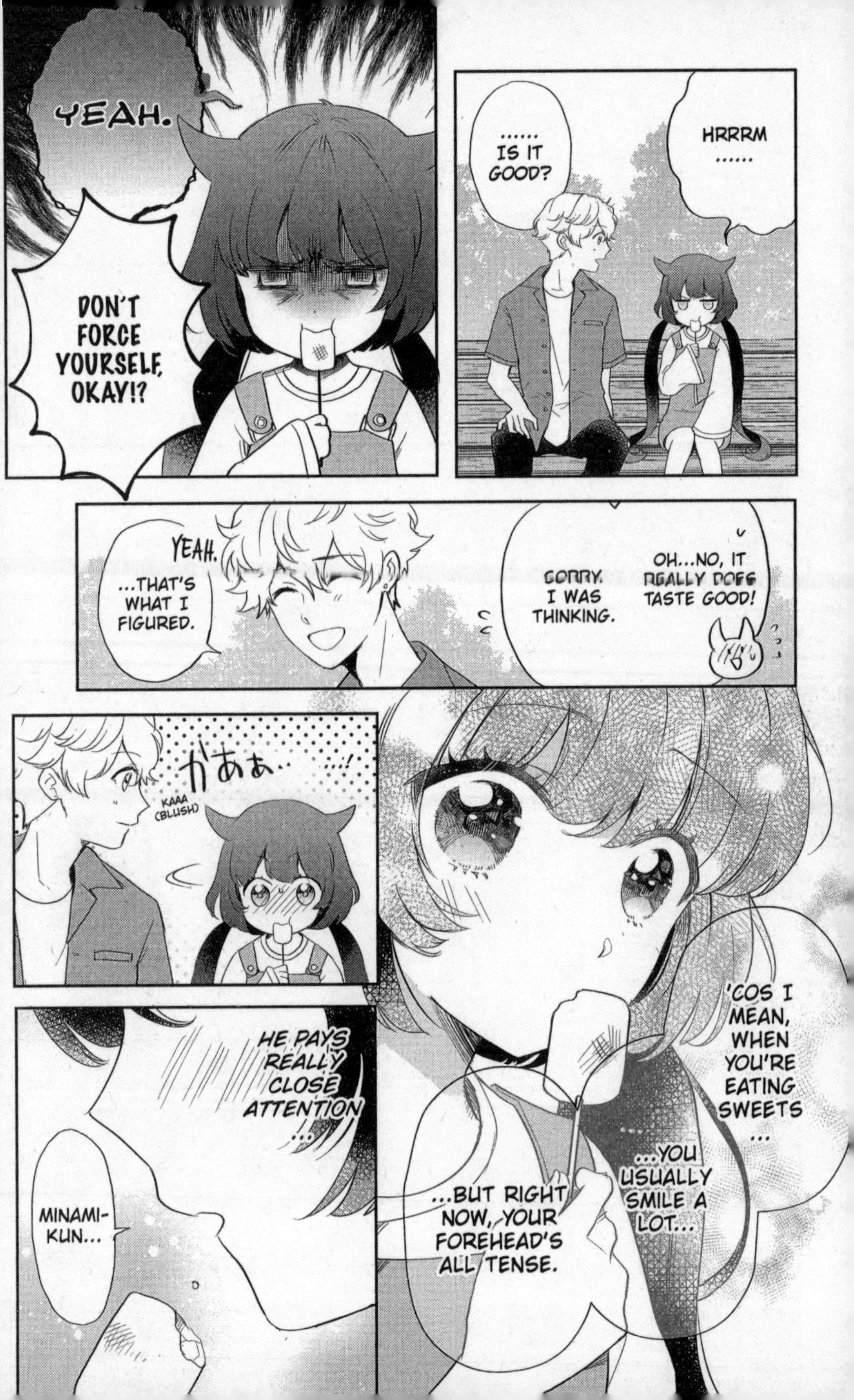
HRRRM ......
...... IS IT GOOD?
YEAH.
DON'T FORCE YOURSELF, OKAY!?
OH...NO, IT REALLY DOES TASTE GOOD!
SORRY. I WAS THINKING.
YEAH. ...THAT'S WHAT I FIGURED.
'COS I MEAN, WHEN YOU'RE EATING SWEETS...
...YOU USUALLY SMILE A LOT...
...BUT RIGHT NOW, YOUR FOREHEAD'S ALL TENSE.
かあぁ
KAAA (BLUSH)
HE PAYS REALLY CLOSE ATTENTION...
MINAMI-KUN...

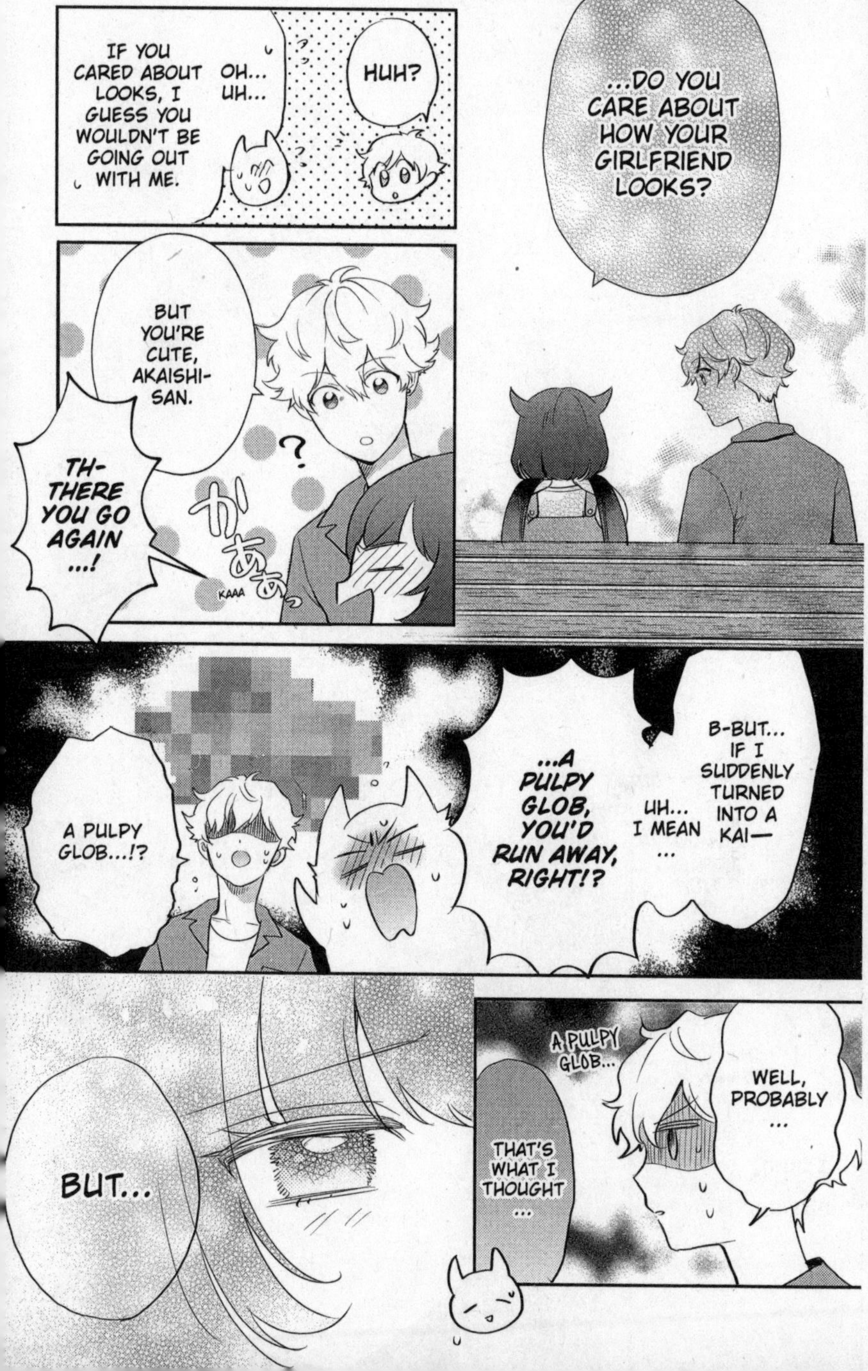
...DO YOU CARE ABOUT HOW YOUR GIRLFRIEND LOOKS?
HUH?
OH... UH...
IF YOU CARED ABOUT LOOKS, I GUESS YOU WOULDN'T BE GOING OUT WITH ME.
BUT YOU'RE CUTE, AKAISHI-SAN.
KAAA
TH-THERE YOU GO AGAIN...!
B-BUT... IF I SUDDENLY TURNED INTO A KAI—
UH... I MEAN...
...A PULPY GLOB, YOU'D RUN AWAY, RIGHT!?
A PULPY GLOB...!?
WELL, PROBABLY...
A PULPY GLOB...
THAT'S WHAT I THOUGHT...
BUT...

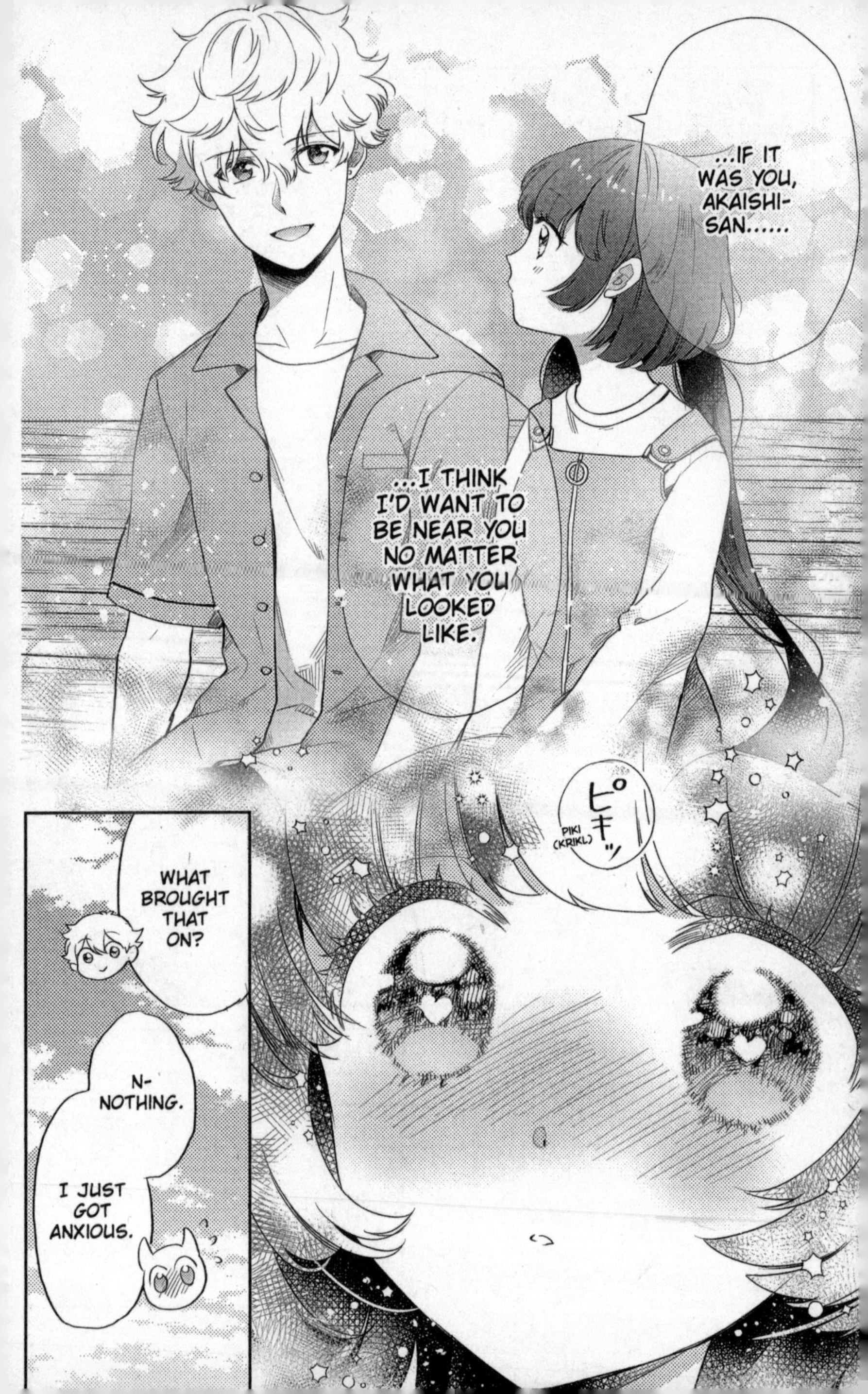
...IF IT WAS YOU, AKAISHI-SAN......
...I THINK I'D WANT TO BE NEAR YOU NO MATTER WHAT YOU LOOKED LIKE.
ピキッ
PIKI (KRIKL)
WHAT BROUGHT THAT ON?
N-NOTHING.
I JUST GOT ANXIOUS.

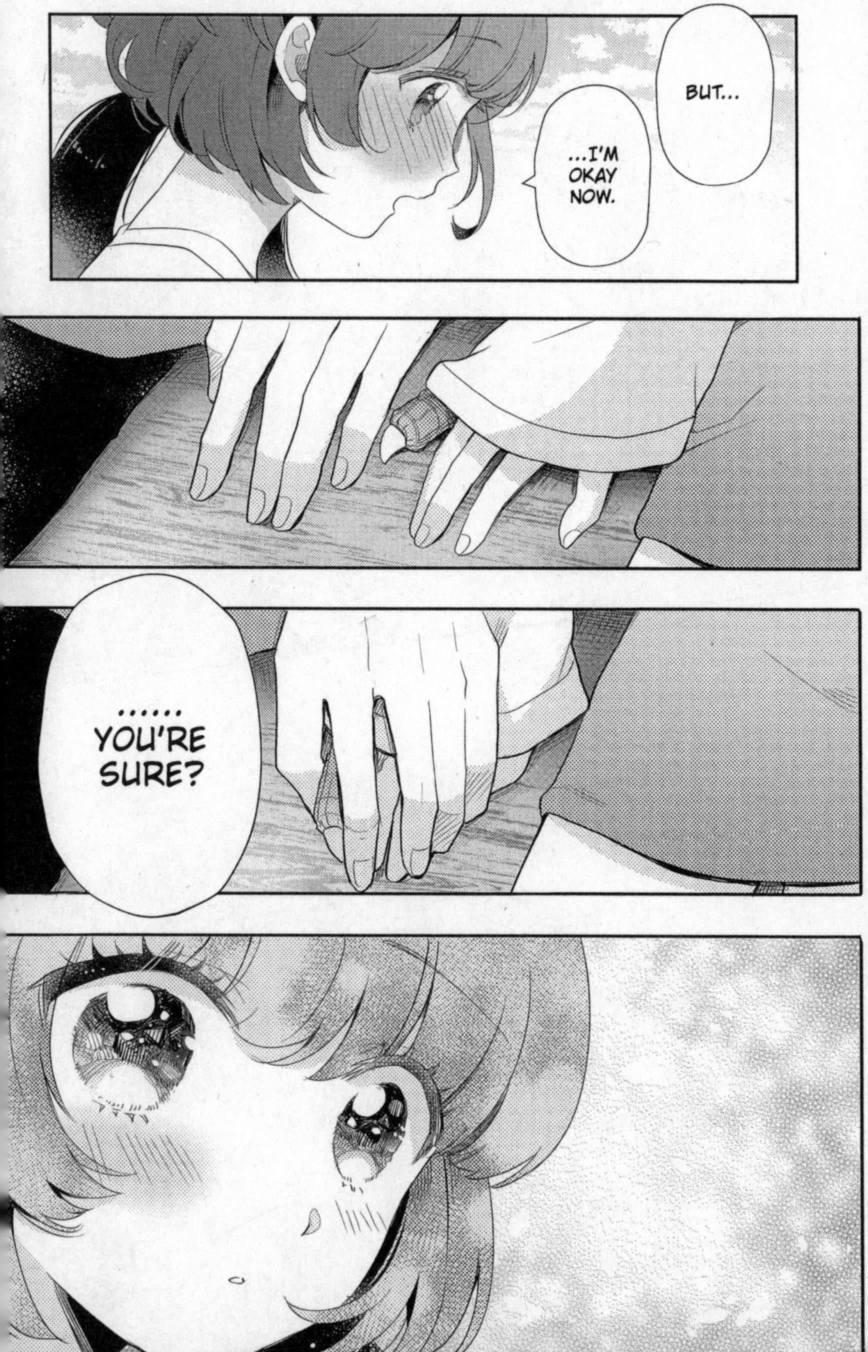
BUT...
...I'M OKAY NOW.
...... YOU'RE SURE?

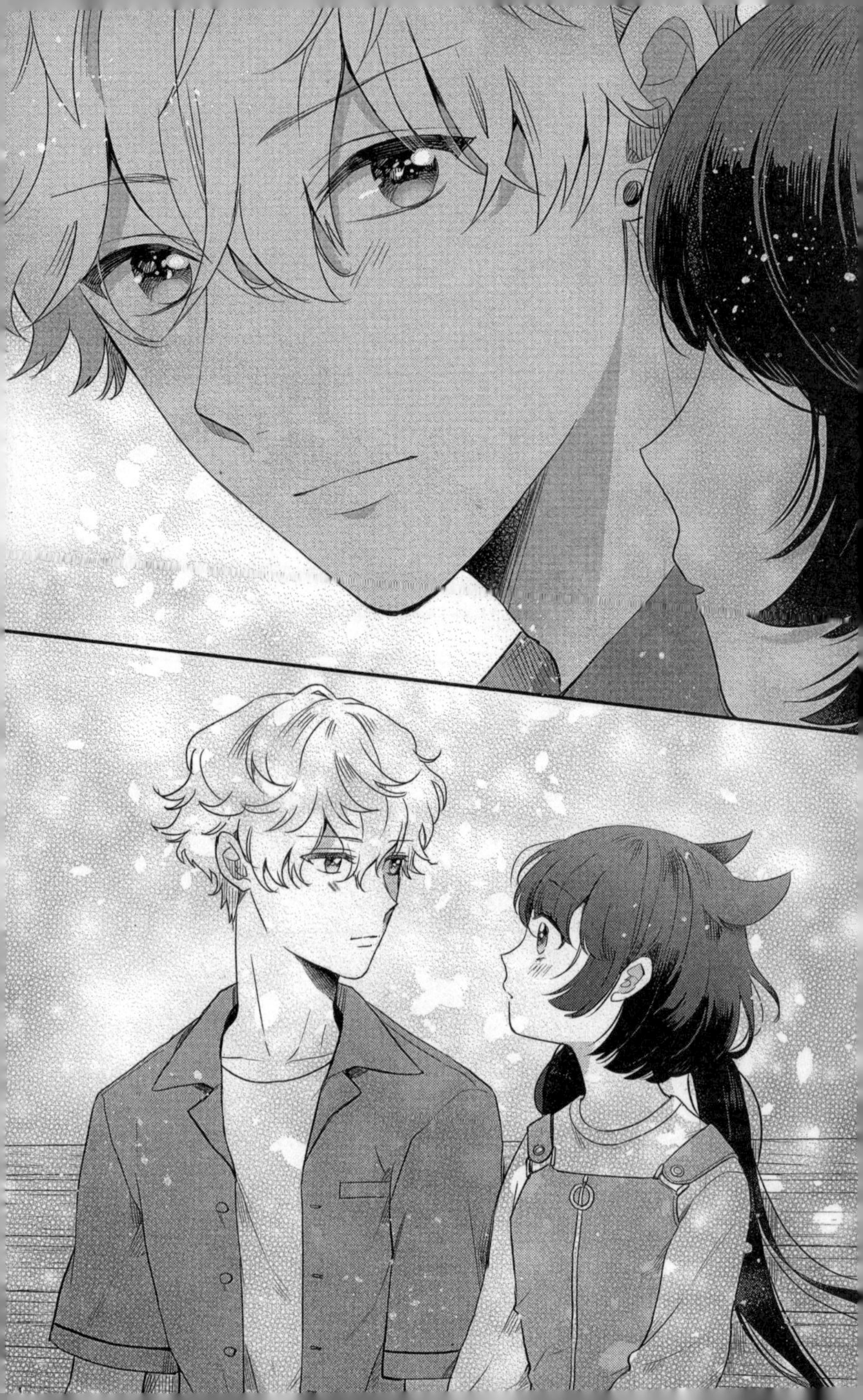

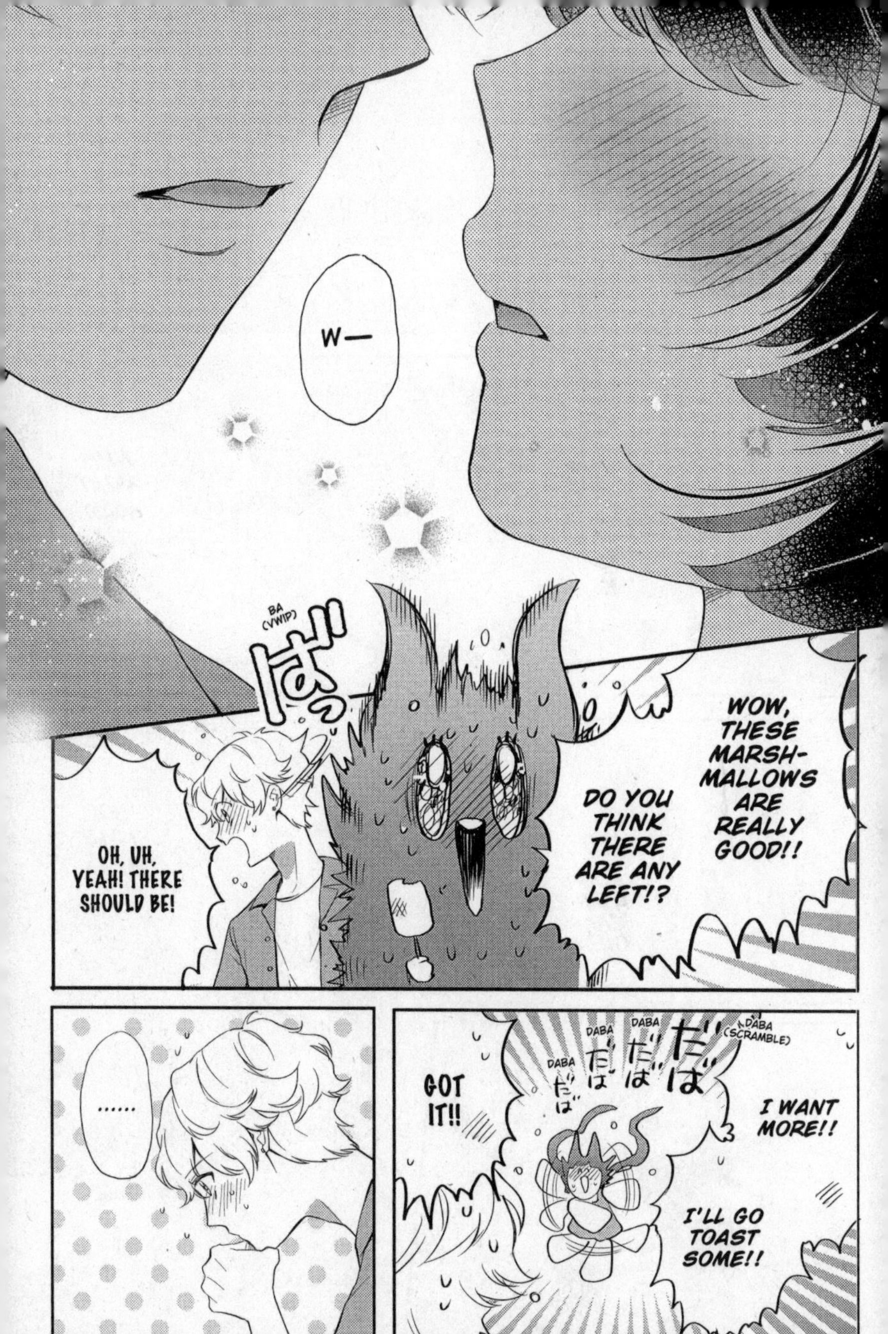
W—
BA (VWIP)
ばっ
WOW, THESE MARSH-MALLOWS ARE REALLY GOOD!!
DO YOU THINK THERE ARE ANY LEFT!?
OH, UH, YEAH! THERE SHOULD BE!
DABA (SCRAMBLE) DABA DABA DABA
だばだばだばだば
I WANT MORE!!
I'LL GO TOAST SOME!!
GOT IT!!
......

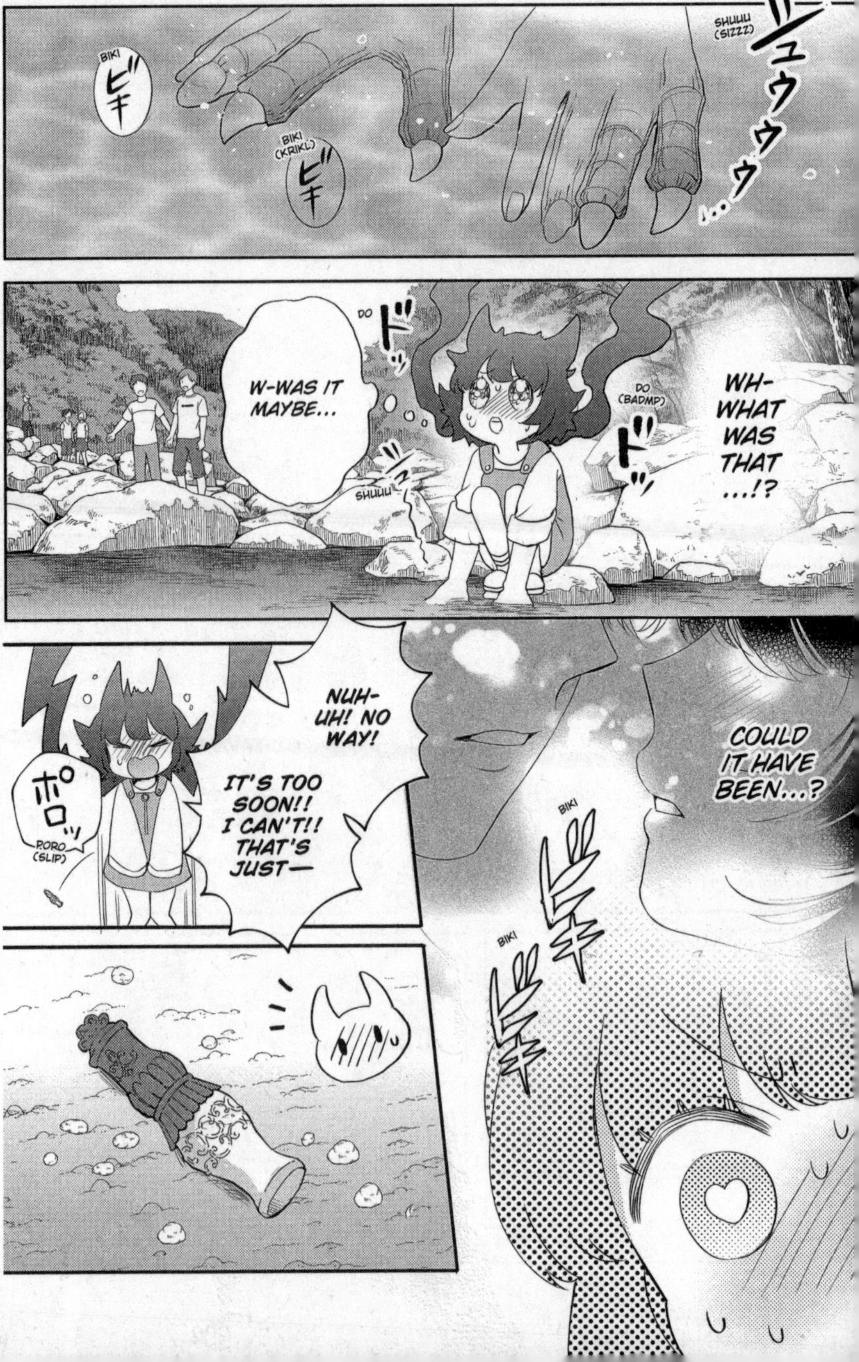
SHUUU (SIZZZ)
シュウウウウ…
BIKI (KRIKL)
ビキ
BIKI
ビキ
WH- WHAT WAS THAT ...!?
DO (BADMP)
ドッ
SHUUU
DO
ドッ
W-WAS IT MAYBE...
COULD IT HAVE BEEN...?
BIKI
ビキ
BIKI
ビキ
NUH-UH! NO WAY!
IT'S TOO SOON!! I CAN'T!! THAT'S JUST—
ポロッ
PORO (SLIP)

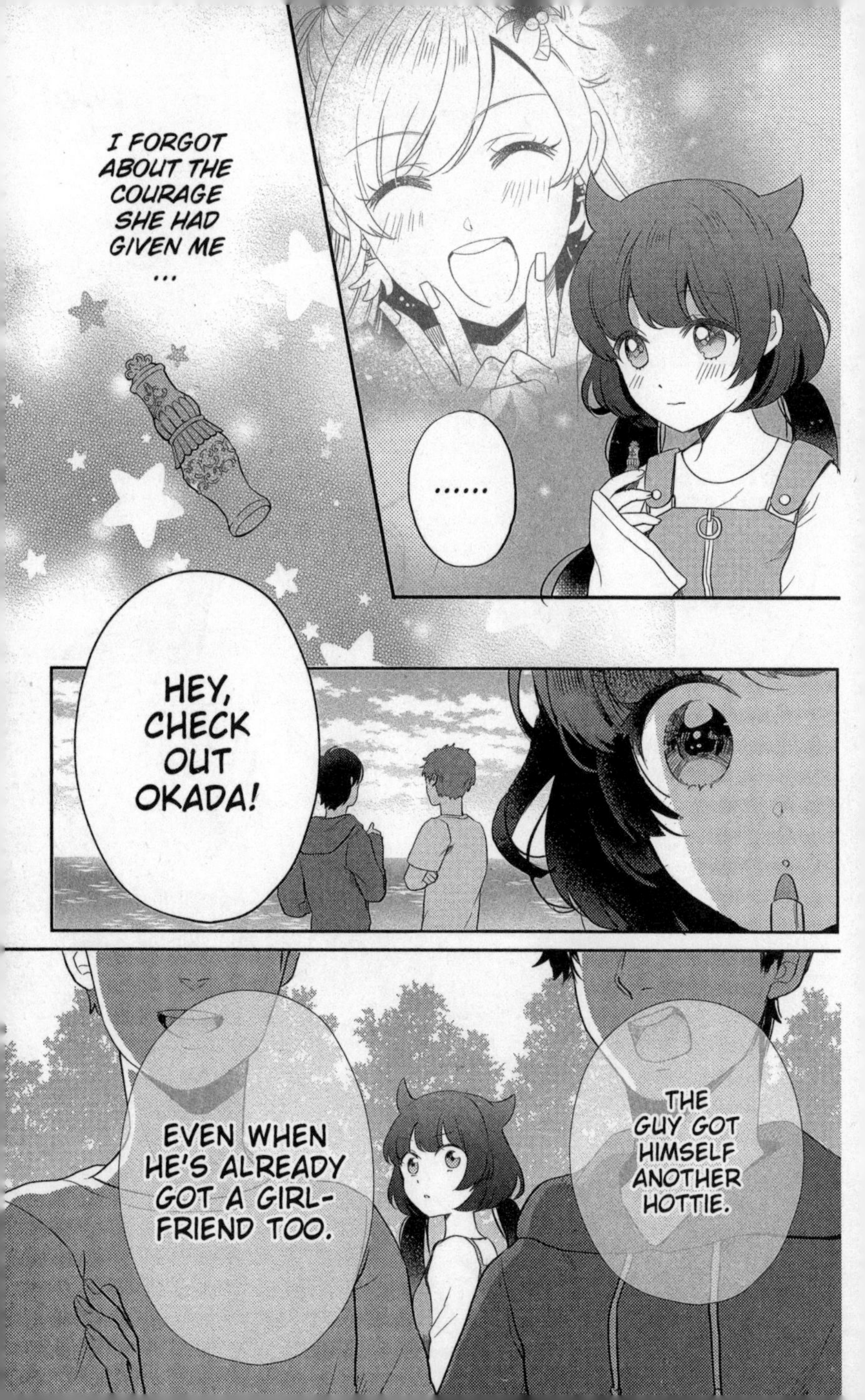
......
I FORGOT ABOUT THE COURAGE SHE HAD GIVEN ME ...
HEY, CHECK OUT OKADA!
THE GUY GOT HIMSELF ANOTHER HOTTIE.
EVEN WHEN HE'S ALREADY GOT A GIRL-FRIEND TOO.

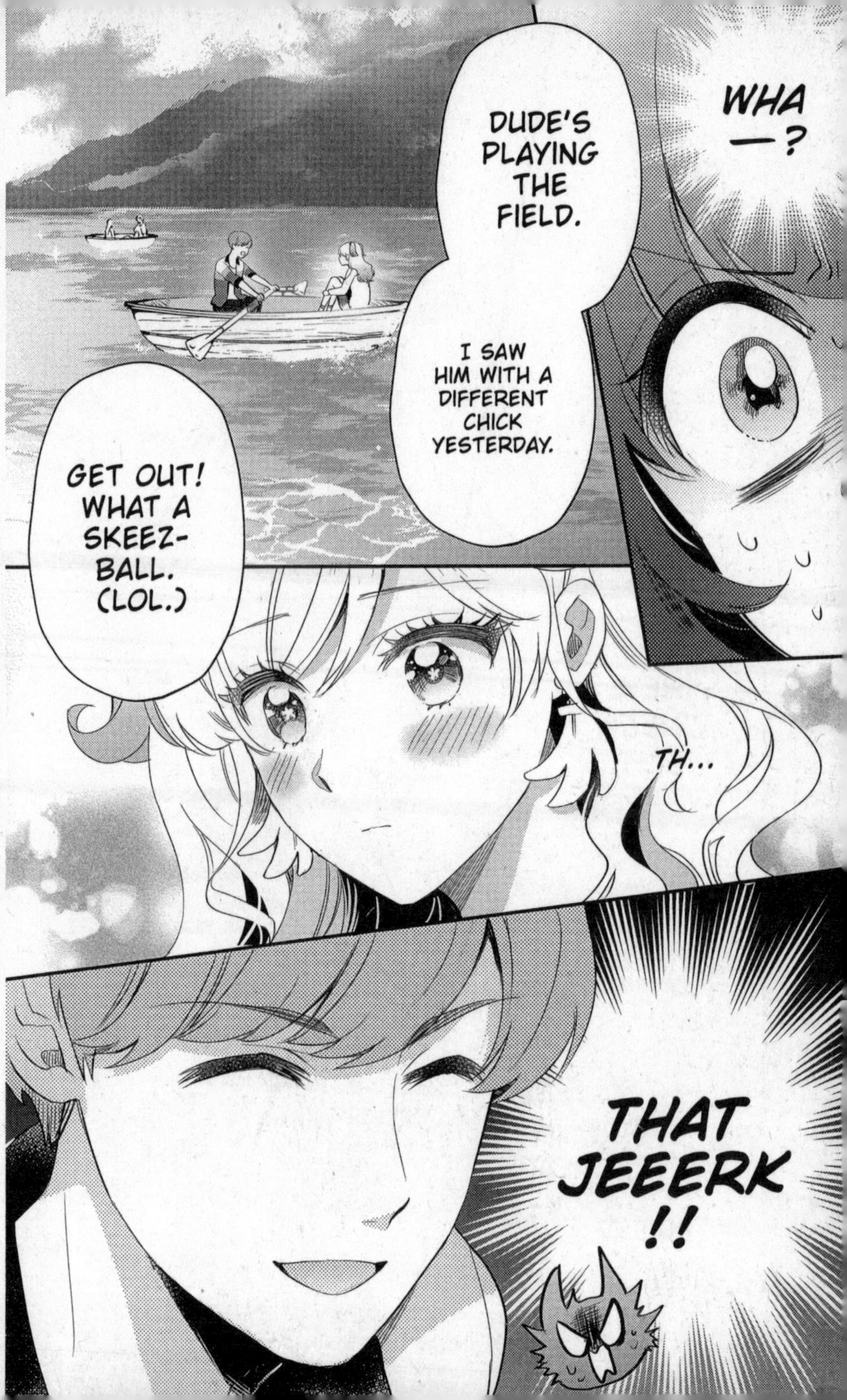
DUDE'S PLAYING THE FIELD.
I SAW HIM WITH A DIFFERENT CHICK YESTERDAY.
GET OUT! WHAT A SKEEZ-BALL. (LOL.)
WHA—?
TH...
THAT JEEERK!!

KAIJU♥GIRL
CARAMELISE

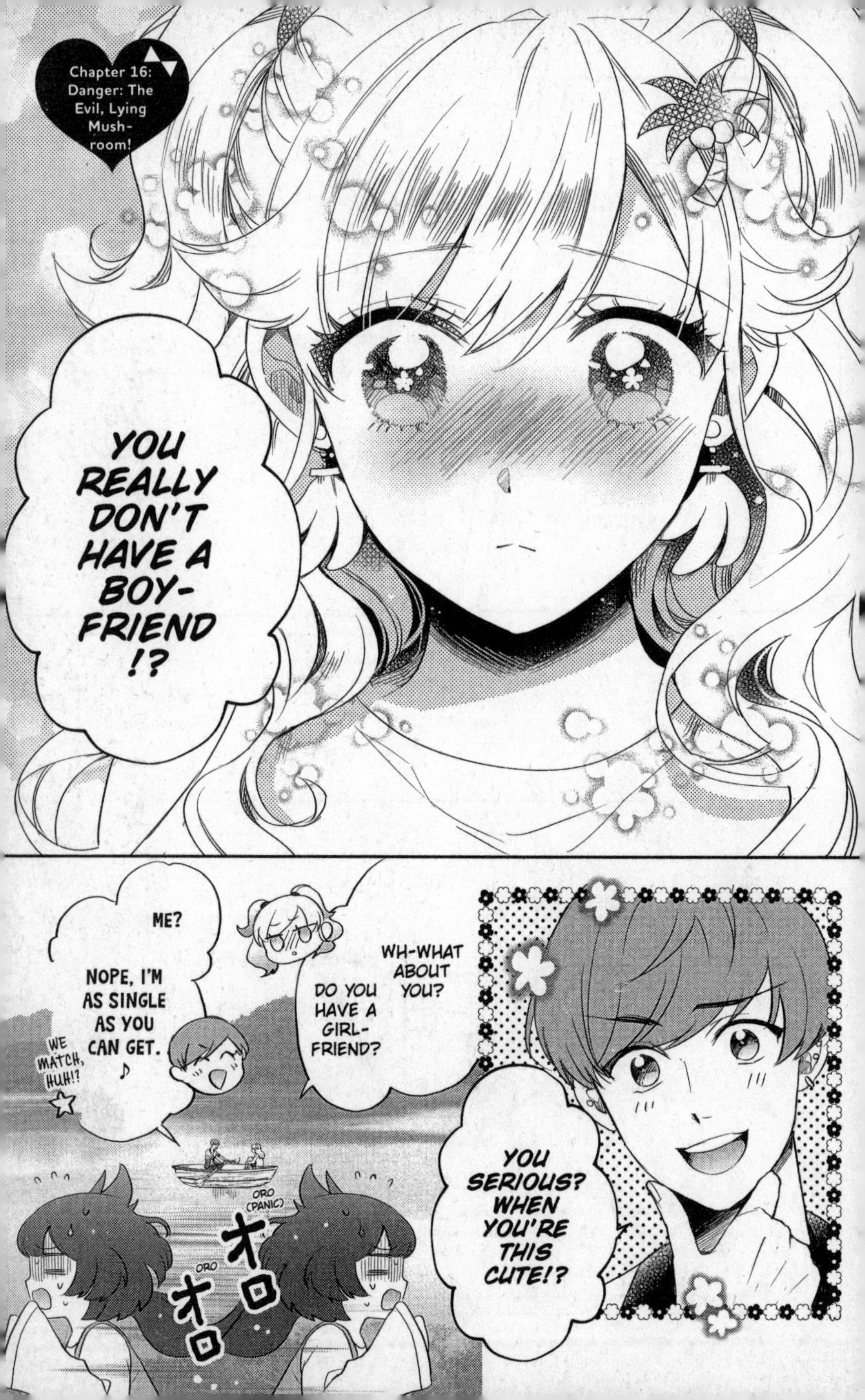
Chapter 16: Danger: The Evil, Lying Mush-room!
YOU REALLY DON'T HAVE A BOY-FRIEND!?
YOU SERIOUS? WHEN YOU'RE THIS CUTE!?
WH-WHAT ABOUT YOU?
DO YOU HAVE A GIRL-FRIEND?
ME?
NOPE, I'M AS SINGLE AS YOU CAN GET. ♪
WE MATCH, HUH!?
ORO (PANIC)
オロ
ORO
オロ

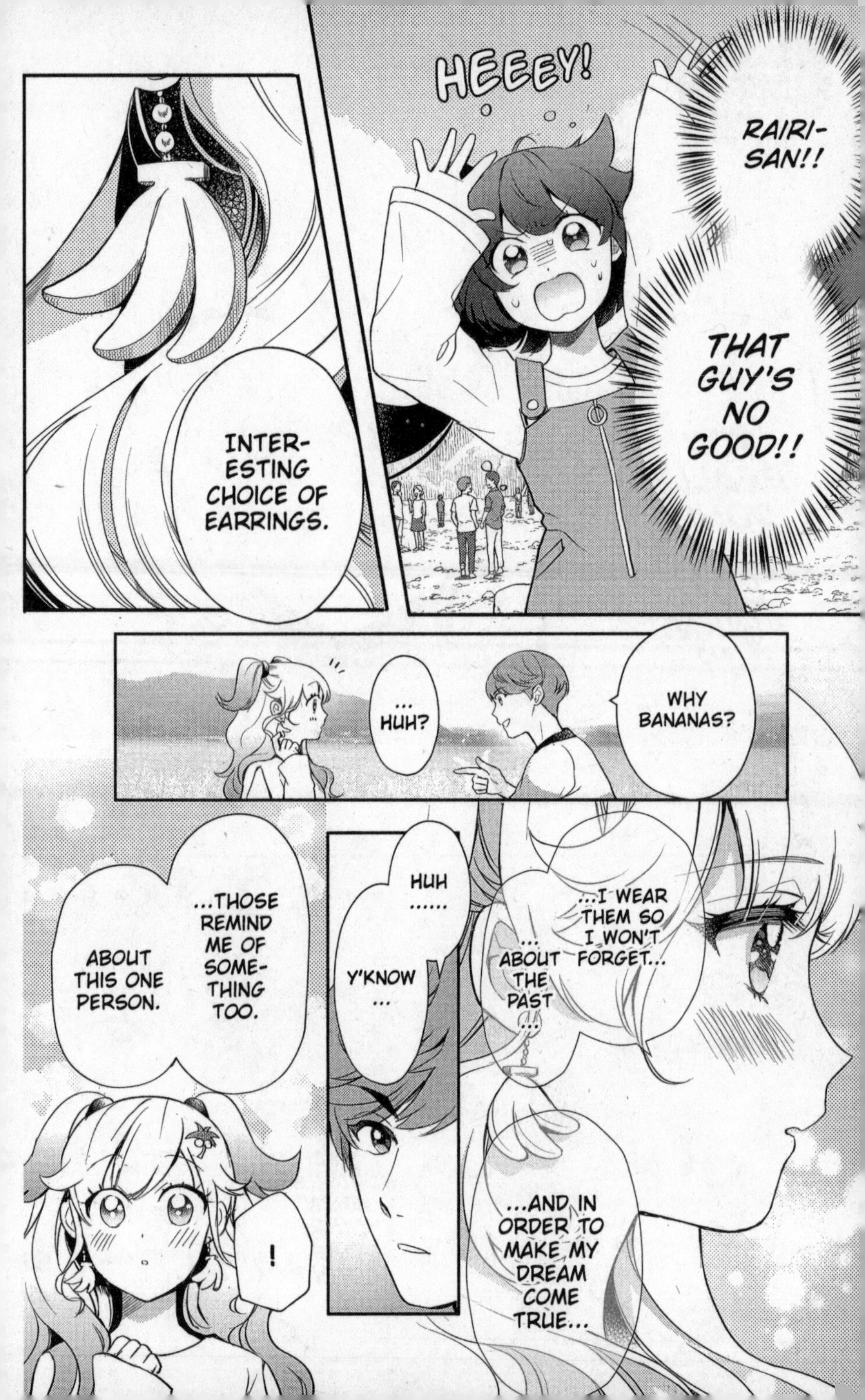
HEEEY!
RAIRI-SAN!!
THAT GUY'S NO GOOD!!
INTER-ESTING CHOICE OF EARRINGS.
WHY BANANAS?
...HUH?
...I WEAR THEM SO I WON'T FORGET...
...ABOUT THE PAST
...AND IN ORDER TO MAKE MY DREAM COME TRUE...
HUH......
Y'KNOW...
...THOSE REMIND ME OF SOME-THING TOO.
ABOUT THIS ONE PERSON.
!

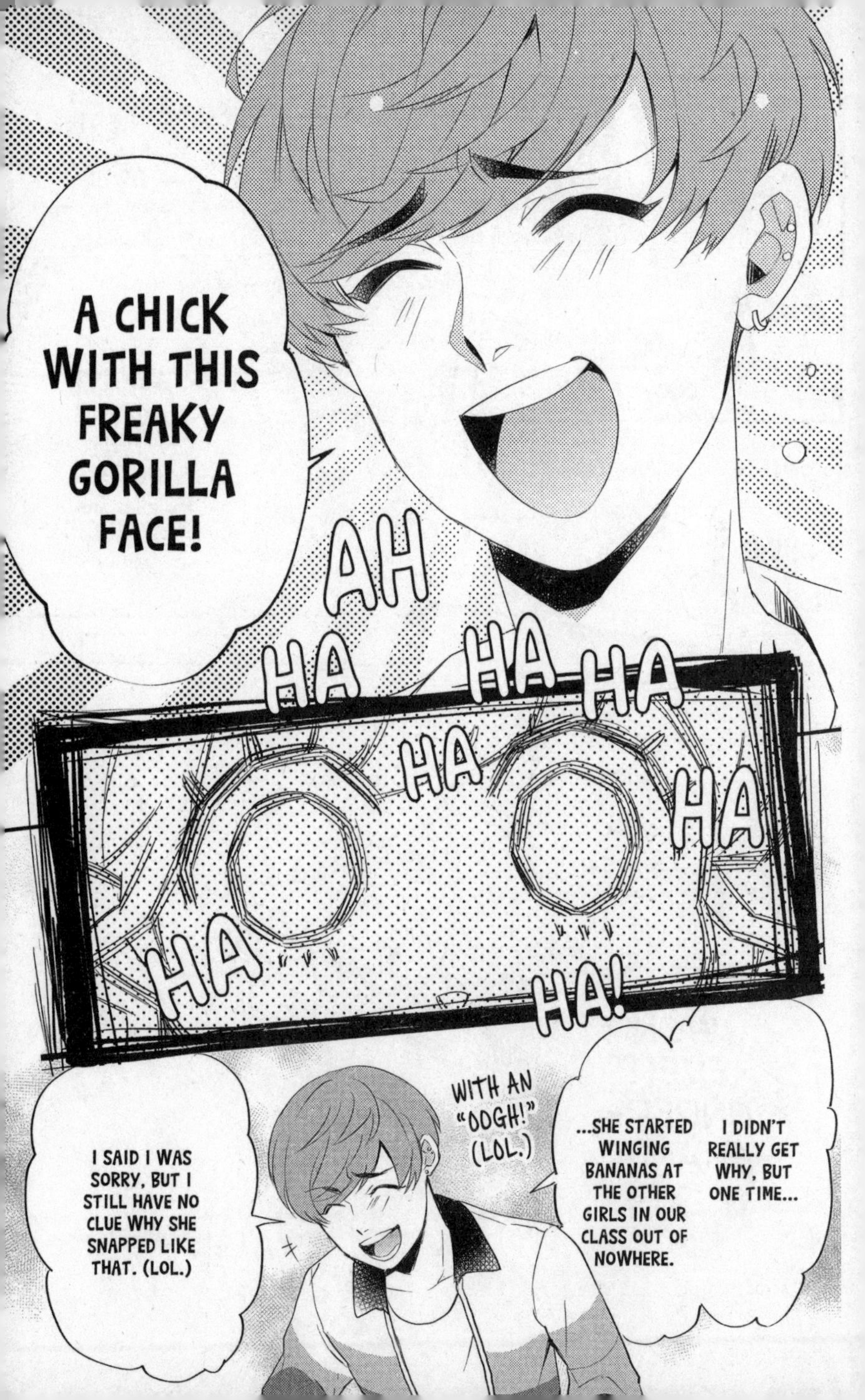
A CHICK WITH THIS FREAKY GORILLA FACE!
AH HA HA HA HA HA HA HA!
I DIDN'T REALLY GET WHY, BUT ONE TIME...
...SHE STARTED WINGING BANANAS AT THE OTHER GIRLS IN OUR CLASS OUT OF NOWHERE.
WITH AN "OOGH!" (LOL.)
I SAID I WAS SORRY, BUT I STILL HAVE NO CLUE WHY SHE SNAPPED LIKE THAT. (LOL.)

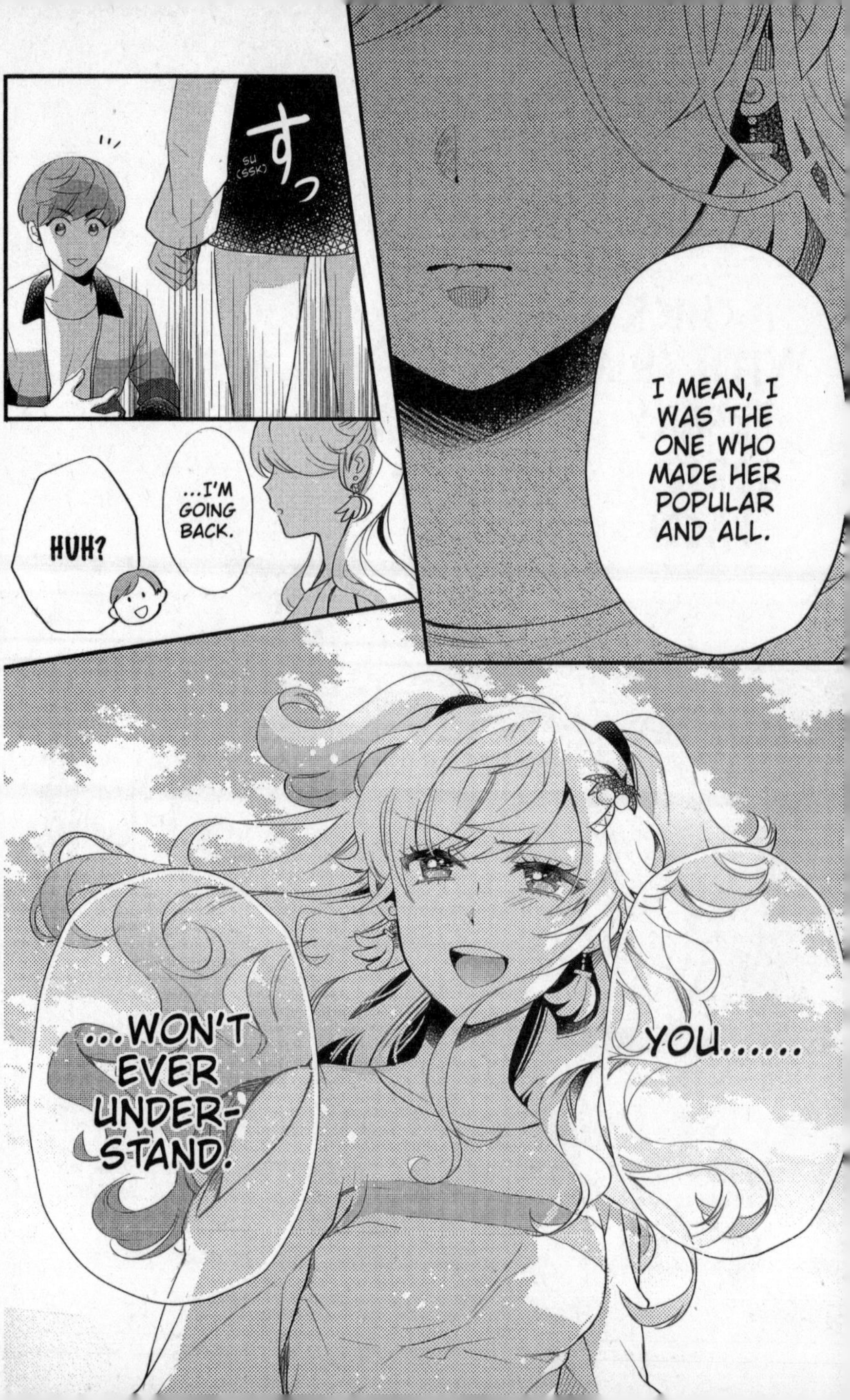

I MEAN, I WAS THE ONE WHO MADE HER POPULAR AND ALL.
すっ
SU (SSK)
...I'M GOING BACK.
HUH?
YOU......
...WON'T EVER UNDER-STAND.

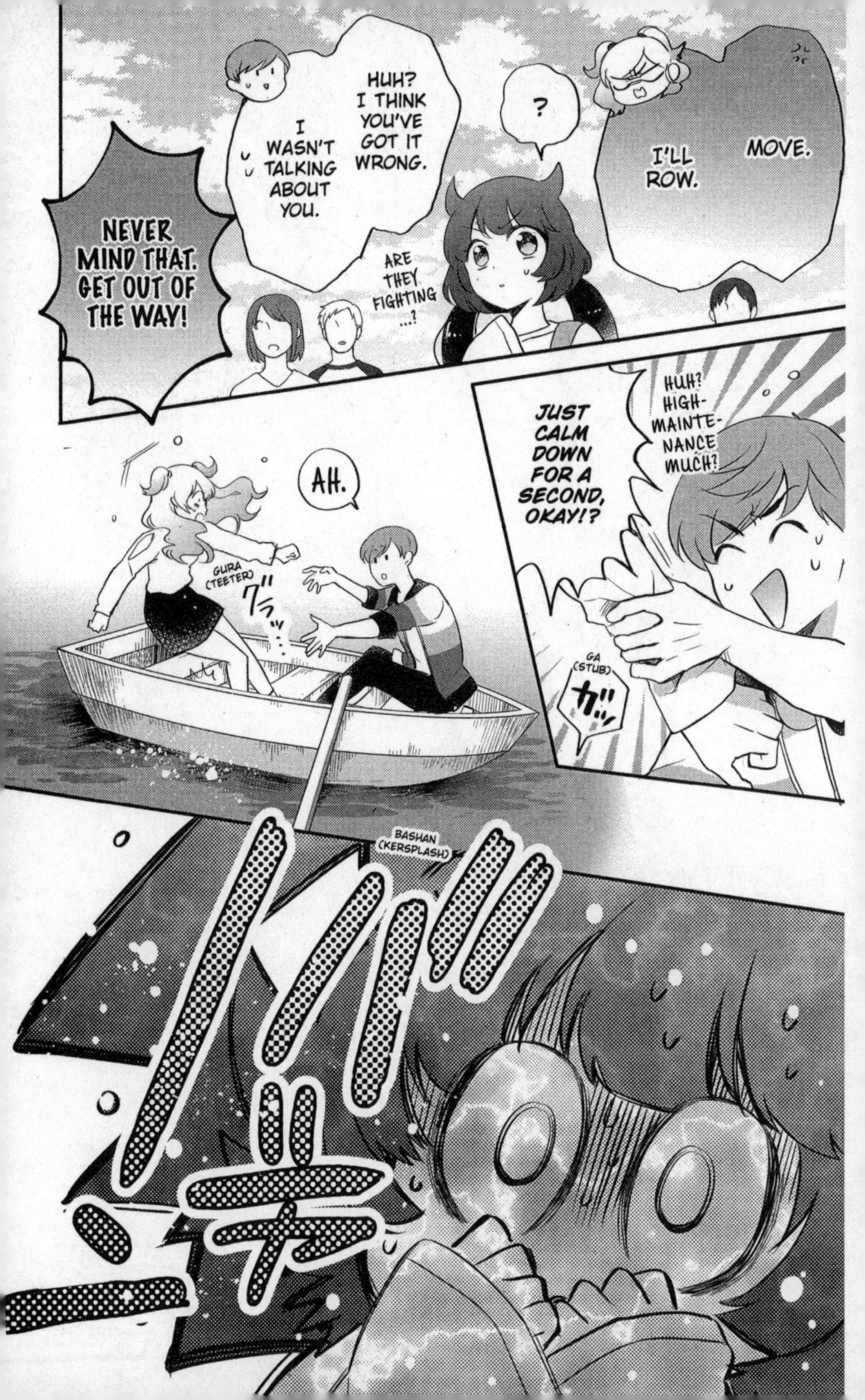
MOVE. I'LL ROW.
?
HUH? I THINK YOU'VE GOT IT WRONG. I WASN'T TALKING ABOUT YOU.
ARE THEY FIGHTING...?
NEVER MIND THAT. GET OUT OF THE WAY!
HUH? HIGH-MAINTE-NANCE MUCH?
JUST CALM DOWN FOR A SECOND, OKAY!?
GA (STUB)
AH.
GURA (TEETER)
BASHAN (KERSPLASH)

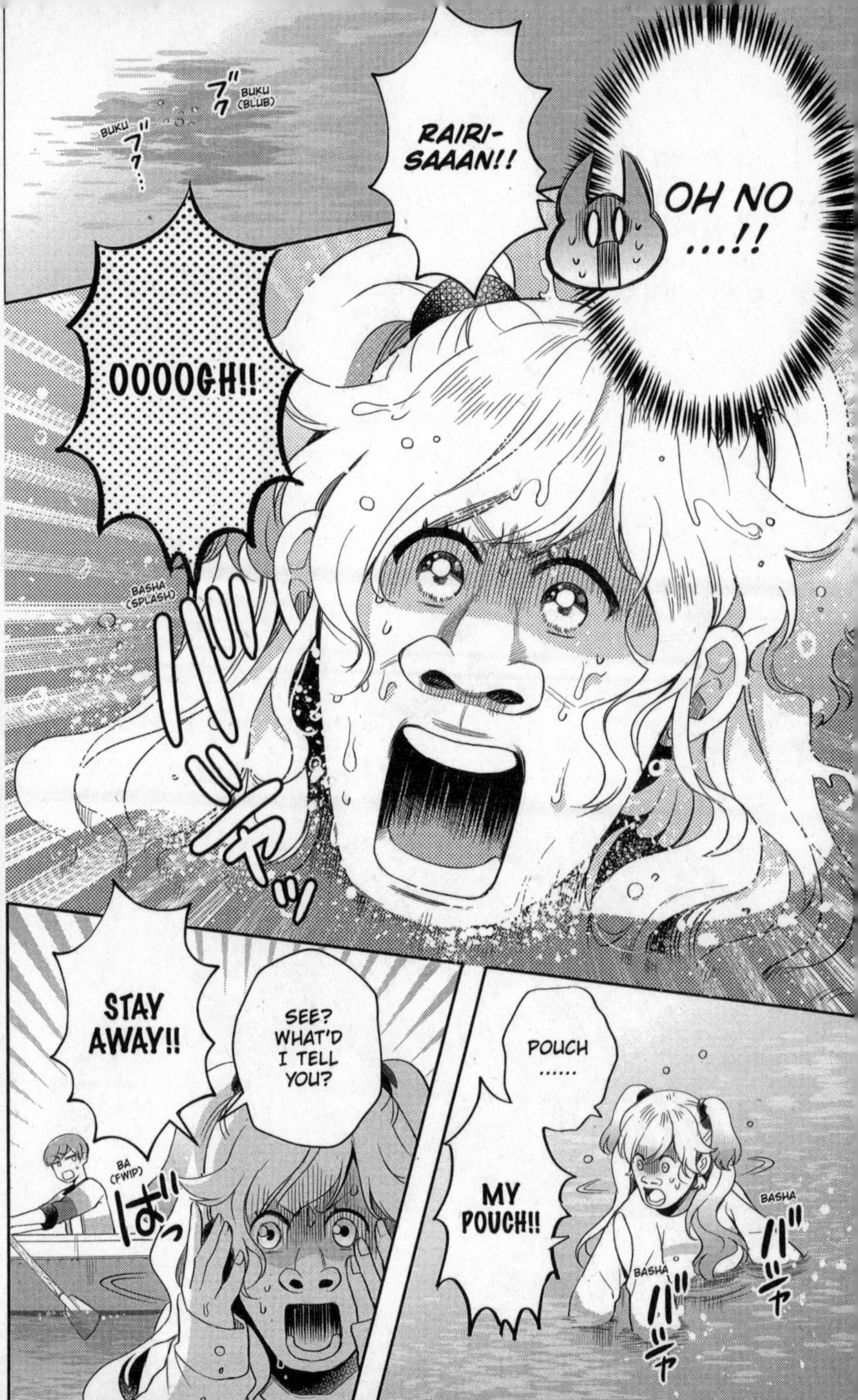
OH NO ...!!
RAIRI-SAAAN!!
BUKU (BLUB)
BUKU
OOOOGH!!
BASHA (SPLASH)
POUCH ......
MY POUCH!!
BASHA
BASHA
SEE? WHAT'D I TELL YOU?
STAY AWAY!!
BA (FWIP)

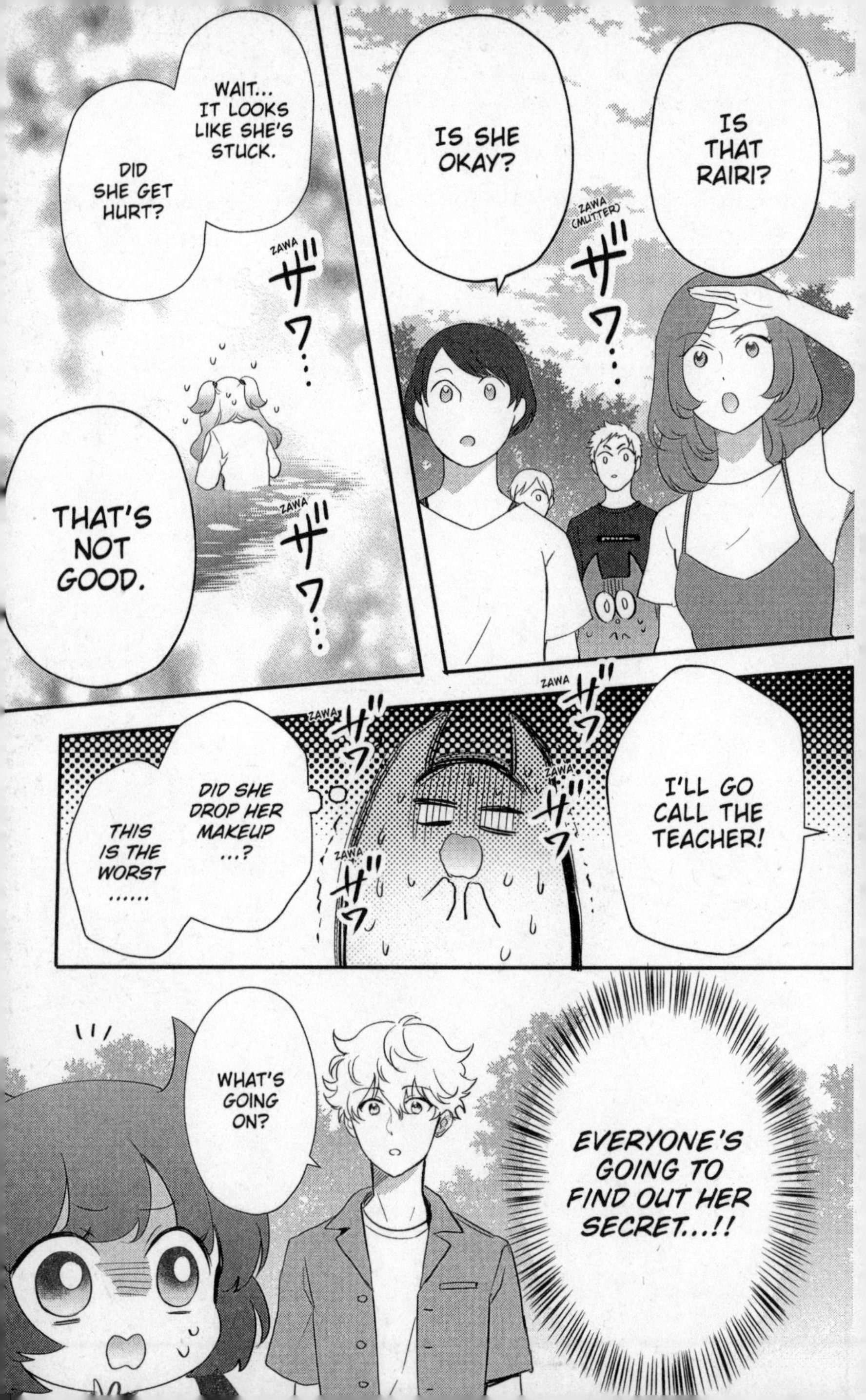
IS THAT RAIRI?
IS SHE OKAY?
ZAWA (MUTTER)
ザワ…
WAIT... IT LOOKS LIKE SHE'S STUCK.
DID SHE GET HURT?
ZAWA
ザワ…
ZAWA
ザワ…
THAT'S NOT GOOD.
I'LL GO CALL THE TEACHER!
ZAWA
ザワ
ZAWA
ザワ
ZAWA
ザワ
ZAWA
ザワ
DID SHE DROP HER MAKEUP ...?
THIS IS THE WORST ......
EVERYONE'S GOING TO FIND OUT HER SECRET...!!
WHAT'S GOING ON?

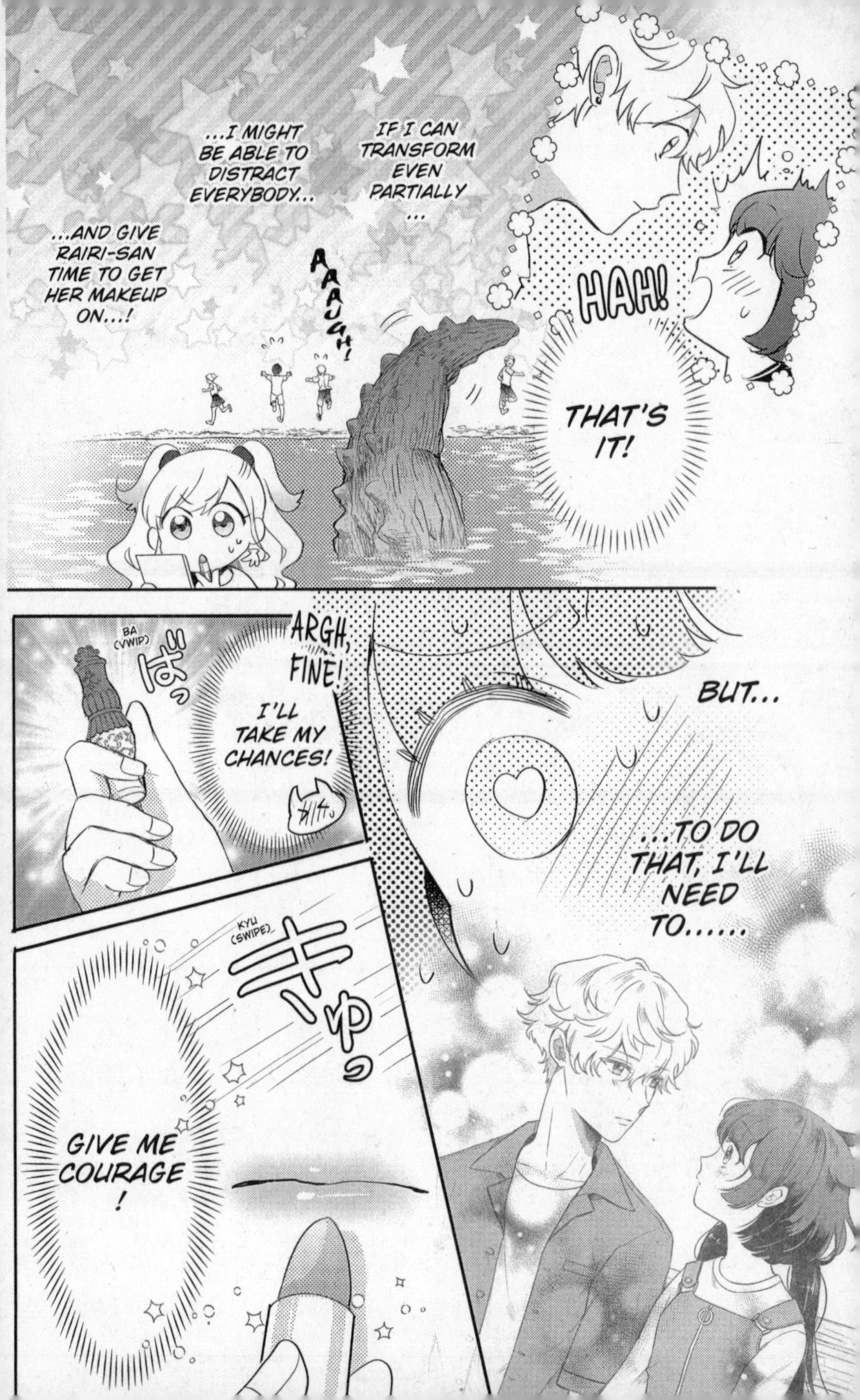
HAH!
THAT'S IT!
IF I CAN TRANSFORM EVEN PARTIALLY...
...I MIGHT BE ABLE TO DISTRACT EVERYBODY...
AAAUGH!
...AND GIVE RAIRI-SAN TIME TO GET HER MAKEUP ON...!
BUT...
...TO DO THAT, I'LL NEED TO......
ARGH, FINE!
I'LL TAKE MY CHANCES!
BA (VWIP)
ばっ
KYU (SWIPE)
きゅっ
GIVE ME COURAGE!

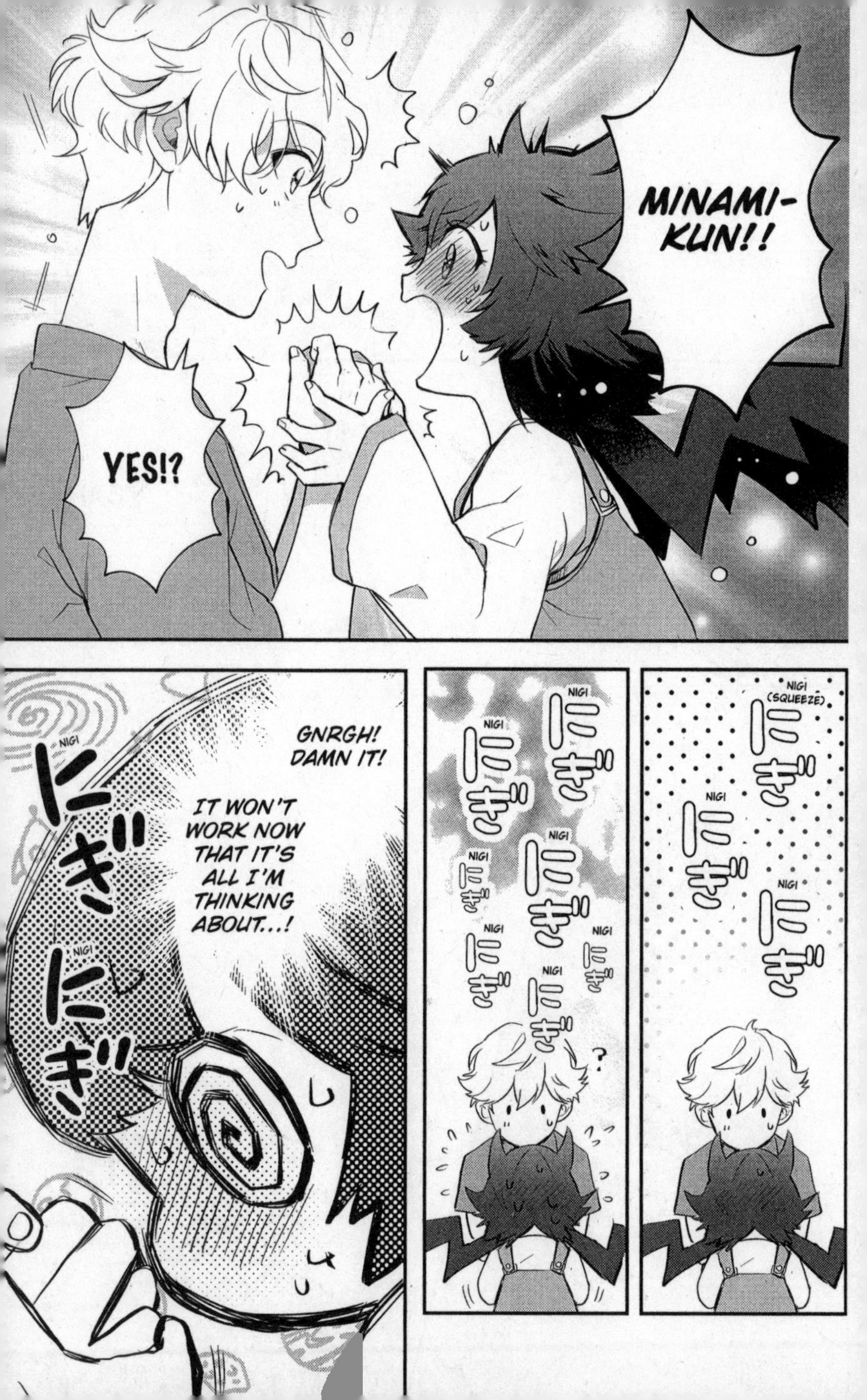
MINAMI-KUN!!
YES!?
NIGI (SQUEEZE)
にぎ
NIGI
にぎ
NIGI
にぎ
NIGI
にぎ
NIGI
にぎ
NIGI
にぎ
NIGI
にぎ
NIGI
にぎ
NIGI
にぎ
NIGI
にぎ
GNRGH! DAMN IT!
IT WON'T WORK NOW THAT IT'S ALL I'M THINKING ABOUT...!
NIGI
にぎ
NIGI
にぎ

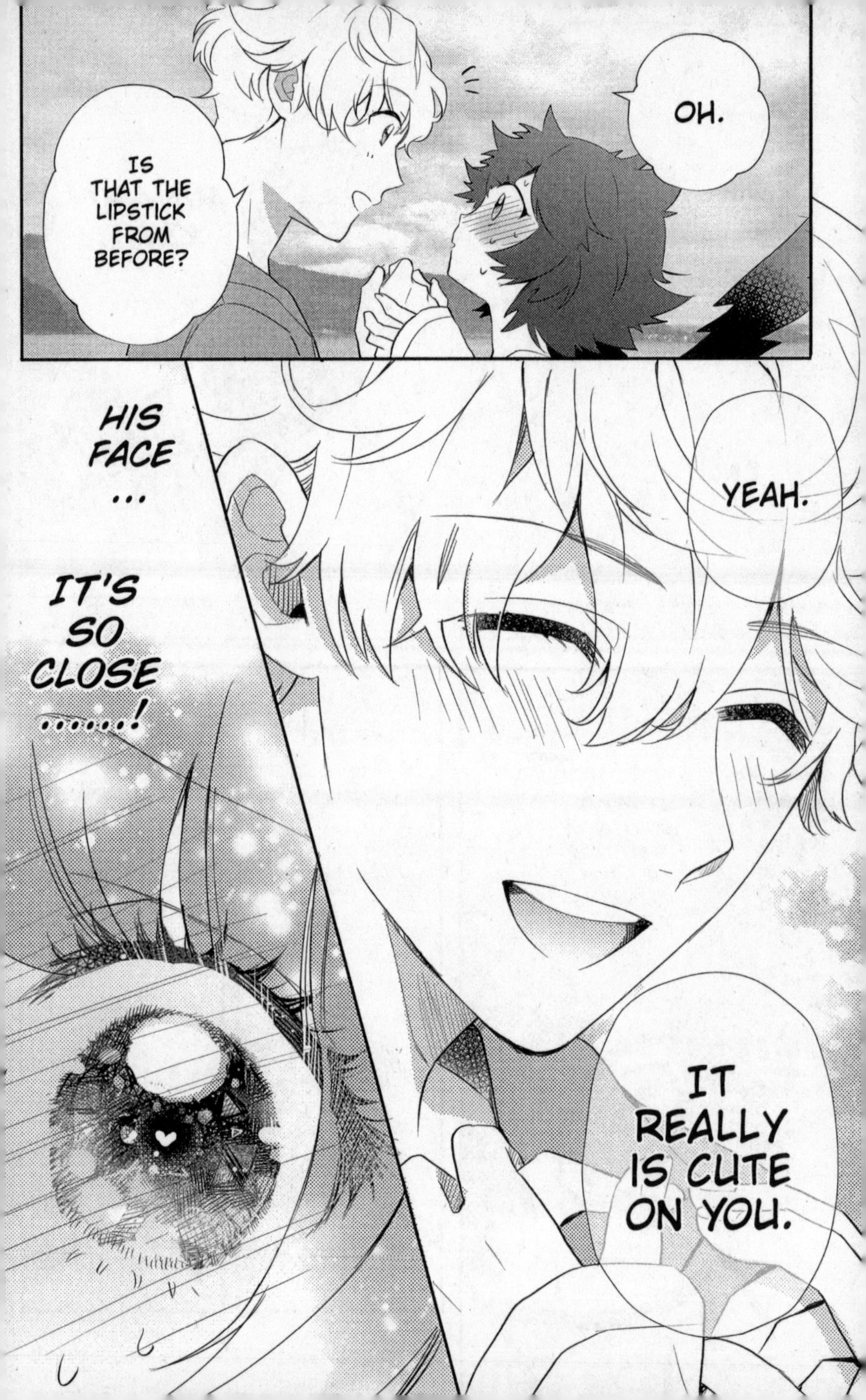
OH.
IS THAT THE LIPSTICK FROM BEFORE?
YEAH.
IT REALLY IS CUTE ON YOU.
HIS FACE...
IT'S SO CLOSE......!

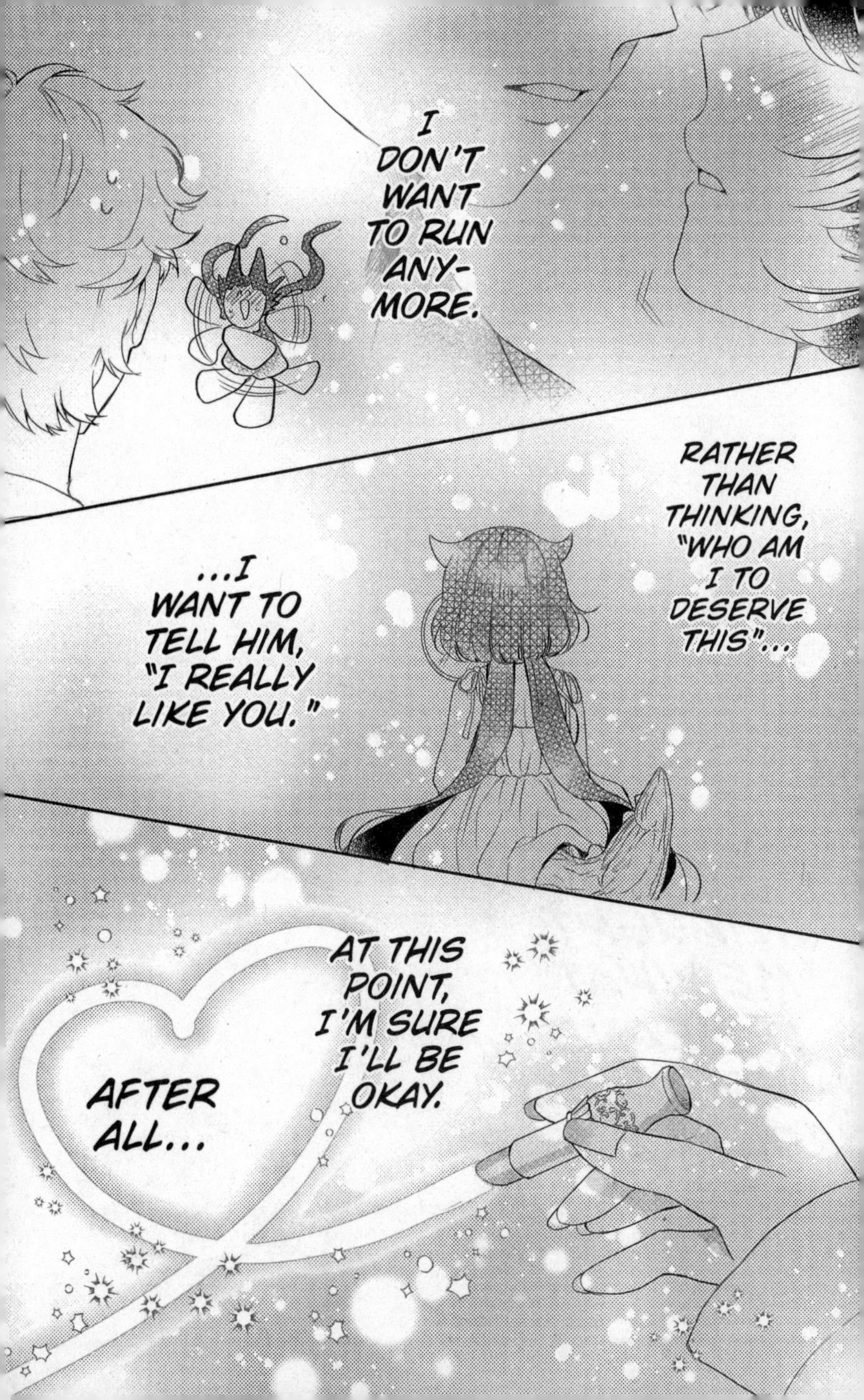
I DON'T WANT TO RUN ANYMORE.
RATHER THAN THINKING, "WHO AM I TO DESERVE THIS"...
...I WANT TO TELL HIM, "I REALLY LIKE YOU."
AT THIS POINT, I'M SURE I'LL BE OKAY.
AFTER ALL...

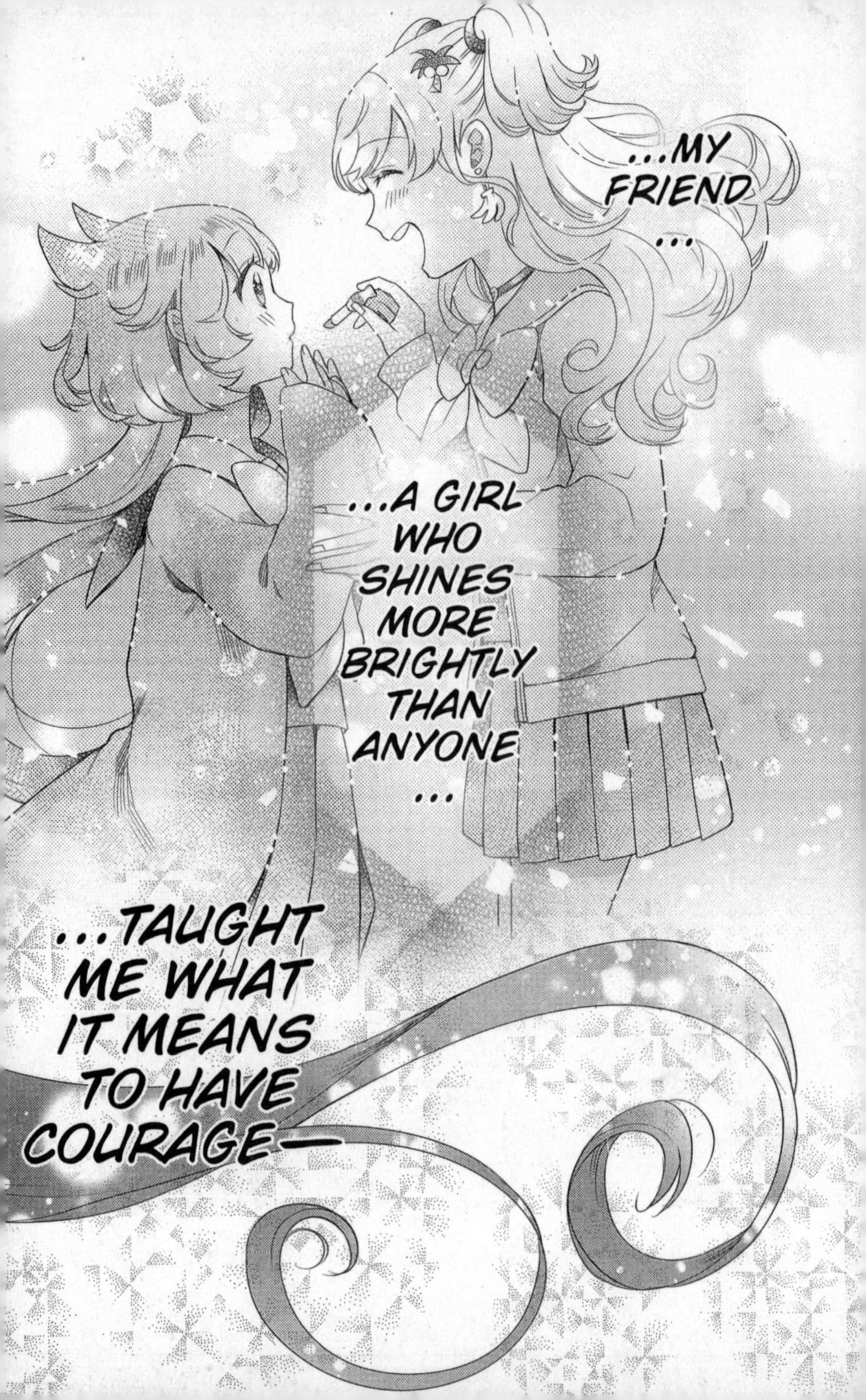
...MY FRIEND...
...A GIRL WHO SHINES MORE BRIGHTLY THAN ANYONE...
...TAUGHT ME WHAT IT MEANS TO HAVE COURAGE—

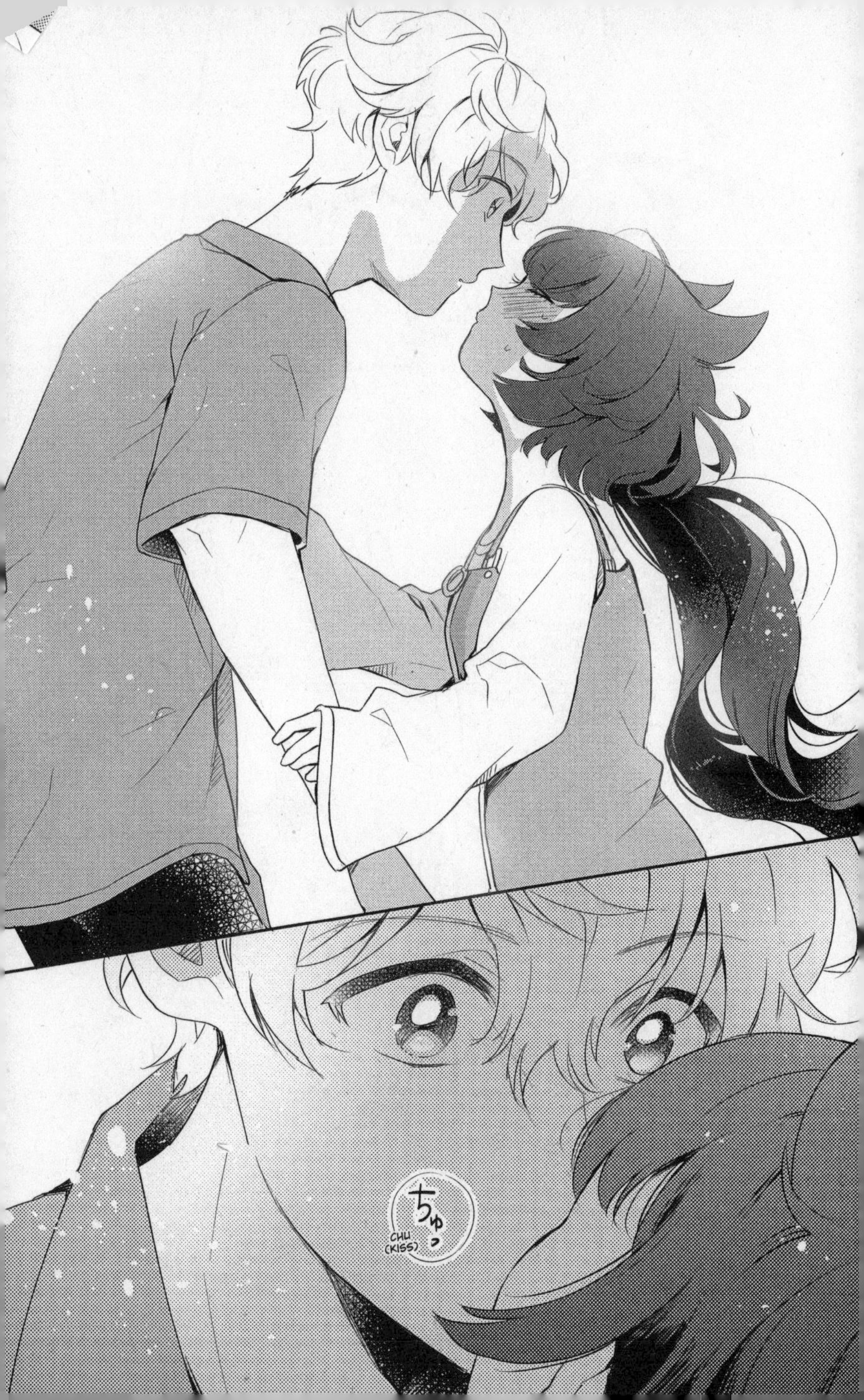
ちゅっ
CHU (KISS)

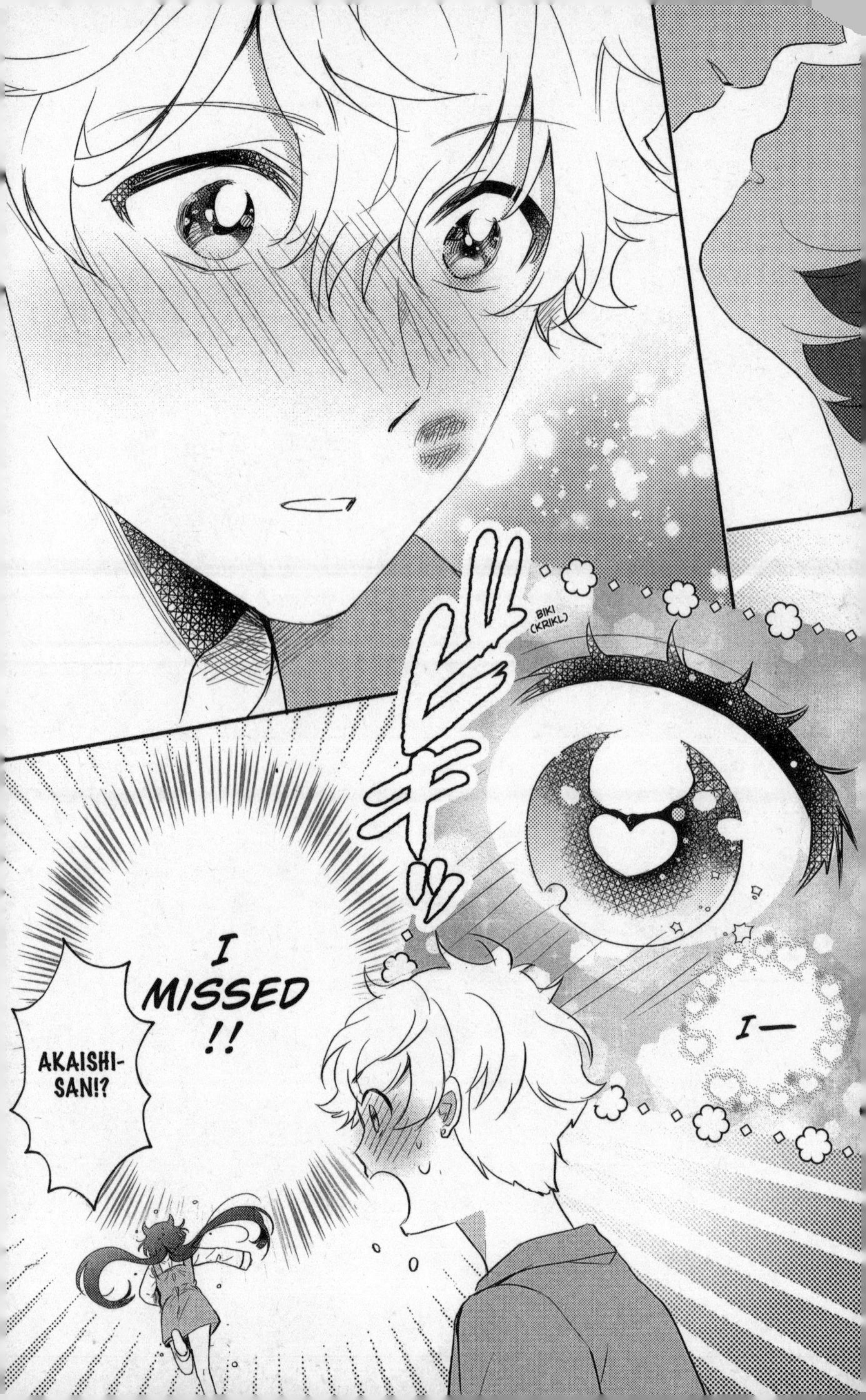
BIKI (KRIKL)
I—
I MISSED !!
AKAISHI-SAN!?

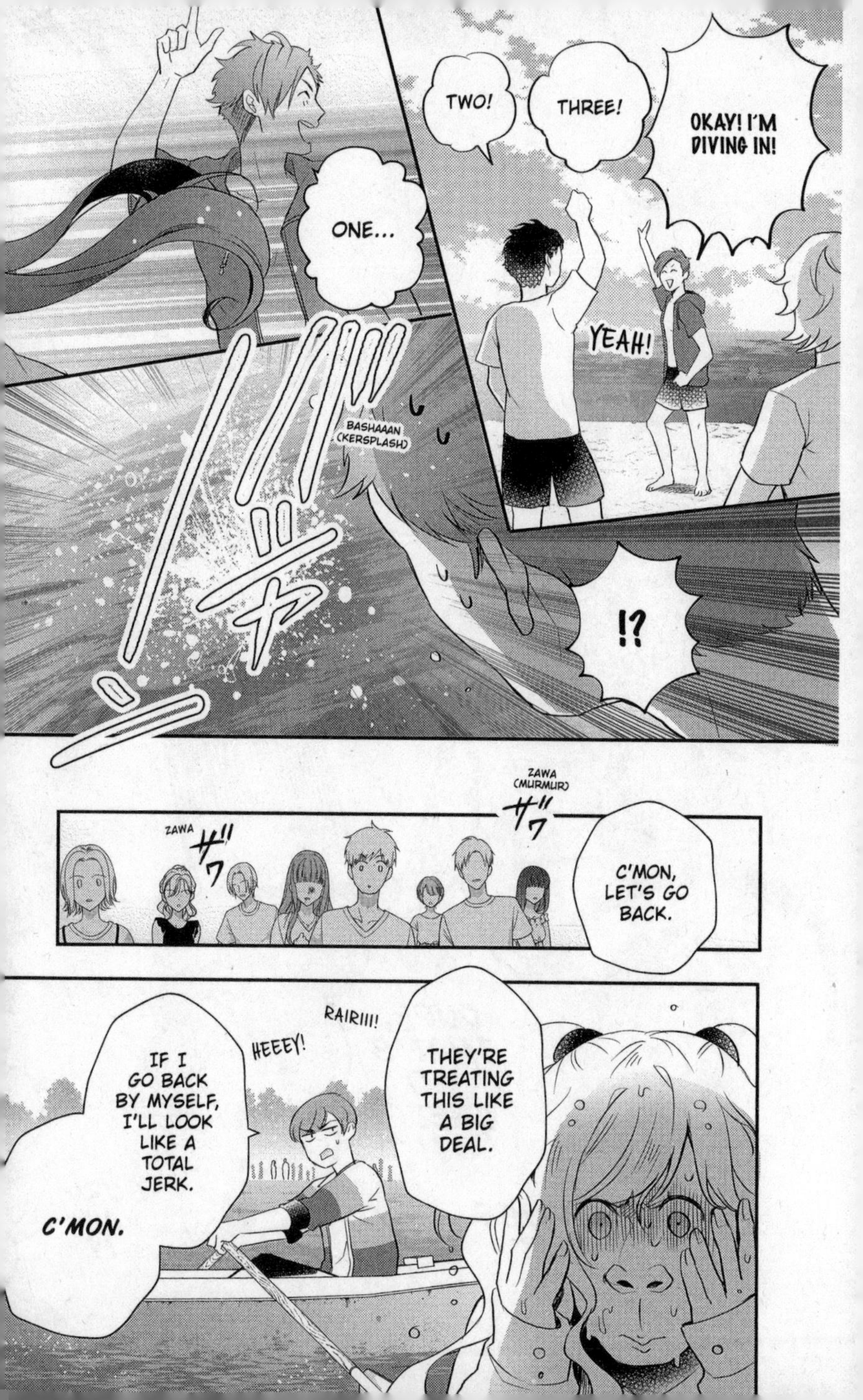
OKAY! I'M DIVING IN!
THREE!
TWO!
YEAH!
ONE...
BASHAAAN (KERSPLASH)
!?
ZAWA (MURMUR)
C'MON, LET'S GO BACK.
ZAWA
THEY'RE TREATING THIS LIKE A BIG DEAL.
RAIRIII!
HEEEY!
IF I GO BACK BY MYSELF, I'LL LOOK LIKE A TOTAL JERK.
C'MON.

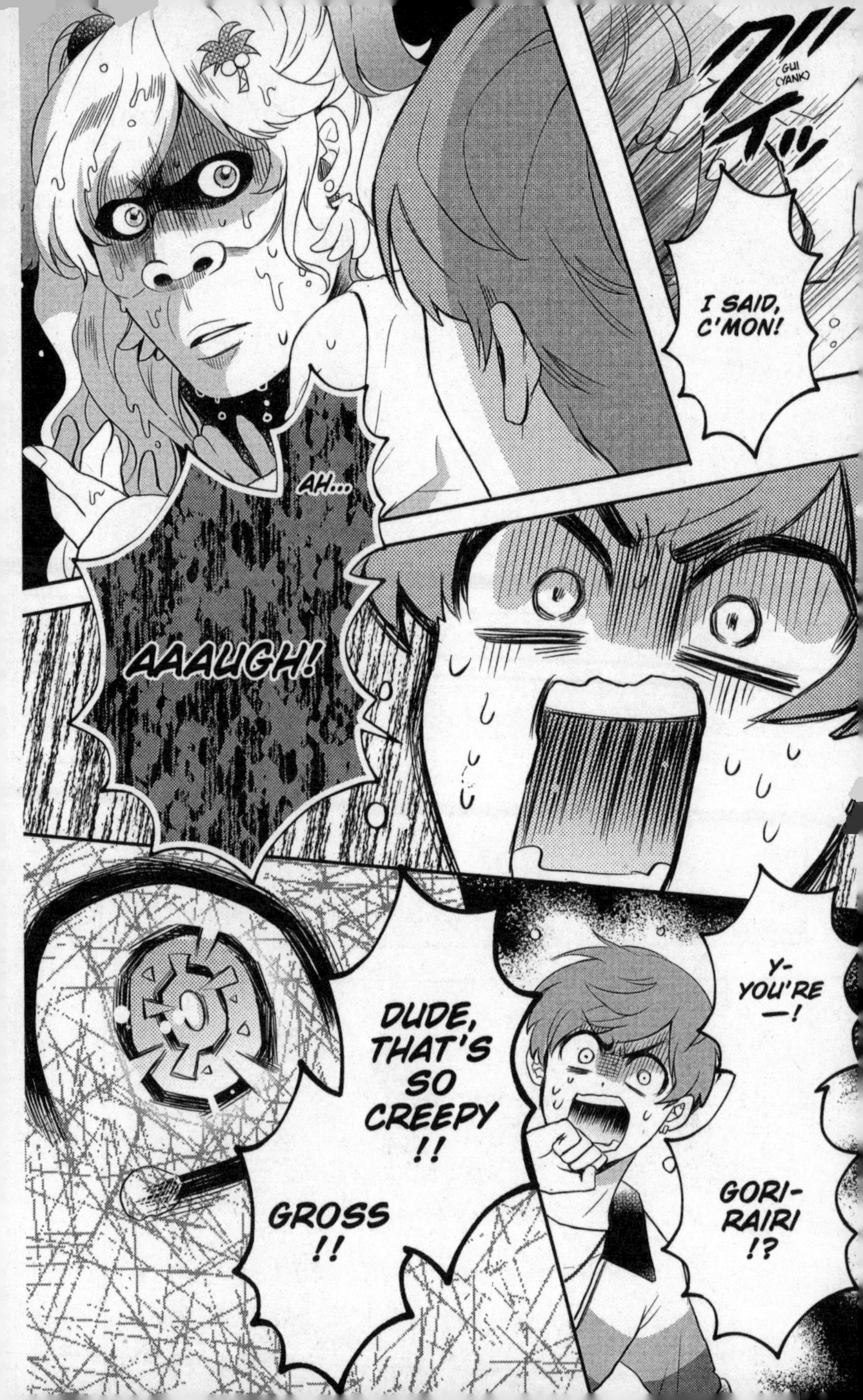
GUI (YANK)
I SAID, C'MON!
AH...
AAAUGH!
Y-YOU'RE—!
GORI-RAIRI!?
DUDE, THAT'S SO CREEPY!!
GROSS!!

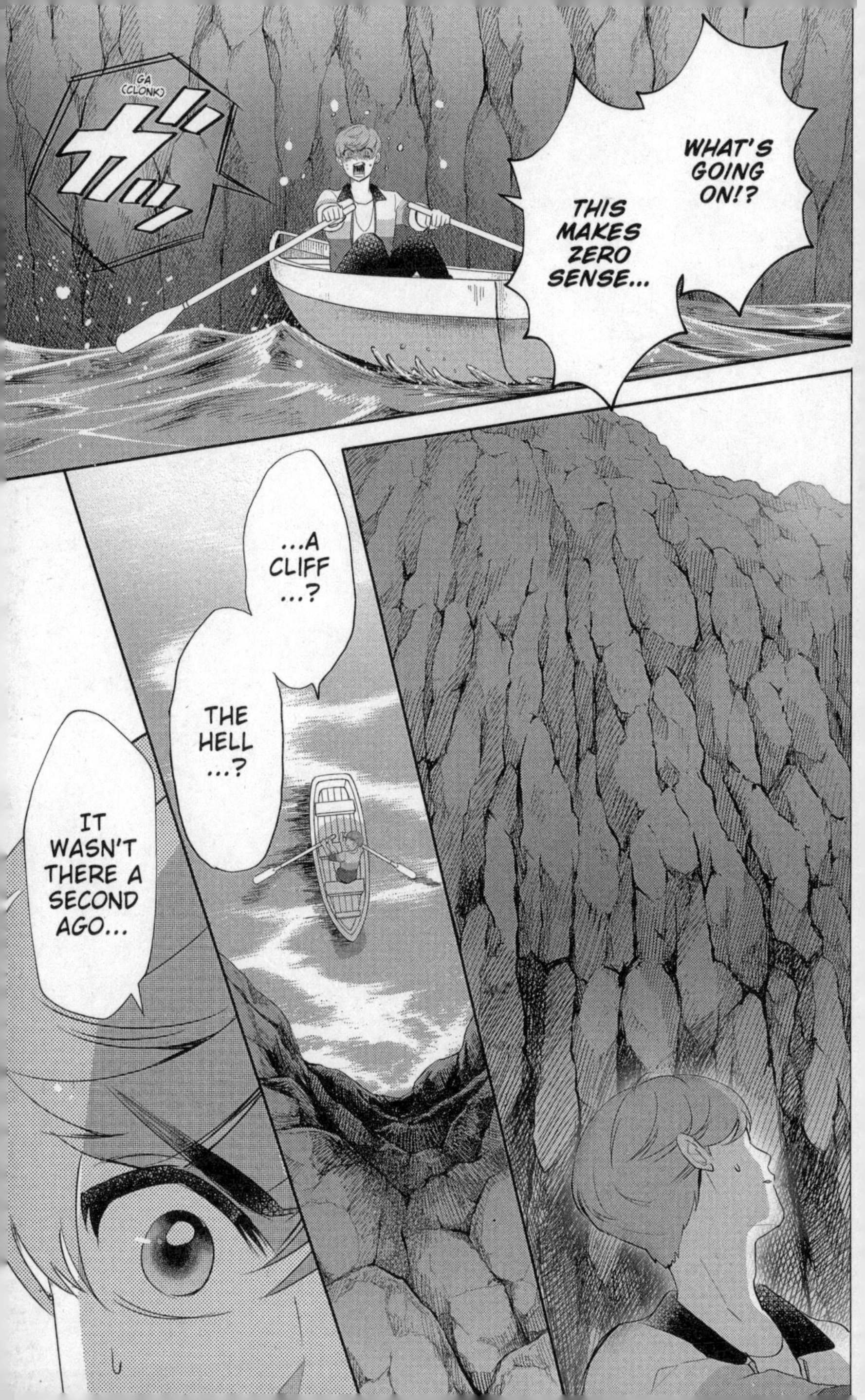
WHAT'S GOING ON!?
THIS MAKES ZERO SENSE...
GA (CLONK)
...A CLIFF ...?
THE HELL ...?
IT WASN'T THERE A SECOND AGO...

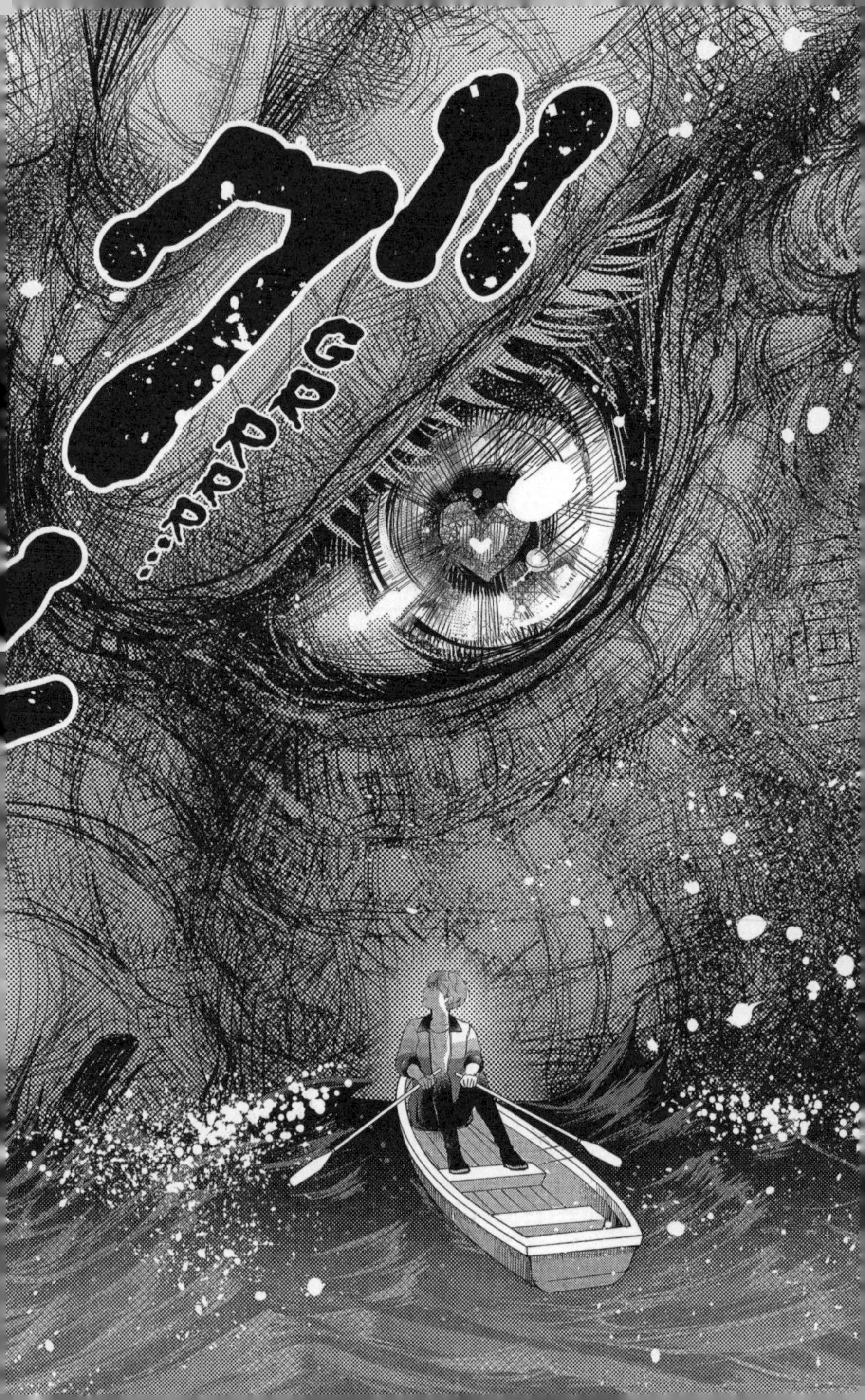
GRRRR...

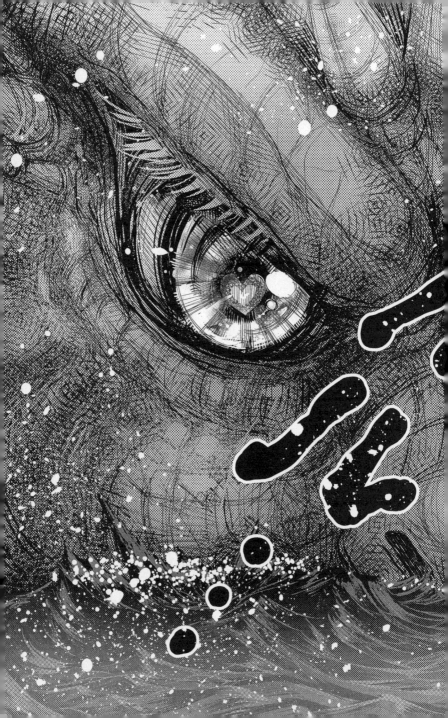

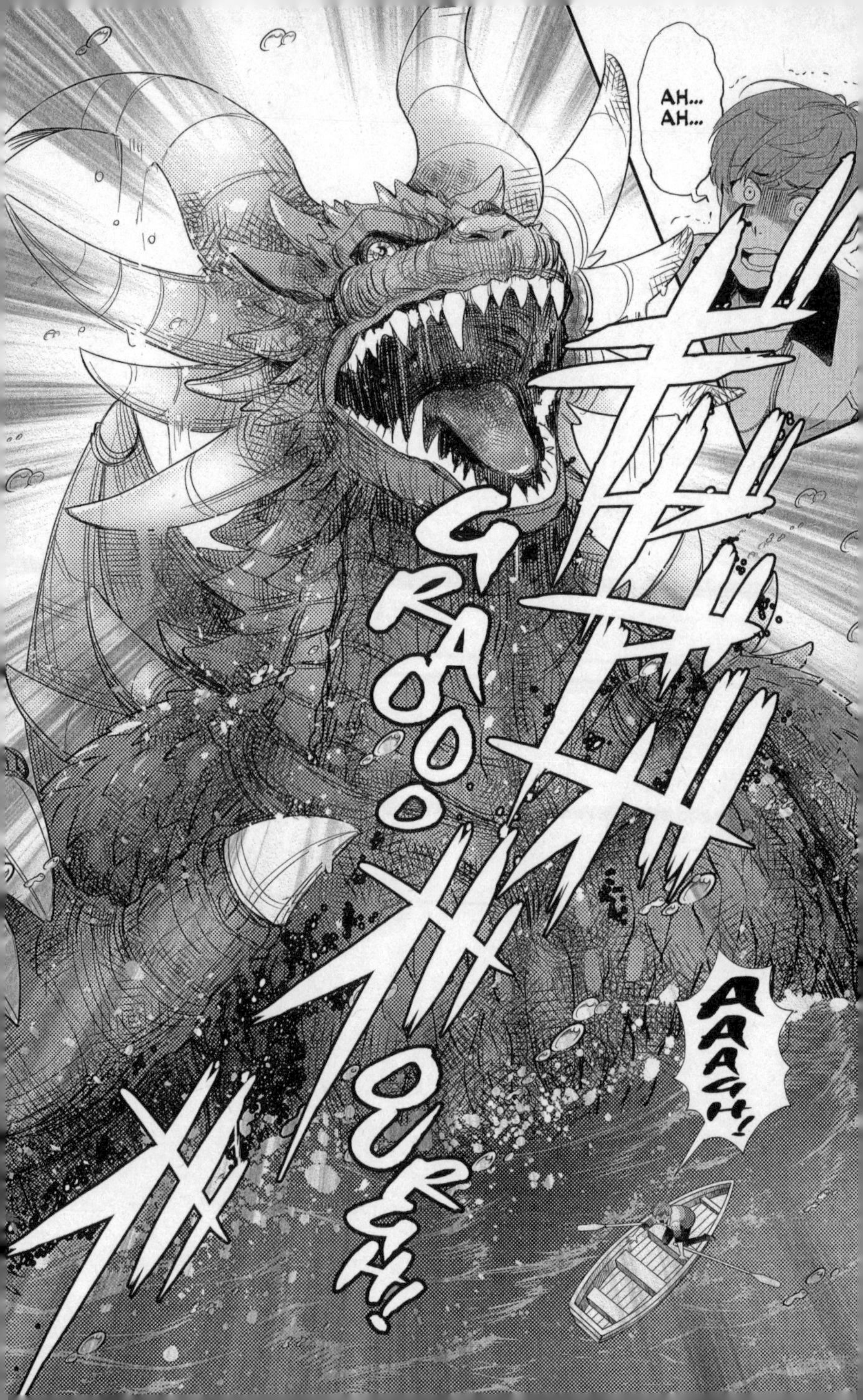
AH... AH...
GRAOOOOURGH!!
AAAGH!

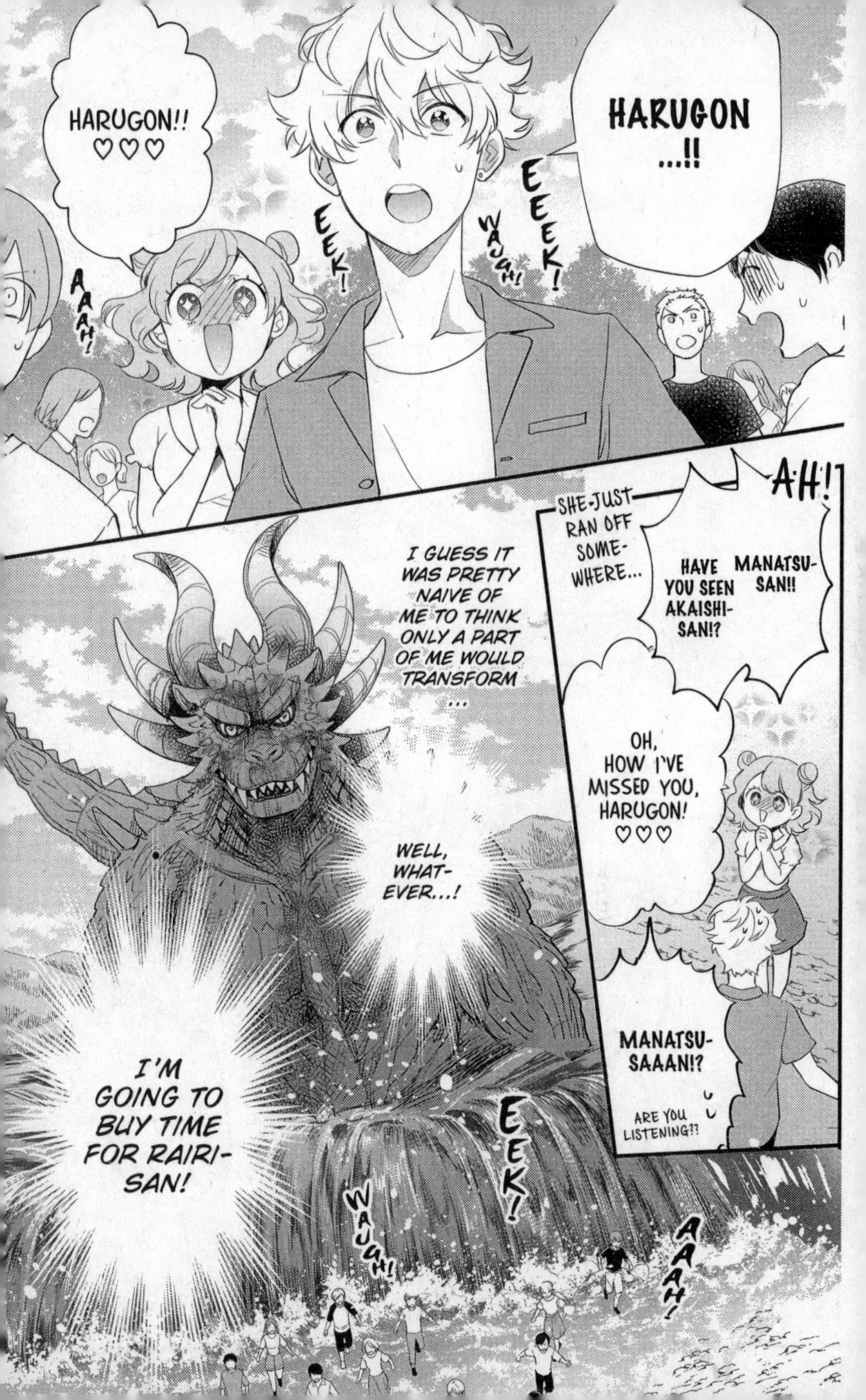
HARUGON ...!!
EEEEK!
WAUGH!
EEK!
HARUGON!! ♡♡♡
AAAH!
AH!
MANATSU-SAN!!
HAVE YOU SEEN AKAISHI-SAN!?
SHE JUST RAN OFF SOME-WHERE...
OH, HOW I'VE MISSED YOU, HARUGON! ♡♡♡
MANATSU-SAAAN!?
ARE YOU LISTENING??
I GUESS IT WAS PRETTY NAIVE OF ME TO THINK ONLY A PART OF ME WOULD TRANSFORM...
WELL, WHAT-EVER...!
I'M GOING TO BUY TIME FOR RAIRI-SAN!
AAAH!
EEEK!
WAUGH!

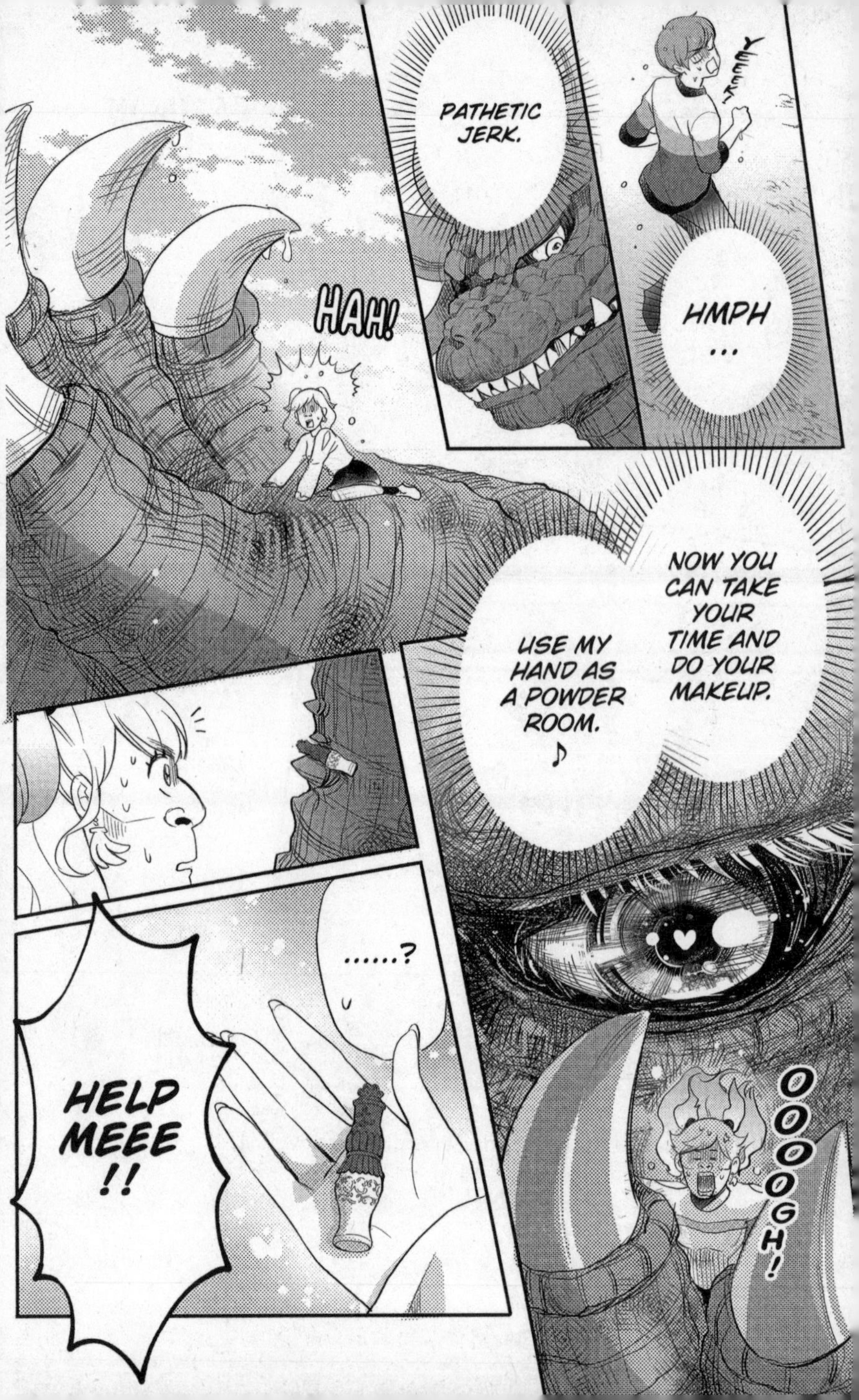
YEEEK!
HMPH...
PATHETIC JERK.
HAH!
NOW YOU CAN TAKE YOUR TIME AND DO YOUR MAKEUP.
USE MY HAND AS A POWDER ROOM. ♪
OOOOOGH!
......?
HELP MEEE!!

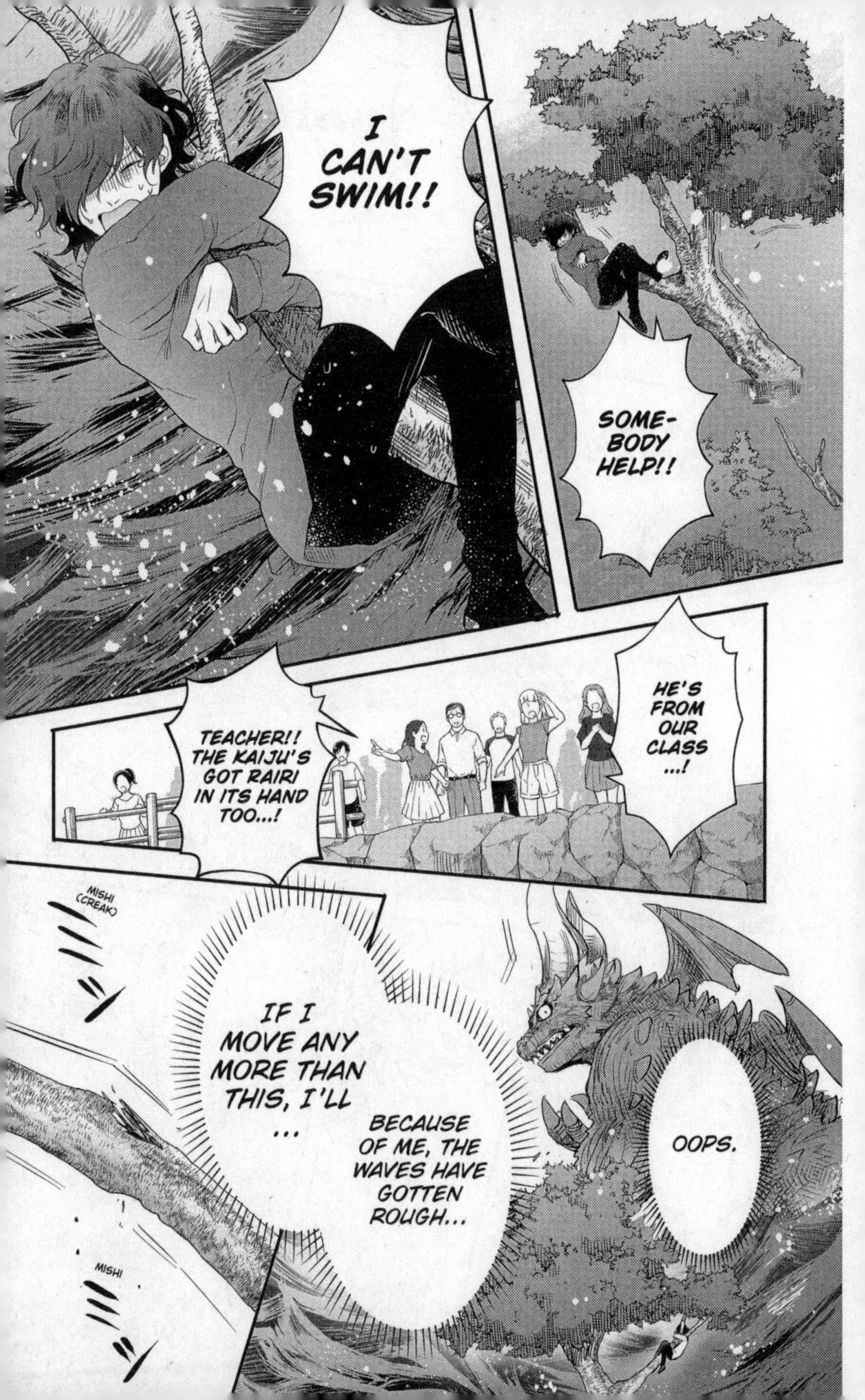
SOME-BODY HELP!!
I CAN'T SWIM!!
HE'S FROM OUR CLASS ...!
TEACHER!! THE KAIJU'S GOT RAIRI IN ITS HAND TOO...!
OOPS.
BECAUSE OF ME, THE WAVES HAVE GOTTEN ROUGH...
IF I MOVE ANY MORE THAN THIS, I'LL ...
MISHI (CREAK)
MISHI

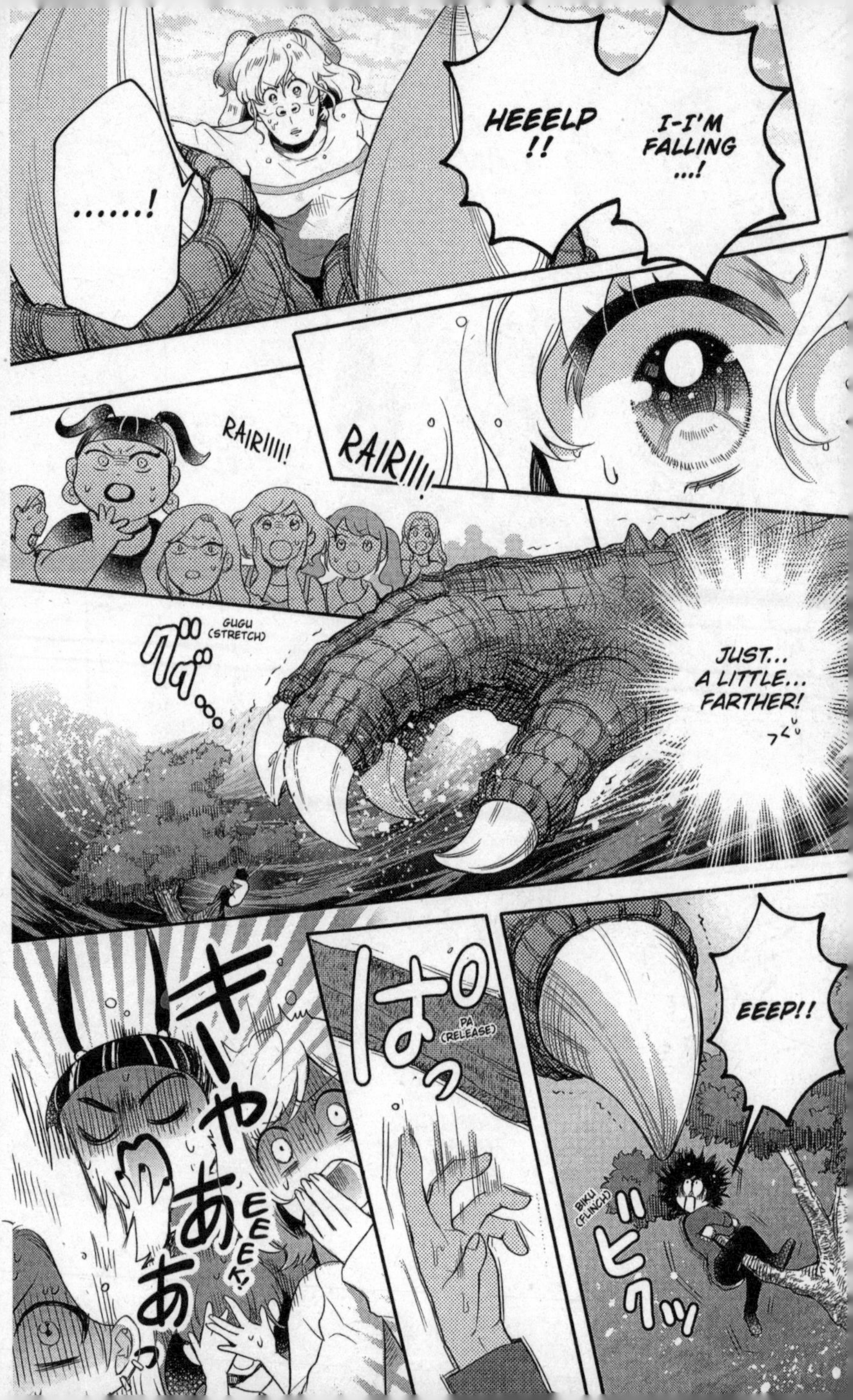
HEEELP!!
I-I'M FALLING...!
......!
RAIR!!!!
RAIR!!!!!
JUST... A LITTLE... FARTHER!
GUGU (STRETCH)
EEEP!!
ビクッ
BIKU (FLINCH)
ぱっ
PA (RELEASE)
きゃああ
EEEEK!

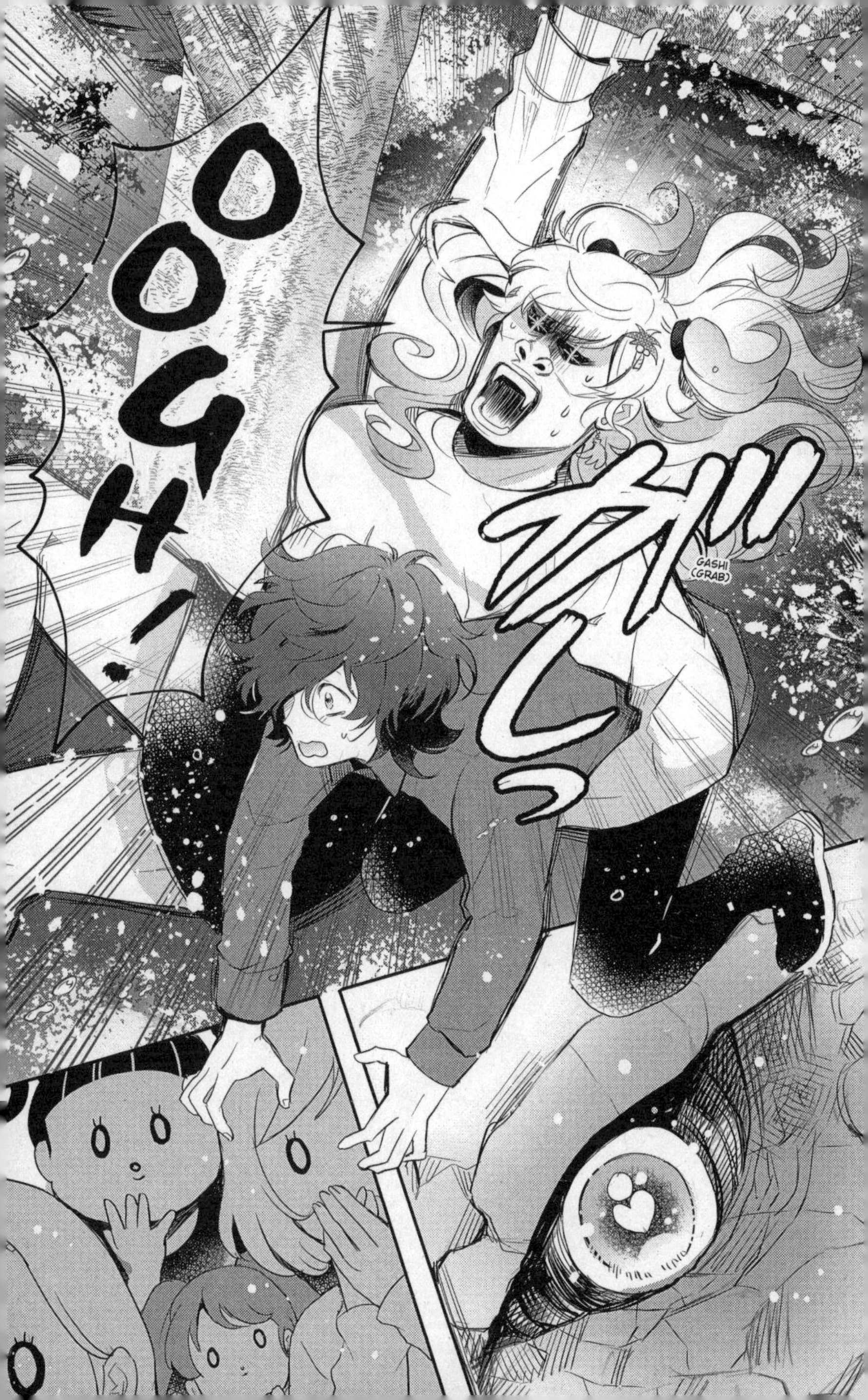
OOGH—!
GASHI (GRAB)

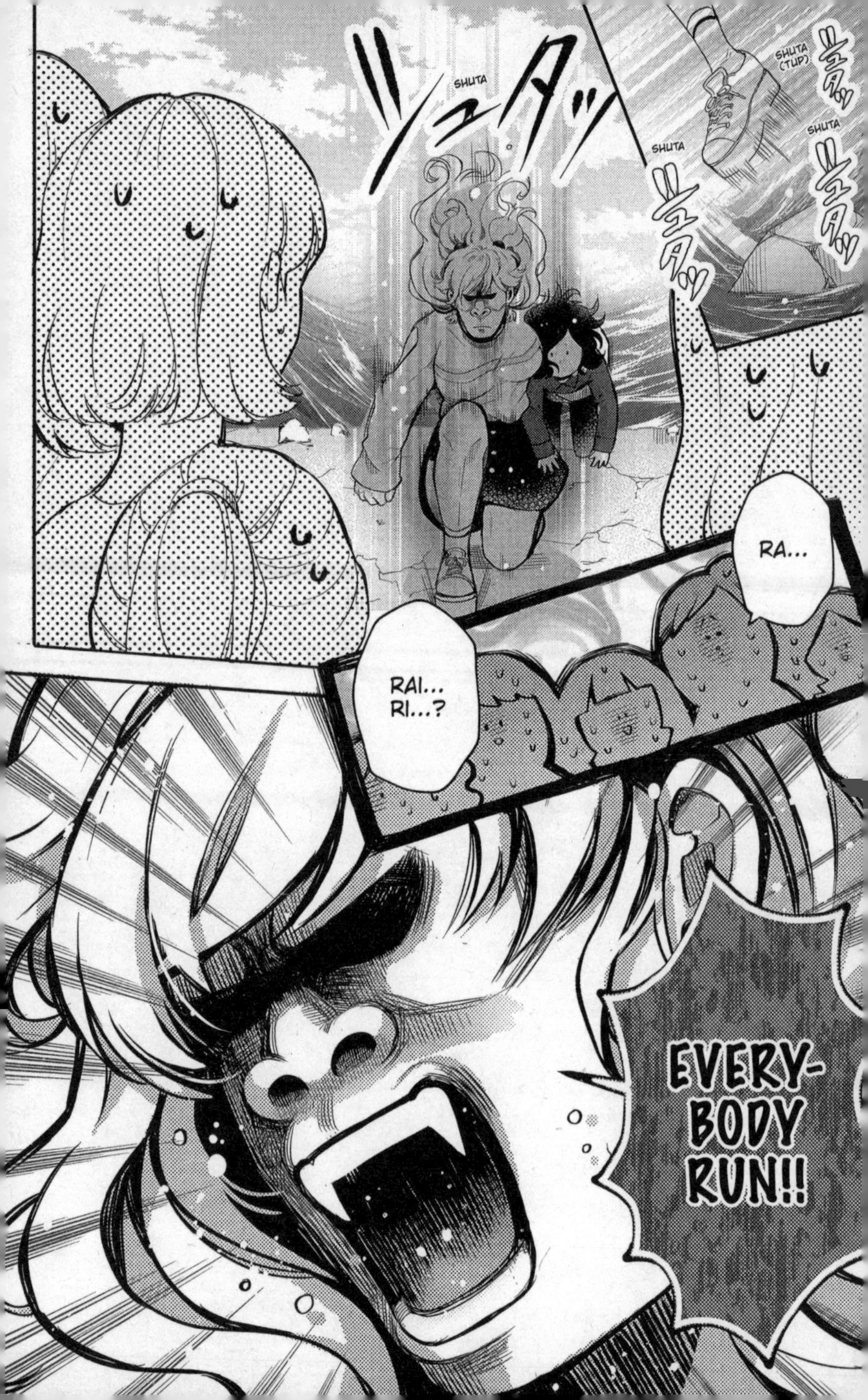
SHUTA (TUP)
SHUTA
SHUTA
SHUTA
RA...
RAI... RI...?
EVERY-BODY RUN!!

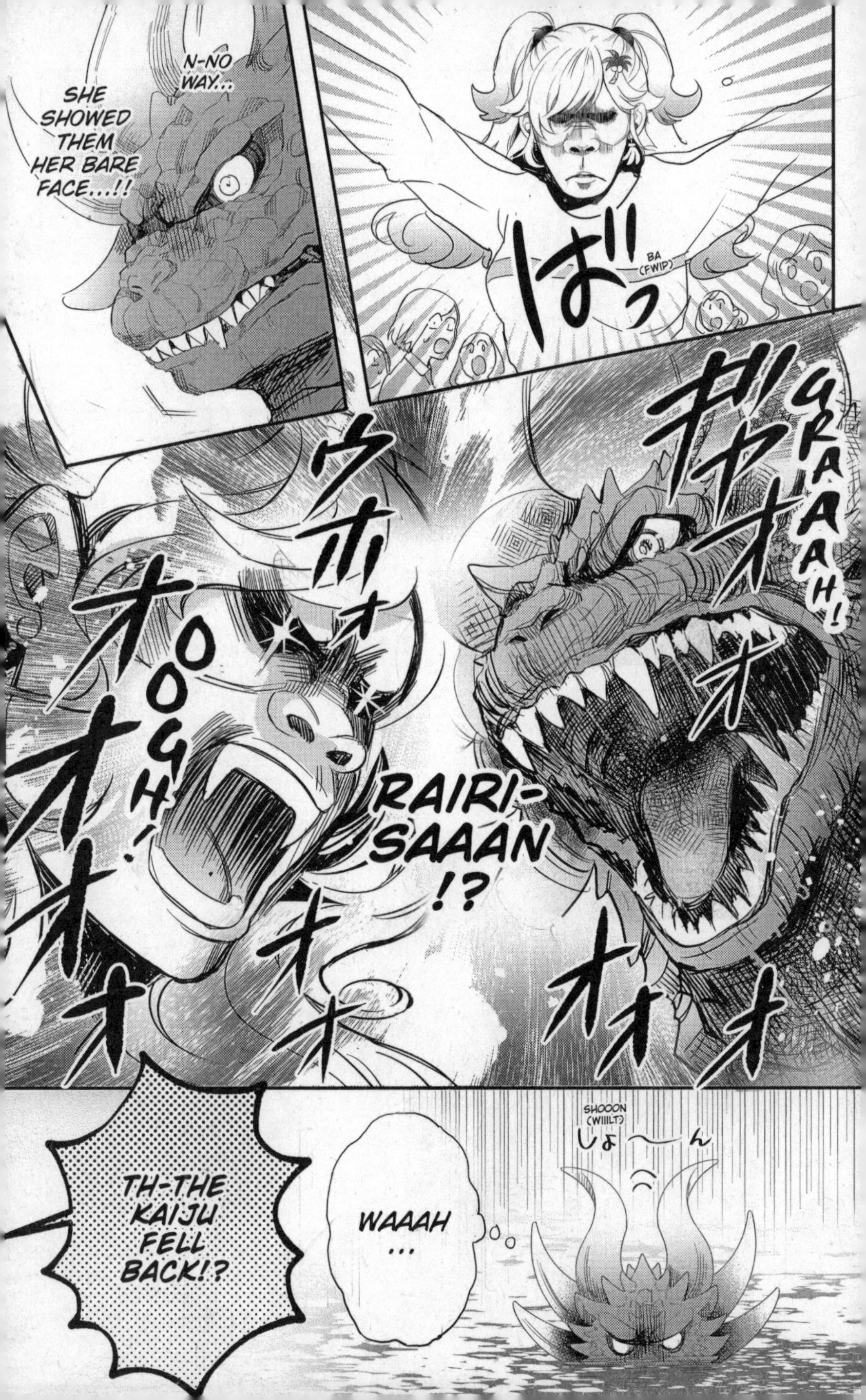
ばっ
BA (FWIP)
N-NO WAY...
SHE SHOWED THEM HER BARE FACE...!!
ギャオオオ
GRAAAAH!
RAIRI-SAAAN!?
ウホオオオ
オオオ
OOOGH!
しょ〜ん
SHOOON (WIIILT)
WAAAH...
TH-THE KAIJU FELL BACK!?

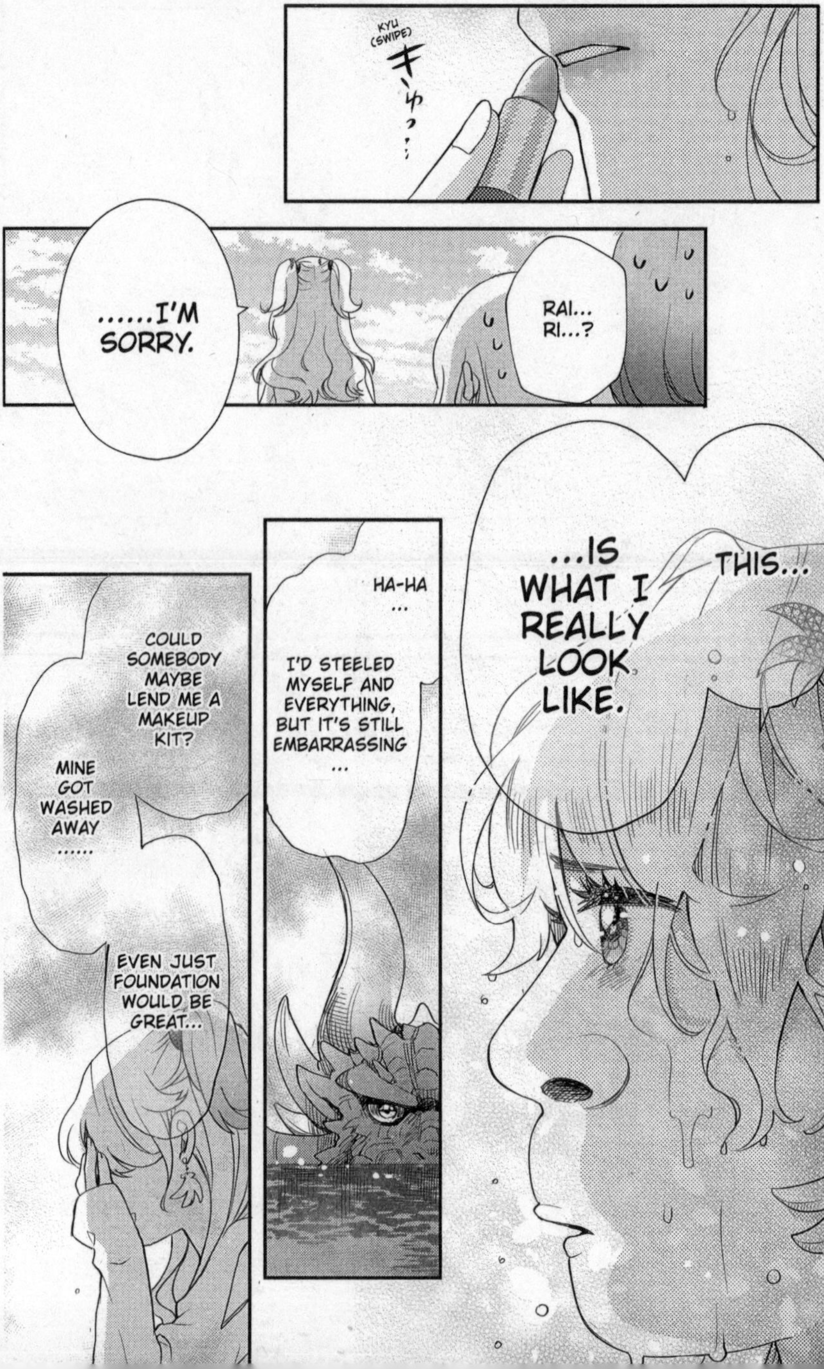
KYU (SWIPE)
キゅっ
RAI... RI...?
......I'M SORRY.
THIS...
...IS WHAT I REALLY LOOK LIKE.
HA-HA ...
I'D STEELED MYSELF AND EVERYTHING, BUT IT'S STILL EMBARRASSING ...
COULD SOMEBODY MAYBE LEND ME A MAKEUP KIT?
MINE GOT WASHED AWAY ......
EVEN JUST FOUNDATION WOULD BE GREAT...

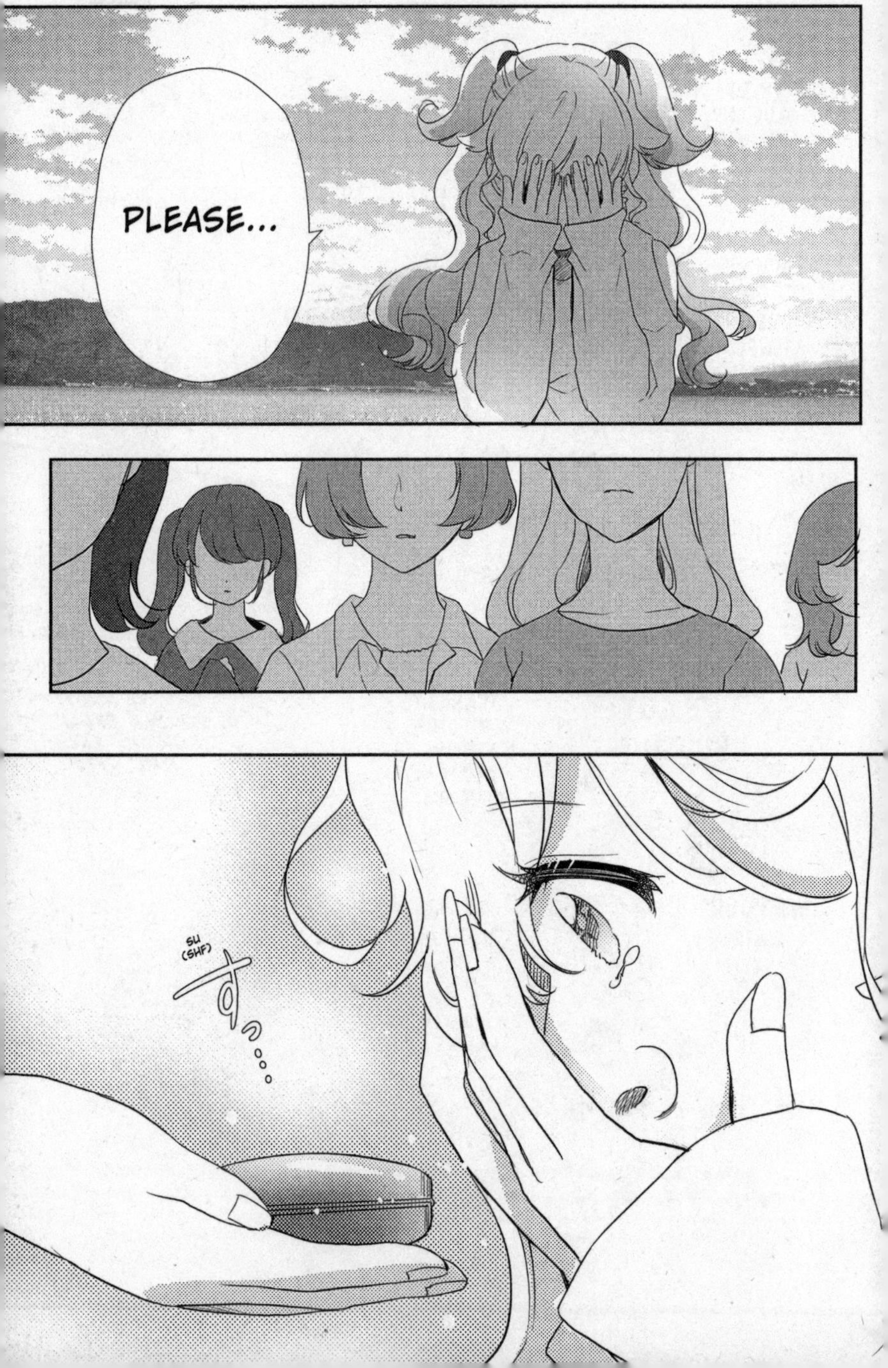
PLEASE...
SU
(SHF)
すっ。。。

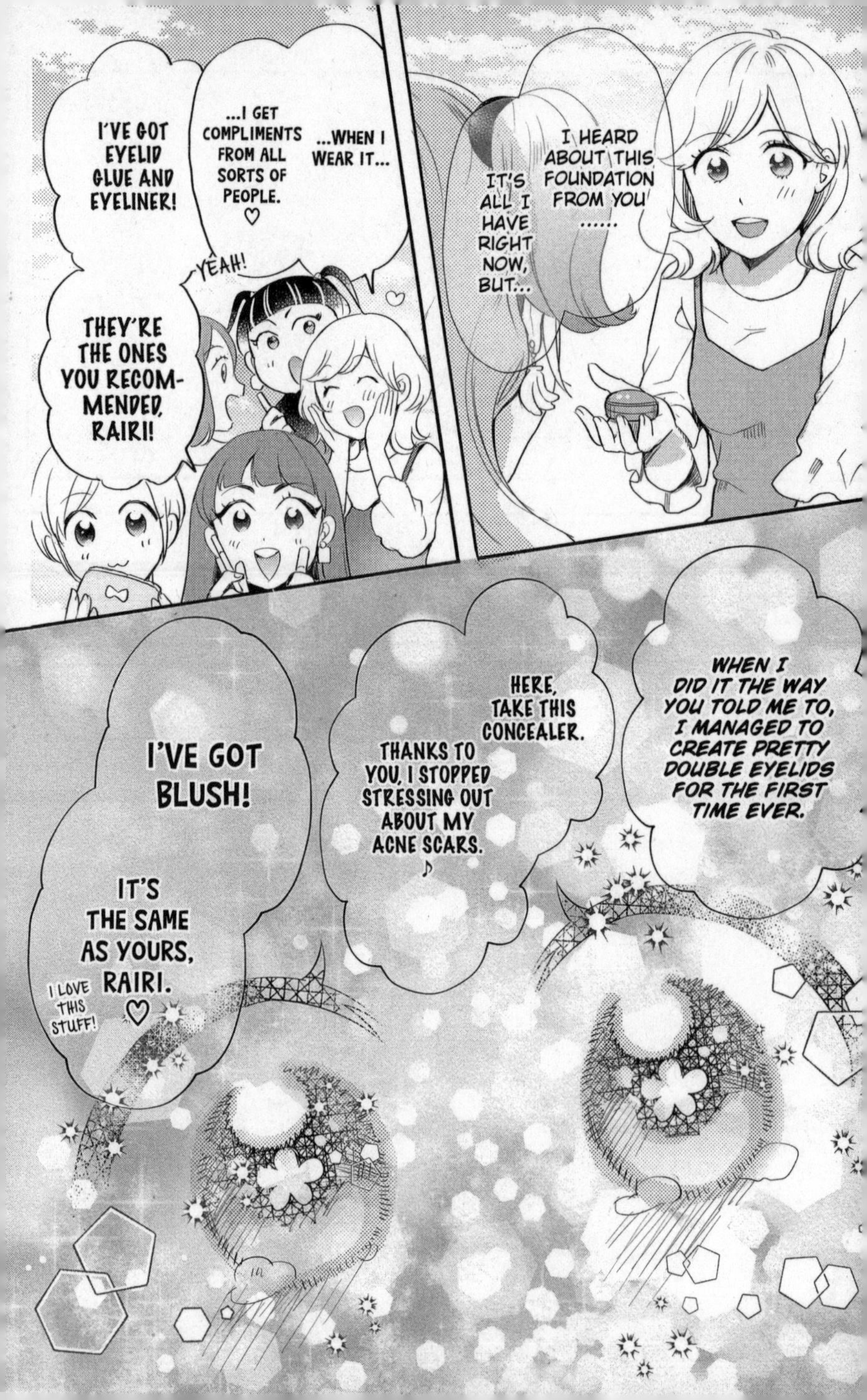
I HEARD ABOUT THIS FOUNDATION FROM YOU......
IT'S ALL I HAVE RIGHT NOW, BUT...
...WHEN I WEAR IT...
...I GET COMPLIMENTS FROM ALL SORTS OF PEOPLE. ♡
I'VE GOT EYELID GLUE AND EYELINER!
YEAH!
THEY'RE THE ONES YOU RECOMMENDED, RAIRI!
WHEN I DID IT THE WAY YOU TOLD ME TO, I MANAGED TO CREATE PRETTY DOUBLE EYELIDS FOR THE FIRST TIME EVER.
HERE, TAKE THIS CONCEALER.
THANKS TO YOU, I STOPPED STRESSING OUT ABOUT MY ACNE SCARS. ♪
I'VE GOT BLUSH!
IT'S THE SAME AS YOURS, RAIRI. ♡
I LOVE THIS STUFF!

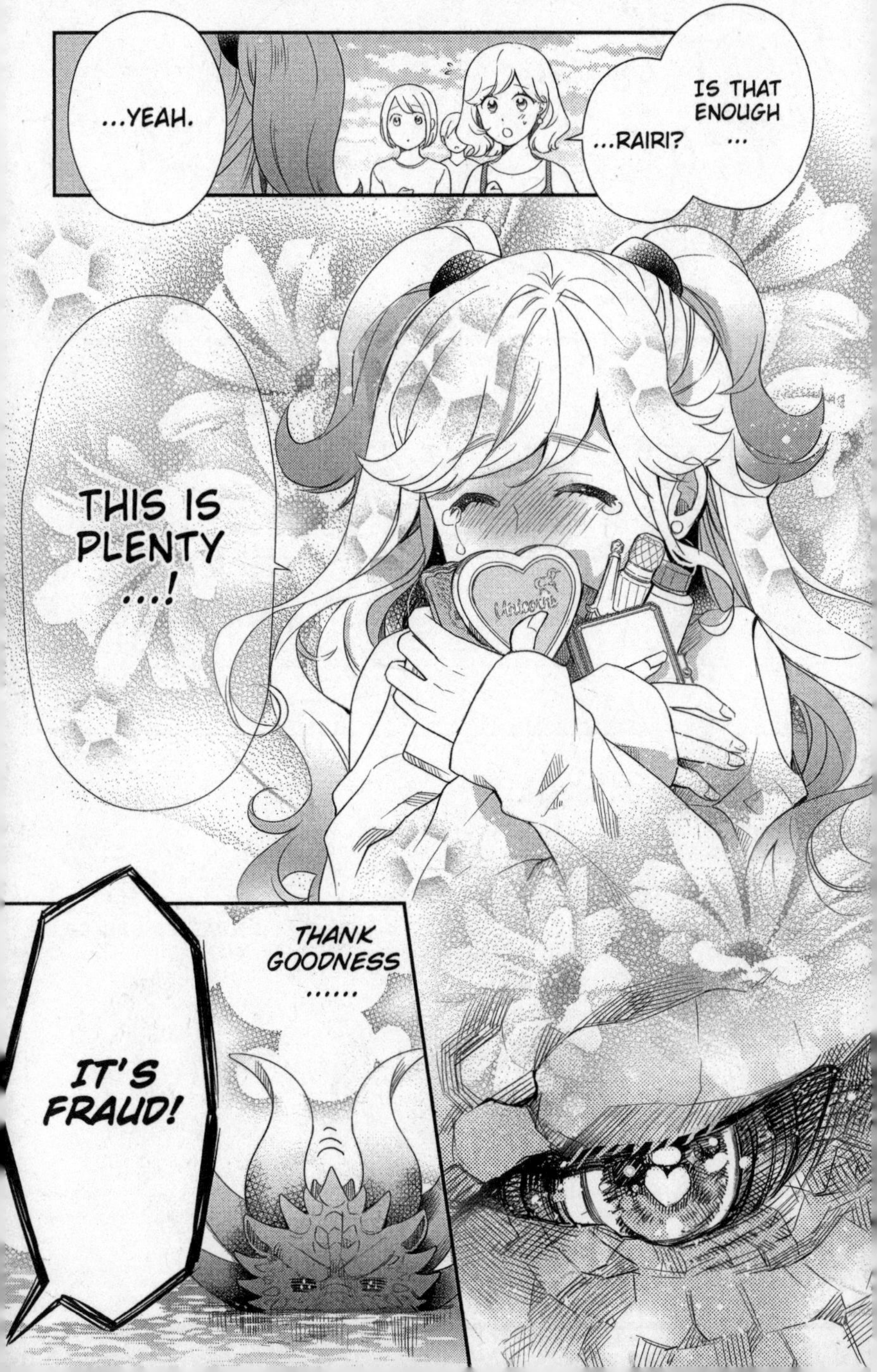
IS THAT ENOUGH ...RAIRI?
...YEAH.
THIS IS PLENTY ...!
THANK GOODNESS ......
IT'S FRAUD!

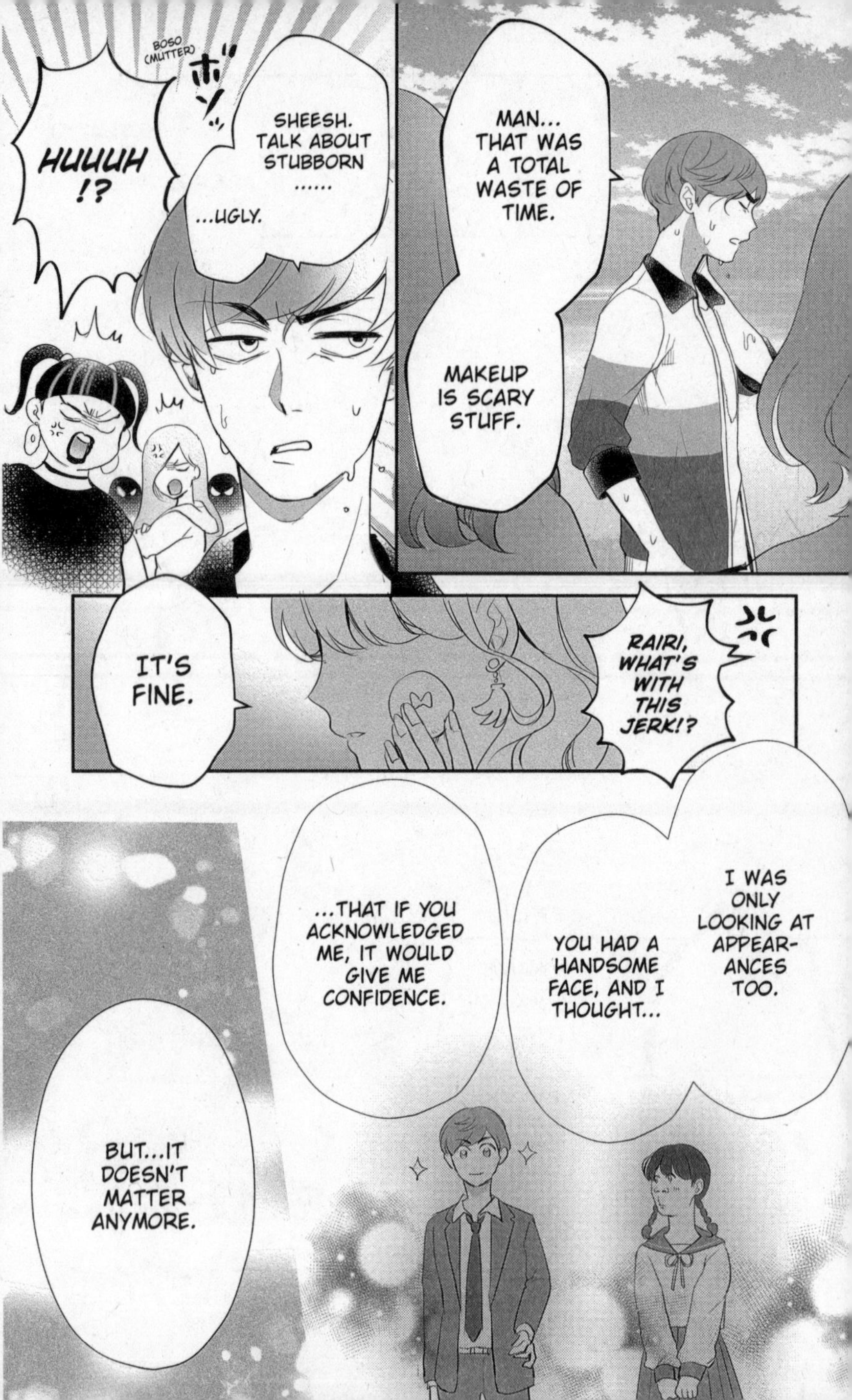
MAN... THAT WAS A TOTAL WASTE OF TIME.
MAKEUP IS SCARY STUFF.
ボソッ
BOSO (MUTTER)
SHEESH. TALK ABOUT STUBBORN ......
...UGLY.
HUUUH !?
RAIRI, WHAT'S WITH THIS JERK!?
IT'S FINE.
I WAS ONLY LOOKING AT APPEAR-ANCES TOO.
YOU HAD A HANDSOME FACE, AND I THOUGHT...
...THAT IF YOU ACKNOWLEDGED ME, IT WOULD GIVE ME CONFIDENCE.
BUT...IT DOESN'T MATTER ANYMORE.

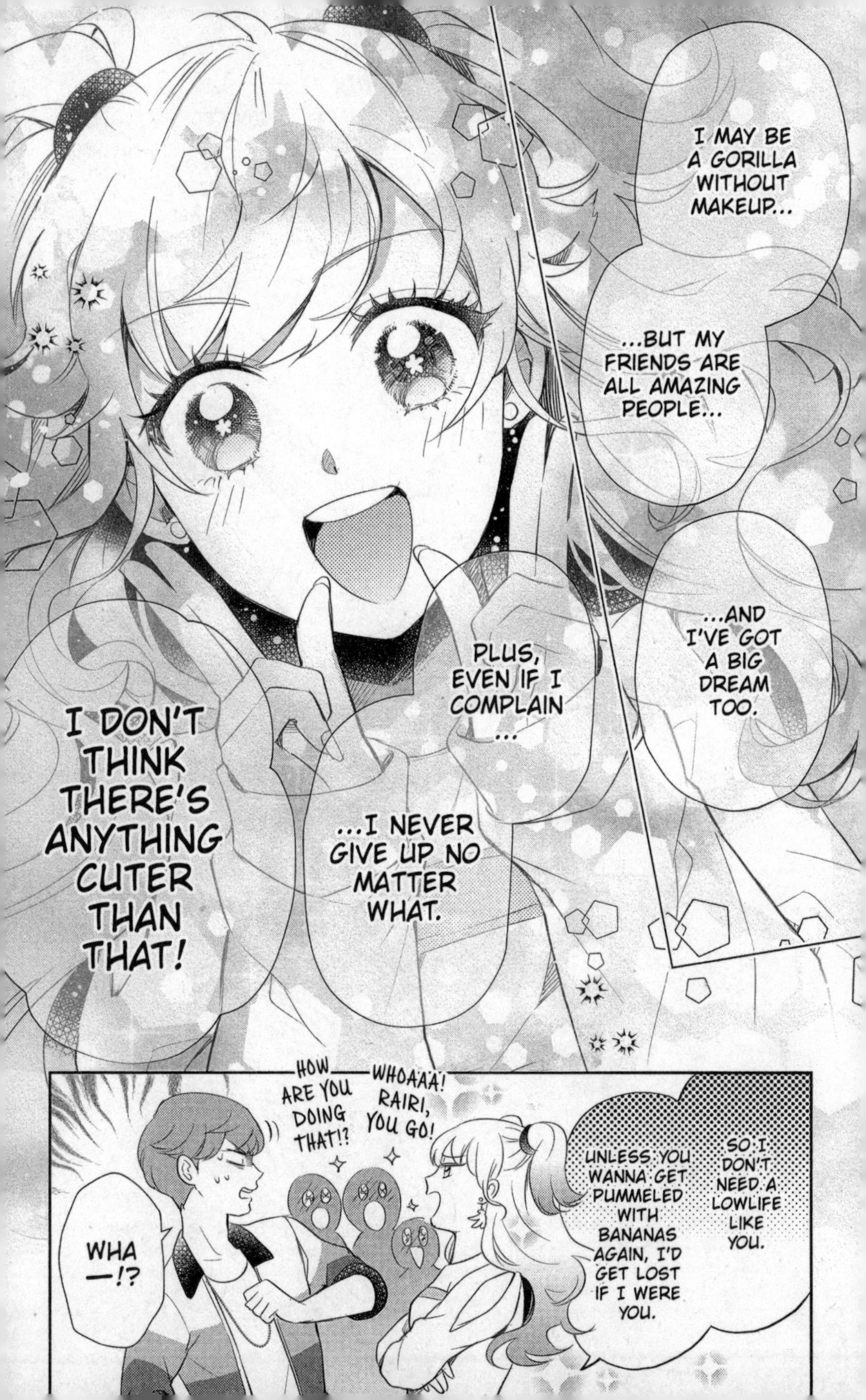
I MAY BE A GORILLA WITHOUT MAKEUP...
...BUT MY FRIENDS ARE ALL AMAZING PEOPLE...
...AND I'VE GOT A BIG DREAM TOO.
PLUS, EVEN IF I COMPLAIN...
...I NEVER GIVE UP NO MATTER WHAT.
I DON'T THINK THERE'S ANYTHING CUTER THAN THAT!
SO I DON'T NEED A LOWLIFE LIKE YOU.
UNLESS YOU WANNA GET PUMMELED WITH BANANAS AGAIN, I'D GET LOST IF I WERE YOU.
WHOAAA! RAIRI, YOU GO!
HOW ARE YOU DOING THAT!?
WHA—!?

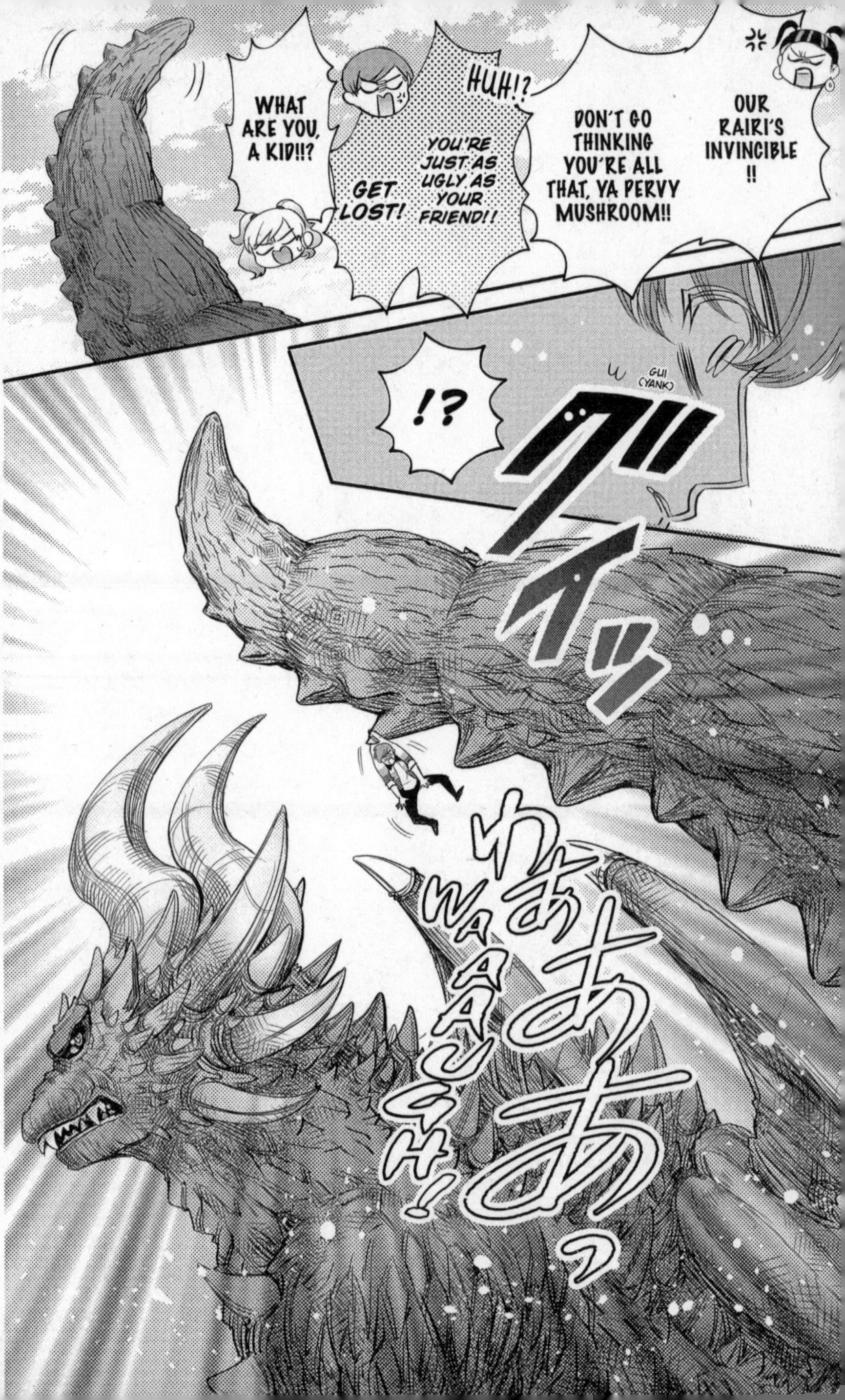

OUR RAIRI'S INVINCIBLE !!
DON'T GO THINKING YOU'RE ALL THAT, YA PERVY MUSHROOM!!
HUH!?
YOU'RE JUST AS UGLY AS YOUR FRIEND!!
GET LOST!
WHAT ARE YOU, A KID!!?
GUI (YANK)
!?
WAAAUGH!

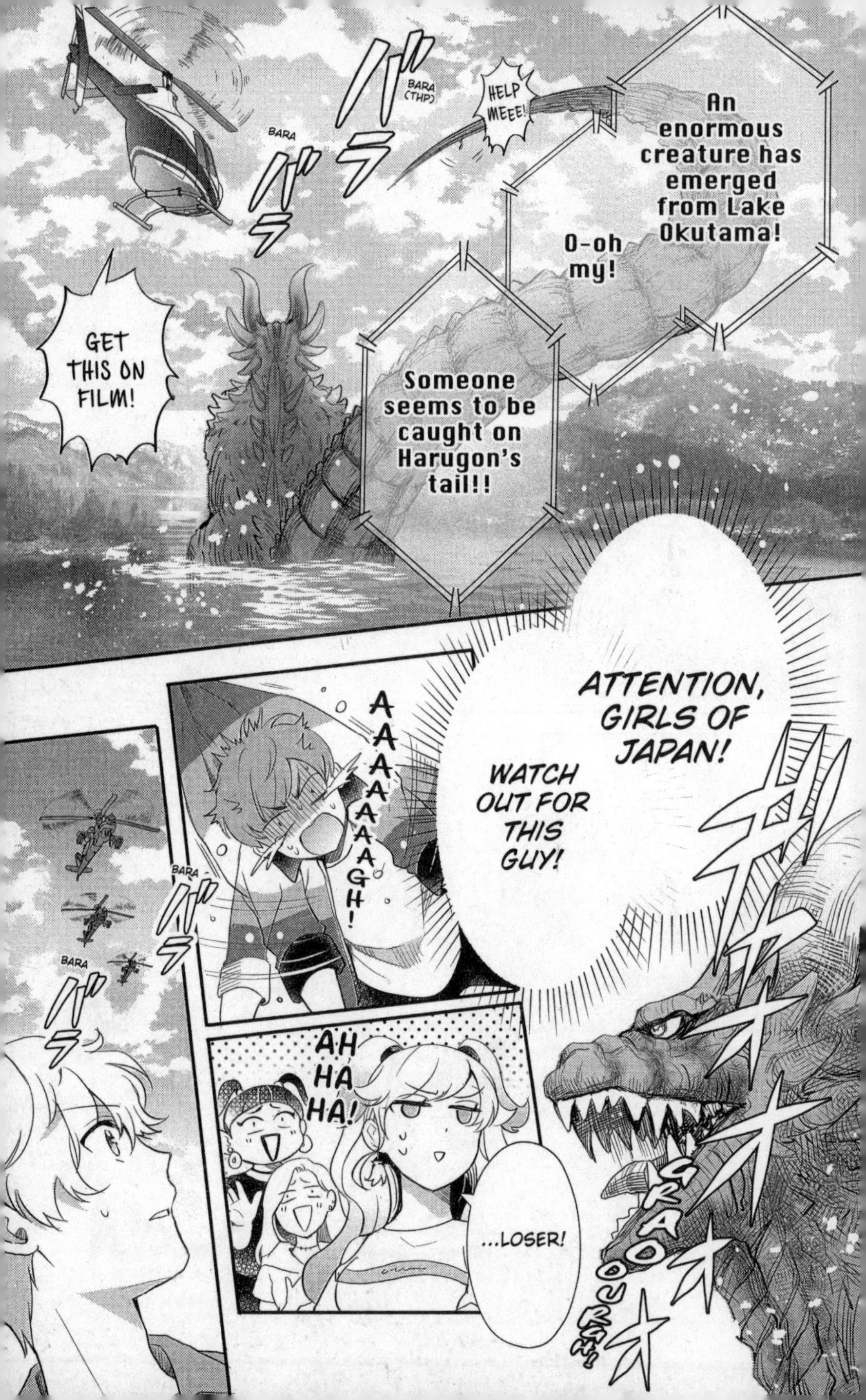
An enormous creature has emerged from Lake Okutama!
O-oh my!
HELP MEEE!
BARA (THP)
BARA
Someone seems to be caught on Harugon's tail!!
GET THIS ON FILM!
ATTENTION, GIRLS OF JAPAN!
WATCH OUT FOR THIS GUY!
AAAAAAAAAGH!
GRAOOUGGH!
AH HA HA HA!
...LOSER!
BARA
BARA

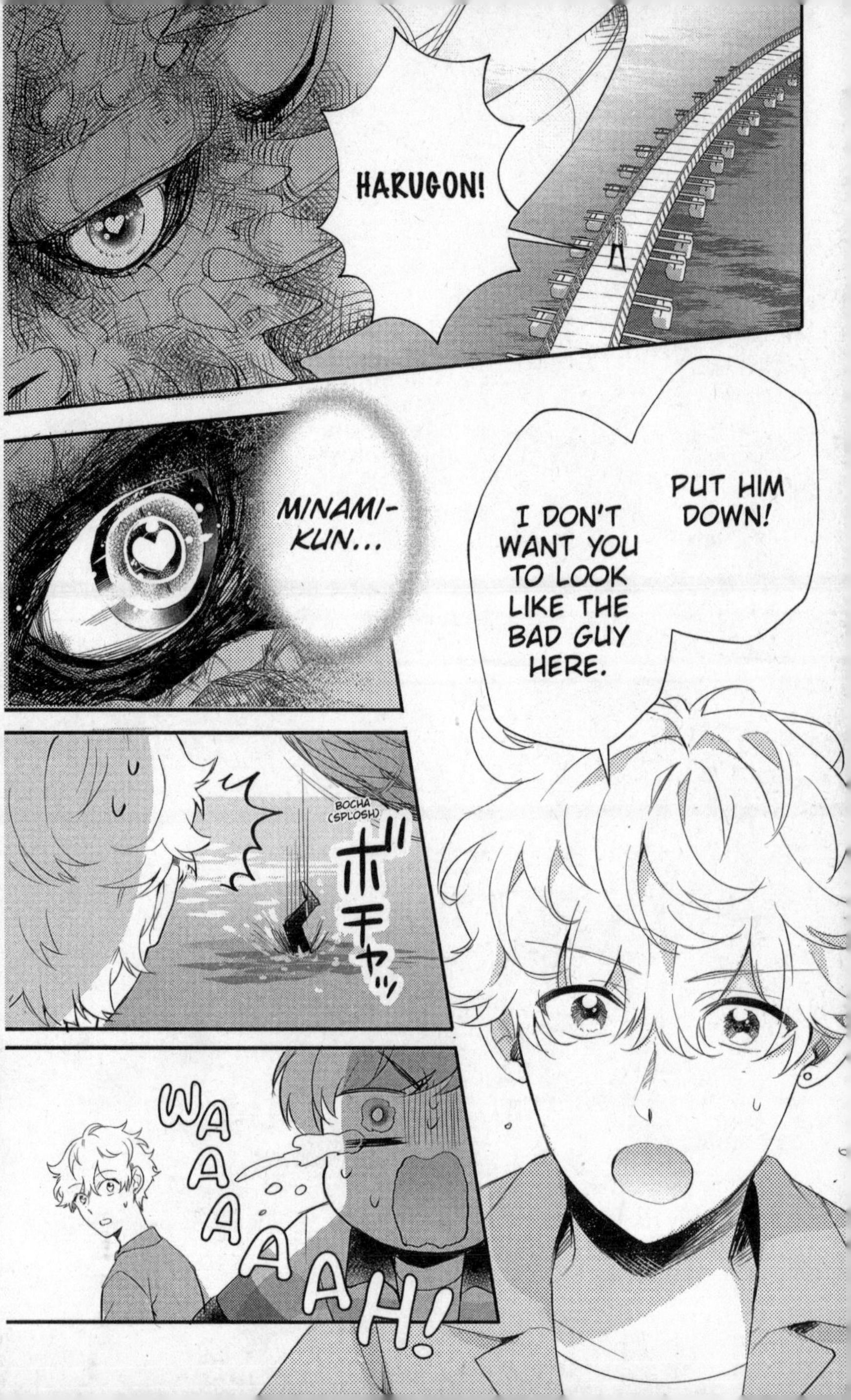
HARUGON!
PUT HIM DOWN!
I DON'T WANT YOU TO LOOK LIKE THE BAD GUY HERE.
MINAMI-KUN...
BOCHA (SPLOSH)
ボチャッ
WAAAAAAH!

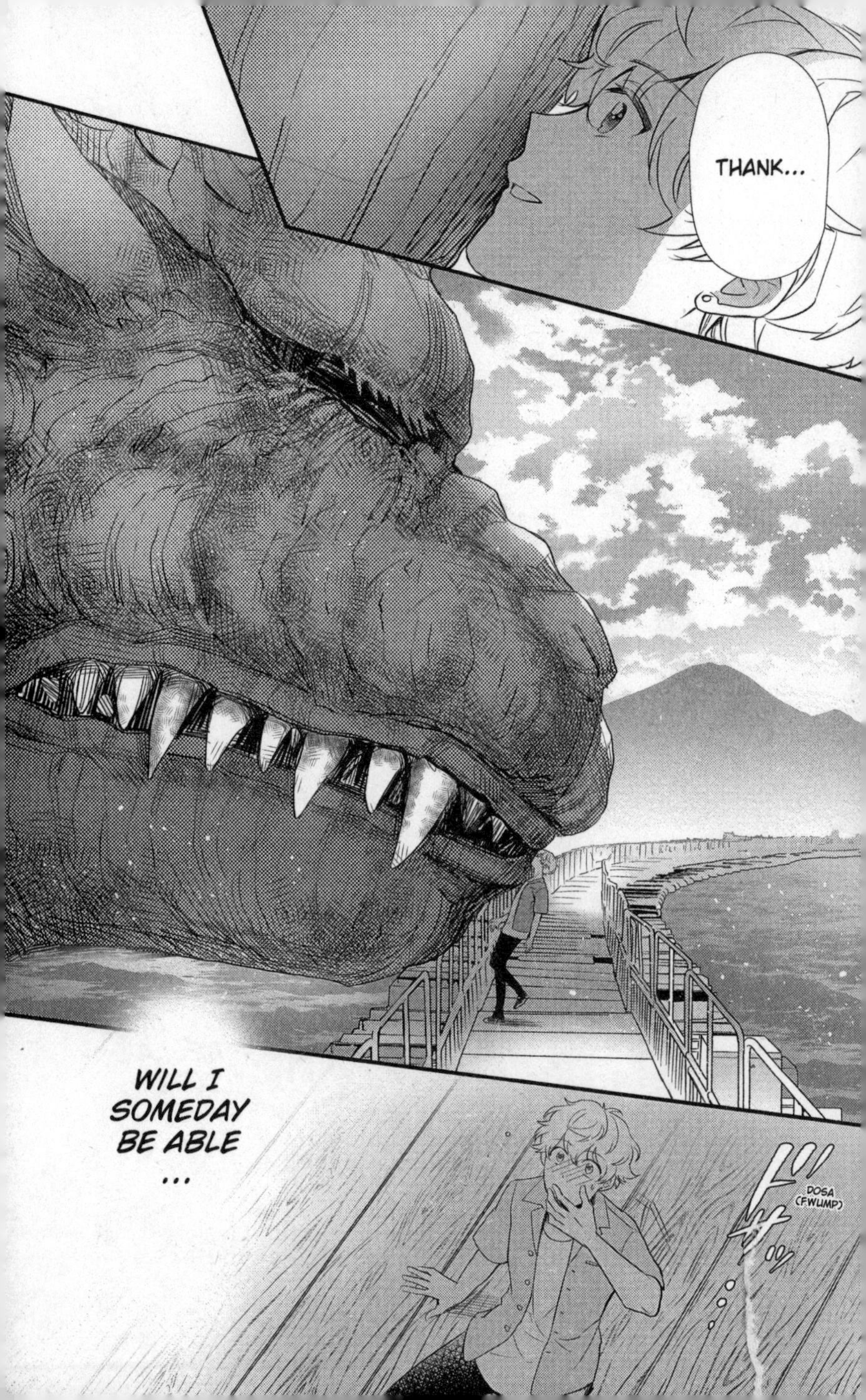
THANK...
WILL I SOMEDAY BE ABLE ...
DOSA (FWUMP)

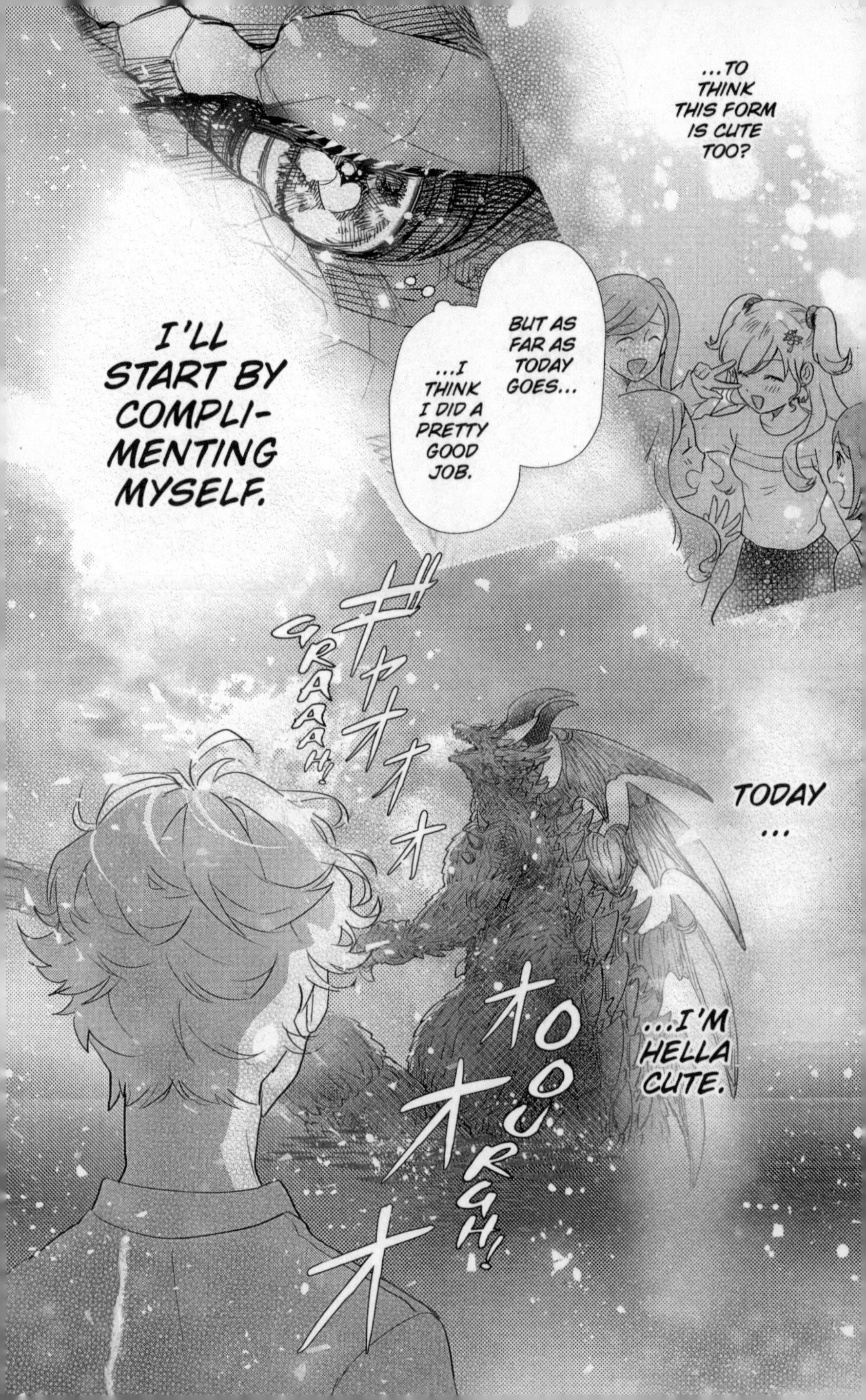
...TO THINK THIS FORM IS CUTE TOO?
BUT AS FAR AS TODAY GOES... ...I THINK I DID A PRETTY GOOD JOB.
I'LL START BY COMPLIMENTING MYSELF.
ギャオオオ
GRAAAAH!
TODAY...
...I'M HELLA CUTE.
オオオ
OOURRGH!

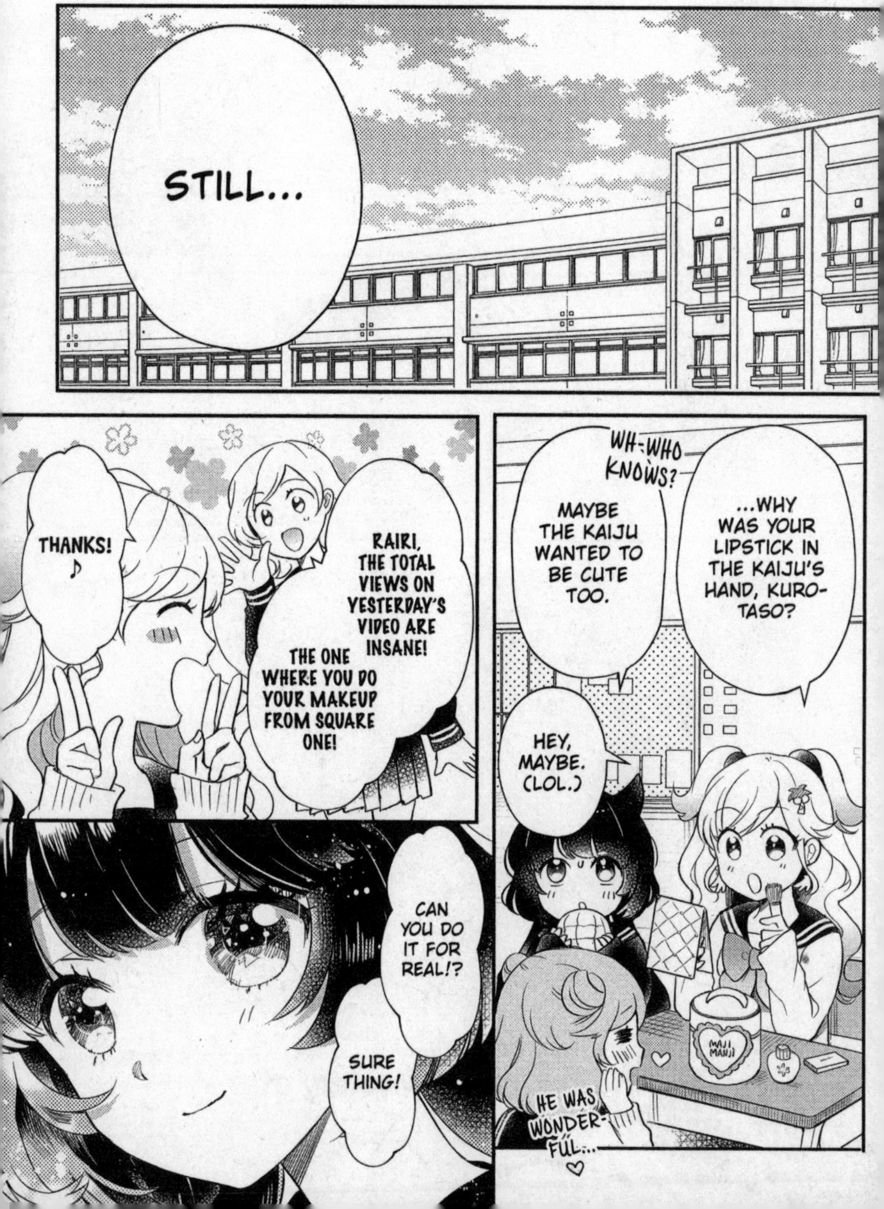
STILL...
...WHY WAS YOUR LIPSTICK IN THE KAIJU'S HAND, KURO-TASO?
WH-WHO KNOWS?
MAYBE THE KAIJU WANTED TO BE CUTE TOO.
HEY, MAYBE. (LOL.)
HE WAS WONDER-FUL... ♡
RAIRI, THE TOTAL VIEWS ON YESTERDAY'S VIDEO ARE INSANE!
THE ONE WHERE YOU DO YOUR MAKEUP FROM SQUARE ONE!
THANKS! ♪
CAN YOU DO IT FOR REAL!?
SURE THING!
MAJI MANJI

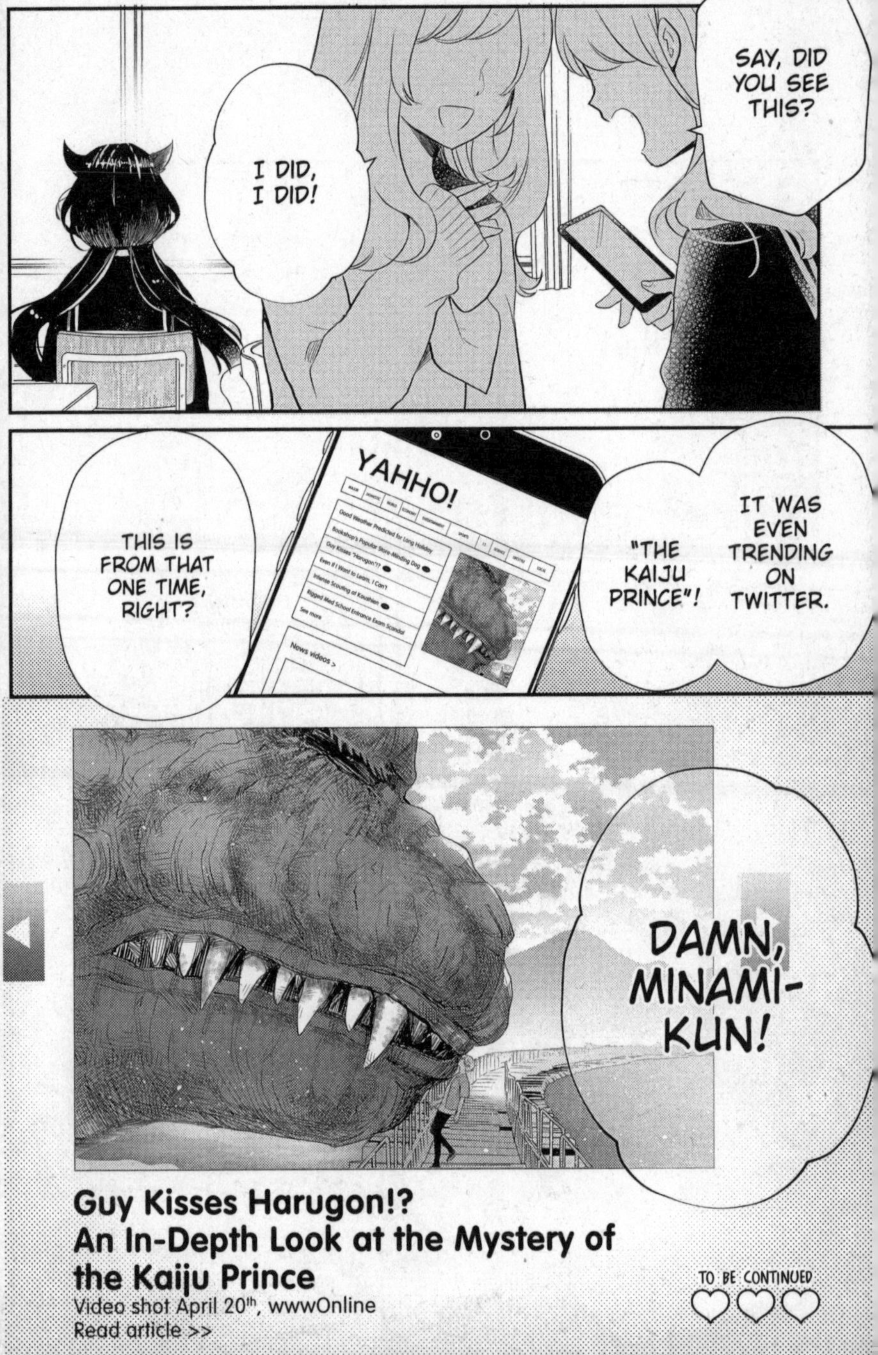
SAY, DID YOU SEE THIS?
I DID, I DID!
IT WAS EVEN TRENDING ON TWITTER.
"THE KAIJU PRINCE"!
YAHHO!
Good Weather Predicted for Long Holiday
Bookshop's Popular Store-Minding Dog
Guy Kisses "Harugon"!?
Even If I Want to Learn, I Can't
Intense Scouting at Koushien
Rigged Med School Entrance Exam Scandal
See more
News videos >
THIS IS FROM THAT ONE TIME, RIGHT?
DAMN, MINAMI-KUN!
Guy Kisses Harugon!?
An In-Depth Look at the Mystery of the Kaiju Prince
Video shot April 20th, wwwOnline
Read article >>
TO BE CONTINUED

TRANSLATION NOTES

COMMON HONORIFICS
no honorific: Indicates familiarity or closeness; if used without permission or reason, addressing someone in this manner would constitute an insult.

-*san*: The Japanese equivalent of Mr./Mrs./Miss. If a situation calls for politeness, this is the fail-safe honorific.

-*kun*: Used most often when referring to boys, this indicates affection or familiarity. Occasionally used by older men among their peers, but it may also be used by anyone referring to a person of lower standing.

-*chan*: An affectionate honorific indicating familiarity used mostly in reference to girls; also used in reference to cute persons or animals of either gender.

-*tan*: A casual honorific that expresses closeness and affection; it is similar to *chan* in that it is used in reference to cute persons.

-*taso*: A casual honorific similar to *tan*. It comes from the fact that *tan* and *taso* look nearly identical when written out in katakana.

PAGE 18
Kanna Hashinomoto is a thinly veiled reference to Kanna Hashimoto, an actress and former idol singer.

PAGE 26
Ginjuuji literally means "silver cross" in Japanese.

PAGE 46
Rairi actually says, "Posi-peace," a catchphrase coined by idol singer Kazumi Takayama from the group Nogizaka46. It's a portmanteau of the words "positive" and "peace," and it's used to brighten the mood when things get gloomy or ugly.

PAGE 49
In Japan, it can be considered rude to freely start talking to someone without an introduction. Kuroe is being very brave by inviting others to do so.

PAGE 50
Banila is a monster in the *Ultraman* franchise.

PAGE 51
Astromons is yet another *Ultraman* villain. He has an enormous flower in the center of his chest that looks like the ones drawn behind Manatsu in this panel.

PAGE 55
Etude Room is a play on Etude House, a Korean cosmetics company that is very popular in Japan.

PAGE 89
Okutama is located in the Okutama Mountains, to the west of Yokohama.

PAGE 162
Isekai, or "different world," is a popular fantasy subgenre in Japan in which the protagonist is either transported to a world that's very different from their own or dies and is reincarnated into said world with an unusual ability.

AFTERWORD

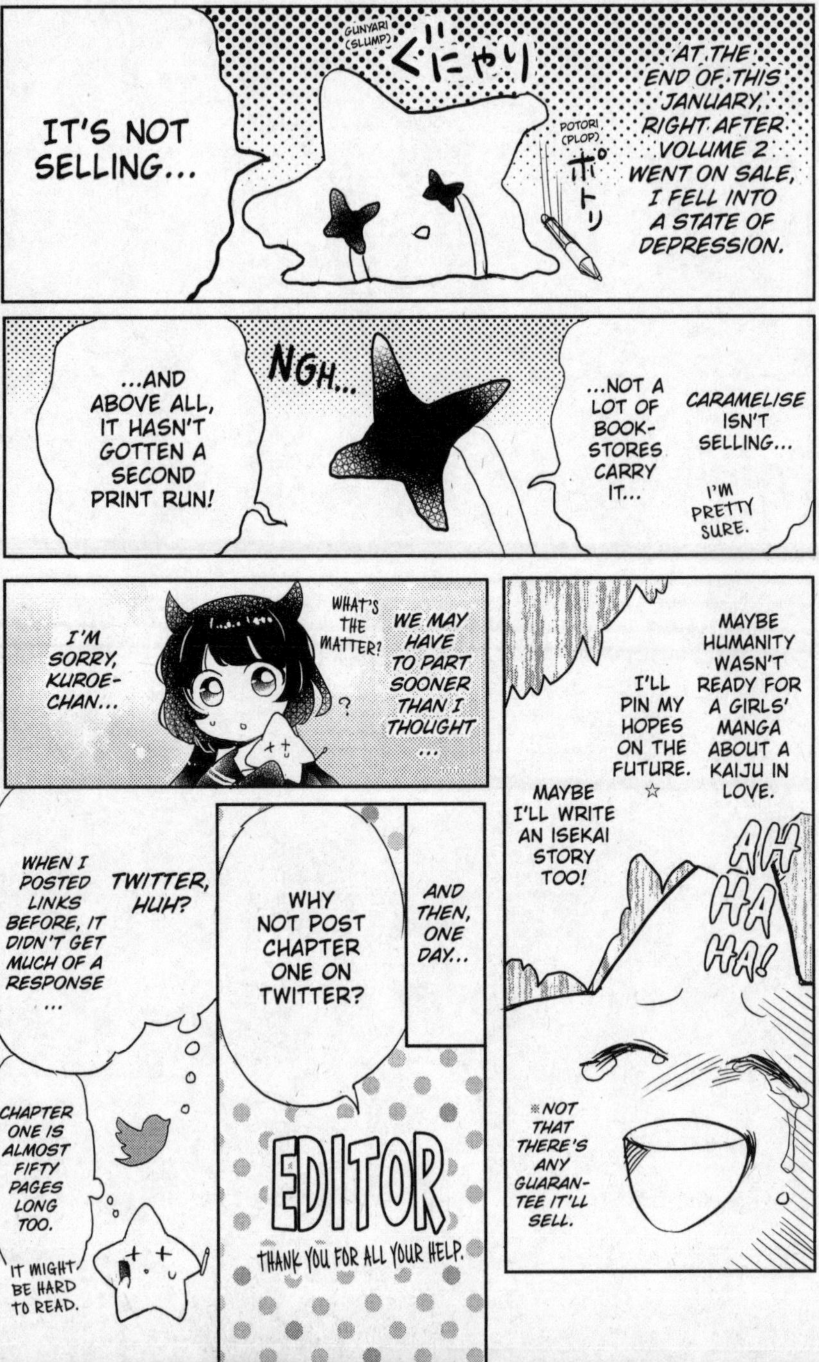
AT THE END OF THIS JANUARY, RIGHT AFTER VOLUME 2 WENT ON SALE, I FELL INTO A STATE OF DEPRESSION.
GUNYARI (SLUMP)
ぐにゃり
POTORI (PLOP)
ポトリ
IT'S NOT SELLING...
CARAMELISE ISN'T SELLING...
I'M PRETTY SURE.
...NOT A LOT OF BOOK-STORES CARRY IT...
NGH...
...AND ABOVE ALL, IT HASN'T GOTTEN A SECOND PRINT RUN!
MAYBE HUMANITY WASN'T READY FOR A GIRLS' MANGA ABOUT A KAIJU IN LOVE.
I'LL PIN MY HOPES ON THE FUTURE. ☆
MAYBE I'LL WRITE AN ISEKAI STORY TOO!
AH HA HA HA!
※NOT THAT THERE'S ANY GUARAN-TEE IT'LL SELL.
WE MAY HAVE TO PART SOONER THAN I THOUGHT...
WHAT'S THE MATTER?
?
I'M SORRY, KUROE-CHAN...
AND THEN, ONE DAY...
WHY NOT POST CHAPTER ONE ON TWITTER?
EDITOR
THANK YOU FOR ALL YOUR HELP.
TWITTER, HUH?
WHEN I POSTED LINKS BEFORE, IT DIDN'T GET MUCH OF A RESPONSE...
CHAPTER ONE IS ALMOST FIFTY PAGES LONG TOO.
IT MIGHT BE HARD TO READ.

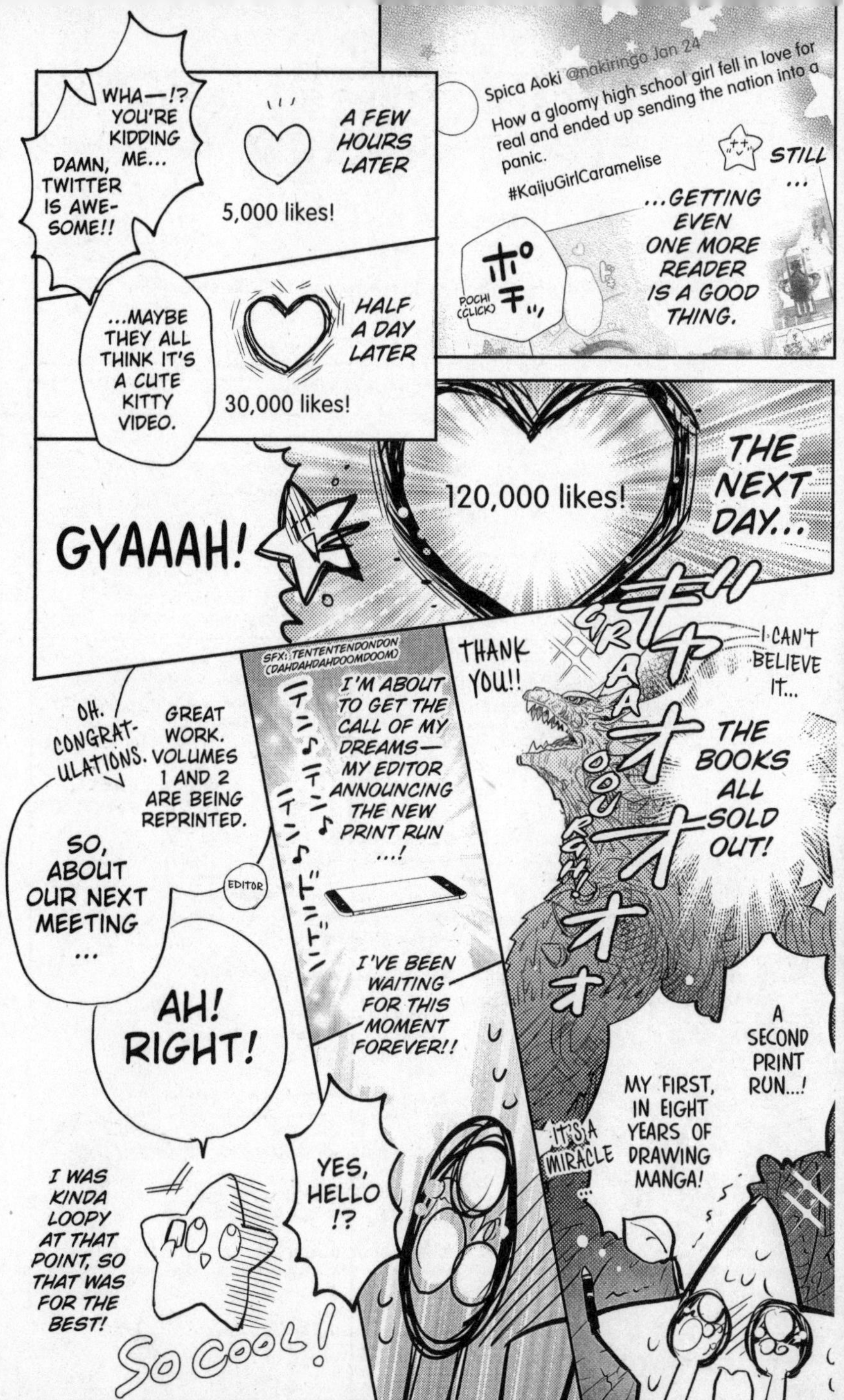
Spica Aoki @nakiringo Jan 24
How a gloomy high school girl fell in love for real and ended up sending the nation into a panic.
#KaijuGirlCaramelise
STILL...
...GETTING EVEN ONE MORE READER IS A GOOD THING.
ポチッ
POCHI (CLICK)
A FEW HOURS LATER
5,000 likes!
WHA—!? YOU'RE KIDDING ME...
DAMN, TWITTER IS AWESOME!!
HALF A DAY LATER
30,000 likes!
...MAYBE THEY ALL THINK IT'S A CUTE KITTY VIDEO.
THE NEXT DAY...
120,000 likes!
GYAAAH!
I CAN'T BELIEVE IT...
THE BOOKS ALL SOLD OUT!
THANK YOU!!
GRAAAOOOURGH!
A SECOND PRINT RUN...!
MY FIRST, IN EIGHT YEARS OF DRAWING MANGA!
IT'S A MIRACLE...
SFX: TENTENTENDONDON (DAHDAHDAHDOOMDOOM)
I'M ABOUT TO GET THE CALL OF MY DREAMS—MY EDITOR ANNOUNCING THE NEW PRINT RUN...!
I'VE BEEN WAITING FOR THIS MOMENT FOREVER!!
YES, HELLO!?
GREAT WORK. VOLUMES 1 AND 2 ARE BEING REPRINTED.
OH. CONGRATULATIONS.
SO, ABOUT OUR NEXT MEETING...
EDITOR
AH! RIGHT!
I WAS KINDA LOOPY AT THAT POINT, SO THAT WAS FOR THE BEST!
SO COOL!

KAIJU ♥ GIRL CARAMELISE 3

Spica Aoki

TRANSLATION: Taylor Engel ♥ LETTERING: Lys Blakeslee

OTOMEKAIJU CARAMELISE Vol. 3
©Spica Aoki 2019
First published in Japan in 2019 by KADOKAWA CORPORATION, Tokyo.
English translation rights arranged with KADOKAWA CORPORATION, Tokyo through TUTTLE-MORI AGENCY, INC., Tokyo.

English translation © 2020 by Yen Press, LLC

Yen Press
150 West 30th Street, 19th Floor
New York, NY 10001

Visit us at yenpress.com ♡ facebook.com/yenpress ♡ twitter.com/yenpress ♡ yenpress.tumblr.com ♡ instagram.com/yenpress

First Yen Press Edition: April 2020

Yen Press is an imprint of Yen Press, LLC.
The Yen Press name and logo are trademarks of Yen Press, LLC.

The publisher is not responsible for websites (or their content) that are not owned by the publisher.

Library of Congress Control Number: 2019935205

ISBNs: 978-1-9753-0860-5 (paperback)
978-1-9753-1016-5 (ebook)

10 9 8 7 6 5 4 3 2 1

BVG

Printed in the United States of America